American Trade Politics

Third Edition

I. M. DESTLER

American Trade Politics

Third Edition

INSTITUTE FOR INTERNATIONAL ECONOMICS
Washington, DC

and

THE TWENTIETH CENTURY FUND
New York, NY

April 1995

I. M. Destler, *Visiting Fellow*, is Professor and Acting Dean (1994–95) at the School of Public Affairs and Director of its Center for International and Security Studies. He was Senior Associate at the Carnegie Endowment for International Peace (1977–83) and the Brookings Institution (1972–77); and Visiting Lecturer at Princeton University (1971–72) and at the International University of Japan (1986). He is the author or coauthor of ten books on American foreign policymaking and US–Japan economic relations including *Dollar Politics: Exchange Rate Policymaking in the United States* (1989), *Anti-Protection: Changing Forces in United States Trade Policy* (1987), *Our Own Worst Enemy: The Unmaking of American Foreign Policy* (1984).

INSTITUTE FOR INTERNATIONAL ECONOMICS
11 Dupont Circle, NW
Washington, DC 20036-1207
(202) 328-9000   FAX: (202) 328-0900

C. Fred Bergsten, *Director*
Christine F. Lowry, *Director of Publications*

THE TWENTIETH CENTURY FUND
41 East 70th Street
New York, NY 10021
(212) 535-4441

Richard C. Leone, *President*

Cover design by Michelle M. Fleitz
Typesetting by Sandra F. Watts
Printing by Automated Graphic Systems

For reprints/permission to photocopy please contact the APS customer service department at CCC Academic Permissions Service, 27 Congress Street, Salem, MA 01970

Printed in the United States of America
97 96 95   5 4 3 2 1

Library of Congress Cataloging-in-Publication Data

Destler, I. M.
    American trade politics / I. M. Destler.—3rd ed.
        p. cm.
    Includes bibliographical references and index.
    1. United States—Commercial policy.
I. Title.
HF1455.D48   1995
380.1′3′0973—dc20   94-44644
                                           CIP

ISBN 0-88132-215-6

Marketed and Distributed outside the USA and Canada by Longman Group UK Limited, London

The views expressed in this publication are those of the author. He wrote this book under the sponsorship of The Twentieth Century Fund, as part of the research program of the Institute for International Economics. It does not necessarily reflect the views of individual members of the Board or the Advisory Committee of the Institute, or of the Trustees or staff of The Twentieth Century Fund.

Contents

II Erosion

Foreword

One of the seeds of the American revolution was the "trade policy" of the British empire. American foreign policy in the 19th century is often seen in terms of protectionism of "infant industries." Later, America was a key participant in the trade wars of the 1930s, and the main architect of the post–World War II liberal trade regime. More recently, the United States has frequently been accused of jeopardizing through its "aggressive unilateralism" the very multilateral system that it had built.

The salience of trade issues is reflected in many volumes prescribing the best trade policy for the United States. While this book does not dodge the question, its primary focus is on the people, politics, and institutions that set tariffs, apply dumping rules, and negotiate trade treaties. *American Trade Politics* thus crosses the terrain of both politics and history, offering a supplement to the econometric models that generally dominate discussions of trade and related issues.

Mac Destler shows in these pages that the United States has created over time a complex process for dealing with international trade. It is a robust mechanism that protects Congress from protectionist appeals, presses trading partners to open markets, and offers some relief to industries hit hard by imports. This system depends on both congressional restraint and presidential leadership, and Destler shows vividly how executive passivity, especially during the early and middle 1980s, created turmoil here and abroad—and how executive aggressiveness did so a decade later.

This third edition of *American Trade Politics* arose from the success of the original as well as from major developments since its publication. The first edition was awarded the American Political Science Association's Gladys M. Kammerer Award in 1987 for the best book on public policy and is already considered a classic in its field. In light of that achievement, the Institute for International Economics and The Twentieth Century Fund asked Destler to revise—and now revise again—his original work to encompass the many trade policy events that have transpired since 1986.

The recent years have been remarkable. The United States has pursued the Uruguay Round of multilateral trade negotiations to a successful conclusion, while at the same time completing both the Canada–United States Free Trade Agreement and the North American Free Trade Agreement. The American Congress passed the Omnibus Trade and Competitiveness Act of 1988—the most comprehensive legislation in this field in the postwar period—after more than three years of intense debate, and then extended the president's fast-track negotiating authority in 1991. Efforts to achieve free trade in both the Asia Pacific Economic Cooperation (APEC) forum and a Free Trade Area of the Americas have been launched. Destler weaves these events together and sets out a series of new ideas for conducting trade policy as we enter the 21st century.

This book began in 1983 when The Twentieth Century Fund asked Professor Destler to undertake a comprehensive study of the politics of American trade policy; the completed manuscript was subsequently published jointly by the Fund and the Institute for International Economics after the author joined the staff of the Institute. The second and third editions were supported by the Fund and the Institute and were written at the latter organization. Like the first two, this third edition is a fully collaborative venture.

The Institute for International Economics is a private nonprofit institution for the study and discussion of international economic policy. Its purpose is to analyze important issues in that area and to develop and communicate practical new approaches for dealing with them. The Institute is completely nonpartisan.

The Institute is funded largely by philanthropic foundations. Major institutional grants are now being received from the German Marshall Fund of the United States, which created the Institute with a generous commitment of funds in 1981, and from the Ford Foundation, the William M. Keck, Jr. Foundation, the Korea Foundation, the Andrew Mellon Foundation, the C. V. Starr Foundation, and the United States–Japan Foundation. A number of other foundations and private corporations also contribute to the highly diversified financial resources of the Institute. About 12 percent of the Institute's resources in our latest fiscal year were provided by contributors outside the United States, including about 5 percent from Japan.

The Board of Directors bears overall responsibility for the Institute and gives general guidance and approval to its research program—

including identification of topics that are likely to become important to international economic policymakers over the medium run (generally, one to three years), and which thus should be addressed by the Institute. The Director, working closely with the staff and outside Advisory Committee, is responsible for the development of particular projects and makes the final decision to publish an individual study.

The Institute hopes that its studies and other activities will contribute to building a stronger foundation for international economic policy around the world. We invite readers of these publications to let us know how they think we can best accomplish this objective.

For over seventy-five years, The Twentieth Century Fund has supported research and writing on important public policy issues. The founder of the Fund, Edward A. Filene, hoped that its studies would raise the level of public debate, influence the making of policy, and ultimately contribute to the progress of the American nation. Throughout this century, the Fund has been concerned with the health of the American economy and the nation's role in the larger world. Mac Destler's book is a distinguished contribution to that effort. Moreover, the Fund plans to continue to support studies of trade policy and to examine the broader implications of the new global economy.

We are indebted to Mac Destler for this new edition of *American Trade Politics*. As the United States enters a new international era with the end of the Cold War, global economic issues are high on the public agenda. Americans will debate and decide how their nation will compete in the vigorous contest for markets and power. Destler's book will inform that argument and the choices we make about trade policy in the uncertain years ahead.

C. Fred Bergsten
Director
Institute for International Economics
February 1995

Richard C. Leone
President
The Twentieth Century Fund
February 1995

Preface

As this third edition goes to press, the political health of US trade policy appears rather good. In December 1994 Congress approved, by lopsided House and Senate margins, the most comprehensive trade liberalization agreement (the Uruguay Round) since the establishment of the postwar GATT system. This followed, by 13 months, the dramatic ratification of US entry into the North American Free Trade Agreement, after the most contentious national trade debate since the Smoot-Hawley Tariff Act of 1930. And the administration of President Bill Clinton had committed the United States to the elimination of trade barriers through a projected free trade agreement for the Western Hemisphere and a similar arrangement within the framework of the Asia Pacific Economic Cooperation (APEC) forum.

But as always, new threats are not hard to find. The Republican sweep of midterm congressional elections has brought to Washington a large group of new legislators who lack their senior colleagues' internationalist commitment. This became evident when Mexico plunged from peso devaluation to broad economic crisis and Clinton sought Capitol Hill authorization of a broad "Mexican rescue" initiative. Despite the backing of Senate leader Robert Dole and House Speaker Newt Gingrich, the measure met a firestorm of rank-and-file criticism, and the president chose to withdraw it rather than risk defeat or serious delay. He was able to implement an alternative package of guarantees for Mexico under his own authority, but the crisis continued. At the very least, American industry's hopes for substantial near-term gains from NAFTA would have to be seriously scaled back. Meanwhile, new records were being registered for the global US trade deficit, and for the bilateral deficits with China and Japan.

The United States was still running huge budget deficits—a prime source of the trade deficits—notwithstanding the significant tax-and-spending package the president pushed through Congress in 1993 and the Republicans' commitment to deficit reduction (albeit with tax reduction) in 1995. The administration ended 1994, moreover, with no "fast-track" authority (or any other authority) for future trade negotiations. It had failed to secure such authority as part of the Uruguay Round implementing legislation. The controversy that contributed to this failure continued, over whether the United States should use this authority to negotiate on trade-related labor and environmental issues. And this controversy divided legislators along partisan lines, just what US trade policy leaders had long sought to avoid.

These issues posed continuing challenges for the president and Congress, and for US trade policy institutions. They also establish the framework for this third edition of *American Trade Politics*, which tells the stories of the great trade successes of 1992–94 and updates the author's broader analyses and prescriptions. Readers of earlier editions will find the core chapters largely as before, with modest corrections and updating. But they will also find an entirely new chapter 9 covering NAFTA and the Uruguay Round, as well as other trade action in the first two Clinton years. They will find also a reshaped prescriptive chapter (now 10), which makes specific proposals for the 104th Congress of 1995–96 and updates my comprehensive recommendations to take account of new developments. To lower the cost of the book, I have omitted this time the long appendices summarizing antidumping and other trade remedy cases. But we did bring the count of case submissions and outcomes through those initiated in 1993, and these data are presented to the reader.

The book remains one man's interpretation of postwar American trade policy experience. It is informed by considerable research, including interviews and discussions with many trade policy practitioners—a number of them conducted specifically for the third edition. Hard information has been sought where available: in compiling, for example, as thorough as possible a count of unfair trade practice cases brought to the US Department of Commerce since 1980. But ultimately, the most important events are *sui generis*, so their aggregation into larger patterns becomes a qualitative, interpretive enterprise. The true test of this edition—like the first two—will be whether it captures the issues and patterns of trade politics accurately enough to shed useful light on the difficult policy and procedural choices the United States now faces.

During my work on this edition, I have accumulated a range of debts. The greatest, once again, is to Director C. Fred Bergsten of the Institute for International Economics for his support of this enterprise and his cogent critiques of successive drafts. He continues to lead a think tank that is exceptional in both the stimulus it offers and the standards of quality and relevance it imposes. The Twentieth Century Fund provided support once again, for which I am grateful, especially to Richard C. Leone, for continuing the research and publication partnership begun over a decade ago. Colleagues at the University of Maryland School of Public Affairs and its Center for International Security Studies at Maryland (CISSM) have provided a congenial intellectual environment for me since I joined the faculty in 1987. For this edition, I profited from insights gained in CISSM's US–Japan study, which I codirected with Professor Hideo Sato of the University of Tsukuba. And I owe a continuing debt to my wife, Harriett Parsons Destler, for her encouragement and support throughout my scholarly career.

Indispensable for updating data on trade remedy cases, and for helping me track trade politics through the hectic year of 1994, was the good work of my University of Maryland student and IIE research assistant, Steven Schoeny. Steve played a role for this edition equivalent to the major contributions of Diane Berliner for the first edition and Paul Baker for the second.

C. Michael Aho, C. Fred Bergsten, Robert C. Cassidy Jr., William L. Diebold Jr., Gary N. Horlick, Gary Clyde Hufbauer, Lawrence B. Krause, Harald B. Malmgren, Gary W. Nickerson, Pietro S. Nivola, Jeffrey J. Schott, Gilbert R. Winham, and Alan Wm. Wolff all read the original manuscript for the first edition and provided many helpful suggestion. Others offered good, oft-corrective commentary on specific draft chapters for this edition or previous ones: Thomas O. Bayard, Steve Charnovitz, Barber B. Conable, Kimberly Ann Elliott, J. Michael Finger, Jeffrey Frankel, William Frenzel, Ellen R. Frost, Claud L. Gingrich, Carl J. Green, C. Randall Henning, Alan Holmer, John H. Jackson, Julius Katz, Charles Levy, Stephen Marris, Robert Matsui, Marcus Noland, Ernest Preeg, Myer Rashish, William Reinsch, J. David Richardson, Richard R. Rivers, Howard Rosen, Susan C. Schwab, John Williamson, Rufus Yerxa, and Robert Zoellick.

Finally let me express my appreciation to the Publications Director Christine Lowry and the editor Valerie Norville, who were efficient and helpful in bringing *American Trade Politics*, third edition, into print. As before, any mistakes must be charged to my account.

I.M.D.

The Twentieth Century Fund sponsors and supervises timely analyses of economic policy, foreign affairs, and domestic political issues. Not-for-profit and nonpartisan, the Fund was founded in 1919 and endowed by Edward A. Filene.

To My Mother

Katharine Hardesty Destler

Who Got Me Interested in Politics

ORIGIN

1

Trade Politics: The Root Problem, the Continuing Crisis

Sixty years ago, an assistant professor at Wesleyan University published a book on the politics of trade. Its full-blown title was *Politics, Pressures and the Tariff: A Study of Free Private Enterprise in Pressure Politics, as Shown in the 1929–1930 Revision of the Tariff*. The author sought to explain why, in enacting the now-famous Smoot-Hawley bill, the United States Congress had ignored the warnings of experts and had raised import duties to record levels. The reason, he found, was that the combined power of special interests seeking import protection had dominated the legislative process. . . . The "history of the American tariff," he concluded, "is the story of a dubious economic policy turned into a great political success. The very tendencies that have made the legislation bad have made it politically invincible."[1]

The book became a classic, and its author rose to the pinnacle of his profession. He became president of the American Political Science Association in 1956–57, and, to this day, the E. E. Schattschneider Award is presented biennially by that organization "for the best doctoral dissertation in the field of American government."

As prophecy, Schattschneider's book was a failure. He found "no significant concentration of forces able to reverse the policy and bring about a return to a system of low tariffs or free trade." Yet before his manuscript had even reached print, Congress passed a bill, the Reciprocal Trade Agreements Act of 1934, that began a historic shift of US policy toward lower trade barriers. But if the author wrongly concluded that the tariff was "politically invincible," he was right on target in his depiction of the root political problem that advocates of international trade

---

1. E. E. Schattschneider, *Politics, Pressures and the Tariff* (New York: Prentice-Hall, 1935), 283.

would have to overcome. "Although . . . theoretically the interests supporting and opposed to tariff legislation . . . are approximately equal," he wrote, "the pressures upon Congress are extremely unbalanced. That is to say, the pressures supporting the tariff are made overwhelming by the fact that the opposition is negligible."[2]

□ □ □

Most people benefit from international trade, for the same general reasons that most people benefit from the division of labor within nations and within localities. By participating in a broader community within which individuals and groups sell what they can produce with the greatest (comparative) efficiency, people can secure a far greater quantity and variety of goods than each individual could possibly obtain if he had to produce every one himself. There are, of course, many instances when blocking or limiting trade can bring advantages to particular groups at the expense of the broader society. But the more these groups succeed in enforcing such restrictions, the lower the standard of living and the slower the pace of economic growth for the community as a whole.[3]

As with communities, so too with nations. Specific interests can gain from import restrictions, and economic theory even recognizes a few cases in which a trade barrier might leave an entire nation better off, albeit at the expense of other nations. In most circumstances, however, open trade—by maximizing economic efficiency—enhances the welfare and the standard of living of the nation and of the wider world.

But the costs of international trade are concentrated. They bear particularly on those firms and workers whose home markets will be diminished by foreign competition. Trade policy must respond to their concerns as well, and some form of action constraining some imports will inevitably be part of that response. Free trade purists deplore this, seeing a "slippery slope" on which protection for one industry leads to protection for others. But free trade, however attractive it may be as a goal, is unreachable as practical policy.

A more attainable aim is not to avoid all import restrictions but to keep those who seek them from dominating the policy process. Through much of American history, these special interests did dominate: trade policy responded to their concerns all too well. The reason for this was highlighted in Schattschneider's book: there is a chronic political imbalance between those who benefit from trade protection and those who pay the costs.

It is an imbalance in intensity of interest and, as a result, in political

---

2. Ibid., 285.

3. For development of this argument, see Mancur Olson, *The Rise and Decline of Nations: Economic Growth, Stagflation, and Social Rigidities* (New Haven, CT: Yale University Press, 1982).

organization. Producers and workers threatened by imports tend to be concentrated, organized, and ready and able to press their interests in the political arena. Those who benefit from trade are diffuse, and their stake in any particular trade matter is usually small.

It is also an imbalance between clear, present benefits and possible future benefits. Exporters who would profit if increased US imports allowed foreigners to buy more from us are unlikely to expend the same effort to achieve a conjectural gain as their adversaries will to preserve a current market.

Finally, it is an imbalance between those who are doing well and those who are facing trouble. Firms with expanding markets and ample profits tend to concentrate on business; their worry is that government may get in their way by placing constraints on their flexibility and their profits. It is the embattled losers in trade who go into politics to seek trade protection.

Under our Constitution, the Congress has primary responsibility for regulating "commerce with foreign nations." Congress is a decentralized, undisciplined institution, particularly susceptible to pressure from organized interests. So if it "does what comes naturally," if the politics of benefit seeking and log-rolling goes unimpeded, the result will be a high level of trade barriers, to the benefit of certain groups and the detriment of the nation as a whole.

For a politician who must respond to concentrated interests, a vote for lowering trade barriers is therefore, as one former official put it, an "unnatural act."[4] If he is to vote this way—and if Congress, more generally, is to divert or turn back the pressures for trade protection—counterweights have to be built into our policymaking system. These counterweights can be ideas, such as the view espoused by Cordell Hull, Franklin D. Roosevelt's secretary of State, that liberal trade promotes peace among nations. They can be processes: means of setting tariffs that insulate Congress from direct responsibility. They can be institutions: an executive branch agency that measures its success in terms of how well it copes with trade-restrictive pressures and thus allows international commerce to flourish.

The main story in the politics of American trade during the years since Schattschneider's classic statement of the problem has been the development of just such antiprotectionist counterweights, devices for diverting and managing trade-restrictive pressures. Such devices, taken together, have constituted an American "system" for trade policymaking that not only has opened up the US market and fueled our postwar prosperity, but also has served as a pillar of our global economic leader-

---

4. "Outline for Remarks by William R. Pearce, before the Committee on Foreign Relations" (Des Moines, Iowa, 11 December 1974; processed), 6. Pearce was Deputy Special Representative for Trade Negotiations in 1972–73.

ship. The fact that during this period the United States was pursuing, credibly and persistently if not always consistently, policies that aimed to reduce its own import barriers made it possible for this country to take the lead internationally and to press others to do likewise. Thus our domestic trade policymaking system was a necessary foundation for building an international regime of relatively open trade under the auspices of the General Agreement on Tariffs and Trade (GATT), negotiated in the late 1940s and implemented in the decades thereafter. This international trade-negotiating process was, in turn, useful in American domestic politics as an argument against trade restrictions.

Postwar trade liberalization did not institute "free trade" or anything close to it. Visible and invisible national barriers to imports remained widespread. But it did bring freer trade, contributing to an explosion in the volume of international commerce and an era of unprecedented global prosperity and growth.

The regime of freer trade had strong domestic support. For the American trade policymaking system benefited from the rise of international economic liberalism among the emerging government and business elite. During the early New Deal, liberalism was simply one contending viewpoint on trade. But in the decades that followed it became the dominant viewpoint. As the world slid into war in the 1930s, and as the war was fought and won, a powerful consensus formed among the American internationalists who took the lead in postwar reconstruction. That consensus was, in important part, Wilsonian: a world open for commerce would be a world at peace. Hull espoused this view explicitly. So did the talented new leadership generation that came to Washington during and after World War II.

In this consensus, the Smoot-Hawley Tariff Act of 1930 played the same role for economic affairs that Munich played for military. Just as British Prime Minister Neville Chamberlain's sincere search for "peace in our time" had only strengthened those who made war, so too had congressional use of trade barriers to aid Depression-hit American producers backfired, postwar leaders believed. Other nations had retaliated, exports had plummeted even more than imports, and the world economic catastrophe helped to spawn both Adolf Hitler's Nazi regime in Germany and aggressive militarism in Japan. Only by building a more open world could we prevent the sort of mutually destructive, beggar-thy-neighbor competition that had produced national economic disaster and international bloodshed. This meant reducing barriers to trade, and to cross-border economic transactions in general. And in the first two postwar decades, as Judith Goldstein has written, success confirmed the liberal ideology, just as the Great Depression had discredited protectionism.[5]

---

5. Judith Goldstein, "Ideas, Institutions, and American Trade Policy," *International Organization* 42, no. 1 (Winter 1988): esp. 187–88.

Public opinion polls underscored this elite support. When the Gallup organization, in June 1953, asked "a cross-section of people listed in Who's Who in America" whether they would "favor lowering tariffs from their present level," 67 percent said yes and only 11 percent expressed opposition. There were still prominent people in Washington in the 1940s and 1950s who called themselves "protectionists," just as there were still "isolationists," but they were on the defensive, politically and ideologically.

"Free trade" was never especially popular among the mass public. When Gallup polled citizens in the 1940s and 1950s about whether they favored higher or lower tariffs, a plurality did back the latter.[6] But when a 1953 Roper poll inquired, "Would you rather see this country import more goods from foreign countries than we do, or put more restrictions on goods imported into this country from abroad," 37 percent opted for restrictions and only 26 percent for the goods.[7] What really mattered, however, was that trade was not high on the list of public concerns. So governmental leaders had the leeway to press the policies they felt were needed.

Liberal trade policies were further buttressed by a concern that was at the top of almost everyone's list: countering the threat of communism. Military alliances with Western Europe and Japan became the prime US instrument for containing the Soviet Union and the People's Republic of China.

Both the internal stability and the external alignment of our allies depended importantly on their economic recovery and prosperity. The United States provided massive aid to facilitate this recovery, permitting recipients to buy needed capital goods in the American market. But our allies' return to self-sufficiency also depended on their ability to sell in our market. To make this possible, not only did the United States grant market access, following the general nondiscriminatory trade rules of the newly established GATT regime, but it also acquiesced in substantial de facto discrimination against itself—in the maintenance of import and exchange controls while these countries recovered, and thereafter in the formation of a common market in Western Europe.

Such one-sided concessions were relatively painless for the United States for, in the years following World War II, the American economy dominated the world as never before or since. It was competitive in all major industrial sectors. It was prosperous, as the anticipated postwar depression never arrived. It was insulated, with its merchandise imports totaling, prior to 1960, only about 3 percent of its gross national product.

---

6. The Gallup Poll, *passim*.

7. Raymond A. Bauer, Ithiel de Sola Pool, and Lewis Anthony Dexter, *American Business and Public Policy: The Politics of Foreign Trade* (Chicago: Aldine-Atherton, 1972), 85.

And finally, exchange rate stability avoided one source of trade risk that would become important in later years.

All of these factors—the "lesson" of Smoot-Hawley, the Cold War imperative, US economic predominance, and prosperity—contributed to one crucial underpinning of the American trade policymaking system: the fact that trade barriers were not a major source of conflict between the Republican and Democratic parties during the postwar period.

This was emphatically not the case in earlier decades. Before 1932, Republicans had used their support of the tariff to help build the broad business backing that made them the dominant party. In the early Franklin Roosevelt administration, almost all Republicans opposed trade-liberalizing legislation, while the great majority of Democrats were in favor. But by the end of World War II, partisan trade divisions were waning. In the quarter-century thereafter, neither party while out of office singled out trade policy as a primary point of difference with the administration in power.

This meant there could be continuity across administrations. Presidents, regardless of party, could champion liberal trade, for both foreign and domestic policy reasons. This White House support was a key to making the system work.

Such was the broad political and policy context within which American trade-policy institutions developed and evolved. But if the early postwar years were years of creation, the more recent period has been one of erosion, of system weakening, which began in the 1970s and accelerated in the 1980s.

One cause was the opening up of American political institutions. As the Congress, for example, became more democratized, more responsive to the initiatives of individual members, it became harder for it to resist the demands of special interests. Prominent among these interests, as ever, were elements of business and labor seeking protection from "foreign imports."

Also contributing to pressures on the system was the internationalization of the American economy, as trade doubled as a share of total US output of goods. This exposed more and more firms and workers to foreign competition, increasing the number of "trade losers" to whom officials would have to respond.

American anxiety about foreign competition grew as the relative position of the United States declined. The striking success of nations like Japan sowed seeds of doubt about liberal doctrine. Here was a nation that seemed committed to a "mercantilist" trade strategy, pushing exports and discouraging imports, and doing very well indeed. Other rising East Asian newly industrializing countries (NICs), Korea and Taiwan, in particular—appeared to be following Japan's example. Might they know something the United States didn't?

Concern was also growing about the direct support that foreign governments gave to chosen industries. Subsidizing steel was the rule, not the exception, in both Old World Europe and the newly industrializing countries. Official trade agencies "targeted" growth sectors like semiconductors and computers. It was hard to determine how substantial such foreign industrial subsidies were; available data suggested that in the strongest trading nations they were not particularly large. Still, US businesspeople were alarmed: "We can compete against foreign companies," they would say, "but not against national treasuries."

In this atmosphere of broad trade frustration, many became deeply skeptical about the liberal image of a world growing more and more open, governed increasingly by common rules of nondiscrimination in trade. What they came to see was an "unfair" world where other nations played loose with the rules and "nice guys" were likely to finish last. They were willing to compete, but they demanded a "level playing field," not one tilted against the United States.

Compounding these problems in the early and middle 1980s was the remarkable and unanticipated rise in the value of the dollar. It went up 70 percent within five years, to a level 40 percent above that at which US firms were broadly competitive, before beginning to decline in 1985. The strong dollar might be good for Americans traveling abroad, but for producers it was equivalent to a 40 percent tax on exports and a 40 percent subsidy to competing imports. Foreign goods poured in as never before, and the United States suddenly faced a trade imbalance without parallel in its modern history. The US trade policymaking system was not in good shape to cope. Imports rose to more than 50 percent above exports, and the US trade deficit swelled beyond $100 billion and kept growing. In response, restrictions on imports increased, their legitimacy grew, and protectionist proposals proliferated. The dollar's subsequent decline brought some relief for producers fighting imports and triggered a surge in American exports. But the rapid rise and slow decline of the trade imbalance left a legacy of skepticism and frustration about the benefits of liberal trade.

This weakening of our capacity to pursue liberal trade policies poses a severe threat to the world standing of the United States. Internationally, relatively open trade relations remain a central element in the network of economic, political, and security relations among advanced industrial nations, a network that is, with the fading of the Cold War, more critical than ever to America's position in the world. Yet the collapse of the common enemy has made this network harder to maintain. Domestically, the problems posed by imports, fair or unfair, pale before those that large-scale import restrictions would bring. For protection would, in the preponderance of cases, mean greater stagnation. It would reinforce the inefficient, and thus bring further deterioration of our relative competitive position in the world economy.

The need then is to combat the erosion of our trade policymaking institutions. The question is how. One route to insight is to examine in detail how our trade policymaking system used to work, exactly how it has deteriorated, and how it might be repaired or—if necessary—replaced. Can the system of the past be restored, in reasonably close approximation? Or must we move on to other means of dealing with protectionism?

This book opens its analysis of these questions by setting forth the main features of the American system for managing trade pressures as it has evolved in the decades since 1934. Subsequent chapters focus on changes in the primary institutions that deal with the politics of trade—Congress, the executive branch, the quasi-judicial procedures—and on changes in the broader economic and political environment. In the final three chapters, the author considers what all this means and what might be done about it.

2

The Old System: Protection for Congress

Sixty-five years ago, the United States Congress took final action on the most famous trade law in American history. The Tariff Act of 1930, better known as "Smoot-Hawley," amended "specific tariff schedules for over twenty thousand items, almost all of them increases."[1] It established "the highest general tariff rate structure that the United States [had] ever experienced," with duties actually collected reaching, by one estimate, 60 percent of the value of dutiable imports.[2]

What followed is well-known. The law quickly "occasioned," as one contemporary critic put it, "more comment, more controversy, more vituperation in the national as well as in the international sphere than any other tariff measure in history."[3] Country after country raised its tariff barriers in retaliation. World trade stagnated: for the United States, imports dropped from $4.40 billion in 1929 to $1.45 billion in 1933, and exports plunged even more: from $5.16 billion to $1.65 billion.[4] The Great

---

1. Robert A. Pastor, *Congress and the Politics of US Foreign Economic Policy, 1929–1976* (Berkeley: University of California Press, 1980), 77–78.

2. John M. Dobson, *Two Centuries of Tariffs: The Background and Emergence of the United States International Trade Commission* (Washington: US International Trade Commission, December 1976), 34.

3. Joseph M. Jones Jr., *Tariff Retaliation: Repercussions of the Hawley-Smoot Bill* (Philadelphia: University of Pennsylvania Press, 1934), 1.

4. US Department of Commerce, Bureau of the Census, *Historical Statistics of the United States: Colonial Times to 1970, part 2* (Washington: US Department of Commerce, 1975), 884. Much of this fall, of course, reflected the Depression's sharp price and output decreases. But even after adjustment for these changes, exports fell, as a share of total US goods production, by more than 20 percent between 1929 and 1933.

Depression—already well under way in 1930—deepened and became truly global. World War II followed less than a decade later.

Not as well-remembered today is the fact that Smoot-Hawley was the last general tariff law ever enacted by the United States Congress. From the "Tariff of Abominations" denounced by Andrew Jackson and John C. Calhoun in 1828 through the McKinley Tariff of 1890 and the Fordney-McCumber Act of 1922, such comprehensive tariff bills had been prime congressional business and the level of US import barriers one of the hottest issues between the Republican and Democratic parties. The tariff, "more than any other single topic, had engrossed [congressional] energies for more than a hundred years."[5] And high rates of duty had been the rule, not the exception.

But barely four years after Smoot-Hawley, our national legislature enacted an entirely different sort of trade law. The Reciprocal Trade Agreements Act of 1934 began a movement of tariffs in the opposite—downward—direction, by authorizing the president to negotiate and implement pacts with other nations in which each agreed to cut tariffs on items of interest to the other. With this authority, he could reduce any US tariff by up to 50 percent without further recourse to Congress. And the authority was renewed in 1937, 1940, and 1943.

Secretary of State Cordell Hull lost no time in exploiting this authority. By 1945, the United States had entered 32 such bilateral trade agreements with 27 countries, granting tariff concessions on 64 percent of all dutiable imports and reducing rates by an average of 44 percent.[6]

In the immediate postwar period, trade negotiations went multilateral. The reciprocal negotiating authority was updated in 1945 to allow further reductions of up to 50 percent from that year's rates. Under American leadership, the General Agreement on Tariffs and Trade (GATT) was negotiated. Its articles provided guidelines for national trade policies and a framework within which the United States and its major (primarily European) trading partners could enter a series of global negotiating "rounds" resulting in further tariff cuts.

This approach began to flag in the 1950s: item-by-item tariff negotiations produced diminishing returns; protectionist pressures regained strength in the United States; and the European Common Market, created in 1957, posed a new challenge. Congress responded in 1962, on President John F. Kennedy's recommendation, by authorizing negotiations to cut tariffs across the board. The resulting "Kennedy Round," completed in

---

5. James L. Sundquist, *The Decline and Resurgence of Congress* (Washington: Brookings Institution, 1981), 99.

6. John H. Jackson, et al., *Implementing the Tokyo Round: National Constitutions and International Economic Relations* (Ann Arbor: University of Michigan Press, 1984), 141; and John W. Evans, *The Kennedy Round in American Trade Policy: The Twilight of the GATT?* (Cambridge: Harvard University Press, 1971), 7.

1967, produced further cuts in US protective duties averaging 35 percent.[7]

When, in the early 1970s, it became clear that impediments other than tariffs were becoming the prime barriers to international trade, Congress authorized the executive branch to bargain yet again—by entering a broad multilateral trade negotiation (MTN), the Tokyo Round, to work out "codes" to regulate government practices that affect trade in such areas as product standards, government procurement, and government subsidies. The result was the MTN agreements of 1979.

Smoot-Hawley remained on the books, in form still the basic US trade law. But because of negotiations authorized by subsequent Congresses, its average tariff level on dutiable imports had been reduced from 60 percent in 1931 to 5.7 percent in 1980.[8]

Total US exports did not return to their pre-depression level until 1942. But thereafter they grew rapidly: to $10.2 billion in 1950, $20.4 billion in 1960, $42.6 billion in 1970, and $216.7 billion in 1980.[9] The parallel figures for imports were $8.9 billion in 1950, $14.7 billion in 1960, $40.0 billion in 1970, and $244.9 billion in 1980.

These numbers reflect, of course, the unprecedented postwar rise in overall national production, compounded by inflation. But they reflect more: between 1933 and 1980, for example, "real" (price-deflated) exports more than doubled as a share of US goods production.

The increase in global commerce was even greater. This unprecedented trade explosion was a prime contributor to a remarkable era of world prosperity. It also contributed to something the 20th century had not previously seen: four decades and more of peace on the European continent.

How was it possible, politically, for the United States to reduce its own trade barriers and persuade the world to do likewise? As noted in the opening chapter, E. E. Schattschneider had demonstrated how politics must drive Congress to respond to producer pressures and raise levels of protection. By what political magic had "Schattschneider's law" been repealed?

The short answer is that Congress legislated itself out of the business of making product-specific trade law. There were exceptions, of course.

7. Evans, *The Kennedy Round in American Trade Policy*, 283.

8. Dobson, *Two Centuries of Tariffs*, 34; US Department of Commerce, Bureau of the Census, *Statistical Abstract of the United States, 1982–83* (Washington: US Department of Commerce, 1982), 844.

9. US Department of Commerce, *Historical Statistics of the United States*, 884, and US Department of Commerce, Bureau of the Census, *Statistical Abstract of the United States, 1984* (Washington: US Department of Commerce, 1985), 831. These data differ slightly from the Commerce Department data employed later in this study in discussions of contemporary US trade flows.

But, as a general rule, Congress as a collective body was as assiduous in avoiding specific trade barriers after 1934 as it had been in imposing them the century before.

A new system for trade policymaking came into being. Like any ongoing set of policy processes, it was not created by any one actor at any single time. It evolved, not only because of creative leadership from men like Cordell Hull, but also because it served the political interests of those senators and representatives most responsible for trade policy.

Protecting Congress From Trade Pressures

Article I of the United States Constitution grants Congress sole power "to regulate commerce with foreign nations." It also provides Congress authority "to lay and collect . . . duties," and the tariff supplied about half of federal revenues as recently as 1910.[10] The Constitution grants the president no trade-specific authority whatsoever. Thus, in no sphere of government policy can the primacy of the legislative branch be clearer: Congress reigns supreme on trade, unless and until it decides otherwise.

Beginning in the mid-1930s, Congress did decide otherwise, changing the way it handled trade issues. No longer did it give priority to protecting American industry. Instead, its members would give priority to protecting themselves: from the direct, one-sided pressure from producer interests that had led them to make bad trade law. They would channel that pressure elsewhere, pushing product-specific trade decisions out of the committees of Congress and off the House and Senate floors to other governmental institutions.

The instruments for accomplishing this goal developed and changed with time, and political protection was never, of course, the sole congressional motive. What moved some legislators was a conviction that trade regulation had become too complicated and too detailed for Congress to be handling its specifics. For Secretary of State Cordell Hull and some of his fellow Democrats—historically the lower tariff political party—the aim was to reduce trade barriers in any way that was practical. As a Tennessee congressman during World War I, the secretary himself had become convinced that "unhampered trade dovetailed with peace; high tariffs, trade barriers, and unfair economic competition, with war."[11] And without the combination of his determination and an economic crisis that produced lopsided Democratic majorities in Congress,

---

10. Dobson, *Two Centuries of Tariffs*, 31. In fiscal year 1984, by contrast, customs duties comprised just 1.7 percent of total federal budget receipts.

11. *The Memoirs of Cordell Hull*, vol. 1 (New York: Macmillan, 1948), 81.

the historic shift of 1934 would not have come about—at least not then. Twenty years later, a landmark trade policymaking study could report that protectionists "shared in the consensus that somebody outside Congress should set tariff rates or impose and remove quotas."[12] But no such bipartisan consensus existed in the 1930s.

The shift did not mean that legislators abdicated all responsibility for trade. They continued to set the guidelines, regulating how much tariff levels could be changed, by what procedures, and with what exceptions. Individual members also remained free to make ample protectionist noise, to declaim loudly on behalf of producer interests that were strong in their states or districts. In fact, they could do so more freely than ever, secure in the knowledge that most actual decisions would be made elsewhere.

1934 was not the first year in which Congress delegated specific trade authority to the president. The US Tariff Commission (USTC) had been created in 1916 as a nonpartisan, fact-finding agency. And the "flexible tariff" position of the Fordney-McCumber Act of 1922 empowered the president, at the commission's recommendation, to raise or lower any tariff by up to 50 percent in order to equalize the production costs of domestic firms and foreign competitors. (If fully applied, which it never was, this provision would have eliminated "comparative advantage," the primary economic reason for trade, since it is such differences in production costs that make trade profitable!)[13]

But as long as Congress was expected to pass comprehensive bills adjusting tariffs every few years, such measures could never keep protectionist wolves from the Capitol's doors. For those affected knew that Congress would shortly be acting on their specific products, in a process that gave priority to their interests. This could only encourage them to press all the harder, for greater and greater protection. As Hull put the matter,

> it would have been folly to go to Congress and ask that the Smoot-Hawley Act be repealed or its rates reduced by Congress. This [approach had], with the exception of the Underwood Act in 1913 . . . always resulted in higher tariffs because the special interests enriched by high tariffs went to their respective Congressmen and insisted on higher rates.[14]

What was required was a system that would make the buck stop somewhere else. In the 1930s, the legislative and executive branches began to construct such a system.

---

12. Raymond A. Bauer, Ithiel de Sola Pool, and Lewis Anthony Dexter, *American Business and Public Policy: The Politics of Foreign Trade* (Chicago: Aldine-Atherton, 1972), 39.

13. Dobson, *Two Centuries of Tariffs*, 87–95.

14. *Memoirs of Cordell Hull*, vol. 1, 358.

The central need was obvious: to delegate specific tariff setting. But meeting this need required answers to two basic questions. First, how could Congress rationalize giving up such a major power? And second, would not whoever was delegated this power be subject to the same unbalanced set of pressures, with similar policy results?

The "Bargaining Tariff"

The need for a rationale for the delegation of congressional power was answered by linking tariff setting to international negotiations, a clear executive branch prerogative. To borrow the phrase of Joseph M. Jones Jr., a strong advocate of this approach, the United States moved decisively from an inflexible, statutory tariff to a "bargaining tariff."[15] The president could reduce rates by up to 50 percent, but only after negotiating bilateral agreements in which the United States "got" as well as "gave."[16]

Another way that Congress rationalized the delegation of authority was by making it temporary. As Dean Acheson noted many years later,

> unlike almost all of the New Deal economic legislation once regarded as radical, the executive power to negotiate trade agreements has not been permanently incorporated in American legislation, but only extended from time to time for short periods with alternating contractions and expansions of scope.[17]

By its answer to the first question—the rationale for delegating power—the Reciprocal Trade Agreements Act of 1934 also addressed the second: how to avoid unbalanced trade pressures. In the process of trade negotiation, "getting" and "giving" were defined in terms of producers, not consumers. But the "bargaining tariff" shifted the balance of trade politics by engaging the interests of export producers, since tariff reductions could now be defended as direct means of winning new markets for American products overseas. Export interests had long been an influence on US trade policy, but usually they were no match for producers threatened by imports. The bargaining tariff strengthened the exporters' stakes and their policy influence, creating something of a political counterweight on the liberal trade side.

---

15. Joseph M. Jones Jr., *Tariff Retaliation*, 303ff.

16. The delegation of tariff-setting authority to encourage "reciprocal" concessions was not unprecedented. The barrier-raising McKinley Tariff Act of 1890 gave the president authority to adjust tariffs on sugar and other specified commodities according to the "reciprocity" shown American exports by particular Latin American countries. See David A. Lake, *Power, Protection, and Free Trade: International Sources of U.S. Commercial Strategy, 1887–1939* (Ithaca, NY: Cornell University Press, 1989), esp. 100–02.

17. Dean Acheson, *Present at the Creation: My Years at the State Department* (New York: W. W. Norton, 1969), 10.

Thus, partly as a genuine objective (we did want other countries to lower their trade barriers) and partly as a political device, the "bargaining tariff" was an essential ingredient in the emerging American trade policymaking system. And since, from the 1920s onward, the United States regularly extended bilaterally negotiated tariff cuts to its other trading partners (under the unconditional "most favored nation" [MFN] principle), country-by-country deals were an effective means of reducing trade barriers across the board.

In 1934, legislators could grant the new authority tentatively, experimentally. Hull had wanted it to be unbounded in time, but Congress limited it to an initial three years (however, the agreements negotiated during this period would remain in effect indefinitely). Hull also would have liked to bargain multilaterally, but he settled for "the next best method," bilateral negotiations, because "it was manifest that public opinion in no country, especially our own, would at that time support a worthwhile multilateral undertaking."[18] Yet in one crucial respect the executive authority to negotiate trade agreements was unconstrained by the traditional limits: Congress did not insist on approving the specific agreements that were negotiated.

In subsequent decades, presidents would employ tariff-negotiating authority more ambitiously—to negotiate multilaterally (after World War II) or to bargain on general tariff levels rather than item by item (the Kennedy Round). And in the Trade Act of 1974, Congress would grant new authority to negotiate agreements on nontariff trade distortions, though these would require subsequent congressional approval. Always there were limits in time and in the range of negotiation. Nevertheless, Congress continued to respond to new trade policy demands by shifting the basic pressure and responsibility onto the president.

The "Bicycle Theory" and "Export Politics"

One political effect of trade negotiations was to divert some trade policymaking attention from the problems of the American market to the benefits of opening up markets overseas. In fact, the very existence of ongoing negotiations proved a potent rationale for deferring protectionist claims. It gave negotiators (and their congressional allies) a strong situational argument: to impose or tighten an import barrier now, they could assert, would undercut talks aimed at broader American trade advantages. Conversely, the unavailability of this argument in periods between major trade negotiations strengthened the hands of those seeking protection. Trade specialists came to label this phenomenon the "bicycle theory": the trade system needed to move forward, liberalize further, or

---

18. *Memoirs of Cordell Hull*, vol. 1, p. 356.

else it would fall down, into new import restrictions. It could not stand still.

Even in the absence of major negotiations, trade officials sought ways to shift from "import politics" to "export politics." Since the late 1960s, for example, every US administration has had to cope with severe pressures generated by rising sales from Japan. Although interest-group pressures would tend to skew the balance heavily toward curbing imports, officials have regularly, with congressional cooperation, shifted the focus to exports, to opening up the Japanese market. Responding to arguments that other countries' trading practices were unfair, US trade negotiators did not have to defend those practices or point to the beams in our own eyes. Instead, they could demonstrate their toughness by demanding market-opening concessions from our trading partners.

But to delegate power over specific trade barriers with reasonable confidence, Congress needed more than an international negotiating process. It also needed two sorts of executive agents: a *broker* who would be responsive to legislators' concerns domestically even as he pushed for bargains internationally, and *regulators* who would technocratically apply statutory import relief rules to a set of exceptional cases.

The Executive Broker

In preparing Smoot-Hawley, the House Ways and Means Committee "accumulated 11,000 pages of testimony and briefs in forty-three days and five nights," but no one came to speak for the executive branch.[19] At hearings for the 1934 act, by contrast, 7 of 17 witnesses represented the Roosevelt administration.[20] Congress would not have adopted such a law without executive branch leadership. And if the new American trade policymaking system were to work, Congress needed a focal point for trade policy management within the executive branch, an official who could balance foreign and domestic concerns.

For the first decade, the position of trusted executive agent was admirably occupied by a man from Capitol Hill, Secretary of State Cordell Hull. While he tilted trade policy in the market-expanding direction as much as was politically feasible, he retained his sensitivity to congressional concerns. He moved immediately and aggressively to exploit the new bargaining authority. At the same time, he never forgot that the hand that had granted this authority could also take it away.

Hull resigned in 1944, leaving a gap on the trade scene that would not be filled in any durable way for nearly 20 years. In the immediate

---

19. E. E. Schattschneider, *Politics, Pressures and the Tariff* (New York: Prentice-Hall, 1935), 36.

20. Pastor, *Congress and the Politics of US Foreign Economic Policy*, 88.

postwar years it did not really matter. Europe and Japan were devastated. Triumphant and economically dominant, the United States was in a position to sell abroad far more than the world could sell us in return. Thus, it was logical—and politically feasible—for trade policy to be subordinate to the broader American foreign policy of constructing a free world coalition founded on a liberal world economic order. And it was logical for the State Department, staffed by such talents as Under Secretary Will L. Clayton, to continue to play the lead trade-negotiating role.

But in the 1950s, as resurgent international competition once again began to threaten American industries, attacks on State stewardship increased. The department was charged with favoring foreign interests over American interests, with bargaining away US commercial advantages in the interest of good political relations or other diplomatic goals. For a time, State managed to keep the primary negotiating responsibility, and it could play this role aggressively when its senior economic official was someone like Under Secretary C. Douglas Dillon. However, in 1953, President Dwight D. Eisenhower found it necessary to join Congress in setting up a commission, chaired by Clarence B. Randall, to develop recommendations for his overall trade policy. Randall was then brought into the White House as a special trade adviser to implement the commission's report. And the Kennedy administration developed its major trade expansion program in the White House, under a temporary staff headed by Howard C. Petersen.

So when, to meet the challenge of the new European Economic Community (EEC), that administration went to Congress seeking broad new authority to reduce tariff rates across the board (not item by item), it was not surprising that House Ways and Means Chairman Wilbur D. Mills (D-AR) raised the question of whether State could be trusted with this new authority. Should it not be given instead to a negotiator who would be responsive at least equally to domestic clients? No existing agency was a good candidate. The Commerce Department was, in Mills's view, incompetent. Moreover, Mills and another well-placed critic of State, Senate Finance Committee Chairman Harry F. Byrd Sr. (D-VA), thought Commerce insufficiently responsive to agricultural interests. So perhaps there should be a new presidential negotiator who could balance domestic and foreign concerns.

Mills proposed, therefore, that the president designate a special representative for trade negotiations (STR). An important figure in developing and brokering this idea was Myer N. Rashish, a Mills aide in the late 1950s, who was serving as Petersen's White House deputy in preparing the Trade Expansion Act. Rashish suggested that the Petersen office itself was an appropriate model. He believed that conflicting bureaucratic interests made it impossible for the administration to initiate such a reorganization proposal; however, if Mills proposed it, the president would consider reorganization an acceptable price to pay for the broad new negotiating authority he was seeking. And Kennedy did accept it, but reluctantly; like most presidents, he resisted efforts to establish special-purpose offices in "his" Executive Office.

Congress not only created its own agent in 1962; it protected and strengthened the special representative a decade later. When the Nixon administration proposed to place the STR under its Council on International Economic Policy (CIEP) staff, Ways and Means responded by voting to make the office of the STR (not just the representative) statutory, in an amendment to what became the Trade Act of 1974. By the time the Senate finished its work, the office had been placed formally in the Executive Office of the President, and, on the proposal of Finance Committee Chairman Russell B. Long (D-LA), its head was given cabinet rank. Long underscored legislators' sense that they owned a piece of this White House trade operation when he suggested, during the confirmation hearings of Jimmy Carter's STR, Robert S. Strauss, that "it might be a good idea for us to ask" the secretaries of State and Treasury to meet with his committee "so that there can be no misunderstanding" about which official was to have trade primacy.[21]

Organizationally, the STR was an anomaly. Though housed in the Executive Office of the President, few of its heads had close personal contact with the chief executive (Strauss was in fact the prime exception). For presidents were politicians who, like members of Congress, wanted to limit their direct responsibility for decisions that went against important trade constituencies. Neither was trade negotiating the normal type of White House activity. In fact, it was the sort of day-to-day operating function usually housed in a cabinet department. But no appropriate department existed.

The White House location offered flexibility, balance, and (sometimes) power. During the Kennedy Round, STR Christian A. Herter and his deputies, W. Michael Blumenthal and William M. Roth, enhanced their leverage by initiating close working relationships with State—which then retained authority for most trade negotiations outside the Kennedy Round—and with the international economic component of the National Security Council staff. In the early 1970s, when influence in such matters shifted to the economic side of the White House, STR William D. Eberle and his deputies William R. Pearce and Harald B. Malmgren made their presidential connection through George P. Shultz, secretary of the Treasury and "economic czar" of the Nixon administration. But whatever the specific relationships of the STR, the White House location—combined with special status and separation from the White House political staff—offered him flexibility in working with legislators across as well as along

---

21. US Congress, Senate Committee on Finance, *Hearing on Nominations,* 95th Cong., 1st sess., 23 March 1977, 4.

party lines, drawing in some interests to balance others, and keeping the trade policy game as open as possible.

The office of the STR allowed executive branch trade officials to do what Hull had done three decades before: employ their leeway to tilt trade policy in the liberal, market-expanding direction. Sensitive to the political winds, they could lean at least moderately against them, recognizing that congressmen who bucked interest group demands to them did not always require their full satisfaction. The STR-led executive branch certainly advocated US interests in international negotiations—it had to do so to retain credibility at home. But the role of such negotiations in US trade politics was to keep the game open, to limit protection, and to respond to the trade problems of specific industries with market-expanding solutions.

Domestically, American trade policymakers were noninterventionist. Unlike their counterparts in Japan's Ministry of International Trade and Industry (MITI), for example, they did not aspire to nurture those industries at home that promised future competitiveness abroad. But when it came to international trade barriers, they were definitely not policy-neutral. They wanted to limit such barriers insofar as was possible. This made them trade policy activists, for when they feared being trapped by one-sided pressure for protection, they would look for countervailing interests and encourage them to weigh in on the other side. This approach created frequent tension with legislators championing particular industries. But most congressional trade leaders, most of the time, sympathized with the broad objective of liberal trade and, free of direct responsibility themselves, often connived with their executive counterparts to steer the political game in the direction of trade expansion.

"The Rules"

As legislators worked with executive branch leaders to construct a system to protect themselves from trade pressures, they also sought a different sort of administrative institution, one modeled on quasi-judicial regulatory procedures. For there remained broad agreement that, under certain exceptional circumstances, American industries ought to have recourse to trade protection. Unless "objective" procedures could be devised to provide such protection, these industries would demand specific statutory action. Thus, US law and practice maintained a set of "trade remedies" designed to offer recourse to interests seriously injured by imports and to those up against what were considered "unfair" foreign practices.

The major legal trade remedies originated well before the Reciprocal Trade Agreements Act of 1934. A law dating from 1897 required the secretary of the Treasury to impose a special, offsetting duty if he found that foreign governments were subsidizing exports with a "bounty or grant." The Anti-Dumping Act of 1921 called for similar measures if foreign sellers were determined to be unloading goods in our market at prices below their home market price. (After World War II, GATT Article VI authorized and regulated national antidumping and countervailing duty [CVD] measures.)

There remained the problem of industries injured by import competition they did not, or could not, claim to be "unfair." If, for example, a US tariff reduction led to an unexpectedly large surge in imports, should not competing domestic producers have the right to seek at least temporary trade relief? Congressional trade specialists generally thought they should; Congress was worried about the uncertainty inherent in the international negotiations it had authorized, and wanted some form of insurance for domestic interests. In the 1943 agreement with Mexico, the United States, drawing on pre-1934 precedents, included an "escape clause" allowing an affected industry to appeal for temporary import relief if it could prove injury from the results of US trade concessions. This approach was incorporated in Article XIX of the GATT.[22]

Seeking to retain executive discretion, State officials proposed to include such a clause in all future US trade agreements, and President Harry S Truman issued an executive order in 1947 setting forth procedures by which injured firms could seek relief. This deferred statutory action for a while, but by 1951 Congress had found this insufficient, so legislators incorporated a general "escape clause" provision in an act extending presidential trade-negotiating authority.

By making protection the "exceptional" recourse in the "normal" process of trade-barrier reduction, the escape clause kept the quasi-judicial form of the old flexible tariff but turned the substance on its head. Protection-minded legislators sought to counter this with so-called peril point requirements that were incorporated in the 1948 law and intermittently thereafter. These required the Tariff Commission to estimate the point beyond which tariffs could not be reduced without "peril" to specific industries; their aim was to pressure the executive not to negotiate rates below that level.

If regularly followed, the peril point principle would have made protection the norm and trade liberalization the exception. And in fact, with this and other devices, Congress in the 1950s slowed the momentum of trade liberalization to a crawl: by grudging, sometimes single-year extensions of presidential negotiating authority; by escape clause criteria that made it fairly easy for industries to qualify for relief; by a 1958 provision allowing Congress, with a two-thirds vote in both houses, to compel the

---

22. For background on American and GATT law, together with case examples, see John H. Jackson, *Legal Problems of International Economic Relations: Cases, Materials and Text, American Casebook Series* (St. Paul: West Publishing Co., 1977), 617–64.

president to implement a Tariff Commission escape clause recommendation; and by limiting the range of future tariff reduction. In the "Dillon Round" negotiation of 1960, for example, authority for tariff cuts was limited to 20 percent. In fact, only a 10 percent reduction was achieved.

The Trade Expansion Act of 1962 brought major revision and codification to the escape clause. An interest seeking relief had to demonstrate serious injury, the major cause of which was an increase in imports due to US tariff concessions. If the Tariff Commission found that a particular interest met this rather tough test, the president had a choice whether or not to accept the commission's recommendations for tariff or quota relief. If he did not, Congress could override his negative decision by a majority vote in both houses. But while the administration had to swallow this "legislative veto" provision, it was able to beat back a Senate floor amendment adding a "peril point" requirement. (And in fact, the veto was never exercised.)

During congressional debate, President Kennedy illustrated the political utility of the escape clause by implementing a Tariff Commission recommendation to increase tariffs on Belgian carpets and sheet glass. When the European Community retaliated, Kennedy stuck to his decision, adding that if his bill were already law, he "could have then offered an alternate package [of compensating tariff reductions] which . . . would have prevented retaliation."[23] He was thus able simultaneously to demonstrate his readiness to help injured industries and to argue that trade-liberalizing legislation offered a better way to do so.

The 1962 act also added an innovative approach to injury from imports—that of "trade adjustment assistance" (TAA). The idea was originally suggested, it appears, in a Council on Foreign Relations planning paper prepared during World War II, and it was given broad public exposure when proposed to Eisenhower's Randall Commission by David J. McDonald of the United Steelworkers union in 1953. The TAA idea offered an alternative, or a supplement, to tariff relief. Workers or firms hurt by imports could apply for government financial, technical, and retraining assistance—including relocation allowances—that would help the firms to become more competitive and the workers to move to other lines of endeavor. The political aim was to weaken support for trade restrictions by offering a constructive alternative to those hurt by imports.

The Randall Commission had rejected the idea, by a 16-to-1 vote. But it was picked up by several senators in the 1950s, including one John F. Kennedy. When he became president, Kennedy favored its adoption on both substantive and political grounds, since it was something to offer AFL-CIO leaders to help secure labor support of his Trade Expansion

---

23. Pastor, *Congress and the Politics of US Foreign Economic Policy*, 114.

Act. TAA was, moreover, consistent with his administration's emphasis on worker retraining as a response to unemployment.

By the 1960s, therefore, a number of administrative remedies were available to companies and workers injured by increased import competition. Substantively, their goal was equity—an established set of procedures, available to all, offering insurance against damage from trade liberalization or offsets for trade-distorting foreign practices like subsidies. Politically, the administrative remedies were another means by which Congress could divert trade pressures elsewhere. Legislators could say to those seeking statutory remedies, "Have you looked into the escape clause?" or "It sounds like a dumping case to me—can I make an appointment for you at Treasury so you can learn the procedure for relief on that?" Rather than trying to arbitrate the many trade claims, legislators could point to "the rules" under which firms and workers were entitled to relief. And officials of the executive branch could do likewise.

But in practice, the administrative remedies could not satisfy the largest trade-impacted industries. These industries wanted greater assurance of relief, and their political power gave them reason to believe they could do better by applying direct pressure at both ends of Pennsylvania Avenue.

Deals for "Special Cases"

International negotiations brought executive branch officials and export interests more effectively into trade politics; remedy procedures offered the injured a recourse other than going to Congress for new legislation. There remained the "special cases": those large, import-impacted interests that saw in open trade more threat than promise, and that were powerful enough not to settle for such relief as the regular rules might afford. The trade policymaking system also needed means to cope with them, or they might join together in a protectionist coalition and overthrow the liberal order. And even if that were beyond their immediate reach, they could certainly do much to impede an administration's trade-expanding initiatives.

In the postwar period, the most important "special case" was textiles (including apparel), followed by certain agricultural products[24] and steel.

---

24. Agricultural interests sometimes won specific statutory protection for products like meat and sugar through legislation that moved through the House and Senate agriculture committees (which never fully joined in the tradition of congressional self-denial on trade). At other times they won import relief through executive action under legal authorities like Section 22 of the Agricultural Adjustment Act of 1933, which authorized the president, on the recommendation of the Tariff Commission and the secretary of Agriculture, to impose quotas or fees to the extent that imports were interfering with a domestic commodity program designed to buttress prices and limit production.

Oil imports were a prime issue until a 1955 statutory compromise authorized the president to restrict imports in cases in which they threatened to impair the national security, and President Eisenhower imposed oil import quotas four years later. The auto industry remained committed to open trade until the late 1970s. But the textile-apparel coalition, with its two and a half million workers and firms located in every state of the union, had sufficient concern about trade and sufficient political power to threaten the general trade policymaking system unless its specific interests were accommodated.

For the first nine postwar years, the textile industry was relatively inactive. It shared the benefits of the artificial economic dominance the war had provided the United States. So confident were its leaders that in 1946, they endorsed and cooperated in a mission to Japan—a fierce prewar trade competitor—to aid in reconstructing that country's textile industry during the American occupation. But in 1955, suffering a depressed market at home and resurgent sales from across the Pacific, and seeing in the debate over reciprocal trade renewal an opportunity to make the industry's weight felt:

> Textiles entered the legislative battle in full force. Letters poured in on the congressmen from the textile districts. The Georgia and Alabama delegations, long-time mainstays of Southern free-trade sentiment, went over to the protectionist side.[25]

At that time, US cotton textile exports exceeded imports, and the latter were less than 2 percent of domestic production. But if the industry's substantive case for relief was a bit overstated, its power was taken very seriously. In the House of Representatives, it took an enormous personal effort by House Speaker Sam Rayburn (D-TX) to beat back efforts to open the trade authority bill of 1955 up to protectionist amendments. A year later, a proposal for rigid textile quotas failed by just two votes in the Senate. The Eisenhower administration got the message, and Japan was pressured to limit its cotton textile exports. When the US textile industry found this "voluntary" Japanese restraint insufficient, Congress added Section 204 to the Agricultural Act of 1956, authorizing the president to negotiate bilateral export limitation agreements with foreign governments on "textiles or textile products." The Eisenhower administration moved promptly to exercise this authority.[26]

For a comprehensive survey of "special protection," see Gary Clyde Hufbauer, Diane T. Berliner, and Kimberly Ann Elliott, *Trade Protection in the United States: 31 Case Studies* (Washington: Institute for International Economics, 1986).

25. Bauer, Pool, and Dexter, *American Business and Public Policy*, 60.

26. For an extended treatment of textile policymaking, especially vis-à-vis Japan, see I. M. Destler, Haruhiro Fukui, and Hideo Sato, *The Textile Wrangle: Conflict in Japanese-American Relations, 1969-1971* (Ithaca, NY: Cornell University Press, 1979).

What was clear to President Eisenhower was clearer still to President Kennedy. As senator from a declining textile state, he knew both the industry's power and its interests. As presidential candidate, he had promised action to control textile imports from Hong Kong and elsewhere, which—now that Japanese sales were limited—were growing in volume. As president, he wanted to deliver on this promise. He recognized also that unless this key industry were appeased, Congress was unlikely to approve general trade-expanding legislation.

The result was a special multilateral deal for the industry, known officially as the Long-Term Arrangement Regarding International Trade in Cotton Textiles (LTA). This pact was completed in 1962 under GATT auspices, although it constituted a massive exception to normal GATT rules. The LTA set guidelines within which importing nations could negotiate detailed, product-by-product quota agreements with exporters. And once negotiations for the LTA were well under way, the American Cotton Manufacturers Institute returned Kennedy's favor by endorsing his trade legislation: "We believe that the authority to deal with foreign nations proposed by the President will be wisely exercised and should be granted."[27]

This pattern was repeated eight years later, albeit at considerably greater international cost. At industry insistence, the Nixon administration embarked on a fractious, three-year negotiation with Japan, eventually threatening use of the "Trading with the Enemy Act" to force that nation to broaden its export restraints to include textiles of wool and man-made fibers. Then, in 1973, this too was multilateralized in a Multi-Fiber Arrangement (MFA), which succeeded the LTA. Not entirely by coincidence, Congress completed action on President Nixon's trade expansion proposal the following year.

And in the late 1960s, with the steel industry feeling growing import pressure, the State Department shepherded an arrangement among Japanese, European, and American producers to limit the volume sales of the major foreign exporters to the US market. This arrangement was abandoned in the 1970s, in part because of uncertainty about its legality under American antitrust law, and in part because dollar devaluation (plus an economic boom) brought a temporary easing of US steel-trade problems. But in 1977, the Carter administration would respond to renewed pressure from the steel industry with a new form of ad hoc import limit, the "trigger price mechanism" (TPM).[28]

These special deals circumvented both national and international rules.

---

27. Bauer, Pool, and Dexter, *American Business and Public Policy*, 79.

28. See Hideo Sato and Michael Hodin, "The U.S.-Japanese Steel Issue of 1977," in I. M. Destler and Hideo Sato, eds., *Coping with U.S.-Japanese Economic Conflicts* (Lexington, MA: D. C. Heath, 1982), 56–70.

Typically, they involved pressuring foreign governments—primarily Japan in the 1950s and 1960s—to enforce "voluntary" export restraints (VERs). This device got around the domestic rules for proving injury and limiting the duration of protection. For the United States, VERs had the international benefit that, unlike measures taken directly against imports, they were not subject to the GATT proviso allowing other nations to impose equivalent trade restrictions unless the United States offered "compensation" in the form of offsetting tariff reductions. In both of these ways, they undercut the American trade policymaking system, for they showed how easily its rules could be avoided by those with power to do so.

Yet at the same time, special deals reinforced the protection for Congress that was the system's political foundation. They kept industry-specific protection out of our trade statutes. They gave executive officials significant leeway to cooperate with exporting countries in working out the form that protection would take, thus limiting the risk of retaliation. They let congressmen play the role they preferred: that of making noise, lobbying the executive branch for action, but refraining from final action themselves. (And for foreign firms they had one major benefit that tariffs or US import quotas did not have—they allowed them to raise their prices, thus pocketing the "scarcity rents" available because they were selling fewer goods than the market wished to buy. This was the real "compensation" provided, and it was one that directly benefited the industry hurt by the restraint.)[29]

Strong Congressional Committees

Last but not least, Congress needed internal safeguards. For the various means of diverting trade pressures shared one fundamental weakness: Congress could always override them by enacting a trade-restrictive statute, since it did not, and could not, yield up that fundamental power to make any law "to regulate commerce with foreign nations." Thus, since the political interests of an individual senator or representative continued to be tilted in the direction of supporting the claimant for protection, there was always the danger that, if forced to an up-or-down vote, legislators would impose statutory trade restrictions.

There was therefore a need for internal procedures and institutions that would keep this from happening. Insofar as possible, product-specific bills and amendments had to be kept off the House and Senate floors.

---

29. C. Fred Bergsten and his colleagues argue for replacing VERs with tariffs or auction quotas that would allow the United States to capture these rents. See Bergsten et al., *Auction Quotas and United States Trade Policy*, POLICY ANALYSES IN INTERNATIONAL ECONOMICS 19 (Washington: Institute for International Economics, September 1987).

This required strong committees. Fortunately, trade policy had long been the province of two of the most powerful congressional panels: Senate Finance and House Ways and Means. They were the tax committees and their jurisdiction over foreign commerce derived originally from the tariff's revenue function. From the 1930s onward, their power was enhanced by jurisdiction over Social Security. As tax committees, they had broad authority, close links to domestic interests, and the reputation for being hard-nosed, realistic, and slightly conservative. Unlike Senate Foreign Relations or House Foreign Affairs, they were unlikely to be disparaged by their colleagues as soft on foreign interests. Because they had other major legislative fish to fry, they were content with a system that delegated trade details, and satisfied with considering major trade authority bills just once every few years.

Particularly pivotal was House Ways and Means. In comparison with the House of Representatives, the Senate was smaller, more informal, and more personality-dependent in its mode of operation. It had always allowed individual members more sway—more opportunity to delay action with unlimited debate, more leeway to propose amendments to legislation being considered on the floor. Once an influx of liberal activists broke down the informal dominance of southern seniors in the 1960s, the Senate became a very open place, where leaders reigned but did not rule. Senate rules did not require an amendment to be "germane" to the pending legislation. Therefore if a trade-restrictive amendment was suddenly sprung on the floor for attachment to a semirelated bill, the Finance Committee chairman often lacked the ability to block it.

But the Ways and Means chairman could. Because of its size, the House was inevitably more dependent than the Senate on formal institutions, rules, and procedures. And after the power of the House leadership had been limited by the revolt against Speaker Joseph G. Cannon (D-IL) in 1910, committee chairmen—chosen by seniority—rose to dominance. In fact, "the zenith of committee government occurred between the years 1937 and 1971,"[30] precisely the period in which the American trade policymaking system flourished. A strong and skillful Ways and Means leader could virtually ensure that the full House considered only those trade proposals that his committee wished to place before it. He could also place a strong personal imprint on whatever his committee recommended.

The most artful practitioner of this power was Wilbur D. Mills (D-AR), Ways and Means chairman from 1958 to 1974. He kept his committee relatively small by House standards—25 members—and resisted the formation of subcommittees. Working closely with these members, he dom-

---

30. Roger H. Davidson, "Subcommittee Government: New Channels for Policy Making," in Thomas E. Mann and Norman J. Ornstein, eds., *The New Congress* (Washington: American Enterprise Institute, 1981), 103.

inated his panel not by arbitrary action—although he valued and used the chair's prerogative—but by his superior grasp of both substance and politics. He was always listening: to committee members, to lobbyists, to administration leaders and staff experts. In his committee, he knew how to put together bills that had consensus support. And he was determined not to take the slightest risk that a Ways and Means bill would lose on the House floor, or that it would be subject to an amendment the committee could not abide.

On trade, this meant playing the game of protecting his colleagues: blocking floor votes, diverting pressure elsewhere, pushing an administration to work out special deals when the heat got too strong. And while Mills was a free trader by personal conviction, he was clever enough not to seem insensitive to import-affected petitioners. He would listen to them sympathetically and make sure that they had access to the proper procedures. Simultaneously, he would maneuver to avert statutory protection of any sort for specific products.

A classic example of how Mills made the system work was his response to mounting textile-industry pressure in the years following the Kennedy Round. In 1968, a junior South Carolina senator, Ernest F. Hollings (D), proposed, as an amendment to the Johnson administration's pending tax bill, that statutory quotas be established for textile and apparel products. The full Senate approved the amendment, and the vote was not close. Mills, in alliance with the White House and the State Department, refused to accept it when the bill went to the Senate-House conference committee; he insisted, as a matter of constitutional propriety, that such provisions should originate in the House (trade was tariffs; tariffs were revenue measures). Senate conferees receded, as they did normally in such cases in those days, and so the quota proposal died without House members ever having to vote on it.

But Mills did not rest here. Realizing that the rise of then-uncontrolled imports of man-made fiber textiles meant that the industry was very likely to win some form of protection eventually, Mills began to advocate it—in the nonstatutory form of restraints negotiated with Japan and the other major East Asian suppliers. And while his goal was to prevent direct congressional action, he buttressed the Nixon administration's bargaining position by introducing his own quota bill. If "voluntary" restraints were not achieved, Mills declared repeatedly, Congress would be forced to act.

Mills was playing a game familiar to trade practitioners: hyping the "protectionist threat" from Congress so as to create pressure on foreign governments to come to terms and to render legislative action unnecessary. The administration, in turn, was supposed to talk about the threat of legislation but stop short of supporting it. However, President Richard M. Nixon broke this unwritten rule in June 1970 when, frustrated by Japan's failure to carry through on high-level promises to come to terms, he "reluctantly" endorsed the statutory quota bill Mills had introduced.

The chairman was now in a bind. He had no choice but to move forward with a "Mills bill" that he did not really want enacted. But it somehow took until late November for the House to complete floor action, and although supporters rushed the bill to the Senate floor in December, they were unable to force a vote. Finance Chairman Russell Long played his part by attaching to the bill a controversial Social Security–welfare reform package, so that it was subject to twin filibusters: by liberal traders and by welfare reform critics. The bill died when the 91st Congress adjourned.

Then, in early 1971, in order to avoid having to travel the same road again, Mills encouraged the Japanese textile industry to develop its own unilateral plan to restrain exports. It did so, and though the limits were far less stringent than those the administration had been seeking, Mills endorsed the plan immediately upon its announcement.

In the end, this Japanese industry plan did not resolve the US-Japan textile dispute. But it did achieve both of Mills's objectives: removing the threat of legislation and providing some relief to the US industry.[31] Thus Mills protected the Congress. He also protected the nation's capacity to pursue generally liberal trade policies.

The fact that it regularly diverted proposals for statutory protection of specific industries did not mean that Congress never employed its independent legislative authority in matters of trade. When, every few years, presidents proposed major trade-negotiating legislation, Ways and Means and Finance were anything but administration rubber stamps. They held lengthy hearings; they reworked executive branch drafts from beginning to end. But the most thorough academic study of the House panel pointed out that in the typically closed Ways and Means markup sessions, "executive department representatives not only attend . . . but are an integral, active part of the discussion."[32] And markups focused on adjusting the details of the system of delegation—setting the range and limits of negotiating authority and refining the rules for trade remedies. With rare exceptions, general trade bills did not include product-specific protection.

Trade as a Nonparty Issue

As it operated in the decades following the 1934 legislation, the American trade policy system provided protection for Congress with a range of devices: the bargaining tariff, the executive broker, the quasi-judicial

---

31. See Destler, Fukui, and Sato, *The Textile Wrangle,* esp. chap. 11.

32. John F. Manley, *The Politics of Finance: The House Committee on Ways and Means* (Boston: Little, Brown, 1970), 348.

"trade remedies," the "special deals," and the strong congressional committees that worked with liberal-leaning executive branch leaders to make the system work. It also benefited enormously from the fact that trade was not a primary focus of partisan political competition.

This had not been true for most of American history. Schattschneider went so far as to argue that "the dominant position of the Republican party before 1932 can be attributed largely to the successful exploitation of the tariff by this party as a means of attaching to itself a formidable array of interests dependent on the protective system and intent upon continuing it."[33] In the early Roosevelt administration, the great majority of Democrats had supported the reciprocal trade legislation, and virtually all Republicans had opposed it. (In 1934, 1937, and 1940, no more than five Republican votes were cast in favor of reciprocal trade in either house.)

But beginning with the wartime extension of 1943, and increasingly in the late 1940s and 1950s, Republicans began to support final passage of liberal trade legislation, although they often backed restrictive amendments.[34] And by the early 1970s, members of the GOP were increasingly aligned in favor of liberal trade, as was logically consistent with their general skepticism about intervention in the domestic economy.

By this time, the Democrats had begun to move in the opposite direction. Policy logic might have inclined them toward protectionism in the 1930s, since in the New Deal they were the party that became committed to aggressive intervention in the US economy. Instead, throughout the 1940s and 1950s they maintained their low-tariff tradition as exemplified by Cordell Hull (who had fought New Deal interventionists seeking to restrict trade), even though textile-industry pressure created a shift among representatives from the South, historically the strongest free trade area. And after President Kennedy had appeased that industry, members of his party voted overwhelmingly in support of his Trade Expansion Act of 1962. Only when organized labor left the liberal trade camp in the late 1960s did substantial numbers of northern Democrats begin to defect.

Thus, in the quarter-century after World War II, neither party, while out of office, singled out trade policy as a primary point of difference with the administration in power. This contributed to cooperation on Capitol Hill: Ways and Means, whose deliberations over taxes were characterized by sharp party division, handled trade in a bipartisan, consensus manner as the issue "lost its partisan character nationally."[35]

---

33. Schattschneider, *Politics, Pressures and the Tariff*, 283.

34. For the main votes through 1958, see Pastor, *Congress and the Politics of US Foreign Economic Policy*, 97.

35. Richard F. Fenno Jr., *Congressmen in Committees* (Boston: Little, Brown, 1973), 207.

Presidential candidates would, of course, target appeals to particular interests—Kennedy sought votes from textile states with industry-specific promises in 1960, and Nixon, bested in that encounter, emulated him eight years later. But the basic open-market orientation of overall policy was not challenged. "Protectionism" remained a discredited concept, and while a politician who advocated it might win gratitude from specific interests, he would lose respect in the broader public eye.

This meant that presidents of both parties could tilt in favor of open trade, as they had to for the system to work. There were variations in their degrees of personal commitment: on balance, Gerald R. Ford's was greater than Richard M. Nixon's, and Lyndon B. Johnson and Jimmy Carter were more devoted free traders than John F. Kennedy. But all proved willing to play the role of tilting policy in the liberal direction—in the decisions they made themselves and in the appointments they made to key trade positions. And all proved able to play this role, for they knew that they were not thereby subjecting themselves to broad, partisan assault. They could take some of the interest group heat. This continuing presidential commitment made it possible for the Congress to buck responsibility, and for the "brokers" in the bureaucracy to do their trade-expanding work.

The System's Advantages and Limits

Operating within the broader context just described, the American trade policymaking system had enormous advantages—not just for trade, but also for the major governmental participants. The president could generally treat trade policy as a component of US international leadership. Yet he could occasionally respond to specific industry constituencies, and he could avoid making very many decisions against particular producers, except those taken in broader negotiations that brought compensating benefits to other producers.

If presidents could pick and choose among trade issues while tilting generally in the liberal direction, members of Congress had even greater leeway. The majority were free to make noise, to give "protectionist" speeches or introduce bills favored by particular constituencies, secure in the knowledge that nothing statutory was likely to result. Or they could respond sympathetically to constituents and point to all the possibilities for help available elsewhere, sending them "downtown" to the Tariff Commission or the STR. Members of the trade committees could use their potential influence over trade legislation to press the executive branch to do something for particular constituencies, on either the export or the import side. All could avoid final responsibility for product-by-product trade action, and thus avoid the choice between what they felt to be good politics and what they believed to be good policy.

For the senior trade officials of the executive branch agencies, the system was cumbersome, inefficient, and frustrating on a day-to-day basis. There were always interest groups to respond to, or interagency battles to fight, or technical problems to thrash out with foreign officials who had their own full agendas of political and operational problems. But over the longer term the system "worked"; maneuvering within it, trade officials could manage issues and negotiations so as to limit trade restrictions. They could give priority to bargaining about foreign trade barriers. They could bring in countervailing interests if a US industry's campaign for protection threatened to overwhelm them. And by timely domestic brokering, they could prevent the formation of a protectionist coalition seeking broad, Smoot-Hawley–type restrictions. Thus they could avoid negative actions that might reverse the continuing growth of trade that was bringing profit to producers worldwide.

Finally, the American trade policy system benefited from the checks and balances built into our governing charter. Since the prime need was to prevent restrictive action, it proved helpful that much in our Constitution is designed to inhibit rash governmental action of any kind. Division of power between branches and within the Congress meant that bad proposals might be stopped at several points. A president could resist or veto legislation. A strong House committee chairman might kill it. The two houses might not agree on details. This constitutional bias was particularly important in those relatively rare instances—like that of textiles in 1969–71—when a president became so committed to achieving a particular trade restriction that his support for the overall liberal system was compromised. For it meant that an adroit legislator—like Wilbur Mills—could come to the rescue.

The system had, of course, important limits. It never provided "free trade," nor did its proponents seriously claim it did. What they sought and achieved was relative openness, but the exceptions could prove significant and expandable. On textiles, for example, what began as "voluntary" Japanese restraints on sales of cotton products grew, by stages, into an elaborate network of bilateral agreements that subjected sales of any textile or apparel item from any substantial developing country to tight quota limits.

The system was weak also in the area of agricultural trade. Here the controlling legislation went through the House and Senate agriculture committees, and the farm legislators did not always play by the same rules. Despite an increasingly favorable overall trade balance in agricultural products, the United States imposed quotas on imports of products such as sugar, cheese, and beef. In fact, to reconcile such restrictions (and broader US crop production programs) with GATT rules against quotas, the United States sought and obtained in 1955 a waiver exempting such measures from GATT coverage. Today, when heavy subsidies and quota restrictions deny American farmers substantial markets in Europe and Japan, they have cause to rue this precedent, which is regularly cited by European Union trade negotiators defending their agricultural trade barriers.

Another limitation was that, nationally and internationally, the system dealt primarily with direct trade measures such as tariffs and quotas, tending to neglect broader national policies that had an important trade impact. There had been one major effort to go further, by creating an International Trade Organization (ITO). The Havana Charter, signed in March 1948, provided for an organization that would not be limited to regulating trade barriers, but would also address such matters as international commodity agreements and domestic full-employment policies. But when the charter came up for legislative ratification, its broad scope alienated not only congressional protectionists but pro-trade "perfectionists" who feared it would encourage government actions that inhibited business enterprise. The ITO charter was never ratified.[36] So these issues had to be addressed ad hoc, under the auspices of a GATT originally conceived as a temporary arrangement.[37]

The system also depended, to a considerable degree, on favorable economic conditions for the nation as a whole and for specific industries. Textile protection began in a decade—the 1950s—when that industry faced stagnant domestic and international demand. Increased demand for trade restrictions tended to rise with the level of unemployment and the overvaluation of the dollar.

And the system could be shaken if a key player departed from the script. After Richard Nixon "reluctantly" supported statutory quotas for the textile industry in 1970, the House voted to enact them.

The Contradictions of the System

More important than these particular kinds of limits, which no system could have avoided, were some deeper contradictions. In several respects, the American trade policymaking system would become the victim of its success, as its accomplishments weakened the instruments that had made success possible.

The "Bargaining Tariff" as Vanishing Asset

As long as the primary trade policy business involved the traditional barriers—tariffs and quotas—international negotiations could focus on

---

36. William Diebold Jr., "The End of the ITO," *Essays in International Finance*, 16 (Princeton, NJ: Princeton University Press, October 1952), esp. 11–24.

37. In fact, trade bills in the 1950s regularly included a clause reading as follows: "The

limiting and reducing them. This made for efficient international negotiations, as national delegations had clear and measurable things to trade off against one another. They could point to concrete results and monitor implementation without great difficulty. And the prospect of barrier reduction abroad served as a brake on pressures at home—protection for an industry could be denied or limited on the grounds that it would undercut the chance to gain export benefits for other industries.

Tariff negotiations also facilitated the delegation of congressional power. Legislation could specify in advance the range of permitted reductions, and the executive branch could negotiate and the president proclaim them without Congress having to ratify their specifics. And to the degree that trade policy was tariffs, the jurisdiction of the "tax" committees, Finance and Ways and Means, was hard for Hill competitors to contest.

However, the more trade negotiators accomplished, the lower were the remaining tariffs. Attention shifted to nontariff trade distortions, which were harder to define and whose removal was more fractious to negotiate internationally; it was hard to point to clear, measurable results.

Domestically, there were two major complications. First, Congress could not simply authorize a negotiation and let an administration take it from there, since legislation could not fully anticipate the sorts of changes in US law that would be required to implement an agreement. So Congress would have to enact trade legislation at both ends of the process. Second, to the degree that trade negotiations explicitly involved many things other than tariffs, the control of the trade committees would be weakened. They would be under pressure to share jurisdiction; subjects like product standards and government procurement regulations were the province of other, competing committees.

International Openness Versus Domestic Intervention

The demise of tariffs as the key trade issue exacerbated another contradiction built into the postwar GATT regime—that between the drive to lower economic barriers among nations and the increasing governmental intervention within them.[38] For if one lesson of the Great Depression was the folly of protectionism, an even more powerful one was that national economies, left to themselves, would not necessarily provide

---

enactment of this Act shall not be construed to determine or indicate the approval or disapproval by the Congress of the Executive Agreement known as the General Agreement on Tariffs and Trade." See Jackson, *Legal Problems of International Economic Relations,* 408–10.

38. See John Gerard Ruggie, "International Regimes, Transactions, and Change: Embedded Liberalism in the Postwar Economic Order," *International Organization* (Spring 1982): 379–415.

full employment, much less ensure equitable income distribution and personal economic security. So almost all "capitalist" governments entered the postwar period determined to conduct activist, interventionist economic policies at home. Their electorates expected them to do so and held them accountable for the results.

As long as trade policy involved tariffs—a distinct, separable instrument—nations could reconcile barrier reductions with activist policies at home. They could be "liberal" on cross-border transactions and interventionist within the home market. But their "domestic" economic actions had considerable impact on trade, and the lowering of tariffs made this impact more visible. Inevitably, American producers began to focus less on tariffs and more on other nations' domestic steps: the subsidies benefitting Europe's state-owned steel companies, or the buy-Japanese policies of the government telecommunications agency in Tokyo.

The many asymmetries in what various governments were doing made it hard to put together packages of "reciprocal" national concessions on nontariff trade issues. Pressures on nations to change their domestic subsidy, regulation, and procurement policies struck at the policy tolerance that had been a central, if largely implicit, element of the international consensus that created and maintained the GATT. For many nontariff barriers (NTBs), like product standards or systems of taxation, negotiations raised sensitive questions of national sovereignty.

Within the United States, attention to NTBs fueled charges of "unfairness," the political Achilles's heel of the liberal trade consensus at home. From the numerous specific cases in which foreign governments intervened in trade to the disadvantage of particular American producers, it was easy to construct a broad general argument that Uncle Sam had become "Uncle Sucker"—that our competitors were taking away with oft-invisible domestic policies the trade opportunities they apparently granted in tariff negotiations.

Success as Multiplier of Trade Pressures

To the degree that the postwar regime brought about expanded trade, it created another problem for the policymaking system. For it increased the number of "losers," producer interests adversely affected by foreign competition and driven to seek help. It was one thing when the major trade-impacted industries were few and predictable: textiles, steel, shoes. But when imports rose from less than 5 percent of GNP to more than 10 percent, the ranks of the "injured" multiplied. Large industries previously ranked among America's finest—consumer electronics, automobiles, machine tools—began coming to Washington with their problems. The system, accustomed to facing only a handful of specific pressures, now had to cope with a basketful.

There were also, of course, an increased number of American producers who were profiting from the export side of international trade, not to mention importers and retailers with a stake in foreign products. But for all the traditional reasons, they did not so readily join the political arena. If trade "losers" go regularly into politics to seek relief, trade "winners" generally stick to business. Trade officials and politicians could work to involve them, and they regularly did so, but this only increased their leadership burden.

The Dilemma of the Rules

A final contradiction was one built into the trade-remedy procedures. These procedures were, in principle, an important escape valve, diverting pressures at least temporarily away from Congress (and the executive branch). Yet to remain credible, they had to result—reasonably often—in actual trade relief.

Viewed from overseas, actions granting such relief were viewed as departures from liberal trade policy, signs that the United States was "going protectionist." The fact that our foreign competitors were imposing their own (often less visible) trade restrictions did not seem to lessen their propensity to express alarm about ours. Moreover, if the trade-remedy procedures regularly resulted in restraining trade, they would in fact have a protectionist result. Thus, relief procedures that were credible domestically weakened US trade leadership internationally.

In the 1960s this dilemma was resolved by rules that made escape clause relief hard to obtain, and by lax administration of the countervailing duty and antidumping laws. In the short run, this facilitated international trade leadership, but it brought petitioners back to congressional doorsteps. And relief under the new TAA program, which might have absorbed some of the pressure, proved as hard to qualify for as relief under the escape clause. So in the 1970s legislators, seeking continued protection for themselves, responded by rewriting the trade-remedy laws so that relief would be easier to obtain.

This meant that more escape clause petitions came to the president with recommendations from the US International Trade Commission for favorable action. This forced the dilemma onto the president personally. He had to choose between credibility for the trade procedures at home and international leadership abroad. To the degree that he tilted toward the latter, he undercut the rules further, creating pressures to reduce presidential discretion and to move toward "special case" treatment for more industries.

It also meant more cases in which US petitioners alleged unfair foreign trade practices. These were particularly sensitive abroad, because they challenged national sovereignty over economic policy and because they combined "moral" claims (allegations of foreign unfairness) with what foreigners saw as rules and procedures weighted against them. At home, these cases reduced the leeway of trade policy managers, because the countervailing duty and antidumping statutes granted them less discretion to balance industry-specific with broader concerns.

□ □ □

From the 1930s through the 1960s, the main story of American trade policymaking was the story of the construction and elaboration of a pressure-diverting policy management system. No one planned this system in its entirety. It evolved from a mix of strong executive and congressional leadership and ad hoc responses to particular pressures. It gave the American body politic not only an unaccustomed capacity to resist new trade restrictions, but remarkable success in reducing old ones, as evidenced by a series of negotiations that culminated in the Kennedy Round agreements of 1967.

This chapter has sought to describe the "old system"—how we got it and how it worked. The body of this book, however, is concerned with how this system has been shaken in the 1970s and 1980s, not only by pressures and contradictions such as those described above, but also by more turbulent economic times—for the United States, its major competitors, and the international trading system. The next chapter treats the global changes to which trade policy has been forced to respond. Thereafter, the book looks at how specific institutions and processes— Congress, the executive branch, the rules—have actually responded to this new world.

EROSION

3

A Tougher World: Changes in the Context of Trade Policy

The years since 1970 brought far-reaching changes to the world economy. US firms and workers became much more exposed to foreign competition in both home and overseas markets. The relative position of the United States declined, as European rivals were joined by Asian ones—first Japan, then rapidly industrializing countries such as Korea. The rules of the international trading regime, the General Agreement on Tariffs and Trade (GATT), grew less effective. The advanced industrial economies, buffeted by two oil shocks, entered a period of stagflation, combining rapid price increases with sluggish growth. Fixed exchange rates among currencies could not hold, and the world moved to a floating rate regime, featuring massive financial flows and severe and protracted misalignments. Last but not least, the collapse of the Soviet Union reinforced the long-standing trend toward tripolarity in the global economy. The United States had to share power with the European Union and Japan. And all three needed to cooperate without the glue that Cold War security alliances had heretofore provided.

15 August as Prologue

The new era was heralded by a US policy action both dramatic and unexpected. On 15 August 1971, at the urging of Treasury Secretary John B. Connally, President Richard M. Nixon took several related steps aimed at reducing the value of the dollar. He suspended the US commitment to support its currency by selling gold reserves on demand; he called upon other major nations to raise the value of their currencies against the dollar; and, to get everybody's attention, he imposed a temporary 10 percent "additional tax" on imports. The aim, Nixon declared, was to ensure "that American products will not be at a disadvantage because of unfair exchange rates. When the unfair treatment is ended, the import tax will end as well."[1]

The financial context of the 15 August actions was the increased vulnerability of the dollar in foreign-exchange markets. Since the late 1950s, the United States had been running regular deficits in its international balance of payments, and these deficits had generated intermittent concern, in Washington as well as overseas, about the dollar's long-term strength. Under the Bretton Woods system, the dollar was the unit against which other nations defined their currency values, and concern about the dollar was therefore synonymous with concern about the viability of that broader international monetary system. Until 1971 the dollar's value had been sustained by a variety of cooperative efforts among the US, European, and Japanese central banks. The speculative pressure that summer, however, was of an entirely new order of magnitude.[2]

The trade context of 15 August was a shift in the overall US export-import balance. Merchandise trade surpluses had been a constant feature of the postwar American economic landscape, averaging more than $5 billion annually in the early 1960s. In 1968 and 1969, however, the US surplus dropped below $1 billion, and critics like Senate Finance Committee Chairman Russell B. Long (D-LA) argued that US commercial trade was actually in deficit, since export statistics included more than $2 billion financed by foreign aid.

An increasing number of economists saw the trade shift as evidence that the dollar had become overvalued. Its exchange rate with other

---

1. This action was aimed importantly at getting the US economy moving, without worsening inflation, before the 1972 election. It also included, therefore, domestic economic stimulus measures and wage and price controls.

For an account of the Nixon decision in historical perspective, see Robert Solomon, *The International Monetary System 1945–1976: An Insider's View* (New York: Harper and Row, 1977), chaps. 11 and 12. For comprehensive analyses of the forces behind this major policy change, see John S. Odell, *U.S. International Monetary Policy: Markets, Power, and Ideas as Sources of Change* (Princeton, NJ: Princeton University Press, 1982), chap. 4; and Joanne Gowa, *Closing the Gold Window: Domestic Politics and the End of Bretton Woods* (Ithaca, NY: Cornell University Press, 1983). For a thorough analysis of American policy interests during this period, see C. Fred Bergsten, *The Dilemmas of the Dollar: The Economics and Politics of United States International Monetary Policy* (New York: New York University Press or the Council on Foreign Relations 1975), esp. part 2.

2. In the first nine months of 1971 . . . US liabilities to foreign monetary authorities increased by more than $21 billion." Solomon, *International Monetary System,* 184. These authorities' increased dollar holdings reflected the movement of other holders out of dollars into other currencies. The average annual increase in such foreign official dollar holdings in the late 1960s, by contrast, was only $637 million. *Economic Report of the President, 1974,* table C-88.

currencies reflected a postwar preeminence that no longer existed. American industry and labor were experiencing greater foreign competition as a result, and official Washington was under new pressure for trade restrictions. Hardly was the ink dry on the Kennedy Round tariff-cutting agreement when a range of industries began pushing for new protection. These included textile and apparel manufacturers, alarmed by the growing imports of man-made fiber products, and steel firms and workers concerned about competition from resurgent European and Japanese competitors. Organized labor, which had endorsed the Kennedy Round, was arguing by 1970 that a new competitive situation had "made old 'free trade' concepts and their 'protectionist' opposites increasingly obsolete." Labor now called for policies aimed at "*orderly* expansion of world trade."[3] As recounted in chapter 2, these pressures, combined with the Nixon administration's mismanagement of the textile issue, led the House of Representatives to pass a restrictive import quota bill in November 1970.

The overvalued dollar put the United States in an economic policy bind. Through the 1960s, devaluation was considered impractical—even unthinkable—because it would undercut the dollar-based exchange rate system established in 1944 at Bretton Woods. President John F. Kennedy told his advisers he did not want the subject mentioned outside of his office; for Kennedy, devaluation "would call into doubt the good faith and stability of this nation and the competence of its President."[4] The traditional medicine for righting one's trade balance without devaluation was to depress overall demand. This would, however, drive up unemployment and generate increased pressures for trade restrictions. (And in fact, the Johnson administration did the opposite in the late 1960s. Its inflationary policies—increasing spending for the Vietnam War years before new taxes were enacted to finance it—made the trade balance worse.)

The United States could also support the dollar with measures that would limit capital outflows and discourage other activities requiring its conversion to foreign currencies. The Kennedy and Johnson administrations employed a variety of devices to this end: an interest equalization tax, limits on foreign direct investment, reduction of the value of duty-free goods that traveling Americans could purchase overseas, even a "balance of payments" program to cut official US overseas staffing. But these palliatives had no durable impact.

Nixon and Connally broke the United States free from this bind in a way that was deeply disruptive of the postwar economic system. Not only was the content of their actions unsettling; their rhetoric generated

---

3. Statement of the AFL-CIO economic policy council, as reported in *New York Times*, 22 February 1970. Emphasis added.

4. Theodore G. Sorensen, *Kennedy* (New York: Harper and Row, 1965), 408.

strong doubts in foreign capitals about whether the United States could still be counted on to support the international monetary and trade regimes its leaders had fostered. Connally actively provoked such anxieties, in part to increase US leverage: Europeans and Japanese might yield more if they saw their concessions as the only way to bring a suddenly rogue America back onto the international economic reservation.

Within four months and three days, however, agreement was reached on a new set of exchange rates that effectively devalued the dollar by about 10 percent against other major currencies. Within two years, the dollar went down substantially further, and the major trading nations were forced to abandon the system of fixed exchange rates altogether. By the mid-1970s, in fact, it seemed that the net effect of the "Nixon shocks" had been not to bury international economic cooperation but to give it new life. Realignment of exchange rates restored the US capacity to pursue open trade policies and press others to do likewise. The US trade balance began to improve in early 1973, just as legislation to authorize the new Tokyo Round made its way through the House of Representatives. With their competitiveness thus buttressed, firms and workers were less disposed to press for protection against foreign products and more conscious of the opportunities a new trade round might bring. When the oil crisis hit later that year, the floating rate regime made it easier for the world to make the wrenching adjustments forced by the fourfold increase in the price of that critical commodity.

Nonetheless, the world Americans faced after 15 August 1971 was clearly one of greater economic insecurity and turmoil. Seven intertwined features of this world stand out:

- increased exposure of the US economy to trade;
- the relative decline of the United States, real and perceived;
- the rise of new (particularly East Asian) competitors;
- the erosion of the GATT international trade regime;
- the worsening of "stagflation," with the United States and its European trading partners facing a combination of slow economic growth, high unemployment, and rapid price increases;
- the move to floating, and oft-misaligned, exchange rates;
- and, most recently, the end of the Cold War and the emergence of a tripolar economic world.

All of these developments put new strains on an American trade policymaking system shaped in more insular economic times.

Table 3.1 United States: merchandise imports, exports and trade balance, 1960–94 (billions of current dollars)

Year	Exports[a]	Imports[a]	Balance
1960	19.7	14.8	4.9
1965	26.5	21.5	5.0
1970	42.5	39.9	2.6
1971	43.3	45.6	-2.3
1972	49.4	55.8	-6.4
1973	71.4	70.5	0.9
1974	98.3	103.8	-5.5
1975	107.1	98.2	8.9
1976	114.7	124.2	-9.5
1977	120.8	151.9	-31.1
1978	142.1	176.0	-33.9
1979	184.4	212.0	-27.6
1980	224.3	249.8	-25.5
1981	237.0	265.1	-28.0
1982	211.2	247.6	-36.5
1983	201.8	268.9	-67.1
1984	219.9	332.4	-112.5
1985	215.9	338.1	-122.2
1986	223.3	368.4	-145.1
1987	250.2	409.8	-159.6
1988	320.2	447.2	-127.0
1989	362.1	477.4	-115.2
1990	389.3	498.3	-109.0
1991	416.9	491.0	-74.1
1992	440.4	536.5	-96.1
1993	456.9	589.4	-132.6
1994	502.8	669.1	-166.3

a. Export data are f.a.s (free alongside ship); imports are customs value. Both exclude military transactions.

Sources: Economic Report of the President, 1992, 1995; and US Department of Commerce News Release, 17 February 1995.

The Trade Explosion

In 1960, exports of US merchandise to the rest of the world totaled $19.7 billion; in 1990, they totaled $389.3 billion (table 3.1). During this same period, US global merchandise imports shot up from $14.8 billion to $498.3 billion. The numbers are in current prices and ballooned by inflation, but on a price-deflated, constant-dollar basis exports rose more than sixfold, and imports nearly eightfold.[5] Perhaps the most important indicator, however, was the growth of trade in proportion to the US economy.

---

5. US Commerce Department data, as reported in *Economic Report of the President,* 1991, table B-102, and US Congress, Joint Economic Committee, *Economic Indicators,* June 1991, 36. The growth of real exports and imports is calculated from the constant (1982) dollar figures in table B-21 of the *Economic Report of the President,* 1991.

In 1950, the United States exported just 6.3 percent of its total production of goods. This percentage rose modestly for two decades—to 7.7 percent in 1960 and 9.2 percent in 1970. Then it shot up to rates more than double that: 19.1 percent in 1980 and 18.2 percent in 1990. The corresponding figures for imports were 5.6, 5.8, and 8.7 percent for the earlier years, and 21.3 percent and 23.2 percent for 1980 and 1990.[6]

The expansion of trade with the United States' primary overseas trading partner was even more dramatic. In 1960, the United States sold $1.4 billion in goods to Japan, and bought $1.1 billion. By 1990, it was exporting $48.6 billion and importing $89.7 billion.[7] When adjusted for price increases, this amounted to an elevenfold increase in US exports to Japan over this period and a nineteenfold increase in imports.

The causes of the trade explosion were many: reduced international transportation and communication costs; reductions in tariff barriers; the broader internationalization of the US economy; the ballooning cost of oil imports, which required an expansion of foreign sales to pay for them. A thorough examination of these causes goes beyond the scope of this book. But the effects of the trade explosion are an important part of our story, and they were substantial.

First and perhaps most significant, the expanded inflow of foreign products brought an inevitable political response. Measured by any standard, US firms were facing significantly more import competition in the 1970s and 1980s than at any previous point in the 20th century. Of course, exports also rose during this period. But the firms that benefited from exports were by no means comparably aggressive in the political arena, though exporters (and import users) did act to limit protectionism when their own specific interests were at stake.

Furthermore, there was great disparity in the impact of the trade explosion on various industries and regions. During the 1970s—the period of greatest relative increase in US trade—producers of farm and high-technology products reaped great benefits. Overall, "in high-technology industries in which U.S. comparative advantage continue[d] to increase," the US trade surplus "grew from $15 billion in 1973 to $52 billion in 1980."[8]

But those who made standard producer and consumer goods suffered, whether their business was steel or autos or television sets. And the suffering was regional as well as sectoral. In the United States as a

---

6. Percentages obtained by dividing total merchandise exports (or imports) by total production of goods, as reported in *Economic Report of the President,* 1991, tables B-102 and B-6, and US Congress, Joint Economic Committee, *Economic Indicators,* June 1991, 36.

7. US Department of Commerce.

8. Robert Z. Lawrence, *Can America Compete?* (Washington: Brookings Institution, 1984), 95. Between 1980 and 1985, as spelled out later in this chapter, virtually all US product sectors, including agriculture and high-technology industries, were hurt by the rise in the dollar, and many were helped, in turn, by its subsequent decline.

whole, employment in manufacturing stayed roughly the same between 1973 and 1980. But in the rust belt states from New York to Michigan, it declined by 10 percent to 15 percent. Within the highly unionized basic industries concentrated within this region, laid-off workers faced, on the average, substantial drops in their income levels even after they found new jobs outside those industries. As William H. Branson has noted, this meant that the greatest adjustment was being forced upon those very "workers and companies . . . in the best position to bring pressure on trade policy."[9] With their plight as concrete evidence, they could claim that a major American achievement of the earlier 20th century, the bringing of industrial workers into the middle class, was now being threatened by foreign competition.[10]

Scale

The "Decline" of the United States

The nation that was suddenly more exposed to world trade was also comparatively less well off. As late as 1960, the incomes per capita of the United States' major "trilateral" competitors—France, Germany, Japan, and the United Kingdom—ranged from 30 percent to 68 percent of its own. By 1979, their per capita incomes had risen to between 64 percent and 86 percent of the United States'.[11] The US share of world trade had also declined, albeit much less dramatically, and in the context of rapidly growing absolute trade flows. In 1950, US international commerce ac-

---

9. William H. Branson, "The Changing Structure of U.S. Trade: Implications for Research and Policy," paper prepared for Washington Conference of the National Bureau of Economic Research, 9 March 1984, processed, 9.

10. Defining a middle-class income as within 30 percent of the median for the economy, Lawrence finds that, according to census data, the proportion of manufacturing workers earning such incomes declined from 44.6 percent in 1969 to 39.3 percent in 1979. But this drop was not, apparently, a product of a shift of jobs from traditional to high-technology industries, as some have hypothesized, for in both years the proportion of high-technology workers earning middle-class incomes was slightly higher than the overall manufacturing average: 47 percent in 1969 and 41.8 percent in 1979. Lawrence, *Can America Compete?* 80.

More generally, "the earnings of less skilled American men began dropping in real terms after 1973 and fell precipitously during the 1980s." This was "a striking break with [the] historical pattern," for " [f]rom 1900 through the 1960s the real earnings of less skilled American workers grew substantially." See McKinley L. Blackburn, David E. Bloom, and Richard B. Freeman, "The Declining Economic Position of Less Skilled American Men," in Gary Burtless, ed., *A Future of Lousy Jobs? The Changing Structure of U.S. Wages* (Washington: Brookings Institution, 1990), 31.

11. Irving B. Kravis, Alan Heston, and Robert Summers, *World Product and Income: International Comparisons of Real Gross Product* (Baltimore: Johns Hopkins University Press [for the World Bank and the United Nations Statistical Office], 1982), 15. Figures are for "gross domestic product per capita," in terms of actual purchasing power.

counted for fully one-third of the trilateral total. This portion dropped to 27 percent in 1960, 23.5 percent in 1970, and 22.1 percent in 1980.[12] Or, to take another indicator, the US share of total *world* trade dropped from 15.0 percent in 1960 to 14.4 percent in 1970 and 12.4 percent in 1980, though it was back up to 14.6 percent in 1989.[13]

As some of these statistics suggest, most of the decline in the US share of world production and trade took place before the 1970s. Moreover, a major goal of postwar US foreign policy had been to restore its European and Japanese allies to economic health. Since 1970, broad indicators suggest that the United States has been holding its own economically vis-à-vis Western Europe; for example, between that year and 1989, the US index of industrial production rose 76 percent, compared with just 48 percent for the European Community. And while Japanese industrial production grew by 110 percent over the same period, the difference between the real annual economic growth rates of the United States and Japan was only 1.7 percent a year in 1976–90—compared with an average annual difference of 7.9 percent in the 1960s.[14]

By these broad indicators, the US "decline" came mainly in the 1950s and 1960s, and could be seen as an inevitable correction of the abnormal and unsustainable preeminence created by World War II. But the full impact was felt in the 1970s and 1980s. Industrial sectors that were once world leaders came under intense trade-competitive assault: first steel and consumer electronics, then automobiles, then microelectronics. By the late 1980s, concern about the apparent erosion of America's economic and geostrategic position had made Paul Kennedy's heavy work of world history into a surprise best seller.[15] And such concerns were reinforced by a separate phenomenon that was frequently, albeit oversimply, interpreted as reflecting an *accelerating* decline. This was the onset of regular merchandise trade deficits.

Every year from 1894 through 1970, the value of the goods the United States sold on world markets exceeded the value of those that Ameri-

---

12. Calculated by Robert O. Keohane from *UN Yearbook of International Trade Statistics,* 1981. See his *After Hegemony: Cooperation and Discord in the World Political Economy* (Princeton, NJ: Princeton University Press, 1984), 199.

13. These percentages are computed from International Monetary Fund, *International Financial Statistics: Supplement on Trade Statistics,* no. 15, 1988; and International Monetary Fund, *Direction of Trade Statistics Yearbook,* 1990.

14. *Economic Report of the President,* 1991, tables B-107 and B-110.

15. Paul Kennedy, *The Rise and Fall of the Great Powers: Economic Change and Military Conflict from 1500 to 2000* (New York: Random House, 1987). Kennedy's argument triggered numerous rebuttals, including those by Joseph S. Nye Jr., *Bound To Lead: The Changing Nature of American Power* (New York: Basic Books, 1990), and Henry R. Nau, *The Myth of America's Decline: Leading the World Economy into the 1990s* (New York: Oxford University Press, 1990).

cans bought. The inflow of funds from these merchandise trade surpluses was offset, in important part, by an outflow of funds for investment overseas. But beginning in 1971, the year of Nixon's policy bombshell, the pattern changed: the United States ran a merchandise trade deficit that year, and in all but 2 of the 20 years thereafter. And the numbers looked increasingly alarming. The negative balance of $2.3 billion in 1971 was succeeded by records of $6.4 billion in 1972, $33.9 billion in 1978, and $159.5 billion in 1987.[16] Bilateral deficits with the United States' most-watched trading partner, Japan, grew apace, with records of $4 billion in 1972, $11.6 billion in 1978, and $56.3 billion in 1987.[17]

The deficits of the 1970s were not unreasonable for a mature industrial economy. What the United States was doing, essentially, was using the income from its foreign investments to finance a higher level of consumption than its current production would have allowed. Once it ceased being a consistent net capital exporter, simple mathematics dictated that modest "structural" trade deficits (amounting to less than 10 percent of total US trade) would be its normal condition, to offset net returns on overseas investment.[18] And the United States could do this while still running, on the average, an approximate balance in its current account, which includes not only merchandise trade but services and investment income. In other words, US trade deficits were no larger than what its overseas earnings could finance; the United States was not going into debt to pay for imports.[19]

However, this was hardly the way the deficit was characterized in US politics. Rather, it was treated as offering clear evidence that the United States was losing out in the world marketplace.[20] This had several re-

---

16. *Economic Report of the President,* 1991, table B-102.

17. Japan Economic Institute of America, *Yearbook of U.S.-Japan Economic Relations in 1982* (Washington: JEI, 1983), 129.

18. No one, of course, "decided" that the United States should do this, and it could have made its future returns even greater by continuing the substantial net capital exports of the 1950s and 1960s.

19. The same could not be said of the genuinely alarming trade deficits of 1984 and thereafter, treated later in this chapter.

20. This was certainly how the matter was viewed by Russell Long (D-LA), chairman of the Senate Finance Committee throughout the 1970s. Long argued persistently, in fact, that the Commerce Department's preferred method of valuing imports—"customs value," or f.a.s.—led to understatement of the real US trade deficit, because it excluded the cost of shipping those imports. To get people to use what he considered the "right" numbers, Long attached to the major trade legislation of 1979 a provision requiring that import statistics be reported on the c.i.f. (cost, insurance, and freight) basis "no later than 48 hours before the release of any other government statistics" on imports or the balance of trade (Trade Agreements Act of 1979, sec. 1108 [a]). He expected the numbers released first to the press to become the ones most used—and his expectation was borne out. Thus, during the height of the trade imbalance, the annual deficit number com-

lated and constraining effects on executive branch policymakers and on the broader political environment.

First of all, it undercut the argument—already very weak in American politics by 1970—that the United States should absorb costs to its specific trade interests in order to help maintain the broader international trading system (and US alliances that were intertwined with that system). The belief that "we could no longer afford" such generosity was hardly limited to Richard Nixon's demanding secretary of the Treasury, John Connally; in the 1970s and 1980s, it became nearly universal.

Second, merchandise trade deficits increased political receptivity for claims that American firms and workers were facing unfair foreign competition, broadly defined. In many instances, foreign governments subsidized products destined for export and restricted imports more than the United States did for comparable products. One plausible—albeit analytically incorrect—explanation for trade deficits was that foreign markets were less open than the US markets.[21] Once we equated negative trade balance figures with a decline of the United States, it was more comfortable to blame this on foreign nefariousness than on domestic inadequacies.

Third, deficits placed American trade negotiators on the defensive because they suggested a negative market judgment on prior US trade bargaining: the United States had not been tough enough with foreign governments, and its producers were being battered as a result.

All of these constraints forced US negotiators to assume a more demanding international trade posture, by pushing for more concessions overseas and offering fewer in return, at a time when US power in the world was diminished. This seemed, at a minimum, a recipe for increased trade conflict, as US leaders were driven to ever more demanding exercises in "export politics."

The Rise of New Competitors

The relative decline of the United States meant, by definition, the rise of other nations. Foremost among them was Japan. That story is well known, and it is underscored by the dramatic rise in US-Japan trade that was noted earlier in this chapter. But a few other numbers are worth recalling as well.

In 1960, after recovery from World War II, per capita income in Japan

---

monly cited was inflated by roughly $18 billion, and the monthly number by about $1.5 billion.

This requirement was repealed by the Omnibus Trade and Competitiveness Act of 1988, sec. 1931 (a), enacted after Long's retirement. This returned Commerce reporting to the practice, preferred by most economists, of treating shipping as a service.

21. For the full argument on why, in a floating exchange rate regime, the US trade balance is not fundamentally a function of market openness here or overseas, see chap. 9.

stood at just 30 percent of the US level in terms of purchasing power—about equal that of Mexico, a bit below that of Spain. Nineteen years later, it had grown to 71 percent of the United States', placing Japan squarely in the middle of the more prosperous Western European nations—ahead of Italy and Britain, if still behind France and Germany.[22] And Japan advanced further in the 1980s—by the comparative measure of the Organization for Economic Cooperation and Development (OECD), Japanese GNP per capita had reached 76 percent of the US level by 1989.[23] Between 1960 and 1980, Japan's share of total world GNP increased from 3 percent to 10 percent.[24] By 1989, at current exchange rates, Japan's GNP had reached 54 percent of the US level, and projections based on historical rates of growth and yen appreciation suggested it could exceed that of the United States—a country with twice Japan's population—early in the 21st century.[25]

Japan achieved this rise through phenomenal annual increases in national production and trade. Between 1960 and 1970, its real GNP rose an average of more than 11 percent a year.[26] Its merchandise exports grew even faster: by 17.2 percent annually in the 1960s, and by 8.5 percent (from a much larger base) between 1970 and 1982.[27] Japan's share of world exports rose from 3.5 percent in 1960 to an estimated 8.3 percent in 1985.[28] No other major nation had growth rates anything like these.

Any large country rising so rapidly was bound to cause problems for the world trading system. In fact, Japan had been perceived as a special

22. Kravis et al., *World Product and Income*, 15.

23. Calculated from Organization for Economic Cooperation and Development, Main Economic Indicators (Washington: OECD, July 1991), 175. The OECD figure for 1980 was 67 percent.

24. Keizai Koho Center, *Japan 1984: An International Comparison* (Tokyo: Japan Institute for Social and Economic Affairs, 1 September 1984), 9.

25. If the US economy grew at 2.5 percent a year and the Japanese at 4 percent, and the real appreciation of the yen was against the dollar by 1.9 percent a year (the average in the 1980s), Japanese GNP would overtake that of the United States in 2008.

By 1989, income per capita in Japan already exceeded that in the United States if converted at current exchange rates. But analysts generally find Japan's cost of living (at these rates) to be 40 percent to 75 percent higher than that in the United States. Hence purchasing power parity (PPP) comparisons, like those developed by Kravis et al. and those employed by the OECD, are preferable. For a comprehensive recent analysis, see Robert Summers and Alan Heston, "The Penn World Table (Mark 5): An Expanded Set of International Comparisons, 1950–1988," *The Quarterly Journal of Economics*, 106, no. 2 (May 1991): 327–68.

26. *Economic Report of the President*, 1991, table B-110.

27. World Bank, *World Development Report*, 1984, 235.

28. Percentages computed from International Monetary Fund, *International Financial Statistics: Supplement on Trade Statistics*, no. 15, 1988; and International Monetary Fund, *Direction of Trade Statistics Yearbook*, 1990.

trade problem, and its products subjected to a range of discriminatory barriers, well before its era of double-digit growth began.[29] But there were other problems in absorbing Japan as one of the preeminent players in the world trading system. As the first non-Western nation to achieve industrial success, Japan was culturally different. This traditionally closed and close-knit society had maintained substantial formal barriers to imports throughout the 1960s. The pace at which these barriers were dismantled always lagged behind that which Japanese export success would have allowed; the de facto opening of Japan's markets seemed to lag even further, though the strong yen of the late 1980s brought an enormous surge in imports. Moreover, in contrast to the aggressive business behavior of Japanese firms, the standard style of the Tokyo government in trade diplomacy was not to take the initiative but to await foreign pressure for trade liberalization and to open up markets, bit by bit, in response to this pressure.[30]

Hence, there developed a widespread perception of Japan as a "free rider" on the international trading system, exploiting market opportunities abroad while only grudgingly making changes at home. It also seemed clear that Japanese producers benefited from some special form of government-business cooperation, although experts differed sharply over its precise nature and impact. By the 1970s and 1980s, when American firms complained about what they perceived to be unfair trade practices —whether producers dumping television sets or governments promoting development of future export industries—Japan was most often their target. They could compete against companies, US business executives argued, but not against the government of a major economic power. Making matters more sensitive was the fact that Japan was the first nation, since the rise of mass-production manufacturing processes, to challenge the United States for industrial preeminence across a wide range of industries. Books that highlighted this phenomenon, like Clyde Prestowitz's *Trading Places*,[31] won wide circulation and broad credence.

Trade concerns triggered by Japan were magnified by the rise of "new

---

29. Gardner Patterson devoted an entire chapter to the various ways that other major trading nations developed special barriers against Japan in *Discrimination in International Trade: The Policy Issues* (Princeton, NJ: Princeton University Press, 1965).

30. American trade negotiators, by contrast, were prone to take the initiative, in part to channel trade pressures in the export-expanding, rather than import-restricting direction. Hence, "officials in both governments" have recurrently employed "intense, highly visible United States pressure as a catalyst for Japanese policy change." Report of the Japan-United States Economic Relations Group, prepared for the President of the United States and the Prime Minister of Japan (Tokyo and Washington, January 1981), 101. See also I. M. Destler and Hideo Sato, eds., *Coping With U.S.-Japanese Economic Conflicts* (Lexington, MA: Lexington Books, 1982), esp. 279–81.

31. Clyde V. Prestowitz Jr., *Trading Places: How We Allowed Japan to Take the Lead* (New York: Basic Books, 1988).

Japans": nations that were following Japan's rapid-growth, export-expanding path. The most impressive single example, perhaps, was the Republic of Korea, whose exports increased annually by 35 percent in the 1960s and 20 percent in the 1970s, and whose growth in income paralleled Japan's, albeit at lower levels.[32] Taken together, the share of world trade of the "four tigers" of East Asia—Hong Kong, Korea, Singapore, and Taiwan—rose from 1.9 percent in 1963 to 7.7 percent in 1988.[33] Thus, from the 1970s onward, American firms faced a trading world very different from the bipolar (US-EC) one of the Kennedy Round.

The Erosion of the GATT

Even as these new competitors were emerging, the system of rules for regulating international trade was weakening. In the first two postwar decades, the GATT had provided a surprisingly effective framework for negotiating trade liberalization and disciplining import restrictions. But its impact diminished thereafter.[34]

One reason for its erosion was the identity of the new competitors. The GATT had originated as a North American–European enterprise, shaped by leaders who drew common lessons from the prewar (and wartime) experience. Nations from these two continents continued to provide the GATT's primary political leadership through the 1970s, but the rise of other nations meant that the lead trading states now formed a less homogeneous community, making it harder to maintain agreement on trade policy norms. And since the new competitors were slow to assert leadership in multilateral trade negotiations, there was a growing divergence between the locus of trade-political activism and the locus of trade-economic power.

A second reason for the GATT's weakening was, ironically, its enormous success at what it did best: multilateral tariff-cutting negotiations. As noted in chapter 2, the remarkable postwar reductions in customs duties forced international trade relations onto the harder ground of nontariff trade barriers: harder to measure and negotiate, more inter-

---

32. By the estimates of Kravis et al., gross domestic income per capita for Korea rose from 8.15 percent of the US level in 1960 to 24.8 percent in 1979. *World Product and Income*, 15. Korean export statistics are drawn from World Bank, *World Development Report*, 198, 235.

33. Marcus Noland, *Pacific Basin Developing Countries: Prospects for the Future* (Washington: Institute for International Economics, 1990), 5.

34. For a good summary of the original GATT system and its evolution, see Miriam Camps and William Diebold Jr., "The Old Multilateralism and What Became of It," *The New Multilateralism: Can the World Trading System Be Saved?* (New York: Council on Foreign Relations Press, 1983), chap. 1.

twined with issues of domestic policy and national sovereignty, and not well defined by the original GATT rules. The Tokyo Round, or MTN, of the 1970s resulted in agreement on a number of "codes" addressing such subjects as subsidies, dumping, product standards, and government procurement. But not all GATT members accepted the obligations of these codes, and enforcement procedures proved slow and cumbersome. The Uruguay Round initiated in 1986, sought to establish GATT-type rules for international investment and services transactions—another task much more complex than the tariff cutting of earlier periods.

A more general problem for the GATT was the erosion of its bedrock principle of nondiscrimination, the core notion that each national government would grant equal treatment to the products of all others adhering to the GATT system. The European Community was one enormous exception; by definition, its members agreed to grant one another more favorable (i.e., duty-free) market access than they granted to outsiders. Tariff preferences for less developed countries were another exception. The Canada–United States Free Trade Agreement of 1988 was yet another, as were the US-Mexico talks initiated in 1990, and the Bush administration's broad Enterprise for the Americas Initiative, which invited nations throughout the hemisphere to seek free trade arrangements with the United States.

Governments discriminated in restricting imports as well as in admitting them. Under the GATT escape clause, Article XIX, members were allowed to impose temporary import barriers for the products of trade-injured industries. But they were supposed to do this on a nondiscriminatory basis. In practice, Article XIX was increasingly circumvented by "voluntary" export restraints (VERs) or orderly marketing agreements (OMAs), in which specific exporting nations agreed to limit their sales. Such arrangements became the norm for trade in textiles and apparel; they spread to steel and automobiles; and, in particular, they were employed to limit the sales of such rapidly rising competitors as Japan and the East Asian newly industrializing countries (NICs).

For American trade policymakers, the erosion of the GATT weakened one important postwar source of leverage in domestic trade bargaining: the argument that a particular restrictive action would undercut the international trading system from which the United States derived great benefits. For the more the international trade regime was viewed as ineffective and riddled with exceptions, the less credible were claims that US interests were served by following its rules.

Stagflation

The GATT also faced growing strain because, from the 1970s to the mid-1980s, the United States and its advanced industrial trading partners were beset with what became known as "stagflation": slow growth and high unemployment coexisting with high inflation. The United States sowed the seeds of the stagflation era when, for several years, Lyndon B. Johnson refused to seek a tax hike to finance the Vietnam War. Richard M. Nixon made matters worse with his overstimulation of the American economy in the election year of 1972. In both cases, the United States pursued fiscal and monetary policies that increased overall demand at a time when production was at or near capacity. The immediate result was price rises, which proved contagious. By early 1973, inflation in the United States was running at double-digit levels.

Then came the October War in the Middle East. Seizing the opportunity presented by tight supply conditions, members of the Organization of Petroleum Exporting Countries (OPEC) quadrupled the price at which they offered their crude oil on world markets. This generated enormous new inflationary pressure, driving up costs for productive enterprises and gasoline-dependent consumers. At the same time, the oil shock depressed demand in all the advanced industrial countries, since paying for needed oil imports at the new prices forced a massive shift of funds from consumer to producer countries. The world plunged from a 1973 boom to a 1974 recession—the deepest of the postwar era. In 1979, revolution in Iran led to the second oil shock, a near-tripling of the OPEC export price. Again, inflation rates rose and the world economy plunged into recession.

Once under way, stagflation proved endemic. The higher the US rate of inflation became, the greater the level of unemployment that was needed to wring expectations of future inflation out of the economy. Hence, in 1979, the Federal Reserve Board under Chairman Paul A. Volcker began to pursue consistently tight money policies, even as growth flagged and the number of jobless increased. What economists and journalists came to label the "misery index"—the sum of the unemployment and inflation rates—rose to new heights.

Statistics once viewed with alarm came to be seen as normal, even encouraging. In the United States in 1957, a 3.6 percent rise in the consumer price index (CPI) had alarmed the Eisenhower administration; for more than a decade thereafter, the country did not again see a year-to-year increase above 3 percent. But the 1970s and early 1980s brought four years of double-digit price inflation, and President Ronald Reagan could claim victory when the 1983 CPI was "only" 3.2 percent above that of 1982.[35] Prior to 1975, the highest annual postwar rates of civilian unemployment were 6.8 percent in 1958 and 6.7 percent in 1961. By 1982, unemployment reached 9.7 percent. Expectations in the United States were so reduced that, in a year when unemployment averaged

---

35. *Economic Report of the President,* 1985, tables B-54 and B-55.

7.5 percent, Reagan could be credited with an impressive economic recovery and ride to a landslide reelection victory.[36]

The trade problems of key industries were exacerbated by their failure to adjust to this less congenial environment. Management and labor continued to negotiate hefty wage increases, notwithstanding slower domestic growth and stiffer international competition: "In 1970 hourly compensation for auto and steel workers was about 30 percent higher than the average compensation in manufacturing. By 1981 the difference had grown to 70 percent for steel workers and 50 percent for auto workers."[37] Only after both industries faced massive layoffs were significant wage and benefit concessions forthcoming.

Coming together with stagflation, as both cause and effect, was a decline in the rate of economic growth. Not only did the United States experience five negative growth years between 1970 and 1982 (there were none from 1959 to 1969), but its average GNP growth also fell by a percentage point despite an exceptional increase in the labor force.[38] This reflected a sharp decline in productivity growth. As a result, the average real wages of the American worker stopped growing around 1973, in dramatic contrast to their near doubling over the 25 previous years.[39] Moreover, income inequality rose over the 1970s and 1980s.[40] Nor were such changes affecting the United States alone. All advanced industrial nations found the going harder after the early 1970s. Average Japanese growth of 4.4 percent in 1971–83 might look good to Americans and Europeans, but it was a big drop from the 11.7 percent of the decade preceding.[41] The worsening in US unemployment looked bad until the much steeper proportionate rises were considered in Germany, France, Canada, and above all, Britain, whose jobless rate leaped from 3 percent in 1970 to 12 percent in 1984![42] The middle and late 1980s did bring

---

36. Ibid., table B-29. By the end of 1985, Reagan (and the US economy) were beginning also to benefit from an oil glut, precipitating a sharp decline in oil prices and undermining the always tenuous OPEC effort to buttress prices through national production quotas. In the ensuing years, driven by sharp US growth in 1984 and moderate growth thereafter, the average civilian unemployment rate declined to 5.3 percent in 1989 before rising with the 1990–91 recession.

37. *Economic Report of the President,* 1984, 92.

38. Average US GNP growth was 3.8 percent in 1961–70, 2.7 percent in 1971–84. Yet the labor force grew by 29 percent in 1971–80, much more than in either previous postwar decade. See *Economic Report of the President,* 1991, tables B-109 and B-32.

39. The best work on this subject is Frank Levy, *Dollars and Dreams: The Changing American Income Distribution* (New York: Russell Sage Foundation and W. W. Norton, 1988).

40. Bartles, *A Future of Lousy Jobs?* 1.

41. *Economic Report of the President,* 1991, table B-110.

42. Ibid., table B-108.

some good economic news for Americans. Inflation fell substantially: from 1982 through 1989, it never exceeded 4.6 percent, whereas it was above that level every year from 1974 through 1981. US economic growth averaged 3.5 percent in 1984–90, compared with 2.5 percent in 1976–83. There was a rebound in the productivity growth of manufacturing (though not service) industries. And toward the decade's end Europe also experienced a surge in growth, as did Japan.

By 1990–92, the United States was back in recession, a problem which in short order also beset Europe and Japan. Thus, other nations would not be very receptive to American demands that they give the United States more in international trade talks than they were likely to get in return. This was even more true in 1993–94, as the US economy took a strong upward turn while recession lingered elsewhere.

Floating Exchange Rates and Dollar "Misalignment"

The monetary regime within which the United States faced these new difficulties was no longer the Bretton Woods system of fixed exchange rates pegged to the dollar, but one in which the dollar's relative price— the single most important determinant of US producers' trade competitiveness—was being set and reset, day by day, in foreign-exchange markets.[43]

As noted at the outset of this chapter, the end of Bretton Woods initially made life easier for US trade policymakers. The "Nixon shock" of 15 August 1971 had begun the process, and devaluations of roughly 10 percent followed in December 1971 and February 1973. Renewed currency speculation forced the major trading nations to move to a floating-rate regime a month later, in March 1973. After that, the markets generally kept the real (inflation-adjusted) value of the dollar at or below the March 1973 level through the Nixon, Ford, and Carter administrations.[44] American exports benefited; import competition eased somewhat; the management of trade-restrictive pressures was somewhat less of a burden. And it was at a time of dollar weakness, with US exports expanding rapidly, that the world completed (and Congress approved) the Tokyo Round agreements aimed at reducing nontariff barriers to trade.

However, in the first half of the 1980s, this exchange rate situation reversed itself with a vengeance. From its level in 1980 to its peak in late

---

43. For a general analysis of the challenges this posed for US policymakers, see I. M. Destler and C. Randall Henning, *Dollar Politics: Exchange Rate Policymaking in the United States* (Washington: Institute for International Economics, 1989), esp. chaps. 1–4.

44. In fact, the markets brought the dollar sharply down in the early Carter administration, necessitating a "dollar defense" initiative on 1 November 1978 to reverse this fall.

Figure 3.1 United States: nominal effective exchange rates, 1980–93[a]

1980=100 (annual average)

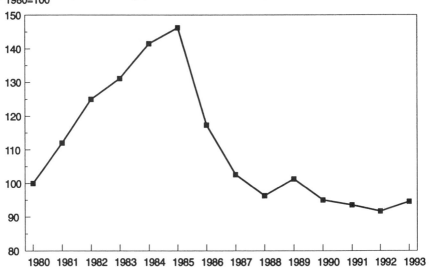

a. The index is based on the International Monetary Fund's Multilateral Exchange Rate Model.

Source: International Monetary Fund, *IFS.*

February 1985, the trade-weighted value of the dollar rose an incredible 67 percent by the MERM index of the International Monetary Fund, and 88.2 percent by the index of the Federal Reserve.[45] (See figure 3.1.) At this point, the dollar was roughly 40 percent above the level that would have brought balance to the US current account. This meant that American producers of internationally traded goods faced a 40 percent cost disadvantage in relation to foreign rivals in US and overseas markets. In terms of trade competitiveness, this was a severe and protracted currency misalignment that had been unseen—and unforeseen—by postwar economists, businessmen, and politicians.[46]

Beginning in March 1985, the dollar turned around again. Given a

45. Destler and Henning, *Dollar Politics,* 22–25. MERM stands for the Multilateral Exchange Rate Model.

46. For a definition of currency misalignments, see John Williamson, *The Exchange Rate System,* POLICY ANALYSES IN INTERNATIONAL ECONOMICS 5 (Washington: Institute for International Economics, September 1983, rev. June 1985), 12. For a proposal to reduce them, see Williamson and Marcus H. Miller, *Targets and Indicators: A Blueprint for the International Coordination of Economic Policy,* POLICY ANALYSES IN INTERNATIONAL ECONOMICS 22 (Washington: Institute for International Economics, December 1987). For a comprehensive analysis of the dollar misalignment's macroeconomic causes and trade consequences, see Stephen Marris, *Deficits and the Dollar: The World Economy at Risk,* POLICY ANALYSES IN INTERNATIONAL ECONOMICS 14 (Washington: Institute for International Economics, December 1985, rev. August 1987).

major push by a joint declaration by the finance ministers of the Group of Five nations (France, Germany, Japan, the United Kingdom, and the United States) in the Plaza Agreement in September 1985, by the end of 1987 the dollar had plummeted to roughly its 1980 level, and it moved within a far narrower range in the years thereafter—as figure 3.1 shows. With both the decline and the subsequent stabilization came renewed cooperation in exchange rate management among the finance ministers and central banks of the advanced industrial nations.[47]

How could the exchange rate shift so much? How was the dollar able to reach a level that rendered many American products uncompetitive, as it had by early 1982, and continue to rise for three more years despite burgeoning US trade deficits, only to plummet over the next three years? A critical underlying source of such currency fluctuations and misalignment was a revolution in world capital markets.

Many international economists had favored a floating exchange rate system well before the world was forced to accept one. Generally, they expected that trade transactions would dominate foreign-currency markets. Since the trade competitiveness of major countries was generally slow to change, this meant that relationships among the strong currencies would be rather stable.[48] Shifts in exchange rates would be gradual, and a function primarily of shifts in trade flows.

What no one anticipated was the impact of the dramatic increase in the magnitude and international mobility of investment capital, particularly "short-term" funds seeking the most rewarding current situation. As one informed observer characterized matters in early 1985:

> The flow of money was now dwarfing the growth of world trade. In 1984, for example, world trade in goods and services was on the order of $2 trillion, while global capital transfers reached $20–30 trillion.[49]

This meant that exchange rates were increasingly driven not by trade transactions, but by whatever might cause those who controlled capital to shift funds from one currency to another. Portfolio managers, responsible for large pools of investment money, became critical participants in the world economy. And while no school of economics could model their behavior with much confidence, they seemed to be motivated primarily by two factors: differences in real interest rate returns between

---

47. See Destler and Henning, *Dollar Politics,* chap. 4, and Yoichi Funabashi, *Managing the Dollar: From the Plaza to the Louvre* (Washington: Institute for International Economics, 1988, rev. 1989).

48. This would not, of course, apply to the currencies of countries experiencing very high inflation.

49. Jeffrey E. Garten, "Gunboat Economics," *Foreign Affairs,* 63, no. 3 (America and the World, 1984): 453. As Garten's broad range suggests, estimates of the magnitude of capital flows were necessarily imprecise.

countries and anticipation as to how, in the near term, a currency's value was likely to move.

When a major country like the United States pursued policies the markets perceived as inflationary—likely to reduce the currency's value and hence the "real" returns on dollar assets—that currency's value plummeted. The swing was exacerbated by the herd instinct of money managers, whose rewards come from calling today's market correctly. Thus the dollar sank in 1977 and 1978.

When, conversely, the United States began its "riverboat gamble"[50] with Reaganomics in 1981, the situation turned around. The United States now needed foreign funds to finance its suddenly mammoth budget deficits. And real US interest rates were strong, spurred by this expanded government borrowing and by the tight-money policies of Federal Reserve Chairman Paul A. Volcker, who had come into office in 1979 determined to squeeze inflation out of the US economy. Foreign money therefore flowed in and drove the dollar skyward. By the end of 1984, a dollar would buy more than twice as many French francs, British pounds, and German marks as it had in October 1978. The dollar could even buy about 40 percent more Japanese yen.

US producers of traded goods found their competitive position demolished, as the currency misalignment made foreign goods far cheaper for Americans to buy and American products very dear for purchasers overseas. Exports stagnated, with the total for 1986 actually below that of 1980. Imports surged. The overall US trade deficit ballooned to $67 billion in 1983 and $159.5 billion in 1987. As former Federal Reserve Chairman Arthur F. Burns noted at mid-decade, such 12-digit deficits were "awesomely different from anything experienced in the past," by any country.[51]

The strong dollar was not the sole cause of the enormous shift.[52] But Secretary of State George P. Shultz stated the consensus view when he blamed it for "over half . . . of the deterioration in the US trade account."[53] From the perspective of producers of traded goods, the strong dollar of the mid-1980s was a devastating source of competitive disadvantage. It was something about which they, as individual economic agents, could do absolutely nothing. And it was something against which traditional intergovernmental trade bargaining was impotent as well.

---

50. The phrase is that of Howard Baker, then majority leader of the US Senate, who guided the Reagan program to enactment.

51. "The American Trade Deficit," *Foreign Affairs*, 62, no. 5 (Summer 1984): 1068.

52. The other major sources were the developing-country debt crisis, which sharply curtailed exports to Latin America, and the fact that the US economy grew more rapidly, in 1983 and 1984, than those of its major trading partners.

53. "National Policies and Global Prosperity," address at the Woodrow Wilson School, Princeton University, Princeton, NJ, 11 April 1985, processed.

But the trade balance _was_ responsive to exchange rate change. And just as the rise of the dollar brought unprecedented trade pain, its rapid fall brought substantial relief. By the end of 1987, the dollar could buy only half as many yen—or marks—as it could in early 1985. With this new price advantage, US exports, stagnant for six years, nearly doubled between 1986 and 1991. Imports maintained their rapid growth for a while, and the annual trade deficit did not begin to decline until 1988. By 1991, however, it had finally dropped well below the $100 billion annual rate; import growth had slackened (with recession an important cause), while the export boom continued.[54]

But if the monthly trade deficits were now lower, deficits they remained. And the United States was still borrowing overseas to finance them.

Economic Tripolarity and the End of the Cold War

Finally, Americans had to digest the fruits of a great victory: the end of the Cold War and the demise of their longtime Soviet adversary. For over 40 years, that global political-military confrontation had dominated American foreign policy. It had also muted economic conflicts, since leading US trade competitors were also its most critical Cold War allies.

Now, suddenly, the Cold War was won, with the collapse of the Warsaw Pact in 1989–90 and the disintegration of the Soviet Union in 1991. The United States emerged as the sole military superpower, flexing its military muscle by leading a United Nations coalition in reversing Iraq's conquest of Kuwait, and extracting major financial contributions in sup-

---

54. The dollar began falling in early 1985, but as Paul R. Krugman noted, "through much of 1987 [trade] imbalances continued to grow, leading to widespread assertions that the traditional international adjustment process no longer worked." In fact, Krugman concludes, the US "export boom . . . happened just about when and in the magnitude that the traditional [economic] models would have predicted." _Has the Adjustment Process Worked?_ POLICY ANALYSES IN INTERNATIONAL ECONOMICS 34 (Washington: Institute for International Economics, October 1991), 1–3, 46. Stephen Marris, on the other hand, writes that "the actual improvement in the US trade balance was about 30 percent less than it should have been according to the D&D model, reflecting an overestimation of the benefits from devaluation (common to most models of the US trade balance extant at the time)." See his essay, "Why No Hard Landing?" in C. Fred Bergsten, ed., _International Adjustment and Financing: The Lessons of 1985–1991_ (Washington: Institute for International Economics, 1992), 250. The "D&D model" is that in Marris's _Deficits and the Dollar_.

Robert Z. Lawrence concludes that the 1980s' experience offers "little support for the pessimists who have claimed that U.S. trade flows would not respond to exchange rate changes." See his "U.S. Current Account Adjustment: An Appraisal," Brookings Papers on Economic Activity (1990:2): 382.

port of this campaign from Tokyo and Bonn. Yet simultaneously it found the going harder on economic issues, as illustrated by the December 1990 breakdown in the Uruguay Round multilateral trade talks, and the rise in trade and economic frictions with Japan.

As recounted earlier in this chapter, the relative US economic position had been receding for decades. But mutual security dependence had kept Europe and Japan responsive to US trade leadership, and made leaders in all three inclined to compromise on trade issues in order to preserve the free world coalition. As Robert Gilpin has noted, "Difficult economic issues dividing the three centers of world capitalism could frequently be resolved through appeals to the need for unity against the common Soviet enemy."[55] Now trilateral economic relations have lost their "security umbrella."[56] Leaders would need to pursue trade and trilateral cooperation for its own sake, or not pursue it at all.

A Tougher World

As these seven changes were intertwined, so too were their political effects. Explosion in the volume of trade meant greater import competition for American producers, and greater pressure for trade restrictions, even in the 1970s when the dollar was comparatively weak. The dollar misalignment of the early and mid-1980s compounded the political problem: it increased the volume of imports and consequent protectionist reaction, while demoralizing export interests because it curtailed their gains from open trade. The dollar decline of 1985–87 brought needed relief, economically and politically. But frustration continued.

The diminished relative position of the United States joined with stagflation and recession to cast a shadow on future American economic prospects. Such unhappy economic outcomes discredited, to a degree, arguments for a continuing commitment to open trade. And the end of the Cold War eliminated the necessity to compromise with allies on economic issues in order to maintain the grand anti-Soviet alliance. More generally, as successive presidents found themselves embattled with economic woes, they had less leeway to press market-opening measures at home, and felt more pressure to restrict imports or to demand that US trading partners buy US exports.

Stagflation and American "decline" were accompanied by the growing

---

55. "The Transformation of the International Political Economy," Jean Monnet Chair Papers (San Domenico, Italy: The European University Institute, 1991), 12.

56. C. Fred Bergsten, "The World Economy After the Cold War," *Foreign Affairs*, 69, no. 3 (Summer 1990): 96–112. See also the articles by Theodore C. Sorensen and Peter Tarnoff in the same issue.

visibility of unfair foreign trade practices, as well as unequal market access in specific product areas. There was an understandable tendency to blame at least some of the "decline" on these foreign trade practices. The weakening of the GATT made it harder to achieve effective remedies for unfair practices within the multilateral system, and pressure for unilateral responses therefore increased. Reinforcing such pressure was the threatening nature of the United States' new competitors—Japan, the NICs—whose trade was growing at historically unprecedented rates, who clearly benefited from some form of government-business cooperation, and whose aggressiveness in exports preceded and exceeded their willingness to open their markets to imports.

Changes of this magnitude would have posed severe problems for the American trade policymaking system even if it had retained its basic postwar character and strength. But it too was changing. This was due in part to the new international economic realities, but also in part to developments that were specific to US politics.

We turn now to these domestic system changes—the primary focus of this book. And we begin with the United States Congress, that central constitutional authority whose interest in protecting itself from trade pressures was the key element in the effectiveness of the old trade order.

4

A Less Protected Congress

For most of the postwar period, the United States Congress was remarkably restrained in the exercise of its constitutional authority to "regulate commerce with foreign nations." Individual senators and representatives engaged in a great deal of trade rhetoric; they lent their names to hundreds of bills proposing trade restrictions for industries that were strong within their constituencies. Congress periodically passed general trade laws to extend, expand, and limit presidential negotiating authority, including the reciprocal trade act renewals in the 1950s, as well as larger authorization acts like those of 1962 and 1974. There were also times when Congress failed to deliver on important executive commitments: to the International Trade Organization charter of 1948, for example, or to the Kennedy Round antidumping agreement signed almost 20 years later.

But product-specific legislative output was sparse. Senators and representatives consistently referred particular cases elsewhere: to the Tariff Commission for assessing injury to petitioning industries, for example, or to the executive for negotiating tariff cuts or arranging limits on the inflow of particularly sensitive commodities. Bills proposing statutory protection for textiles or shoes or steel typically died in committee, often without so much as a hearing. With the exception of a few agricultural quotas, Congress almost never legislated specific import protection.

As outlined in chapter 2, such "voluntary restraint" by the Congress was the central domestic political prerequisite for US international trade leadership. By delegating responsibility to the executive and by helping fashion a system that protected legislators from one-sided restrictive pressures, Congress made it possible for successive presidents to maintain and expand the liberal trade order.

Congressional restraint depended, in important part, on the capacity of legislative leaders to control the action by preventing floor votes on product-specific restrictions. In the words of one prescient analyst in 1974, the House Ways and Means Committee and its chairman were "in effect . . . hired to put a damper on particularism in tax and tariff matters."[1]

However, during the postwar period, Congress was changing. Power was spreading out among the 535 individual members; thus the legislative calendar and output were less subject to leaders' control. This change accelerated in the 1970s, particularly in the House of Representatives. At the same time, trade was becoming more important to the American economy.

Then, in the 1980s, this less protected Congress was hit with unprecedented trade-political pressure, generated mainly by unprecedented trade deficits. And the Reagan administration was slow to respond. So legislators of both political parties seized the initiative, demanding tougher executive action to enter resistant foreign markets, and passing the first congressionally initiated omnibus trade bill since before Smoot-Hawley.

Counter to many predictions, Congress still did not "go protectionist." Nor did legislators reclaim their constitutional power to impose product-specific trade barriers. They continued to delegate broad powers to the executive—in the 1988 act and in the 1991 vote renewing "fast-track" negotiating authority for the multilateral Uruguay Round and for free trade negotiations with Mexico. But they did so more grudgingly, with more detailed demands and timetables, which constrained administration flexibility. They thus put more pressure than ever on the executive branch, making open US trade policies more dependent than ever on the latter's policy commitment and leadership skill.

□ □ □

The tragedy of one man came to symbolize the demise of the old order. In October 1974, even as the Senate Finance Committee was quietly marking up the authorizing legislation for the Tokyo Round, the chairman of its House counterpart became involved in a scandal that would force his resignation. For years, Wilbur D. Mills (D-AR) had been the consummate insider. The central congressional figure on trade and tax policy, he was perhaps the most powerful member of his chamber, yet he was little known to the general public. In a parliamentary regime, he might well have become prime minister. But in the United States, his one quest for national recognition was in a belated campaign for the 1972 Democratic presidential nomination. This campaign had peaked with

---

1. David R. Mayhew, *Congress: The Electoral Connection* (New Haven, CT: Yale University Press, 1974), 154.

a 4 percent vote in the New Hampshire primary, and Mills won a total of 33.8 delegate votes at the convention the following August.

Now Mills's name would become a household word because of a bizarre incident that exposed his heavy drinking and involvement with a woman not his wife.[2] It came at a time when Mills's influence was already in decline. Suffering from a back ailment, he had missed most of the House Ways and Means markups of the Tokyo Round authorization bill the year before. Now his career and reputation publicly disintegrated. He won reelection in November, but the sudden scandal reduced his usually overwhelming majority to 59 percent. By December, he had declared himself an alcoholic and announced that he would not continue as Ways and Means chairman in the next Congress. Two years later, he retired from public office.

Mills was succeeded as chairman by Al Ullman (D-OR). He was replaced by no one. His talented Senate counterpart of the 1970s, Finance Chairman Russell B. Long (D-LA), would develop a formidable personal reputation, as would Long's successors, Robert J. Dole (R-KS) and Lloyd Bentsen (D-TX). In the 1980s, Dan Rostenkowski (D-IL) would restore some of the old luster to Ways and Means. But, from the 1960s onward, the Senate was too freewheeling and democratic to permit the sort of personal policy dominance that Mills had exercised. In the 1970s the House became so as well.

Congressional Reform and the Weakening of Ways and Means

Even before the Arkansan's public fall from grace, the "excessive power" of Ways and Means had been "a major target of reorganization."[3] This was part of a broader challenge to the power of committee chairmen by congressional reformers.

American politics was opening up, and more and more legislators owed their election not to party machines but to personal entrepreneurship. They did not want to run the turtle's race between seniority and senility, by serving quietly as apprentices for the 20 to 30 years it might take to move up the ranks to chair a major committee.

By the end of 1974, it was clear that new House members no longer had to wait. They could aspire to policy influence almost immediately.

---

2. A car in which Mills was riding was stopped (for speeding, without lights) by a National Park Service police cruiser, at which point the woman ran from the car and leaped into the nearby Washington Tidal Basin. The episode received extensive press coverage, particularly in the *Washington Post*, as the "full story" was gradually revealed.

3. Roger H. Davidson and Walter J. Oleszek, *Congress Against Itself* (Bloomington: Indiana University Press, 1977), 179.

The Watergate election brought no fewer than 75 new Democrats into the House. Adding to them the newly elected Republicans and the turnover in the 1972 election, more than one-third of the House members in January 1975 had not been there three years before.

The freshmen joined the veteran reformers to activate the long-moribund Democratic caucus. Exploiting a recently adopted requirement for caucus votes on all House committee chairs, they ousted three and threatened others. The caucus took particular steps to cut the powers of Ways and Means. Its Democratic members were stripped of one special source of power over their colleagues: the role of "committee on committees," deciding who would fill vacancies on all House panels. Ways and Means was also expanded from 25 members to 37 members, making close management in the Mills mode harder for a successor to accomplish.

Not all reform ideas were adopted. One major internal review group, the "Bolling Committee," proposed in 1974 to take away substantial chunks of jurisdiction, moving authority over trade and tariffs, for example, to House Foreign Affairs. This proposal was set aside, and Ways and Means's substantive sphere remained largely intact.

Nevertheless, like other committees, Ways and Means was forced to form legislative subcommittees with separate staffs. This meant that, in the future, its chairman would share primary trade responsibility with the chairman of the Trade Subcommittee. The committee was also subject to new House rules making markups of bills generally open to the public. Bills were subject to procedural changes that made "open rules"—allowing floor amendments—the norm, so that on-the-record, roll-call votes on such amendments were now far easier for proponents to obtain.

In both its sources and its goals, the congressional reform movement was unrelated to trade. But the reformers' twin objectives—decentralization of power and openness of procedures—nonetheless struck at the heart of the old American trade policymaking system. Open US trade policy had been founded, in part, on closed politics, on a variety of devices that shielded legislators from one-sided restrictive pressures. It had prospered under congressional barons—Mills above all—who had enough leverage to manipulate issues and to protect their colleagues from those up-or-down votes that forced a choice between conviction and constituency. As noted in chapter 2, the system did not protect Congress all of the time; for example, agriculture was partly outside its domain. In addition, as illustrated by the "Mills bill" episode of 1970 (see chapter 2), an unfavorable sequence of events could overcome barriers to congressional action. Still, the old system had succeeded in keeping the great bulk of product-specific protectionist proposals from coming to roll-call votes on the House floor.

This was the very sort of thing that reformers wanted to change.

Although they were not thinking specifically of trade, their overall goal was to force policy choices out in the open, by publicizing House actions and members' stands. Believing that "special interests" benefited from the closed system, they reasoned that if Congress were democratized and its operations exposed to the sunshine, then the larger public interest would prevail.

There was both truth and oversimplification in this critique of the cozy old system. Closed procedures could indeed benefit special interests. But they also could offer insulation to members who wanted to resist such interests but were reluctant to do so under the watchful eyes of their lobbyists. For while anyone could attend open meetings, it was typically the lobbyists who did. They came, they saw, and they reported back on what members were doing for (or against) their particular causes. More open floor procedures also offered new opportunities for special interests to press their proposals.[4]

Three textile episodes, spread over three decades, illustrate how more open House processes offered advantages to those seeking protection. In the spring of 1968, to buttress his candidacy for his first full Senate term, Senator Ernest F. Hollings (D-SC) won adoption of a stringent proposal for statutory textile quotas cosponsored by no fewer than 67 colleagues, attaching it to major Johnson administration tax legislation. However, as noted in chapter 2, this proposal stopped at the House door, for Mills, supported by the administration, refused to accept it in conference. The Senate Finance Committee cooperated; indeed, it generally counted on its House counterpart to kill such initiatives. (And Johnson, according to one who served in his White House, added a personal flourish, making Hollings "an offer he couldn't refuse." He told the junior senator that if he pushed for another Senate floor vote the administration would defeat him and then spread the word around South Carolina that Hollings had bungled the textile industry's case.)

In 1978, Hollings won Senate adoption of another extreme industry proposal, one that would require an 11th-hour withdrawal of all the textile tariff reductions offered by the United States in the nearly completed Tokyo Round.[5] Senate Trade Subcommittee Chairman Abraham A. Ribicoff (D-CT) declared this could "ensure the failure of the negotiation." Again the vehicle was a bill that the administration

---

4. John F. Witte draws a similar connection between congressional reform and special-interest tax provisions. See his "The Income Tax Mess: Deviant Process or Institutional Failure?" paper prepared for delivery at the 1985 Annual Meeting of the American Political Science Association, New Orleans (1 September 1985).

5. The industry was hardly in dire straits. The system of negotiated quota agreements had been broadened in the early 1970s from cotton products to those of all major fibers, and this had helped keep the total volume of textile imports in 1976–78 at about 6 percent below its peak in 1971–73.

needed, one that renewed the lending authority of the Export-Import Bank. But now a weaker Ways and Means Committee, in a decentralized House, could not prevent a floor vote. So a much more elaborate procedural shuffle had to be devised to sidetrack the proposal.[6]

In 1985, with imports surging, the textile industry was able to move a highly restrictive quota bill to the House floor through the Ways and Means Committee, notwithstanding the opposition of the chairmen of both the full committee and the trade subcommittee. Sponsored by Representative Ed Jenkins (D-GA), the bill would have imposed quotas on a global and on a country-specific basis. With nearly 300 members signing on as cosponsors, the Ways and Means leadership elected to send it to the floor without recommendation, in the expectation that President Ronald Reagan would veto the measure. Reagan did, and a motion to override failed by eight votes.[7] Similar bills were passed—and vetoed—in 1988 and 1990.

The textile industry campaign of 1978 contributed to the failure of the Carter administration to win enactment that same fall of legislation needed to complete the Tokyo Round of multilateral trade negotiations (MTN): extension of authority to waive enforcement of countervailing duties.[8] The chairman and the ranking Republican of the Ways and Means Trade Subcommittee then conceded defeat, declaring in a public letter to Special Trade Representative Robert S. Strauss that the countervailing duty waiver could not be passed in the next Congress unless the textile exclusion was attached. To prevent this, the administration was forced to buy off that industry with policy concessions in early 1979.

If congressional reform thus weakened the key committees, so also

---

6. The Export-Import Bank measure was formally abandoned, its provisions attached to another bill at 4 a.m. on the last day of the 95th Congress. The textile-tariff proposal was brought to the House floor and adopted overwhelmingly, but as an amendment to a bill President Jimmy Carter could afford to veto—one authorizing the sale of Carson City silver dollars. By design or coincidence, this bill was one of the last two of the session to be formally "enrolled" and sent to the White House, and the presidential veto thus could be delayed until after the mid-term election (the other straggler, also vetoed, provided for meat import quotas).

7. The veto took place in December 1985, but in an unusual action, industry supporters won postponement of an override vote until the following summer so that the threat would toughen the administration's stance in the talks for extension of the Multi-Fiber Arrangement. On this they were, in the main, successful.

8. Europeans had insisted from the start that they would not negotiate under threat of such duties being imposed under the old, pre-GATT US law which did not require that petitioning industries prove injury from imports, at the same time as they were working out a new subsidy-countervail-code agreement under which the United States would impose such a test. Although the Trade Act of 1974 had granted a five-year authorization for the Tokyo Round, it only provided a four-year authority for waiving countervailing duties. This expired on 3 January 1979, just as the negotiations were reaching their climax.

did changes in the content of trade policy. Senate Finance and House Ways and Means were, first and foremost, revenue committees. By historical precedent and recurrent argument, their trade authority was derived from tariffs—the main means of raising revenue during most of the republic's existence. Tariffs' declining importance in trade policy undercut this jurisdictional rationale. The rise of nontariff trade issues in the 1970s—such as government procurement, product standards, and subsidies—inevitably brought other committees into the substance of trade policy.

How then could Congress play its role in the trade system? On one major type of business—authorization and implementation of major trade agreements—it showed considerable creativity by developing new rules for expedited action that led to the overwhelming 1979 vote in favor of the MTN. On product-specific issues, however, Congress had become more vulnerable to special-interest pressures.

Renewing the Delegation of Power: The "Fast-Track" Procedures

From the Reciprocal Trade Agreements Act of 1934 through the Trade Expansion Act of 1962, the means by which Congress delegated authority for trade negotiations remained basically the same. Successive statutes authorized executive officials to negotiate (within specified numerical limits) reductions in US tariffs, in exchange for reductions by its trading partners. When a deal was finally struck, it could be implemented by presidential proclamation, without further recourse to Capitol Hill.

For American trade negotiators, this arrangement had enormous advantages. It gave them maximum credibility abroad, since their power to deliver on their commitments was not in doubt. It also increased their leverage with affected industries at home. Those fearing the effects of particular tariff cuts could and did appeal for congressional backing, but since no formal ratification of the final trade agreement was required, the ultimate decision rested at the northwest end of Pennsylvania Avenue. In theory, of course, lobbyists could prevail on Congress to vote an exception for their product—as the textile industry sought to do in 1978. But this was very much an uphill fight, for it went against the whole system of delegating power and protecting legislators.

When a nontariff trade barrier (NTB) was at issue, however, there was no comparable system of advance authorization, and therefore no assurance that what US representatives negotiated abroad would become law at home. This weakness of the trade system was revealed rather dramatically in the final stages of the Kennedy Round. In exchange for related foreign concessions, the Johnson administration made two important nontariff commitments in 1967: to participate in a new GATT antidumping code and to eliminate the system of customs appraisals called the American Selling Price (ASP), which inflated the duties of certain categories of US imports. Congress had authorized neither of these agreements; in fact, the Senate passed a sense-of-Congress resolution in 1966 opposing their negotiation. And Congress implemented neither of them. In fact, it rendered US adherence to the antidumping code meaningless by insisting that whenever it conflicted with domestic law, the latter would prevail.[9]

These precedents were hardly encouraging. With tariffs now at a fraction of Smoot-Hawley levels, future trade rounds would focus increasingly on NTBs. How could US negotiators be credible internationally? And how could Congress be insulated from pressure to reject or rework what the executive branch had wrought?

The Nixon administration confronted this problem in early 1973 when it sought legislation to authorize a trade round giving priority to nontariff distortions. Not surprisingly, it proposed a procedure nearly identical to that for tariffs. Congress would authorize talks to bargain down NTBs; the president would implement the agreements reached by proclaiming the necessary changes in US domestic statutes, which would go into effect unless either house of Congress vetoed the measure within 90 days. The process was similar to that inaugurated in the New Deal for executive branch reorganization: the president could put forward "reorganization plans," which became law unless the House or the Senate objected.

The House accepted this legislative veto proposal; the Senate did not. It was, argued senior Finance Democrat Herman E. Talmadge of Georgia, "not the way we make laws." This procedure might be all right for government organization, but for substantive policy he was convinced that such an open-ended delegation of power to amend statutes was unconstitutional. Talmadge saw no alternative to affirmative congressional action, after the fact, on all specific, nontariff changes in American law resulting from trade negotiations. And his Finance Committee colleagues agreed.

This seemed to render negotiations impossible: how could foreign governments deal seriously with the United States if Congress might reject or amend the outcome or never take definitive action at all? Fortunately, negotiations among STR leaders, Talmadge, and Finance Committee staff yielded an alternative the senator found acceptable. This was a statutory commitment to an up-or-down vote, within a specified period of time, on

---

9. For detail and documentation on this episode, see Michael J. Glennon, Thomas M. Franck, and Robert C. Cassidy Jr., *United States Foreign Relations Law: Documents and Sources*, vol. 4, International Economic Regulation (London: Oceana Publications, 1984), 1–38.

any legislation implementing an NTB agreement submitted by the president.

As finally enacted, the Trade Act included an elaborate procedural timetable aimed at assuring expeditious legislative action. After consulting with the relevant congressional committees, the president would give notice of intent at least 90 days before entering into any NTB agreement. Once he did so, Congress would act within 60 days of his submitting the implementing bill, under rules barring committee or floor amendments.[10]

This was not a perfect solution for executive negotiators, for they could not assure their foreign counterparts that Congress would deliver. But they could promise a prompt and clear answer.

These new procedures were adopted to facilitate negotiations abroad. Yet, although no one fully realized it at the time, they would also reshape the policy process at home. Specifically, on trade agreements, the procedures allowed the new, "open" Congress to replicate its closed predecessor. With the legislative process limited in scope and time, the stance of the trade committees, Finance and Ways and Means, was once again likely to prove decisive. To be confident of favorable floor actions, the STR's office needed the committees' overwhelming support of the agreements negotiated. This meant paying attention to committee members and aides, whom the legislation made official observers and advisers at the negotiations.

In practice, the Hill's substantive contribution was limited for most of the MTN. But as the end of the talks approached in the spring of 1978, the senior trade expert on the Finance Committee staff, Robert C. Cassidy Jr., posed a procedural challenge. He began pressing for a major congressional role in the drafting of the nonamendable MTN implementing legislation that the president was to propose. Politically, he argued, enactment of such legislation would require a joint commitment by the STR and the trade committees. Operationally, this could best be accomplished if they developed that legislation together.

Insofar as possible, Cassidy proposed, they would replicate the normal legislative process. In sessions with STR Robert Strauss and other executive branch representatives that came to be labeled "nonmarkups," Finance and Ways and Means would advise separately on the implementing bill's substance. They would then reconcile their differences in a "nonconference." Finally, the drafting of the actual statutory language would be an interbranch process, with congressional legal aides working

---

10. For details, see I. M. Destler, *Making Foreign Economic Policy* (Washington: Brookings Institution, 1980), 177–78; Matthew J. Marks and Harald B. Malmgren, "Negotiating Nontariff Distortions to Trade," *Law and Policy in International Business* 7, no. 2 (1975): 338–41; and Glennon, Franck, and Cassidy, *Foreign Relations Law*, esp. 41–65. The maximum time period for action on an "implementing revenue bill" was slightly longer: 90 days.

with counterparts in executive agencies much as they did on normal trade legislation. Only then would the president send the formal, nonamendable implementing bill to Capitol Hill.

There was some initial skepticism at the staff level in STR: Did they really want to give Capitol Hill that strong a role in drafting the president's bill? But ties between the trade office and the Finance staff were strong—STR General Counsel Richard R. Rivers had worked for that committee prior to 1977—and so STR acquiesced. But "unofficially," by one authoritative report, "STR said they still hoped to carry on the bill drafting process without too much congressional interference."[11] So Finance senators summoned STR Strauss and won his personal assent to this procedure, which was quickly confirmed in an exchange of letters. Ways and Means, never a formal party to the arrangement, followed it in practice.[12]

In return for this considerable concession on procedure, the executive branch won near-total congressional approval of the substance of the MTN agreements it negotiated, which were implemented through a single legislative package, the Trade Agreements Act of 1979.[13] On the most sensitive issue—how tough an injury test would be applied in US countervailing duty cases—the code commitment to a "material injury" test survived a strong industry challenge. So strong was Strauss's credibility by this time that he reportedly clinched his argument by declaring that "the French want it" this way. "I don't know why and [Deputy STR Alan Wm.] Wolff doesn't know why and Rivers doesn't know why, but I need you to go along!"[14]

Congressional action was expeditious as well. On 4 January 1979, Presi-

---

11. Glennon, Franck, and Cassidy, *Foreign Relations Law*, 161.

12. See Robert C. Cassidy Jr., "Negotiating About Negotiations," in Thomas M. Franck, ed., *The Tethered Presidency* (New York: New York University Press, 1981), 264–82; I. M. Destler and Thomas R. Graham, "United States Congress and the Tokyo Round: Lessons of a Success Story," *World Economy* (June 1980): 53–70; Destler, "Trade Consensus; SALT Stalemate: Congress and Foreign Policy in the Seventies," in Thomas E. Mann and Norman J. Ornstein, eds., *The New Congress*, (Washington: American Enterprise Institute, 1981), 333–40; and documents in Glennon, Franck, and Cassidy, *Foreign Relations Law*, 153–99.

13. In only one case did its congressional consultations force the administration to alter a previously negotiated accord: the House Small Business Committee protested the proposal to open up to international bidding US government contracts reserved for minority-owned enterprises. Strauss responded by substituting other opportunities for foreign firms to sell to US agencies.

14. One interesting example of a substantial change in US policies resulting from the MTN was the wine-gallon concession, in which American negotiators agreed to thoroughgoing revision of a method of computing excise taxes on distilled spirits that dated from the mid-19th century, and that had the effect, not originally intended, of penalizing imports. For a full description, see Gilbert R. Winham, *International Trade and the Tokyo Round Negotiation* (Princeton, NJ: Princeton University Press, 1986), chap. 7.

dent Jimmy Carter gave the required 90-day notice of intent to conclude the MTN. By 6 March, the Senate Finance Committee had begun its series of nine "nonmarkups," and by 16 May, the House Ways and Means Subcommittee on Trade concluded its 15th such session. Representatives of the two then joined in a "nonconference" on 21–23 May. All these meetings were closed to the public, although hearings were held in both committees and press releases reported major committee decisions as they were made.

Most interesting perhaps was the fact that this quasi-legislative process cut the full Senate and House out of the main action. When a 373-page "committee print" containing proposed statutory language was finally circulated on 1 June, all the major decisions had been made. With a few changes, these same words were what the president proposed to Congress in his nonamendable bill 18 days later. Both chambers passed the bill in July, by votes of 395 to 7 and 90 to 4. One who voted no, reformist Representative A. Toby Moffett (D-CT), gave testimony to how effectively the broad membership had been excluded when he protested that "the speed with which we were expected to get on with this bill did not provide ample opportunity for full analysis."[15]

The Carter administration, with STR Robert Strauss in the lead, had constructed a carefully balanced MTN package that responded to all major US trade interests. Some observers actually felt that Strauss had been too responsive, and cited the overwhelming approval margins as evidence. Ranking Ways and Means Republican Barber B. Conable (R-NY) recalled warning him, "You're buying a landslide," giving away too much. In terms of congressional process, however, the key was that the "fast-track" provisions protected the bulk of legislators from product-specific pressure in 1979 just as effectively as the bargaining tariff, and the closed rule barring House floor amendments, had done in the 45 years previous. The administration, in alliance with the primary trade committees, shouldered the main political burden for the members at large. And the main congressional trade players clearly were pleased with the process, for they included in the implementing act a provision that extended this procedure for negotiating and implementing NTB agreements through 3 January 1988.

Still, there were important differences between the new NTB process and the old one on tariffs, and these differences had policy consequences. One was the fact that Congress now had to pass legislation at both ends of a negotiation. For the Kennedy Round tariff agreements, the Trade Expansion Act of 1962 had sufficed. The Tokyo Round required the Trade Act of 1974 to get it going and the Trade Agreements Act of 1979 to conclude it successfully.

This meant that during the talks, US negotiators had to worry about

---

15. *Congressional Record*, Daily Edition, 13 July 1979, E3582.

the danger that unhappy industries might join together and mobilize a congressional majority to block the implementing bill. In fact, negotiators felt they had to prevent even the formation of such a coalition, since once one came together there was no telling how widely it might spread. Thus in addition to mobilizing maximum support from export interests that stood to gain from a successful MTN, the STR had to show particular sensitivity to the demands of the more powerful among the potential losers, the import-affected industries.

So pressure for special deals increased. Textiles, which had already gotten its Multi-Fiber Arrangement during the runup to the 1974 act, won a tightening of its implementation vis-à-vis the major East Asian exporters and mainland China. The steel industry won adoption of the trigger price mechanism (TPM), through which the US government pledged to initiate antidumping action if foreign products were sold at prices below certain specified minimum levels.

Further policy concessions were included in the 1979 law itself. Though generally consistent with the MTN codes, its drafting was much more than a pro forma implementation exercise. In fact, it grew to exceed the 1974 law in its length, and the key committees used their leeway to press purposes well beyond those the MTN required. As will be recounted in chapter 5, Senate Finance held up final action until President Carter submitted a proposal to reorganize the trade bureaucracy. Even more important for trade policy, steel industry ally John Heinz (R-PA) joined with trade law reformer John C. Danforth (R-MO) to bring about a comprehensive rewriting of the countervailing duty and the antidumping laws, with effects to be set forth in chapter 6.

Finally, the content of the codes meant that Finance and Ways and Means had to acknowledge more explicitly than ever that trade regulation reached into the jurisdictions of numerous competing committees. The 1974 act foreshadowed this recognition, for the fast-track procedures provided only that an implementing bill be referred to "the appropriate committee" in each chamber. The decision to use a single implementation bill for the entire MTN meant that Ways and Means kept its primacy on MTN legislation, and in practice it even proved possible to get the other committees to waive their claim to joint referral. But in return, Trade Subcommittee Chairman Charles A. Vanik (D-OH) invited members of the relevant committees to participate in nonmarkups affecting their jurisdictions. Senate Finance went even farther, passing entire titles on to sister committees and adopting their recommendations as its own.

Most important was the fact that the fast-track procedures solved only half of the "Congress problem" insofar as trade was concerned. They established a new mechanism for authorizing and implementing major international, trade-expanding agreements. Thus, they extended the possibility of US leadership in negotiating such agreements into the post-tariff trade world. In 1984, Congress would authorize negotiation of bilateral agreements under this procedure, enabling the Reagan administration to negotiate free-trade arrangements with Israel and Canada and win expeditious, overwhelming fast-track approval. And in 1988 and 1991, as discussed later, Congress again extended the fast-track time period, both for the Uruguay Round multilateral talks and for bilateral talks with Mexico.

But this procedure did nothing to divert the many other product-specific restrictive proposals that individual members had always put forward and always would. As Congressman Conable phrased it a few months before his retirement at the end of 1984, "Congress has become a participatory democracy. So you can't stop bad proposals as easily as you used to."[16]

Industry-Specific Proposals: The Automobile Case

The textile episodes offer one illustration of Conable's point. Few congressional trade leaders believed that the textile industry needed further protection, but they lacked both the authority and the mechanisms to prevent it.

This did not mean that Congress had become eager to pass statutory restrictions. In most instances, the aim of particular quota bills was still not to get them enacted into law but to demonstrate the sponsor's allegiance to a particular industry, or to pressure the executive branch, the appropriate foreign government, or both. Congress was still acting as a lobby to influence decisions made outside its halls.

In the early 1980s, the most dramatic and visible example was the struggle over trade in automobiles. The second oil shock of 1979 brought gasoline lines and a doubling of the price of motor fuel. As a result, demand shifted sharply toward small, high-mileage models. American car makers were unprepared for this shift: their sales fell off sharply, and imports, three-fourths of which came from Japan, expanded to meet the new demand.[17] Ford and General Motors suffered record losses, and Chrysler needed a governmental rescue to avert bankruptcy. US auto

---

16. Personal interview, 31 July 1984.

17. In absolute numbers, the growth of imports was moderate, from 2 million in 1978 to 2.4 million in 1980. But their market share shot up from 17.7 percent to 26.7 percent, as sales of American-made vehicles plummeted during the same two years from 9.3 million to 6.6 million, the lowest figure since 1961. See Gilbert R. Winham and Ikuo Kabashima, "The Politics of U.S.-Japanese Auto Trade," in I. M. Destler and Hideo Sato, eds., *Coping With U.S.-Japanese Economic Conflicts* (Lexington, MA.: Lexington Books, 1982), 76.

unemployment exceeded 300,000, out of a total of almost 1 million directly employed in the industry.[18]

Long the symbol of US economic supremacy, the auto industry was suddenly in very dire straits. The congressional response went through three distinct stages. The first, extending through most of 1980, was one of spotlighting the problem and hoping that established remedies would produce a solution. Vanik's Trade Subcommittee held hearings, sending a clear signal that some form of protective action might have to be taken. At the same time, legislators supported the United Auto Workers (UAW) in its campaign to get Japanese automakers to build plants in the United States. The June submission of an escape clause petition by the UAW and Ford offered the hope that "the rules" could provide the needed relief. While the US International Trade Commission (USITC) deliberated, President Carter encouraged provision of generous adjustment assistance for laid-off workers, and his electoral rival, Ronald Reagan, promised in September to "try to convince the Japanese that . . . the deluge of their cars into the United States must be slowed."[19]

But the USITC decided in November, by a three-to-two vote, that it could not recommend relief because the major causes of the industry's woes were other than imports. Congress then moved quickly into the second stage, that of pressing for the issue to be treated as a "special case." Vanik rushed to schedule hearings and won House passage, before December adjournment, of a special resolution authorizing the president to negotiate an orderly marketing agreement with Japan.

In the new 97th Congress, the initiative shifted to the Senate. Vanik, a pragmatist frequently sympathetic to trade-impacted industries, had retired and was succeeded by liberal trade champion Sam M. Gibbons (D-FL). On the other side of the Hill, the surprise Republican capture of the Senate made John Danforth chairman of the Finance Subcommittee on International Trade. Automobiles were an important industry in his home state of Missouri, and he lost no time: he held hearings before Reagan's inauguration in January and introduced a bill in February that would impose statutory quotas on Japanese automobile imports for three years.

The aim was not to pass the bill but to pressure the Japanese, and to ensure that Reagan's general campaign promise won out over the liberal trade views of his senior economic advisers. Tokyo was, in fact, willing, but the Japanese Ministry of International Trade and Industry needed strong American pressure as leverage against its auto industry. The Reagan administration, however, wanted to minimize its own formal responsibility for any restrictive outcome. The result was a "look no hands"

---

18. "The U.S. Automobile Industry, 1980," Report to the President from the Secretary of Transportation, January 1981, 83–85.

19. Winham and Kabashima, "The Politics of U.S.-Japanese Auto Trade," 115.

approach that confused Tokyo and increased the need for congressional threats. Finance Chairman Robert J. Dole (R-KS) claimed that he could count two-thirds of the Senate in support of the quota bill, enough to override a presidential veto, and Danforth scheduled a markup for 12 May.

All of this positioning had the intended result. On 1 May, with US Trade Representative William E. Brock in Tokyo, the Japanese government announced a "unilateral" commitment to limit exports for two to three years. This met the Finance Committee's demand for a "multi-year effort,"[20] and in fact the restraints have been extended every year since— through March 1993. It also enabled USTR Brock to satisfy the Japanese political need, by assuring them that, in the light of the plan, there was now no prospect of the quota legislation's passing Congress. Danforth could declare the plan "an important step in the right direction," and set aside his bill.

The second phase thus produced modest protection for autos, and this solution lasted, politically, for about a year. But the US recession deepened, helping move the auto issue into the third phase, in which politics now spilled over outside the trade committees' control.

The impetus came from the United Auto Workers, a union long committed to open trade. Beset with growing unemployment and frustrated by the slow response by Toyota and Nissan to his campaign for Japanese investment in the United States, UAW President Douglas A. Fraser began in 1980 to suggest "local content legislation" as a long-term solution. But the real push came two years later. The continuing recession had caused US auto sales to plunge further, and despite the slightly lower sales forced by export restraints, the Japanese share of the US market edged further upward. The UAW responded with HR 5133, introduced by Representative Richard L. Ottinger (D-NY), which provided a rigid domestic-content formula: the larger the number of cars a company sold here, the greater the portion of their total value would have to come from the United States, up to a maximum of 90 percent. Had it become law, this bill would have slashed future imports of autos and auto parts to a fraction of current levels.

Brock called it "the worst piece of economic legislation since the 1930's," and Danforth exaggerated very little in declaring that "the overwhelming majority" of members saw it as "perfectly ridiculous."[21] By making the bill a litmus test of the allegiance of labor Democrats, however, the UAW was able to win House adoption of a modified domestic-content bill by 215 to 188 votes in December 1982. In November 1983, a House with 26 more Democrats passed a somewhat stronger bill by a slightly

---

20. Finance Committee Press Release 81-9, 29 April 1981.

21. *Congressional Quarterly Almanac*, 1982, 56.

smaller margin, 219 to 199 votes. On both occasions, northeastern and midwestern Democrats voted almost unanimously in favor. The bill never reached the Senate floor, however, and the issue gradually faded from the trade scene as the US auto industry regained sales and strength, albeit at lower levels of employment.

Committee Competition and Policy Entrepreneurship

As important as the progress of domestic-content legislation was the process by which it was achieved. By drafting the legislation as a measure to regulate domestic production, its proponents managed to get it referred to the sympathetic Committee on Energy and Commerce. Ways and Means, the panel with established trade jurisdiction, was limited to sponsoring parallel hearings and urging rejection of the bill—suggesting a further erosion of the procedural checks on industry-specific trade legislation.

Energy and Commerce was chaired by an aggressive old-timer, John D. Dingell (D-MI), who had come to the House in 1955. But by 1982, its next eight ranking members, in terms of seniority, were members of the reformist class of 1975, including Ottinger (with three terms of prior service), Henry A. Waxman (D-CA), and James J. Florio (D-NJ). They were, for the most part, policy activists in the Democratic party mainstream. With energy fading as a national concern, trade policy was a natural focus for their talents.

Ways and Means had also expanded in 1975, as noted at the outset of this chapter. But competition for seats on that committee was much keener, so in 1982 the most senior of its 1975 arrivals, Andrew Jacobs Jr. (D-IN), remained number seven on the committee (Gibbons, who chaired the Trade Subcommittee, had come to the House in 1963.) And the energies of several of the more aggressive mid-level members—James R. Jones (D-OK, 6th in seniority), Richard A. Gephardt (D-MO, 12th) and Thomas J. Downey (D-NY, 13th)—were divided between Ways and Means and the Budget Committee.

The net result in the early 1980s was a certain imbalance of initiative and energy. Dingell and his committee were aggressive and policy-active. Ways and Means continued in the more passive gatekeeper role, but without the power and procedural tools it had possessed a decade before.

Dingell's committee was far from seizing control of trade policy. In fact, when Dan Rostenkowski (D-IL) became Ways and Means chairman in 1981, Dingell faced an adversary whose political skills and concern for "turf" were at least equal to his own. In 1985, Rostenkowski himself would seize the initiative by cosponsoring a trade-restrictive bill targeted at Japan and other nations running large surpluses with the United States.

And from then into the 1990s he was clearly the most important House figure on trade policy. But Energy and Commerce was an active contestant, and it pushed Ways and Means toward activism as well. It gave the Gibbons Trade Subcommittee strong reason to take initiatives about which some senior members were ambivalent, like toughening the trade-remedy laws to demonstrate seriousness about the trade problems of important constituencies.[22] And the full committee sometimes found it prudent to tilt toward the restrictive Energy and Commerce approach, as in the omnibus trade bill of 1986.

Activism in competing committees was also consistent with another congressional trend. Trade issues were becoming, to a greater extent, entrepreneurial issues, as members increasingly saw the subject as worthy of investment of their discretionary time.

Since the 1950s, there had been a sharp rise in policy entrepreneurship on Capitol Hill, particularly among liberals. Senators and representatives would adopt particular issues as their own, seeking both to improve government policy and to enhance their personal reputations. But through the mid-1970s, it is striking how seldom they made trade policy a vehicle for their ambitions. It was seen as a dull, "no-win" issue. Free trade was unappealing to the mass public; protectionism was anathema to the policy community. So neither broad stand was attractive for presentation to a general national or party audience. Legislators (and presidential candidates) generally limited themselves to trade "noise" targeted at specific constituencies. Broader trade advocacy was left to idiosyncratic legislators like Senator Vance Hartke (D-IN), cosponsor of the Burke-Hartke quota bill of 1971. Its fate did not inspire emulation. Nor did the fate of Hartke himself, who was beaten decisively in his 1976 reelection contest.

Even on a central question like trade with Japan, activism was late in coming. It was not until 1977, for example, that a congressman, Democrat Jim Jones of Oklahoma, moved to concentrate his energies on this broad subject, forming a Ways and Means Task Force on US-Japan Trade. And one apparent reason why Senator Lloyd Bentsen (D-TX) suggested a surcharge against Japanese imports in 1979 was that despite the enormous rise in that country's sales to the US market, the senator's staff judged that none of Bentsen's 99 colleagues had yet made Japan "his" issue.

This could not, of course, continue. As detailed in chapter 3, trade was simply becoming too important to the American economy. So congressional debates reflected increasing trade advocacy: between 1975 and 1980, by one measure, the frequency of House and Senate floor refer-

---

22. As an aide to a relatively protectionist senator put it in an interview, "We always figured that the way to get Gibbons to do something was to get Dingell to do something." The trade remedies bill and its politics are treated in chapter 6.

ences to trade went up by 70 percent.[23] And a comprehensive count, based on computerized bill summaries supplied by the Congressional Research Service, indicates a gradual increase in the number of trade-restrictive bills introduced in the House of Representatives: from 127 in the 96th Congress (1979–80) to 137 in the 97th and 144 in the 98th.[24] These included proposals to impose steel quotas or link wine import restrictions to wine export opportunities, and even, in one case, a proposal to establish a dollar ceiling for the bilateral US-Japan trade imbalance.

Many proposals have been in the "export politics" tradition of seeking to solve problems through trade expansion, opening foreign markets. But even here, several of the most prominent, in the words of two expert analysts, "break sharply with traditional US trade policy."[25] In their original form, the "reciprocity" bills sponsored by Danforth and Heinz sought to require restrictions on access to US markets in sectors where major trading partners denied US products comparable market opportunities. More generally, as Raymond J. Ahearn and Alfred Reifman noted at mid-decade, "the most common congressional approaches were based

---

23. This figure was arrived at by comparing the number of columns under "Foreign Trade" in the *Congressional Record Index*, adjusted for the index's overall length.

24. This computation draws on the computerized CRS bill digest file. If one counts only those bills whose primary purpose was to restrict trade, and whose primary apparent motivation was to benefit US producers (for example, excluding bills to bar purchases of Iranian crude oil, Ugandan coffee, etc.), this modest trend disappears: the numbers drop to 62, 56, and 57, respectively. There was a clear upsurge in 1985, however. In the first nine months of that year, 49 such bills were introduced, compared with just 30 in the same period two years earlier.

After this analysis was completed, Raymond J. Ahearn of CRS published a count that was more comprehensive in its coverage, and more detailed for 1985. Using a broader definition of trade, this computer search found 1,089 trade bills introduced in the 96th Congress, 1,150 in the 97th, 1,401 in the 98th, and 879 in 1985, the first year of the 99th. Bill-by-bill inspection of the 1985 group to eliminate nongermane legislation reduced the total to 634, of which 99 were significantly and directly protectionist in purpose and effect. There were also 51 routine bills adjusting tariffs upward, 77 "potentially protectionist" bills that would make it easier to obtain quasi-judicial trade relief, and 109 bills to "restrict trade to achieve nonprotectionist objectives." See Raymond J. Ahearn, "Protectionist Legislation in 1985" (Washington: Congressional Research Service, 31 March 1986, processed).

At this author's request, Ahearn updated his general bill count in 1991: totals were 1,248 for the 99th Congress (1985–86), 1,455 for the 100th (1987–88), and 1,429 for the 101st (1989–90). Over this period—and for the first seven months of the 102nd Congress—trade bills were between 11.5 percent and 12.9 percent of total bills submitted (Ahearn to Destler, memorandum, 12 August 1991).

25. Raymond J. Ahearn and Alfred Reifman, "U.S. Trade Policy: Congress Sends a Message," in Robert E. Baldwin and J. David Richardson, eds., *NBER Conference Report: Current U.S. Trade Policy: Analysis, Agenda, and Administration* (Cambridge, MA: National Bureau of Economic Research, 1986), 104.

on unilateral standards of reciprocity, discrimination, and the threat of retaliation. Successive administrations have opposed similar approaches on the grounds that they violate US international obligations, undermine US global leadership, and are economically counterproductive."[26]

Reinforcing such congressional approaches was a spreading belief that the United States needed to recognize that the liberal trade ideal was impractical and outmoded and to adopt a more sophisticated, interventionist approach to international trade, comparable to that of its trading partners. Intellectual staff aides put forward appealing alternate conceptions: we should no longer pretend that we or anybody else could make market openness the touchstone of commercial relations; rather we should determine the shape of the future economy we want and use trade policy as one tool to bring it about.[27]

More than once in the 1980s and early 1990s, an explosion of specific initiatives signaled to many who followed trade that Congress was at last going to reclaim direct, detailed control over "commerce with foreign nations." In late 1982, the plight of import-impacted industries was exacerbated by an overvalued dollar, with record unemployment fueling worker discontent. Frustration with US trading partners was compounded by seemingly endless market-access negotiations with the Japanese, and by bitterness about European agricultural protectionism, which boiled over at a fractious GATT Ministerial Conference in November. Looking at these trends, and at the number of trade-related bills on the near-term legislative schedule, Senate Finance Chairman Robert Dole predicted that 1983 would be "the year of trade" on Capitol Hill. The *National Journal* rang in that year with a headline, "The Protectionist Congress—Is This the Year That the Trade Barriers Go Up?" "The 98th Congress," it reported, "may be dominated by legislators angered by what they view as unfair European and Japanese trade practices and eager to retaliate in kind."[28]

Two years later, the driving force was the hitherto unimaginable US trade deficit, which shot above $100 billion in 1984 and continued in 12

---

26. Ibid. See also William R. Cline, *"Reciprocity": A New Approach to World Trade Policy?* POLICY ANALYSES IN INTERNATIONAL ECONOMICS 2 (Washington: Institute for International Economics, September 1982). There was some resistance among the leaders of multinational firms. The Business Roundtable warned, for example, that "an improper use of reciprocity could worsen, instead of improve, our economic vitality. If misapplied, the concept has the potential for further undermining an already vulnerable multilateral trading system by triggering retaliation." "Statement of the Business Roundtable Task Force International Trade and Investment on Reciprocity in Trade" (19 March 1982; processed), 2.

27. See, for example, US Congress, House Energy and Commerce Committee, *The United States in a Changing World Economy: The Case for an Integrated Domestic and International Commercial Policy*, Staff Report, September 1983.

28. 1 January 1983, 18.

digits through 1990. Feeling enormous pressure from affected producers, and frustrated by the administration's neglect of both specific trade issues and the overvalued dollar, senators and representatives began in the spring of 1985 by unloading on Japan, passing strongly worded (albeit nonbinding) resolutions by votes of 92 to 0 and 397 to 19. Through this and subsequent moves toward omnibus legislation, they seized the trade policy initiative—and retained it through the end of the Reagan administration.

And in 1991, with the trade deficit reduced but multilateral negotiations stalemated, a new labor-environmental coalition sought to derail the Bush administration's plans to negotiate a free trade agreement with Mexico.

On each occasion, however, Congress made only marginal policy changes. While it forced greater aggressiveness in US trade policy, it refrained from taking clear control, and from imposing protectionism. It stepped back from the abyss. The ferment of 1982–83 culminated in the modest, marginally liberalizing Trade and Tariff Act of 1984. The raging trade fires of 1985–86 were dampened, by and large, in the comprehensive—but only marginally restrictive—Omnibus Trade and Competitiveness Act of 1988. And the debate of 1991 resulted in solid—though not overwhelming—congressional endorsement of the Bush administration's multilateral and bilateral trade initiatives.

The first anticlimax came in 1983. Contrary to Dole's forecast, Congress did little on trade that year, as the long-delayed US economic recovery began, taking some of the bite out of the drive for statutory restrictions. Once again, legislators were willing to channel pressure elsewhere. Even when, in 1984, 201 representatives signed onto a steel quota bill, the predominant view was that it would serve the traditional function of pressuring the executive branch, rather than find its way into the statute books. And the pressure proved successful, as President Reagan ordered USTR Brock to negotiate export restraint agreements with major foreign suppliers. The summer and fall of 1984, however, brought a surge of congressional activity, capped by enactment of the first general trade bill in five years.

The Trade and Tariff Act of 1984: Pressure Contained

The closing months of the 98th Congress saw the policy context worsen.[29] By summer, most experts had come around to C. Fred Bergsten's projection that the US trade deficit would top $100 billion in 1984. This

---

29. The following pages draw substantially on confidential interviews with persons involved in the enactment of the Trade and Tariff Act of 1984. See appendix A of the first edition of this book (1986), for a more detailed account of its enactment.

put advocates of open trade very much on the defensive and made the prospects bleak for the several relatively specialized trade bills on the legislative agenda.

These included one "must" item for the liberal trade community, trade preferences for developing countries (GSP, or Generalized System of Preferences). In the Trade Act of 1974, the United States had, pursuant to an international agreement, granted these countries duty-free access to the US market for a range of their products for a 10-year period ending on 3 January 1985. GSP had precious little support among American economic interests, even though only 3 percent of total US imports were affected—because of the exclusion of sensitive articles (for example, textiles and shoes) and ceilings on benefits available to any one country for a specific product. Organized labor opposed the program, particularly for the "big three" newly industrializing countries—Hong Kong, Korea, and Taiwan—whose products are generally competitive in the United States without special treatment. But Third World nations attached great symbolic importance to GSP. Its abandonment would make it very hard for the United States to negotiate with these countries on matters that were important to interests here—intellectual property protection, for example, and access to their markets.

The prospects for passing GSP extension on its own were dim: the administration had been unable in 1983 to find a single House member to sponsor it. There was on the table, however, a trade proposal that was enormously popular in both Congress (it had 163 House sponsors) and the Reagan White House: a bill authorizing negotiation of a bilateral free-trade agreement with Israel. On 31 July 1984, the Senate Finance Committee voted to combine the two, add a number of other proposals (including Danforth's modified reciprocity bill), and attach the whole package to a minor tariff-adjustment bill (HR 3398) that had already been passed by the other chamber.[30]

USTR Brock welcomed this development. With the House stymied on GSP, this offered the best opportunity for forward movement. Trade Subcommittee Chairman Danforth favored it for this reason, and another: it was the best vehicle for enactment of his reciprocity proposal. But Majority Leader Howard H. Baker Jr. (R-TN), was reluctant to allot Senate floor time to the bill. Danforth had not been able to negotiate a "unanimous consent" agreement limiting time for debate or amendments that might be proposed. The leader feared, therefore, that the bill would be tied up procedurally on the floor, and loaded with protectionist baubles for a wide range of industries.

But because of a House-Senate-administration impasse on budget leg-

---

30. This legerdemain was necessary because of the constitutional requirement that "all bills for raising revenue," and hence bills affecting tariffs, "originate in the House of Representatives" (Article I, Sec. 6).

islation, there was floor time available in mid-September. So Baker gave Danforth his chance. The tacit understanding was that if he lost control, the bill would be pulled off the floor, never to return.

In one sense, Baker's fears were borne out. Danforth never lost control, but to keep it—as debate extended from the anticipated two days to three, then four—he had to accept 6 floor amendments on Monday, 14 on Tuesday, 12 on Wednesday, and 11 on Thursday. The pattern, faintly reminiscent of Smoot-Hawley, was to bargain down but then accept industry-specific protection proposals, and among the successful floor amendments were those favoring producers of copper, bromine, wine, footwear, ferroalloys, and dairy products. When, on the second day of debate, the president made his decision to negotiate voluntary restraint agreements with steel-exporting countries, an amendment was added giving the administration legal authority to enforce such restraints.

But for three factors, the damage would have been even greater. First, on the second day, the Senate did signal that there were limits by rejecting a particularly egregious proposal to reverse a USITC decision and raise the tariff on water-packed tuna. Second, during the final two days, Danforth was supported by the personal presence of Brock, who employed his floor privileges as a former senator to involve himself aggressively in the brokering process. Third, organized labor did essentially nothing, reacting very slowly when the legislation was suddenly taken up. Labor senators proposed neither domestic-content nor anything else for autos. Nor did any senator advance a labor amendment curbing GSP, which might either have passed or forced the extended debate that would have been fatal to the legislation.

So the bill survived, passing the Senate late Thursday by a vote of 96 to 0. The margin reflected the number of interests that had been temporarily "bought off" in the bill itself or through agreements negotiated on the side. An alarmed Washington Post lambasted the result in an editorial entitled "The Anti-Trade Bill": "The losers in every major trade case of the past year have managed to insert language to try to win in Congress what they lost in litigation."[31]

Senate passage broke the Ways and Means logjam, and a week later that committee reported out four separate trade bills: GSP renewal, US-Israel free trade, "steel import stabilization," and "wine equity." Chairman Rostenkowski secured floor time for each under "modified closed rules" that limited amendments. Six days later, on Wednesday, 3 October, the House passed each of the four separately, defeating in the process, by a surprisingly wide 233-to-174 margin, a labor-backed Gephardt amendment that would have eliminated preferences for the big three NICs. It then attached the four bills as amendments to the Senate-passed

---

31. *Washington Post*, 28 September 1984.

HR 3398, along with several previously enacted bills, the most important being the "Trade Remedies Reform Act" developed by Trade Subcommittee Chairman Sam Gibbons. Interestingly, the domestic-content bill was not among them.

By this point, time for compromising House-Senate differences had grown very short: the target for *sine die* adjournment of the 98th Congress was the coming weekend. One question was whether the product-specific amendments in the Senate bill (and to some degree the House bill also) could be deleted, rendering the bill acceptable to President Reagan. Another was whether the House conferees could be persuaded to yield on most other issues where the two bills differed—preferences, procedures for approving the US-Israel agreement, trade remedies. If they did not, Brock and the administration could not accept the bill. But what could House representatives get in return?

The answer, it soon became clear, was in the provisions with which Rostenkowski was personally most identified, those on steel. He had pushed through a bill that, in the name of implementing Reagan's just-announced "national policy for the steel industry," incorporated two proposals advocated by presidential challenger Walter F. Mondale and other Democratic critics of the president's action: a market-share target of 17 percent for steel imports, and an "adjustment" condition for steel firms, which were, as a price for continued protection, required to reinvest all net cash flow in steel operations and allocate 1 percent of earnings to worker retraining. Rostenkowski insisted on retaining these, and was granted most of his demands. One by one the other issues were worked out, in a frenetic 26-hour conference punctuated by both policy and personal tensions. By the conclusion of the Senate-House deliberations Friday afternoon, 5 October, Congress had abandoned its weekend adjournment target, and the compromise bill, labeled the Trade and Tariff Act of 1984, was adopted by both houses the following Tuesday. Somehow, observed the *Washington Post* in a follow-up editorial, "most of the bad stuff got thrown out [in conference] and all of the good stuff stayed."[32]

It had proved possible for Congress to pass a general trade bill that extended an unpopular program (GSP), while omitting or gutting most protectionist provisions. Language designed to benefit copper, ferroalloys, shoes, and dairy products was deleted or neutralized. On preferences, in fact, the bill represented a move in the liberal-internationalist direction, in comparison with the 1974 law that it replaced, by encouraging the administration to negotiate with the NICs for market access and intellec-

---

32. "On Trade, a Happy Ending," *Washington Post*, 12 October 1984. Singled out for special praise was "William E. Brock, who worked mightily and, as it turned out, highly effectively to change the thrust of this bill."

tual property rights, and offered the NICs inducements as well as penalties.[33]

But the bill had restrictive provisions as well.[34] Most serious was one that originated in the administration—the new steel policy. The White House had suggested, in a way that the industry read as a promise, that it would seek to limit total steel imports to a certain level. This cleared the way for the bill to incorporate a global import ceiling, something even the textile industry had been unable to achieve. It was written as a bipartisan compromise—between the 17 percent ceiling favored by Mondale and the 20.2 percent Reagan target—reflecting only the "sense of Congress." But the bill included a future threat, of "such legislative actions concerning steel and iron ore products as may be necessary," if the Reagan program did not "produce satisfactory results within a reasonable period of time."[35] And the entire steel title was enacted hastily, without hearings or serious review of the language in either body.

Still, in 1984, Congress was able to enact a modest, balanced trade law. Legislative success that year was the product of a confluence of particular personalities: Brock, Danforth, and Rostenkowski. Each, in a different way, wanted the omnibus bill to pass, and each was skilled in moving it forward. Each was willing to limit rewards to special interests, and each proved indispensable to its success.

But the way the bill moved through the Congress underscored the weakness of the old institutional checks, particularly in the House. With Ways and Means deadlocked, the Senate had to move on the legislation first, something Wilbur Mills would never have allowed. This exposed the bill to the vagaries of that freewheeling chamber and guaranteed that there would be an enormous amount of cleanup work to do in the House-Senate conference—and little time to do it.

The legislation cleared most current issues on the trade-legislative agenda. So as the 98th Congress completed its work, there was a widespread expectation that its successor would focus on other issues. But the years

---

33. The Reagan administration used this leverage to win policy concessions—getting Singapore, for example, to revamp its intellectual property laws. Then, in the spring of 1988, it revoked trade preferences for Singapore anyway, together with those for Hong Kong, Korea, and Taiwan.

34. For example, it included technical changes in the trade-remedy laws, using such obscure labels as "cumulation," which tilted them in favor of domestic claimants. It also included a watered-down but still objectionable precedent on wine, allowing producers of grapes to challenge wine imports and thus provoking a confrontation with the European Community. The Community won a GATT panel ruling against this law in 1986, and the United States complied, but only because "the law expired." See Robert E. Hudec, "Thinking about the New Section 301: Beyond Good and Evil," in Jagdish Bhagwati and Hugh T. Patrick, eds., *Aggressive Unilateralism: America's 301 Trade Policy and the World Trading System* (Ann Arbor: University of Michigan Press, 1990), 157.

35. Trade and Tariff Act of 1984, Sec. 803.

1985 through 1988 would be the *years* of trade, the period of greatest congressional trade intensity since the 1930s. From the late-January 1985 release of figures showing a $123 billion trade deficit for calendar year 1984,[36] to the presidential signing of comprehensive trade legislation almost four years later, trade leaped to a place near the top of congressional preoccupations. Both House and Senate seized the trade policy initiative, and the second Reagan administration struggled to stay in the game.

1985–88: The Years of Trade

The initial target of congressional activism in 1985 was Japan, the nation with the largest trade surplus with the United States. As recounted in chapter 9, Danforth and his Senate Finance colleagues felt frustrated on a number of fronts. The bilateral imbalance, conservatively measured, had shot up from $19.3 billion to $33.6 billion, making it far higher than any the United States had ever run with any country. At the same time, American negotiators seeking to open Japanese markets felt continuing frustration on all fronts, even in areas like telecommunications, in which there was a long negotiating history and a strong commitment to progress from Prime Minister Yasuhiro Nakasone. And the Reagan administration was declaring itself ready to end voluntary auto restraints. Before the end of March, the Senate had passed, without opposition, a strongly worded Danforth resolution denouncing "unfair Japanese trade practices" and calling for retaliation unless Japan opened its markets sufficiently to American products to offset its anticipated increases in auto sales. The House followed with a parallel resolution, which, although it was directed more at the overall US trade imbalance and its macroeconomic causes, also singled out Japan for priority attention.

The concerns of Danforth and his Republican colleagues involved politics as well as policy. If Republicans did not find a way to get out front on trade, the issue might threaten them in the mid-term elections in November 1986. This fear gained substance in August 1985, when a Democrat who blamed imports for lost jobs won a close race for an open congressional seat, taking particular advantage of his opponent's unthinking rejoinder questioning "what trade had to do with East Texas."

By that summer, three prominent, centrist Democrats on the trade committees—Bentsen of Senate Finance, and Rostenkowski and Gephardt

---

36. The Commerce Department reported trade figures first on a c.i.f. basis, with imports including the cost of freight, as required by the Trade Agreements Act of 1979. The "customs value" deficit figure, preferred by economists, was $107 billion, later adjusted to $114 billion. This study generally uses customs value trade statistics, the norm before 1980 (and after 1988), to facilitate historical comparison.

of House Ways and Means—had cosponsored a bill imposing a surcharge on countries running heavy trade surpluses with the United States. Brazil, Japan, Korea, and Taiwan were the countries potentially affected. In September, House Speaker Thomas P. "Tip" O'Neill (D-MA) could declare with only modest exaggeration: "Based on what I hear from members in the cloak room, trade is the number one issue."[37]

More traditional protectionism flourished as well. A highly restrictive textile quota bill, sponsored by Representative Ed Jenkins, was originally introduced to stiffen the administration's position in the negotiations on renewal of the Multi-Fiber Arrangement (MFA), which regulates imports from developing nations and from Japan. But the bill literally took off, with a majority of senators and nearly 300 representatives signing on as cosponsors. Proponents got the bill through Ways and Means essentially as proposed, despite the opposition of the full committee and trade subcommittee chairs, with the latter, Sam Gibbons, reduced to declaring victory when the House passed it by "only" 262 to 159, less than the number required to override a veto.

Unable to get Finance to take up the measure, Senate sponsors Hollings and Strom Thurmond (R-SC) went around the committee, attaching the legislation to bill after bill on the floor until Majority Leader Robert Dole was forced to cooperate. And in the version passed by the Senate, quotas for shoes were added, as well as a provision calling for voluntary trade restraint on copper. President Reagan vetoed the measure in December, but in the override vote the textile industry managed to increase its House margin to 276 to 149, just 8 votes short of the two-thirds required.

Legislative initiative continued also on other trade fronts. Danforth's proposal to enforce "reciprocity" on telecommunications products was reported out by Finance. A similar bill was approved by the House Energy and Commerce Committee, which challenged the supremacy of Ways and Means on trade by also drafting its own trade-remedy legislation. The House Democratic Caucus formed working groups that made their own proposals, and Senate Democrats did likewise.

But the most important drive was for new omnibus trade legislation. In November 1985, Danforth introduced S 1860, a relatively moderate, 10-title bipartisan proposal with 33 cosponsors, 13 of them from Finance. Early in 1986, the House Democratic leadership launched a more partisan campaign to make trade one of its top priorities. Ways and Means now had to move lest it lose its authority, and by early May it had reported out legislation that curbed presidential discretion in trade-remedy cases, mandated retaliation when other nations did not open their markets (with a separate, specific chapter for telecommunications

---

37. Quoted in *Washington Post*, 19 September 1985.

products), and provided (in the famous "Gephardt amendment") for quotas in cases of countries—Japan, Taiwan, Germany—running large bilateral surpluses with the United States. After being combined with bills reported out of other committees, the omnibus measure passed the House by 295 to 115.

The White House denounced the bill as "pure protectionism," a "rankly political" action that would be "trade-destroying, not trade-creating."[38] This was technically misleading on substance, but all too accurate about the likely results. Unlike the Jenkins bill or Smoot-Hawley, the omnibus measure did not restrict imports directly. But it revised section after section of general US trade laws to make it easier for firms to qualify for import relief and harder for presidents to deny it to them. It also represented a giant step toward unilateralism, establishing new, "made in USA" standards for defining fair and unfair trade that were not sanctioned by GATT rules or by established international practice. The bill therefore merited the label of "process protectionism." The likely outcome, had it become law, would have been a significant rise in de facto US import restrictions, though this was not necessarily the intent of all members who supported it.

Senate Republicans did not share President Reagan's unhappiness with the House bill. Indeed, many of its provisions had counterparts in Danforth's S 1860. Members of the Finance Committee would have liked to move their own trade measure, but they were preoccupied through spring and summer 1986 with major tax-reform legislation: first getting committee agreement, then bringing it to the Senate floor, then working out differences in a conference with the House which lasted until the August recess. Thus, while trade hearings were held as schedule permitted, Finance senators could not get to the actual trade bill–drafting stage until September, a month before adjournment. With the administration opposing any trade action that year, it proved impossible to achieve consensus among committee members on the omnibus legislation's substance and priority, and so the measure died with the 99th Congress in October 1986.

Within a month, however, executive-congressional relations were transformed. The Democrats recaptured control of the Senate, with a surprise gain of eight seats in the mid-term elections. That same month, the Reagan administration was gravely weakened by the exposure of what became known as the Iran-contra scandal. The partisan change had the more direct impact on trade politics. The reason was not that Senate Democrats were more aggressive on trade, or more protectionist, than their Republican counterparts—the difference here was marginal. What mattered was that control of that body had shifted from a leadership whose

---

38. Statement by White House Deputy Press Secretary Larry M. Speakes, 22 May 1986.

job (in important part) was to make life easier for a Republican administration, to one whose job (in major part) was to score points against it. Trade was *the* legislative issue most ready for such use, and Senator Robert Byrd (D-WV), soon to be restored to the majority leadership, lost no time in declaring that trade would be the Democrats' top priority in the 100th Congress of 1987–88.

The Omnibus Trade and Competitiveness Act of 1988

Senate Democrats were eager to move on trade, but the House had to go first. Trade bills remained revenue measures, which the Constitution ordained must originate in the House. The rule had been circumvented in 1984, but now there was no need: the House had acted in 1986, and Jim Wright (D-TX), O'Neill's successor as speaker, was eager to move in 1987. Seeking greater substantive engagement than had most of his predecessors, Wright set an ambitious deadline for action by all interested committees. The omnibus bill that had passed in 1986 was reintroduced as HR 3 and was parcelled out for reworking to 11 House committees, with Ways and Means first among equals.

Seeing the handwriting on the wall, Treasury Secretary James Baker now indicated that omnibus legislation could be useful. Moreover, USTR Clayton Yeutter had won agreement the previous September to inaugurate the multilateral Uruguay Round, so the administration needed extension of the fast-track negotiating authority due to expire in January 1988. The administration now sent down its own draft legislation, as had its predecessors for the Kennedy and Tokyo Rounds. But in sharp contrast to 1962 and 1974, the House ignored the administration's bill,[39] and proceeded on the basis of HR 3.

By April the leadership was merging the 11 separate committee proposals. Wright insisted on excluding product-specific measures: textiles would get a separate vote later, and an Energy and Commerce–reported measure to limit imports of high-quality digital tape recorders was excised from the omnibus legislation. The revised HR 3 passed the House, 290 to 137, on 30 April, with 43 Republicans joining virtually all Democrats in support. Included with the standard trade policy measures—such as authorization for the Uruguay Round, numerous toughenings of trade-remedy laws, strengthening of the authority of the USTR—were several new measures, including the "Bryant amendment," which re-

---

39. In the words of one congressional source, "They never opened the envelope." See J. David Richardson, "U.S. Trade Policy in the 1980s: Turns—and Roads—Not Taken," Working Paper no. 3725 (Cambridge, MA: National Bureau of Economic Research, June 1991), 46.

quired reporting of foreign investment, and provisions on exchange rates and Third World debt; worker retraining; relaxation of national security export controls; agricultural and broader export promotion; and math, science, and foreign language education. (The "omnibus" in the title was not without meaning.)

Included also was the Gephardt amendment, which required imposition of import barriers against countries that failed to reduce their large bilateral trade surpluses with the United States. Unlike in 1986, Ways and Means had not included this amendment in the provisions it reported. This was part of a broader committee effort to produce a more moderate bill; this time, members knew they might actually be writing a law, and they tempered their actions accordingly. But Gephardt won inclusion of his amendment by a floor vote of 218 to 214. The victory helped Gephardt's newly launched presidential campaign, which many members supported. But the narrow margin signaled that the amendment was unlikely to be included in the final legislation.

Meanwhile, the Senate began its work, with new Finance Committee Chairman Lloyd Bentsen in the lead. By early May, his committee reported a bill with broad (19 to 1) bipartisan support, which excluded the Gephardt amendment but which, among its many provisions, imposed new procedural conditions on fast-track authorization for the Uruguay Round, mandated retaliation against unfair foreign trade practices, and curbed presidential discretion in escape-clause cases. Majority Leader Byrd combined this with bills reported by eight other committees, and brought it to the Senate floor in June. (One of these, from Edward Kennedy's [D-MA] Labor and Public Welfare Committee, included a provision requiring firms with over 100 employees to give 60 days' notice before plant closings.) After a month of debate, the omnibus measure passed by a vote of 71 to 27.

The Senate bill included, in a floor amendment, the Senate's alternative to the Gephardt amendment: a measure that would, after conference reworking, become known as "Super 301," and which required the USTR to name and target countries maintaining patterns of import barriers and unfair, market-distorting practices. The bill also contained a ban on all imports from Japan's Toshiba Corporation and a Norwegian defense company, a provision also added on the floor after revelation that the two companies had sold important defense-related equipment to the Soviet Union (in violation of both Japanese law and international export control arrangements). In general, this bill—like its House counterpart—was considerably less restrictive in its likely effects than the omnibus bill of 1986. Moreover, the House bill was more restrictive on some matters, the Senate on others, suggesting that the final result could prove more liberal than either.

Administration trade officials were considerably more engaged in the legislative process in 1987 than they had been in 1986. And White House comments as the bill made its way forward were certainly more moderate than the denunciations of 1986. But officials' access was asymmetric: good in the House, limited in the Senate. Deputy USTR Alan Holmer and USTR General Counsel Judith Bello had prepared the ground carefully with Rufus Yerxa and his associates on the Ways and Means trade staff, spending weekends in 1986 going over issues and possible solutions. Moreover, Chairman Rostenkowski was predisposed to cooperate with the administration. And so even though the House leadership had pushed trade for partisan advantage, Holmer and Bello had good working access to Ways and Means staff and to members' caucuses.

It was chillier for them on the north side of the Hill. Holmer had once served as Senator Packwood's administrative assistant, facilitating good relations with staff aides Leonard Santos and Josh Bolton during his chairmanship. But Packwood's successor, Lloyd Bentsen, was a much sterner critic of administration trade policy, and Jeffrey Lang, who acceded to the key Finance staff position, replicated his boss's reluctance to work closely with USTR officials. Holmer and Bello thus lacked both regular access to Finance senators and the sort of ties to Finance staff that their predecessors had developed in 1974 and 1979. So they worked with whom they could. Particularly important was longtime Danforth aide Susan Schwab, architect of his "reciprocity" legislation and an influential inside player on issues such as Section 301, telecommunications, and Japan.

In general, the administration was less happy with the Senate bill than its House counterpart: USTR Yeutter and Treasury Secretary James Baker urged Senate Republicans to vote against final passage in order to strengthen the prospects for change in conference. In any case, each house had passed a multititle, multicommittee bill roughly 1,000 draft pages in length. To reconcile the two, a 199-member conference committee was appointed—44 senators and 155 representatives. They were split into 17 subconferences responsible for separate sections.

Organizing all this brought the members into October, when a dramatic event intervened: the Dow Jones Industrial Average plunged by over 500 points in a single day. The crash of 19 October, "Black Monday," was blamed in part on the federal budget deficit, and it precipitated a White House–congressional summit on that subject. As this summit dragged on into December, it became the main policy preoccupation of Bentsen, Rostenkowski, and many of their colleagues. Black Monday also made members wary of taking *any* forceful trade action; the markets were jumpy, and anything labeled "protectionist" might drive them further down, with Congress taking the blame!

At the start of 1988, Rostenkowski and Bentsen began to refocus on trade, and they signaled that they were seeking a bill the president would sign. Their readiness to compromise with the administration was underscored when the House conferees proposed dropping all provisions in either version that were directly trade-restrictive, a proposal the Senate eventually accepted. Such action was made easier by the fact that the trade deficit was at last declining, lessening the heat from import-impacted interests and giving exporters the incentive to lobby for moderation to avoid cutting short the now-burgeoning boom in their foreign sales. By the end of March, Subconference I had resolved virtually all *trade* policy issues; a rewritten version of Super 301 supplanted the Gephardt amendment, and numerous specific authorities were transferred from the president to the USTR, although executive flexibility was maintained on the escape clause and the imposition of trade sanctions. The Bryant amendment that threatened foreign investment in the United States was replaced by the Exon-Florio provision, which provided for executive branch review of foreign takeovers that carried national security implications: the president was authorized to block those he found inimical. The ban on Toshiba imports was narrowed to apply only to the offending subsidiary, Toshiba Machine Company, and to its Norwegian counterpart.[40] A broad range of special-interest amendments to the antidumping laws were deleted or neutralized. And fast-track authority was extended in a form the administration found acceptable.

On 20 April 1988, the full conference committee reported out a compromise HR 3, still over 1,000 parchment pages. The House passed it by 312 to 107, and the Senate followed by 63 to 36. The legislation still contained, however, the Senate-initiated provision mandating notification of plant closings by companies employing 100 or more workers. There had been frenetic negotiations on this issue, with Kennedy and organized labor pushing for retention of the provision, and many other Democrats attracted by its political message. But Reagan, backed by organized business, was threatening a veto. To prevent this, Rostenkowski and Bentsen wanted the provision removed, but they did not prevail. Speaker Wright sent the bill to the White House in a Capitol "signing ceremony" featuring television cameras and laid-off workers speaking in support of the measure.

Reagan did veto HR 3 in May, citing in particular both the plant-closing provision and a formerly obscure prohibition of certain oil exports from Alaska. The Senate override attempt fell five votes short. To trade legislators and officials, it looked briefly as if their intensive labors would come to naught. But Democrats soon found an ingenious way to have their cake and eat it too. A new trade bill was prepared, HR 4848, identical except for the excision of the plant closings and Alaskan oil provisions. The plant-closing provision was introduced as a separate mea-

---

40. This result was widely attributed to Toshiba's multimillion dollar lobbying effort. But US firms using Toshiba inputs were also very unhappy with the original ban, and they made their feelings known on Capitol Hill.

sure, and brought quickly to the House and Senate floors. To Democrats' and organized labor's delight, the issue and the bill caught fire, and both chambers passed it with lopsided, bipartisan majorities. Thus put on the (anti-worker) defensive, Reagan let it become law without his signature. In the meantime, the House and then the Senate were passing the slightly slimmer trade bill by overwhelming margins. On 23 August, with Reagan's signature, HR 4848 became Public Law 100-418, the Omnibus Trade and Competitiveness Act of 1988.

The 1988 law was the culmination of four years of congressional activity. It was the first major trade bill initiated by the Congress since the days before Smoot-Hawley. And it was by far the longest trade bill passed by the postwar Congress: the 1,000-plus pages of parchment amounted to 467 statutory pages, compared with 173 pages for the 1979 law, 98 pages in 1974, and just 31 pages for the Trade Expansion Act of 1962. The length reflected the multicommittee process and the many detailed methods by which legislators sought to constrain the executive in the management of trade policy.

There were two important things the bill did not do: it did not impose statutory protectionism, and it did not impose direct congressional control over trade. Rather, it passed the policy ball back to the statutorily enhanced USTR with multiple provisions aimed at setting the USTR's agenda and stiffening its spine. Most important were extension of fast-track authority to cover the Uruguay Round and bilateral negotiations,[41] and language centered on Section 301, which targeted "unjustifiable and unreasonable" foreign trade practices—particularly those impeding US exports. Congress wanted to make retaliation against such practices "mandatory but not compulsory," to quote the delightful phrase that originated at a Finance Committee hearing and was widely repeated thereafter.[42] But as this ambivalent language suggested, members remained more than willing to have the USTR make the tough calls.[43]

---

41. Congress imposed new conditions on fast-track authority, one of which would deny use of the procedures if both houses passed, within any 60-day period, procedural disapproval resolutions declaring that "the President has failed or refused to consult with Congress on trade negotiations and trade agreements in accordance with the provisions of the Omnibus Trade and Competitiveness Act of 1988." Sec. 1103(c)(1)(E)

42. Judith Hippler Bello and Alan F. Holmer, "The Heart of the 1988 Trade Act: A Legislative History of the Amendments to Section 301," in Jagdish Bhagwati and Hugh T. Patrick, eds., *Aggressive Unilateralism*, 59. They report that the phrase originated in an exchange between Chairman Packwood and former STR Robert Strauss.

43. For a broader argument on why senators and representatives may find such behavior in their political interest, see I. M. Destler, "United States Trade Policymaking in the Eighties," in Alberto Alesina and Geoffrey Carliner, eds., *Politics and Economics in the Eighties* (Chicago: University of Chicago Press, 1991); and Destler, "Delegating Trade Policy," in Paul E. Peterson, ed., *The President, the Congress, and the Making of Foreign Policy*, (Norman: University of Oklahoma Press, 1994), 228–45.

The House also accepted, in the end, continuing Ways and Means trade primacy. Speaker Wright was a force at key junctures, and his office was active in intercommittee coordination. But on the details of substance and trade policy bargaining, it was Rostenkowski who emerged supreme in the House—confident in the eighth year of his chairmanship and comfortable in bargaining with colleagues in the House, his counterpart in the Senate, leaders in the administration, and the many private interests engaged.

Ways and Means also played a central role in another important trade measure of 1988: the implementing bill for the Canada–United States Free Trade Agreement. Responding to an initiative from north of the border, and using the bilateral, fast-track authorization contained in the 1984 act, President Reagan notified Congress in December 1985 of his intention to proceed. Frustrated over the administration's lack of responsiveness to its concerns, Senate Finance took up a proposal to block fast-track treatment for the negotiations, rejecting it in April 1986 (by 10 to 10) only after assurances were provided on softwood lumber and other issues.[44] And the negotiations were rushed to completion in the waning months of 1987 so that Congress could be prenotified in early October, as the law required, and the agreement could be signed on 2 January 1988, the very last day that the fast-track authority allowed.[45]

Thereafter, however, the implementing process proceeded smoothly, replicating that for the Tokyo Round nine years earlier. The administration promised not to submit implementing legislation before June, provided congressional leaders agreed to act between then and adjournment in October. "Nonmarkups" were then held in February through May, followed by a "nonconference" to resolve House-Senate differences. Only after agreement was reached was the legislation formally introduced and approved, by 366 to 40 in the House and 83 to 9 in the Senate.[46] Ways and Means's central role in tracking the details was reflected in the fact that, as one administration official later put it, the implementing bill "was written on Mary Jane Wignot's computer" (Wignot was the Ways and Means aide with specific responsibility for US-Canada trade).

---

44. Jeffrey J. Schott, *United States–Canada Free Trade: An Evaluation of the Agreement,* POLICY ANALYSES IN INTERNATIONAL ECONOMICS 24 (Washington: Institute for International Economics, 1988), 13.

45. To legislators' annoyance, and contrary to the law's intent, major substantive provisions of the agreement were defined in the period *between* the October notification and the January signing. In 1991, they extracted commitments from the Bush administration not to repeat this practice in the negotiations with Mexico.

46. For more detail, see David Layton-Brown, "Implementing the Agreement," in Peter Morici, ed., *Making Free Trade Work: The Canada–U.S. Agreement* (New York: Council on Foreign Relations Press, 1990), 28–30.

With approval of the Canada-US FTA in September, the 100th Congress completed its ample trade work. Its successor would not do likewise: legislators in 1989–90 moved on to other issues, limiting their trade activity to monitoring implementation of their 1988 handiwork. In 1991, however, they were suddenly confronted with a new challenge: a vote on extending the fast-track deadline not just for the Uruguay Round, but for a projected FTA with Mexico as well. This brought before Congress the first explicit floor consideration of the legislative procedure that constrained the authority of the rank and file over trade.

Mexico and Fast-Track Renewal

In 1989 and 1990, trade receded on the legislative agenda. Exports continued to surge; import growth moderated; the trade deficit shrank somewhat. Speaker Jim Wright was caught up, in 1989, with a scandal that would force his resignation. Tom Foley of Washington, a liberal trader, was the consensus choice to succeed him, and Foley was succeeded as majority leader by Richard Gephardt (D-MO). In the Senate, Robert Byrd left the majority leader position to become president pro tempore and chairman of the Appropriations Committee, with George Mitchell of Maine his successor.

Trade-minded senators and representatives watched with approval in 1989 as USTR Carla Hills named Japan a "priority foreign country" under Super 301,[47] and as Korea and Taiwan scurried to make enough trade concessions to avoid similar designation. And in 1990, many in both chambers were preoccupied with the extended budget negotiations that began in the spring and continued into late October. Aside from its now-routine passage of textile quota legislation, and the equally routine failure to override President Bush's veto, Congress took little specific trade action. There were no burning statutory issues. Moreover, the enactment of the 1988 act had been a politically demanding enterprise, with Bentsen, Rostenkowski, and their colleagues compelled to respond to and balance an enormous range of pressures and interests. The years that followed offered welcome respite. And even though Super 301 expired in 1990, there was no serious congressional move to extend it.

Such legislative restraint was also consistent with the projected timetable of the Uruguay Round. The multilateral talks were intended to last four years, culminating in an agreement by the end of 1990. The 1988 act reflected and reinforced this timetable, with a bit of leeway, by providing that fast-track approval procedures would be followed if the president signed an agreement by 1 June 1991—provided he gave notice 90 days before.

---

47. Also designated were Brazil and India.

But the Uruguay Round moved slowly. Agreement was particularly elusive on agriculture, where the United States had initially sought a commitment to remove all trade-distorting government policies and was still insisting on major liberalization as a prerequisite for deals on textiles, services, and the many other specific issues on the agenda. A December 1990 GATT Ministerial Conference at Brussels, designed to break the impasse, confirmed it instead.

With the multilateral talks at a stalemate, attention turned to a fallback provision of the 1988 act inserted with just such a contingency in mind. The president could, on or before 1 March 1991, seek a two-year extension of fast-track authority by declaring that progress had been made and additional time might allow the negotiations to succeed. And as the law was written, he could gain the extension unless either house voted against it by 1 June.[48] He would then have until June 1993 to sign a multilateral agreement.

There was one complicating factor. In the spring of 1990, Mexico's reformist president, Carlos Salinas de Gortari, broke with his country's protectionist and anti-*yanqui* tradition by asking President Bush to negotiate a bilateral free trade agreement. Bush agreed, overruling trade advisers who preferred to wait until a Uruguay Round accord was in hand. He sent Congress the required notification of intent in September. When Ottawa expressed concern that a bilateral US-Mexico pact might undermine *Canada's* arrangement with the United States, it was agreed to include Canada in the talks, with the aim of creating a North American Free Trade Agreement (NAFTA). Bush notified Congress of this decision in February 1991.

A fast-track extension would therefore apply to the NAFTA talks as well to the Uruguay Round. Free trade with Mexico had been in no member's mind when the law was enacted in 1988. The act did include a brief section endorsing the procedural, US-Mexico "framework" agreement signed in 1987, but a free trade arrangement was considered a decade off at the very least. Still, the fast-track procedures had been broadened in 1984 to cover bilateral accords, with similar consultation caveats and the same expiration date. And the new timetable in the 1988 act applied to both as well. Hence an extension for the GATT talks would cover Mexico as well.[49]

---

48. In general, legislative vetoes of presidential or agency actions had been rendered unconstitutional by the Supreme Court's *Chadha* decision of June 1983. But the issue here was not statutory substance but legislative procedures, over which the Constitution gave Congress full authority.

49. House Ways and Means or Senate Finance could have blocked fast-track for Mexico by exercising their right to disapprove the negotiations within 60 days of the presidential notification. But neither did so, forcing members to vote up or down on both together.

This prospect alarmed US organized labor and some environmental groups. The former felt particularly threatened by open trade with a "low-wage" neighbor: US workers had already lost many low-skill, mass-production jobs to foreign competition, and a Mexico deal would only exacerbate this trend. Environmentalists worried that competition with Mexico would undercut US environmental regulations by creating a "pollution haven" for US firms south of the border, and leading to a relaxation of US antipollution laws for competitive purposes. Well before 1 March, both were mobilizing against fast-track extension. Their initial success drove Rostenkowski to suggest at one point that it might be necessary to somehow exclude Mexico from coverage in order to salvage authority for the GATT talks. However, the president followed the law (and his interests) in requesting general fast-track extension.

The fast-track procedures had been law for over 16 years, but this was the first time they had held center stage on the House or Senate floor. Previously, their specifics had been worked out in Finance and in Ways and Means, with Congress as a whole ratifying the committees' handiwork when it voted general trade legislation. And this time the issue *could* have been buried in committee—the law provided that a fast-track disapproval resolution could reach the House or Senate floor only if the requisite committee(s) approved. But committee and chamber leaders quickly decided that burial in committee, while perfectly legal, would be viewed as politically egregious and thus discredit both the procedures and any agreements reached thereunder. Disapproval agreements therefore would have to go to both floors, and be voted up or down there.

With critics quick off the blocks, congressional leaders would have normally sought statutory compromise. But on its face the law made this difficult or impossible: the "sole matter" of an "extension disapproval resolution" was to be "That the [House/Senate] disapproves the request of the President for the extension . . . because sufficient tangible progress has not been made in trade negotiations."[50] Moreover, Speaker Foley resisted creative proposals to separate the Mexico negotiations from the Uruguay Round, or otherwise compromise the procedures. He saw them as a pact between Congress and the executive; if Congress changed the rules when acting on the extension, how could it demand that the administration play straight?

Bentsen and Rostenkowski, both strong backers of fast-track renewal, therefore resorted to nonstatutory bargaining. They wrote to President Bush seeking assurances on three key matters: the overall economic impact of a NAFTA; its effects on jobs and worker rights; and its impact on the environment.[51] They needed a reply by 1 May, they declared, so that

---

50. Public Law 100-418; Sec. 1103(b)(5)(A).

51. Bargaining with colleagues was impeded by the fact that some key labor Democrats on Ways and Means (like Donald J. Pease of Ohio) were committed to vote against

Congress could consider it and vote before the 1 June deadline. Gephardt, resisting strong labor pressure and maintaining an undecided posture, wrote a separate letter raising similar concerns.

With everyone's attention on Mexico, the Uruguay Round got something of a free ride. When the Brussels ministerial conference failed, it was thought that a fast-track extension debate would turn the spotlight on those negotiations, with senators and representatives pressing the administration on why progress had been limited and why they expected the next two years to be any better. Congress might even have threatened specific conditions or minimum requirements for a Uruguay Round package. The USTR would presumably have responded by pressing its counterparts in Europe and East Asia, seeking concrete evidence of prospective gains in order to persuade Congress to continue the enterprise. But this did not happen—in fact, the tendency was for members critical of the Mexico accord to say nice things about the multilateral round, to balance their positions and avoid being labeled protectionists.

Responding to the strong, early labor and environmentalist opposition, Bentsen and Rostenkowski pressed business leaders to get moving: if they favored fast-track extension, they had better lobby hard, or else the measure would fail. And business responded. The old pro-trade coalition, demoralized by the Reagan trade deficit and mobilized only for the endgame in 1985–88, was now back in full force—encouraged by the export boom, but concerned that a collapse of the Uruguay Round would unleash protectionism here and abroad. So they went "balls out" for extension, as one Washington insider put it. Mexican representatives were active and effective also, belying their long-standing reputation for inattention to the Washington power game.

Last but not least, the charge was led by a highly competent USTR, Carla A. Hills, backed by a president who wasn't about to see his Mexico initiative go under. Together, the USTR and the White House pressed business to be active; they encouraged (and received) restraint and flexibility from Mexico and Salinas; they brought in a range of arguments, from the future of the world trading system to the interests of the growing population of Hispanic-Americans. And on 1 May the president responded adroitly to the questions posed by Bentsen and Rostenkowski. Pointing to the doubling of US exports to Mexico between 1986 and 1990, the administration declared that "a NAFTA will result in greater prosperity for U.S. workers, farmers, businesses and consumers." Moreover, since "Mexico's economy is 1/25 the size of the U.S. economy . . .

---

extension for Mexico. And labor followed its characteristic strategy of taking a strong stand and refusing to compromise. On trade, this had usually served to minimize labor's influence—with the plant-closing provision of 1988 the major exception; it would do so in 1991 as well.

scenarios of mass dislocations resulting from reduced U.S. trade barriers are not realistic." Nonetheless, the statement promised "adjustment provisions to avert injurious effects," including transition and safeguard mechanisms and an "adequately funded" worker adjustment program providing "prompt, comprehensive, and effective services" for those who lost their jobs as a result of an FTA with Mexico.[52] Bush's statement also praised and supported Mexican efforts to enforce labor standards and worker rights. On the environment, "Mexico and the United States agree that efforts to increase growth through an FTA should be complemented by cooperative efforts to enhance environmental protection." And in addition to pursuing "joint environmental initiatives," the United States would "ensure that our right to safeguard the environment is preserved in the NAFTA."[53]

The statement accelerated a shift by some environmental groups: from opposition to an accord to using the negotiations as an opportunity to advance their concerns. Labor remained in opposition, but once the outcome was clear the AFL-CIO deemphasized the final vote and scurried unsuccessfully for ways to make the outcome less clear-cut. Bentsen and Rostenkowski declared their satisfaction with the White House response. On 9 May Gephardt declared his support, with a "caveat: If the administration sends to this Congress a trade treaty that trades away American jobs, or tolerates pollution of the environment or abuse of workers, we can, and we will, amend it or reject it."[54]

When the votes came, they were anticlimactic. Ways and Means voted 27 to 9 against the disapproval resolution; Finance did likewise by 15 to 3. On 23 May the House rejected the resolution by 231 to 192, a margin that apparently overstated the bedrock opposition to fast-track.[55] The Senate followed the next day by 59 to 36. The split was both partisan and regional. Democrats in the House voted 170 to 91 to veto fast-track, but the leadership backed it, and representatives from California, Florida, and Texas—states with large Hispanic-American populations— voted 64 to 25 in favor.

Critics got one consolation prize. Speaker Foley resisted the idea of

---

52. This represented, at least potentially, a reversal of the deemphasis on trade adjustment in the 1980s. See chapter 6.

53. Quotations are from "Response of the Administration to Issues Raised in Connection With the Negotiation of a North American Free Trade Agreement," Transmitted to the Congress by the president on 1 May 1991, processed, "Overview" section, 1, 3, 6, 9, and 11.

54. Quoted in *Congressional Quarterly*, 11 May 1991, 1181.

55. *Congressional Quarterly* reported that "the opposition total" seemed padded, "since many votes to reject the fast track were made after it was apparent that proponents had the numbers to win." The AFL-CIO vote count had shown "only 140 lawmakers solidly . . . against the fast-track extension." 25 May 1991, 1358–59.

staging separate votes on the Uruguay Round and Mexico, though some members complained they were being forced to oppose the former because of the latter. And efforts by critical legislators to modify the fast-track procedures never came to a vote.[56] But the House did adopt by 329 to 85, *after* rejecting the disapproval measure, a Gephardt-Rostenkowski resolution endorsing the labor and environmental objectives included in the 1 May statement, and calling for close consultation with the administration during the Mexico negotiations.

By fall 1991, it was back to business as usual. Hills was pushing ahead on the Geneva and Mexico fronts; legislators, faced with many competing demands, were only sometimes responsive to opportunities to give advice. The House majority leader had come forth with "a new 'Gephardt amendment' that will put teeth in Super 301," again targeting Japan in particular, to "reduce the discretion the President has not to take action against priority countries and priority practices."[57] But its effect—and perhaps its intent—was more to position Gephardt and like-minded Democrats on the "tough" side of the trade debate (and to balance Gephardt's support of fast-track) than to influence the legislative agenda on trade, at least in the near term. For that awaited the results of the global and hemispheric trade talks (see chapter 9).

1984 and After: The Leadership Difference

Since the early 1980s, Congress has seemed ready on several occasions to reverse postwar liberal trade policies. On each occasion, it refrained from doing so. Product-specific protectionism, so much in prospect in 1982 and 1983, was removed from the law passed in 1984. The explosion of concern about the US trade balance in 1985–86 was brought under control by an administration that first shifted course on the exchange rate—encouraging the dollar to fall—and thereafter bargained hard on the specifics of what became the 1988 Trade Act. And despite strong early opposition, fast-track renewal passed comfortably in 1991. Frustration with the no-amendment procedure was substantial, raising doubts as to whether Congress would agree to it for a post-1993 trade negotiation. But for the present, it once again went along and delegated major authority to the administration.

On each of these occasions, members of Congress showed strong in-

---

56. Representative Sander M. Levin and Senator Donald W. Riegle Jr., both Democrats from Michigan, proposed that the procedures be revised so that Congress could offer a limited number of amendments to a US-Mexico accord. But with the no-amendment rule for the disapproval resolution, they were unable to get a vote.

57. Richard A. Gephardt, remarks at the Institute for International Economics, Washington, 10 September 1991, 4–5.

terest in trade policy, and insisted on making it tougher and more responsive to US-based economic interests—particularly on the export side. But on each occasion, Congress failed to seize authority for itself and instead passed the policy ball back to the other end of Pennsylvania Avenue. Members of Congress were less satisfied with liberal-trade policies than they had once been. And with the reform in congressional procedures, they were less capable of resisting product-specific initiatives. But neither did they wish to succumb to such initiatives, or to take responsibility for their consequences. Delegation to the executive was the natural way out of this dilemma.

But greater congressional skepticism and activism have increased the burden on executive branch trade leaders. Congress's changed role makes the trade policymaking system even more dependent on the liberal trade commitment and the political skill of the senior officials at the other end of Pennsylvania Avenue, who must now delve deeply into the legislative game, arguing and resisting and bargaining with trade activists on Capitol Hill.

USTR Brock and his staff performed this service in 1984, helping to protect Congress from itself. In 1985, when White House attention was elsewhere for most of the year, the administration lost the initiative, and USTR Yeutter was forced to spend the years through 1988 struggling to regain it. Hills did regain momentum for the Bush administration in 1989, but the USTR's longer-term success would depend on what it achieved in the Uruguay Round talks, which would play back into domestic trade politics. For a deeper look at this interplay, we turn now to the subject of the next chapter, the executive branch. Ch 5

An Embattled Executive

From the 1930s onward, the key activator of liberal American trade policies has been the executive branch of government. Whether negotiating abroad or facing pressure at home, US officials responsible for international economic relations have leaned persistently in the direction of reducing barriers and expanding trade. Presidents, while only occasionally involved in day-to-day decisions, have supported governmental experts in this liberal tendency and lent their names and their weight, periodically, to the major steps forward. Hence, the 1960s negotiations were dubbed the Kennedy Round. The successor talks might well have been remembered as the "Nixon Round" had not Watergate rendered that label unappealing.

Successive Congresses not only endorsed executive branch trade leadership, but sought to centralize it in an institution that would balance domestic and international concerns. The Trade Expansion Act of 1962 created the position of president's special representative for trade negotiations (STR). After two Nixon administration efforts to weaken or abolish it, the Trade Act of 1974 made the STR a statutory unit in the Executive Office of the President. Five years later, Congress forced the Carter administration to carry out a trade reorganization that increased the office's size and power and renamed it USTR (for Office of the United States Trade Representative). And in 1983, strong resistance from Senator John C. Danforth (R-MO), chairman of the Finance Subcommittee on Trade, helped block an administration-backed proposal to subsume the USTR in a new cabinet Department of International Trade and Industry.

The White House trade office proved an effective policy leadership institution. It brought the US government successfully through two am-

.tious multilateral trade negotiations. Its leaders got major trade bills enacted by Congress in 1974 and 1979, limited the trade-restrictive damage from the legislation of 1984 and 1988, and won congressional reauthorization of major trade negotiations in 1991. The demands of trade leadership drove the office into close relationship with the key congressional trade committees and into an interest-balancing, coping mode with private groups. The office showed greater sensitivity to protection-seeking forces than did, say, the State Department or the Council of Economic Advisers. Nevertheless, its aim was not to bury liberal US trade policy but to keep it alive.

Presidents of both parties have lent continued support to liberal trade policies. But they have not given consistent backing to the White House trade representative as a person or to the USTR office as an institution. Just as Kennedy was reluctant to have Congress structuring "his" executive office, his successors have been ambivalent, more often than not, about a high-profile White House trade office with which they had limited day-to-day contact. Presidential political aides have been wary as well. In the first Reagan term, Secretary of Commerce Malcolm Baldrige was able to use his White House ties, and the added trade powers given his department in 1980, to pose a strong challenge to USTR William E. Brock.

In the 1980s this presidential ambivalence toward the USTR was joined by a rise in piecemeal protectionism, in steps taken to shield specific industries without offsetting measures on the market-expanding side. President Ronald Reagan, committed in principle to free trade, was driven—in the words of his Treasury secretary—to "grant more import relief to US industry than any of his predecessors in more than half a century."[1] And when the record trade imbalances of the mid-1980s triggered a political storm on Capitol Hill, his administration lost the initiative to a Congress determined to enact tough new trade legislation. Despite a new aggressiveness in pressing export cases overseas, the USTR was mainly reacting at home to a flurry of congressional proposals. Only in 1989—with the legislative battle over—did a new USTR, Carla A. Hills, succeed in recovering the trade policy initiative for the executive branch. But her continued success at home depended on bringing negotiations overseas to a successful conclusion.

□ □ □

From the 1930s through the 1950s, there was little statutory control of the structure and process of executive branch trade policymaking—who should lead in international trade negotiations, for example, or how the counterpart domestic negotiations should be conducted. Inevitably, then as now, a range of departments and agencies were involved, especially

---

1. Remarks of Secretary of the Treasury James A. Baker III at the Institute for International Economics, Washington, 14 September 1987.

Agriculture and Commerce, and interagency committees were the typical means of handling complex policy and operational issues. Yet as late as 1960, a senior State Department official could be so dominant—domestically and internationally—that a tariff negotiation under the General Agreement on Tariffs on Trade (GATT) was given his name.

But the "Dillon Round"[2] was the State Department's last hurrah in multilateral trade leadership. When John F. Kennedy moved to break a political stalemate by going after sweeping new barrier-reducing authority—including a mandate to negotiate across-the-board (as opposed to item-by-item) reductions—Congress, not surprisingly, demanded a change in executive-branch trade structure. Thus was created an "executive broker," the STR, to oversee US participation in the talks.[3]

STR's Early Ups and Downs   *Special Rep. for Trade Negotiations*

Section 241 of the Trade Expansion Act of 1962 established two roles for this new trade official: the STR was to be "the chief representative of the United States" during the authorized negotiations and also chairman of the "interagency trade organization" that was to manage them for the president. It said nothing about his staff or its location, however. Kennedy had insisted on having leeway to define these himself, which he did in Executive Order 11075 of 15 January 1963, placing the new unit within the Executive Office of the President. The new negotiator and his aides were clearly intended to play the "executive broker" role required by the American trade policymaking system—between domestic interests and foreign governments, between the executive branch and Congress, and among the concerned government agencies.

During the Kennedy Round, the STR played this role with a small staff of about 25 professionals and with substantial sharing of specific analytic and negotiating tasks with State and, to a lesser degree, Commerce and Agriculture.[4] President Kennedy filled the post with a prom-

---

2. The official was Under Secretary of State C. Douglas Dillon.

3. Also significant, at least as a harbinger of the future, was a provision making two senators and two representatives accredited members of the US negotiating team for the first time. The STR was also required to seek advice and information from industry, agriculture, and labor representatives. As in previous talks, the administration had to give public notice and hold hearings before agreeing to reduce tariffs for a particular industry. And the Tariff Commission was to advise on the probable impact of such reductions on particular sectors.

4. On the STR's early years, see Anne H. Rightor-Thornton, "An Analysis of the Office of the Special Representative for Trade Negotiations: The Evolving Role, 1962–1974," in *Commission on the Organization of the Government for the Conduct of Foreign Policy*, vol. 3 (Washington: GPO, June 1975), appendix H, 88–104.

inent Republican, former Secretary of State (and Massachusetts Governor) Christian A. Herter. Herter had one deputy for Washington management, William M. Roth, and one for Geneva bargaining, W. Michael Blumenthal. When Herter died from a heart attack in December 1966, President Lyndon B. Johnson designated Roth as his replacement. Neither trade executive spent much time with either president; for example, to prepare for his decision in the crucial climactic stages of the talks in the spring of 1967, LBJ worked mainly with and through his deputy special assistant for national security affairs, Francis M. Bator. Yet with his ultimate acceptance of the final Kennedy Round package, Johnson gave his strong endorsement to what the STR-led team had wrought.

For the next four years, however, the STR went into eclipse. The big trade negotiation was over, and the role of the office in bilateral and product-specific talks was not well established in either law or practice. In early 1969 Richard M. Nixon's secretary of Commerce, Maurice H. Stans, made a strong push to have trade coordinating responsibilities transferred to himself. Congressional and interest-group opposition blocked this; agricultural groups, in particular, feared they would get short shrift. But Stans won two substantial concessions: the right to control who was appointed STR and the lead role in the major trade action of the early Nixon administration, the "textile wrangle" with Japan. The STR became a bureaucratic backwater, weakly led and devoid of presidential support.

There followed a trade policy disaster. Stans bungled the textile negotiation, as his aggressive, insensitive style provoked fierce Japanese resistance. This led to a blunder with Congress: Stans got Nixon to endorse statutory import quotas for textiles. As discussed in chapter 2, this drove Ways and Means Chairman Wilbur D. Mills (D-AR) to push a protectionist bill he privately abhorred. The bill passed the House and got as far as the Senate floor before time ran out in December 1970.[5]

The need to restore central trade policy leadership was now evident, and in 1971 the White House began remedial action by naming a new STR, Idaho lawyer and businessman William D. Eberle. Eberle quickly recruited two strong deputies: William R. Pearce to handle the development of legislation, and Harald B. Malmgren to manage the international negotiations to prepare a new trade round.

But the STR was still not secure in the Nixon administration, for the president also established in 1971 a Council for International Economic Policy (CIEP), whose staff was headed by an assistant to the president for international economic affairs—first Peter G. Peterson, then (in 1972) Peter M. Flanigan. And Flanigan moved, with Nixon's apparent endorsement, to have the STR formally incorporated in CIEP under his direction.

---

5. For details on these events, see I. M. Destler, Haruhiro Fukui, and Hideo Sato, *The Textile Wrangle* (Ithaca, NY: Cornell University Press, 1979), chaps. 3–10.

Many legislators feared that the nonpartisan, "trade expert" character of the STR would be destroyed if it were brought into a more "political" (partisan) White House operation. And they had twice seen the Nixon administration ready to sacrifice the trade representative. So House Ways and Means responded in 1973 by adding to the pending trade legislation a section making the STR a statutory office, something Kennedy had resisted. The Senate bill went two steps further: placing the STR in the Executive Office of the President by law, and giving cabinet rank and salary to its chief. As signed by President Gerald R. Ford, the Trade Act of 1974 included all of these provisions.

Even as these steps were being taken, the STR was asserting de facto leadership, first in drafting the administration's legislative proposals, then in lobbying the Trade Act through the House and the Senate in 1973 and 1974.[6] By the time the bill was enacted, the STR had become a congressional as well as a presidential agent. In 1975 and 1976, the office entered another in-between period, as the trade negotiations it was leading moved slowly at Geneva. But this time its position in the executive branch was stronger and more secure. And the stage was set for a major trade-brokering success story—the completion of the Tokyo Round in 1979 under the leadership of President Jimmy Carter's special trade representative, Robert S. Strauss.

Strauss and the MTN: The STR on Center Stage

Almost alone among senior Carter administration international economic officials, Robert Strauss had no prior experience with trade policy. His forte had been partisan politics. He had served as chairman of the Democratic National Committee, where he had begun with a party bitterly divided by its 1972 debacle and ended with Democrats surprisingly united behind the Carter candidacy. He had made an important personal contribution to this outcome with his ornery, persistent, inclusive style of interpersonal diplomacy. And along the way he had established close relationships with a number of senior senators, including Senate Finance Committee Chairman Russell B. Long (D-LA).

With his flair for the public spotlight, Strauss brought celebrity to the STR job. Skilled at political maneuvering, he led in reenergizing the MTN negotiations abroad and selling them at home. As STR aides he brought in trade or management specialists, not partisan politicos: Geneva Deputy (later to be Carter White House operations chief) Alonzo L. McDonald; Washington Deputy (and former STR General Counsel) Alan

---

6. For a detailed account, see I. M. Destler, *Making Foreign Economic Policy* (Washington: Brookings Institution, 1980), chaps. 10 and 11.

Wm. Wolff; General Counsel (and former Finance Committee aide) Richard R. Rivers. And Strauss promptly demonstrated his ability to act as a broker in sensitive trade issues by negotiating orderly marketing agreements with Korea and Taiwan on shoes, and with Japan on color television sets. He also led in bilateral, market-expanding negotiations with Tokyo.

His handling of Japanese market issues in later 1977 and early 1978 illustrated Strauss's unique blend of verbal hyperbole and political adroitness. Until that fall, other administration officials had been more active than he on US-Japanese economic issues, voicing special concern about Tokyo's growing world trade and current account surplus. Strauss seized the initiative by exaggerating the danger. He declared—with little if any supporting evidence—that US-Japan relations were near the "bursting point," and that Congress would likely go protectionist when it reconvened in January 1978, unless Japan made significant market-opening commitments. Turning aside an initiative from Senate staff aides to hold Finance Committee hearings on US-Japan issues—that might raise the political temperature too much, he thought—he nevertheless urged senators to be very demanding in their private conversations with Japanese trade officials.

When a newly designated Japanese minister for international economic policy flew to Washington in December, Strauss got Finance Committee senators to host a very tough private luncheon. And Strauss himself immediately and "very candidly" declared the minister's offer of tariff and quota adjustments to be "insufficient," falling "considerably short" of what was necessary. This made it possible for Strauss to find an anticipated further concession "promising," and to imply that US toughness was beginning to bear fruit. He traveled to Japan the following month to complete a revised Japanese trade agreement, and, by threatening to fly home without signing, he won further concessions on its language.

When he then reported the deal to senators at a Finance Committee hearing, the first thing Strauss did was to give *them* the credit. He thanked them, "on behalf of the entire nation," for "the strong bipartisan support" they had given to US negotiators. He described the broad result in expansive terms: Japanese Prime Minister Takeo Fukuda had "crossed the political Rubicon," and the specific Japanese commitments in the agreement represented "an entire change of direction and change of philosophy of trade" on Tokyo's part. But he cautioned that implementation was "just beginning."

When Senator William V. Roth Jr., (R-DE, no relation to the former STR) suggested hearings every six months to monitor progress with Japan, Strauss questioned whether that was often enough. "I think I should report to you on a more frequent basis, if you have the time in the Senate to do it." He wanted the Japanese and the Germans and the

European Community "to feel some of the pressure from the Congress that I feel. You know, you are breathing down my neck every day," he told Senator William D. Hathaway (D-ME). "I would like to turn that red hot breath toward the people we are trading with."[7]

The performance was vintage Strauss—part substance, part charade—as his more savvy Senate interlocutors fully realized. But his game was their game too: he was giving them credit for toughness greater than they had actually displayed, and greater credit than they deserved for such negotiating results as were achieved. Yet while deferring to them in rhetoric, he kept the action initiative for himself—just as they wanted him to do. For he was absorbing the political heat, diverting pressure from them. With the Japanese also Strauss was adroit, for although his strong words ruffled their sensitivities, they also gave Tokyo bureaucrats and politicians a credible rationale for making trade concessions. In both cases, Strauss was the consummate activist broker—keeping the game going, getting results that at least defused the immediate crisis, and spreading credit around in a way that enhanced his own central role, rather than diminished it.

Strauss was also playing another old trade game, that of "export politics." The main domestic pressures concerning Japan were coming from import-competing industries like color TVs and steel, and the Carter administration accommodated these pressures with moderate trade-restraining arrangements. But it preferred to push trade-expanding issues. Thus, it encouraged agricultural export interests and then employed these interests as pressure in winning limited, grudging Japanese expansion of beef and citrus quotas. The overall gain was small—no more than $50 million set against a bilateral trade deficit with Japan that would reach $12 billion in 1978. But to the degree that discontent with Tokyo on trade was generalized in nature, such tactics channeled this discontent into pressure for expanding exports, not restricting imports. (The Carter administration also pressed Tokyo to stimulate its economy and to allow the yen to appreciate in order to reduce Japan's growing trade surplus.)

"Export politics" also was prominent in early 1979 when the United States, in order to broaden the coverage of the MTN government procurement code, pressed Tokyo to internationalize the purchases of its government telecommunications agency, Nippon Telephone and Tele-

---

7. US Congress, Senate Committee on Finance, Subcommittee on International Trade, *Hearing on United States/Japanese Trade Relations and the Status of the Multilateral Trade Negotiations*, 95th Cong., 2d sess. (1 February 1978), 9, 12, 13, 22. For a fuller discussion of those negotiations, see I. M. Destler, "United States-Japanese Relations and the American Trade Initiative of 1977: Was this 'Trip' Necessary?" in William J. Barnds, ed., *Japan and the United States: Challenge and Opportunity* (New York: New York University Press [for the Council on Foreign Relations], 1979), 190–230.

graph (NTT).[8] In that case again, US officials, with Strauss in the lead, sought to reinforce domestic interests in export expansion and to counter and limit the influence of those seeking import restriction.

A more comprehensive and structured form of brokering took place within the private-sector advisory committees that were established under the Trade Act to work with US negotiators in setting and implementing MTN goals. In response to complaints from some in the business community about their limited and ad hoc role in the Kennedy Round, Congress had added a detailed section to the 1974 law, setting forth requirements and guidelines to institutionalize "advice from the private sector." Working with Commerce, Labor, and Agriculture, the STR was required to organize general and sectoral committees that would, "so far as practicable, be representative of all industry, labor, or agricultural interests . . ."[9]

Initially, some officials feared that the requirement for such elaborate private-sector consultation would prove a straitjacket, for the law even provided that the STR must inform the advisory committees—and give reasons—when he did not accept their counsel! In practice, however, the advisory network proved a great boon. Membership on the committees gave producers a forum for pressing specific concerns; film manufacturers could argue that a reduction on Japanese tariffs would increase their sales, for example. And committee members knew that trade negotiators would listen and try to respond, since each committee would report independently to the Congress on how it viewed the final MTN agreements. The advisory committee system gave Congress what its members particularly favored: a place away from Capitol Hill where they could refer petitioning interests and assure them that they would get a hearing. Each committee was broad enough (for example, "Industrial Chemicals and Fertilizers," "Nonferrous Metals") to encompass a range of firms and interests. Their exposure to one another gave committee members a broader perspective, and it gave executive officials useful leeway on whose advice they finally took. And because the advisers felt they were taken seriously—and came to understand the constraints faced by their governmental counterparts—they developed sympathy for the larger enterprise and modest personal identification with its success.

As noted by Gilbert R. Winham, broader lessons can be drawn from this experience:

> In delegating the task of constituency relations to the executive, Congress took advantage of the capacity of governmental bureaucracy to take the initiative

---

8. See Timothy J. Curran, "Politics and High Technology: The NTT Case," in I. M. Destler and Hideo Sato, eds., *Coping with U.S.-Japanese Economic Conflicts* (Lexington, MA: Lexington Books, 1982), 185–241.

9. Trade Act of 1974, Sec. 135.

in dealing with constituents. . . . The same [advisory group] system that organized the sectoral interests and gave them influence in government also structured the task of the executive in dealing with those interests. In the words of
one government official, "The SAC system gave STR a series of targets to
shoot at." . . . [It also] meant that communications with constituency groups
generally occurred in an environment defined by trade bureaucracies and not
by the constituents themselves. . . .

To sum up, the Tokyo Round experience demonstrated that channels of
access could be two-way streets: access to the executive by the private sector
could also mean access to the private sector by the executive. In comparison
to Congress, which is the normal arena of interest-group activity, the executive was better able to confront constituency groups with a coordinated plan
of its own for trade policy. . . .[10]

At the final stage of the MTN, Strauss's political skills were tested by a
crisis that was partially of his own making. Europeans had participated
in the MTN on condition that the United States not impose countervailing
duties on EC exports before the subsidies code was negotiated. Congress
had reluctantly granted the secretary of the Treasury the authority to
waive countervailing duties for four years, until 3 January 1979. But when
it became clear that the MTN would not be entirely completed by then,
and Strauss and his Hill allies failed to get the waiver extended before
Congress adjourned for the year in October 1978, Europeans refused to
continue. An intricate rescue was required. At home, the United States
deferred collection of the duties, while Strauss bargained with Congress
to extend the waiver retroactively.[11] In the meantime, the Europeans
agreed to resume talking, but not to sign anything until the waiver extension became law, which it did in March 1979.

In the end, everything came together in one of the Carter administration's major policy successes. Nontariff barrier codes were completed to
regulate government behavior on subsidies, government procurement,
product standards, etc. The United States granted long-sought concessions—abandonment of the American Selling Price system of customs
valuation,[12] and an injury test for the imposition of countervailing duties—in exchange for commitments on a range of trade-distorting foreign practices. Of the 38 private-sector advisory committees, 27 made
positive reports to Congress, with 5 neutral and just 6 tilted toward the

---

10. Gilbert R. Winham, *International Trade and the Tokyo Round Negotiation* (Princeton, NJ:
Princeton University Press, 1986), 315–17.

11. As described in chapter 4, part of this bargain was increased protection for the
textile industry.

12. This was a provision of US customs law, long offensive to America's trading partners, that required duties on certain products (including benzenoid chemicals, rubber
footwear) to be calculated by multiplying the tariff rate not by the price of the import,
the normal procedure, but by the higher selling price of the competing US product. This
inflated actual duties considerably.

critical side. As recounted in chapter 4, the STR collaborated with its congressional counterparts in drafting the implementing bill, which passed overwhelmingly. A triumphant Strauss moved on to other pursuits, as did all of his senior STR colleagues.

The Executive Broker and Its Critics

Strauss was sui generis, but the way he handled trade policy was broadly consistent with the tradition of the postwar system. He aimed to balance pressures, build coalitions, give a little here, get a little there— but above all to keep the overall American and global trade regime moving in a trade-expanding direction. For the ultimate goal of postwar US trade leaders was not maximum US advantage but openness in general, a trade world where American products and firms could compete as freely as possible with others. It was assumed that the United States as a whole would do well in such a world; others would gain, but so would it, and it would remain in the front economic rank. Trade was a positive-sum game, and liberal policies would make everyone better off, the United States included.

Of course, no US trade official could argue openly for brokering as the primary function. If US trade negotiators were to keep their mandate from Congress and product interests, they had to appear tough in advancing and defending specific US commercial interests. And if aggressiveness simply meant being assertive in trade bargaining and going after those foreign trade barriers that blocked promising US trade opportunities, this was fully consistent with the postwar brokering tradition. Successive administration leaders did pursue market openness abroad even as they did so at home. This was the path to expanding the volume of trade. And "export politics" demanded it. Only by convincing industries and firms that there was money to be earned overseas could officials engage them in policy struggles, balancing the ever-active forces that sought import restrictions.

There were political risks, of course. A tough, critical, visible market-expanding campaign—like those of successive administrations toward Japan— might buttress executive credibility, but it would also fuel anti-Japanese sentiment. For in practice the best "leading indicator" of congressional activism on Japan in the 1970s and early 1980s was executive branch activism. Noisy, visible negotiations got congressional attention and drew members and their staffs into the policy game of pressing their demands. And "Japan bashing" by the executive branch legitimized Japan bashing on Capitol Hill, though up to a point this too could be useful to executive brokers, as Strauss demonstrated.

For Strauss and for his less famous predecessors, the flexibility of the STR arrangement was useful, as was its White House location. These features made it easier not just to engage important business interests but to bring into the balance other departments, such as Treasury or State, that were dependably antiprotectionist for economic or diplomatic reasons. But compared with other units within the Executive Office of the President, the STR was an organizational anomaly. First, unlike the coordinating staffs for broad subjects like national security or domestic policy, the STR was a special-purpose operating unit, typically distant from daily presidential business. Second, it was staffed by "professional" trade specialists, in contrast to the more partisan recruitment pattern that became the norm at the National Security Council and its domestic policy counterparts. Yet the STR did have rapid staff turnover, and hence it was not a career bureaucracy with an institutional memory like, say, the old Bureau of the Budget.

These features made the STR a natural target of reorganizers. So did frustration about trade policy. As set forth in chapter 3, the relative position of the United States was, by most measures, declining. Throughout the postwar period, other advanced industrial nations had grown faster, closing the gap in per capita income and individual well-being. Our merchandise trade balance, consistently in surplus through 1970, was almost always in deficit thereafter. Major industries were losing international market share—and not just textiles or shoes, but steel, automobiles, and consumer electronics as well. It was easy to draw from this evidence a broader diagnosis of American industrial decline and to view "trade wars" as a prime contributor to this decline.

There developed an alternative view of US trade policy: that priority had to be given to halting and reversing this decline. Uncle Sam had to stop being the world's nice guy. As Russell Long put it in 1974, the United States could no longer afford to be the world's "least favored nation," exposing our markets while the rest of the world employed "practices which effectively bar our products."[13] Others were taking advantage—Japan in particular—and America had to fight back. Our policy should thus give priority to the relative position of the United States, particularly in the industries of the future. There was also a general belief among congressional trade specialists that the Treasury Department had not, in practice, been carrying out its responsibility to enforce laws aimed at penalizing foreign dumping and subsidies.

These factors combined to generate dissatisfaction with the executive branch trade structure even as Strauss was moving to his triumphant congressional votes. To some, there was a link between the disappointing market results and the dispersion of various trade functions within

---

13. US Congress, Senate Committee on Finance, *Hearings on the Trade Reform Act of 1973*, 93d Cong., 2d sess. (4 and 5 March 1974), part 1, 2. Challenges to the general trade-expanding and brokering tradition in postwar US trade policy are discussed further in chapter 7.

the executive branch. The Senate Finance Committee summarized these concerns:

> Trade is not given a very high priority in terms of commitment of resources and the attention to top governmental policy officials on a regular basis, other than the STR. Additionally, major trade functions are spread throughout the Executive branch making formulation of trade policy and implementation of trade policy haphazard and in some cases contradictory. No single agency exists which clearly predominates in the formulation of trade policy to the extent that people with a trade issue know where in the Executive branch they can turn to find a person who will give their particular problem attention and whom they and the rest of the government can hold accountable. Another problem that has been noted often is that the present organization of the Executive branch with respect to trade has failed to result in retaining experienced trade personnel, so that often the United States is faced with the prospect of entering trade negotiations with other countries who have a tough, seasoned corps of trade negotiators.[14]

The STR had established a clear lead role for major multilateral negotiations and an important one in bilateral and product-specific issues. Yet other trade responsibilities were spread about: Commerce promoted exports, Treasury handled unfair-trade-practice cases, Agriculture dealt with grain sales, and most major departments influenced presidential decisions on escape clause cases.

One proposal for clarifying matters was to consolidate most of these functions within a new Department of Trade. This idea got its first prominent exposure when the author of a study on US international economic policymaking showed a draft proposal to a staff aide of Senator Roth; the aide liked it and so did his boss, who introduced it as a bill and won the cosponsorship of the chairman of the Finance Subcommittee on Trade, Abraham A. Ribicoff (D-CT).[15] So when Finance began meeting on the draft MTN results, it voted initially to recommend that the implementing legislation include a provision establishing a Trade Department.

But the Finance senators' commitment to the idea was less than it seemed: Ribicoff was of two minds, and Russell Long preferred to retain the White House office. Moreover, House Ways and Means members did not favor the departmental approach. So, in the end, a compromise was adopted. The draft trade legislation required the president to consider establishing a Trade Department (along with other options), and to submit a specific trade reorganization proposal to Congress by 10 July 1979. When that date instead found Carter on his famous retreat to Camp David, soliciting insights from a range of national leaders about

---

14. US Congress, Senate Committee on Finance, *Trade Agreements Act of 1979*, 96th Cong., 1st sess. (17 July 1979), S. Rept. 96-249, 268–69.

15. For the story as told by a participant, see Stephen D. Cohen, *The Making of United States International Economic Policy* (New York: Praeger, 2nd ed., 1981), chap. 8.

what had gone wrong with his presidency, Ribicoff held up final Senate action on the MTN package. This had the intended impact. On 19 July, Carter sent forth to Congress a reorganization proposal, which, after further consultation and resubmission, became effective in January 1980.

The Carter Reorganization

The Carter reforms created, in essence, a two-tiered executive branch structure. On top was an enlarged and renamed Office of the United States Trade Representative (USTR). It was assigned "international trade policy development, coordination and negotiation functions," and it included responsibilities previously handled by State regarding the General Agreement on Tariffs on Trade (GATT), bilateral, commodity, and East-West trade matters, as well as policy responsibility for overseeing trade-remedy cases.

At the level of trade administration, Commerce was to become "the focus of nonagricultural operational trade responsibilities." It was therefore given Treasury's authority over countervailing duty and antidumping cases, as well as State's jurisdiction over commercial attachés. The trade committees had, in fact, insisted on the former step, judging Treasury to be insufficiently aggressive in enforcing the unfair-trade statutes. And the adjective "nonagricultural" signaled a bow to political reality: farm interests would never accept the transfer of responsibility and expertise for their products from the Department of Agriculture.

The USTR half of the Carter reorganization reflected the sensible principle that in restructuring government one should start with organizations and processes that work. The Trade Representative's office had completed the MTN with success and with a reputation for effectiveness, and it was better to build on that than to start anew. There was some risk of making its staff too large.[16] This could incline the USTR toward too much in-house detail work, at the expense of reaching out and mobilizing the resources of all agencies. And assigning it difficult tasks outside the GATT-MTN mainstream, such as East-West trade policy coordination, did not necessarily bring added strength. Still, a timely, visible reinforcement of the STR's mandate helped offset the tendency for trade policy power to disperse whenever a multilateral round was completed.

The reasons for strengthening Commerce were more ad hoc. It was there. It already handled certain operational trade functions, such as industry information and export promotion. So it seemed a logical home

---

16. The Carter administration, under substantial congressional pressure, increased the number of permanent USTR staff slots to 131, compared to 59 in the STR.

for other trade tasks whose current management generated dissatisfaction. Moreover, Carter did not want the White House trade office to grow too much, since this would undo his earlier reorganization, which had reduced the total number of Executive Office personnel. So those functions that required an expanded, specialized staff—enforcement of unfair-trade laws, for example—were placed in Commerce.

The overall package was rationalized by an old and largely discredited public administration dichotomy—the separation of policy from operations, with the corollary that the former could control the latter.[17] The USTR, with policy leadership responsibility, would be in charge; Commerce would carry the policy out. This could work, but only if both organizations and their leaders accepted these roles and worked closely and cooperatively, with Commerce deferring to USTR direction.

Under Carter, the system performed adequately; at least there was no major conflict between Commerce and the USTR. Both had to adjust to new leaders. Commerce busied itself with filling a range of new positions, including an under secretary for trade who would oversee the department's renamed and expanded International Trade Administration, which now had no fewer than 17 officials at or above the deputy assistant secretary level. The new USTR was former Florida governor Reubin O'D. Askew, who lacked Strauss's political mastery and close presidential ties; he proved a competent trade policy leader, however, and no single competitor rose to challenge him.

Reagan I: Commerce Versus USTR

Askew's successor, William E. Brock III, was not so lucky. Like Strauss four years earlier, Brock in 1981 had just completed a successful term as his party's national chairman. And once in the trade job, he would demonstrate comparable talents on Capitol Hill.

Yet a month before Brock was named to the USTR, President-elect Ronald Reagan chose as secretary of Commerce a capable, ambitious Connecticut businessman named Malcolm Baldrige. In discussions surrounding the appointment, it became public knowledge that influential Reagan counselor Edwin Meese III, favored abolishing USTR and giving Baldrige the primary trade responsibility. Again, the fact that the trade representative's office was an organizational oddity, a "line" unit (possessing specific policy responsibility) within the president's Executive Office staff, rendered it vulnerable to reformers who sought to streamline structure before they understood substance. Brock, one of the last

---

17. For a more general discussion of the persistence and limits of this approach to foreign policy management see I. M. Destler, *Presidents, Bureaucrats, and Foreign Policy: The Politics of Organizational Reform* (Princeton, NJ: Princeton University Press, 1972), 18–22.

cabinet-level appointees announced by Reagan, had therefore to respond in his confirmation hearings to claims by the incoming Commerce secretary that he, not Brock, would be the central trade policy figure.

Brock replied by reiterating the "indispensible" USTR function: it "must continue to be, for the President and the Congress, the government's principal architect and exponent of trade policy to insure that we act and speak as one." Three successive laws had made the trade representative chairman of the statutory interagency trade committee, so that matter was settled; moreover, he had had "fairly extended conversations with the Secretary of Commerce" and they had "a very healthy and solid commitment to the same goal": an "aggressive" trade and export policy. He was sure they would "work very effectively together."[18] Nevertheless, when the Reagan administration, under Meese's leadership, created its own (nonstatutory) network of coordinating committees, it was Baldrige who chaired the Cabinet Council on Commerce and Trade.

In practice, neither man was able to establish clear predominance in the first Reagan administration. Brock was supported by the precedent of successful leadership by previous STRs. He also had strong policy and political skills and close ties to senators and representatives, having served (as had Cordell Hull) in both chambers. Indeed, when the new Cabinet Council on Commerce and Trade held its first meeting under Baldrige's chairmanship, both the Finance and the Ways and Means chairmen reportedly phoned the president and informed him that this was against the law! Yet the Commerce secretary had political resources also: a stronger relationship with Reagan (and with Meese), the new authorities given Commerce in the Carter reorganization, and the talents of an aggressive under secretary, Lionel H. Olmer. So while Brock handled auto imports from Japan and headed the US delegation at the unsuccessful GATT ministerial talks of November 1982, it was Baldrige who brokered a voluntary export restraint agreement between American steel companies and European governments earlier that same year. Beginning in 1980, Commerce also established the first credible enforcement operation for the unfair-trade laws. (The consequences are addressed in chapter 6.)

Baldrige also continued in his quest for governmentwide trade dominance. His persistence was hardly surprising, for trade was by far the most prominent of his department's substantive responsibilities, and it naturally attracted any aggressive secretary with decent White House connections. And if Maurice Stans had failed egregiously in 1969–71, Baldrige did a bit better 12 years later. In the spring of 1983, despite the opposition of Brock and almost all other senior presidential advisers, President Reagan accepted a Baldrige-Meese recommendation that the administration endorse Senator Roth's proposal for a Department of In-

18. US Congress, Senate Committee on Finance, *Hearing on the Nomination of William E. Brock, III*, 97th Cong., 1st sess. (19 January 1981), 3, 10, 12, 13.

ternational Trade and Industry, with the USTR incorporated therein. The Commerce secretary spent much of the rest of Reagan's first term lobbying to win industry support for that reorganization.

The reemergence of the trade department proposal raised anew the question of whether the brokering function was adequate for trade leadership. Roth's Governmental Affairs Committee argued the negative in its report recommending approval of the legislation: "Trade needs a champion in government. The new Department Secretary will be this champion. The USTR was created as a broker, not an advocate." Or to quote the views of three Democrats:

> USTR was established basically to pull together our position for multilateral negotiations at a time when our major trade problem was coordinating and balancing our own diverse interests, and we had no significant industrial problems. We now have a host of other problems, and most of the negotiating action has shifted into the bilateral arena. We need a more focused effort to deal coherently with trade, industry, and competitiveness questions.[19]

Nonetheless, the Trade Department idea did not move very far on Capitol Hill. To win bipartisan endorsement by his committee, Roth had to accept organizational add-ons that compromised the "lean, mean" department he favored. Most important was an industrial policy mechanism pushed by Democrats: for any trade-threatened sector of national significance, the secretary was to convene an "industry sector competitiveness council" representing business, labor, and government to recommend an action program. This was but a watered-down version of a proposal for a permanent Council on Industrial Strategy, but it nonetheless served to reduce the Reagan administration's enthusiasm for the venture. Pungent opposition by Finance Trade Subcommittee Chairman Danforth delayed, and ultimately prevented, the bill from reaching the Senate floor in 1984. In the House, it never reached the markup stage. Still, the fact that the president was proposing to eliminate his organization could only damage Brock's standing and the credibility of the USTR generally.

USTR and Presidential Ambivalence

Reagan's lack of attachment to the trade office had ample precedent. Kennedy had been reluctant to establish a trade representative in the Executive Office of the President (EOP). Nixon had been willing to reor-

---

19. US Congress, Senate Committee on Governmental Affairs, *Trade Reorganization Act of 1983*, 98th Cong., 2d sess. (3 April 1984), S. Rept. 98-374, 8, 128. The three Democrats were Thomas F. Eagleton of Missouri, Carl Levin of Michigan, and Jeff Bingaman of New Mexico.

ganize it out of existence. As House Trade Subcommittee Chairman Sam Gibbons (D-FL) remarked, with only modest exaggeration, "Every President that comes in wants to throw the USTR Office out of the White House."[20]

Presidents have, traditionally and understandably, resisted establishing units to serve other people's purposes in "their" White House. Presidency scholar Richard E. Neustadt, in his role as transition adviser, warned Kennedy against pressures in this direction. Citing Franklin D. Roosevelt's staffing practices, he urged that JFK start by filling only jobs "for which the President-elect, himself, feels an *immediate and continuing need.*" Neustadt inveighed thereafter against "proliferating advisory staffs in your Executive Office."[21] Kennedy generally followed such advice. And 16 years later, Jimmy Carter's Executive Office reorganization similarly aimed at "limiting EOP, wherever possible, to functions which bear a close relationship to the work of the President."[22]

Kennedy did, of course, accede to the STR's creation. Carter retained it and, under congressional pressure, broadened its functions and enlarged its staff. Yet the office has never had the sort of connection to broad presidential policy business possessed by, say, the National Security Council or the Office of Management and Budget. It is too specialized, too focused on a specific slice of policy substance and ongoing operations.

Had Congress not wanted (U)STR, it is unlikely that any postwar president would have created such an EOP office on his own. Trade policy just has not loomed large enough, and presidents have seen it as, for the most part, second-order, technical business. When it does become first-order, it is usually because it bears upon their nontrade concerns, like foreign relations or partisan politics. Generally, presidents want protection from trade issues for the same reasons that legislators do: they don't like to say "no" to important interests or to choose among them when choice can be avoided.

This presidential coolness has limited the capacity of the trade representative to build personal ties with the man in the Oval Office. Only Robert Strauss attained the status of a close presidential adviser, and he kept his access because he was useful to Carter on a broad range of

20. US Congress, House Committee on Ways and Means, Subcommittee on Trade, *Hearings on Options to Improve the Trade Remedy Laws*, 98th Cong., 1st sess. (16 and 17 March, and 13 and 14 April 1983), Serial 98-14, part 1, 389.

21. "Memorandum on Organizing the Transition" (15 September 1960), 7 (emphasis added), and "Memorandum on the Council of Economic Advisers: First Steps" (19 December 1960), 2. Copies obtained from Neustadt; both are available in the John F. Kennedy Library, Boston.

22. US Congress, "Reorganization Plan No. 1 of 1977," *Message from the President of the United States*, 95th Cong., 1st Sess. (15 July 1977), H. Doc. 95-185.

matters.[23] Trade alone would not have given Strauss enough to talk about with the president and his key aides; however, the universal belief that Strauss was talking regularly with the president was central to his credibility on trade, not only with business and on Capitol Hill, but in foreign capitals as well.

Conversely, those who, like Brock, could not build such strong presidential ties were vulnerable to challenge from executive branch rivals. Some managed to build a presidential base indirectly: Herter and Roth through the national security staff; Eberle and his deputies through Nixon's "economic czar," George P. Shultz. Indeed, one advantage of the (U)STR's Executive Office location is that it makes such relationships easier for its head to develop than they would be for the head of a separate executive department. On the other hand, a high-profile USTR, of the sort needed to manage major international trade talks or domestic trade crises, may be hard for a White House chief of staff to swallow, since the USTR combines independence in day-to-day actions and the White House label. She or he must swear allegiance to Congress as well as the president.

Liberal Words, Protectionist Deeds

In part because of the struggle between Brock and Baldrige, but more important perhaps because of recession and the burgeoning trade imbalance, the first Reagan administration developed a pattern of endorsing liberal trade in principle but tightening protection in practice. The auto quotas initiated in 1981 were understandable, and probably unavoidable, given the industry's sudden crisis. However, they were followed in 1982 by "voluntary" EC steel export restraints, and in December 1983 by toughening of restrictions on textile imports, after Baldrige persuaded the president to overturn an 11-to-1 cabinet committee vote against such a move. Brock's reputation rebounded the following September, as the USTR took the lead in explaining and implementing yet another protectionist step—perhaps Reagan's most significant—his decision to negotiate sales-limiting agreements with all major steel exporters. On the free trade side, Brock also gained by blocking or neutralizing several industry-specific protectionist provisions in what became the Trade and Tariff Act of 1984 (see chapter 4). Brock was frustrated, however, by the failure of the 1982 GATT ministerial talks and the difficulty of winning endorsement, at home and abroad, for a new round of trade negotiations. And as a consequence, Brock lacked the advantage of a central trade negotiation

---

23. The index of Jimmy Carter's *Keeping Faith* (New York: Bantam Books, 1982) has seven references to Strauss. Only two refer to his trade job, and none to the substance of trade policy.

to strengthen his hand within government and vis-à-vis private interests.[24]

At the same time, the trade deficit was ballooning to levels previously unknown. Prominent Democrats were pushing for more protection, not less, and it looked for a while as if trade would become a central issue in the president's reelection campaign. Reagan was hardly the first incumbent to buy some insurance with sympathetic responses to politically potent industries like textiles or steel. The trade policy performance of the first Reagan administration was therefore understandable, if far from ideal.

The second Reagan administration proved very different. In the first eight months of 1985, its behavior can only be described as bizarre. As the trade pressure mounted and mounted, the administration seemed to do nothing, and seemed not even to recognize that there was any problem to address. Then, under new leadership, it launched an 11th-hour campaign to open markets abroad and stave off protection at home.

Reagan II: An Eight-Month Vacuum

First, the president agreed to a 1985 New Year's meeting with Japanese Prime Minister Yasuhiro Nakasone. But despite the urgings of his trade advisers, and despite the fact that the politically sensitive bilateral deficit was rising to an unheard-of $33.6 billion for calendar year 1984, he decided not to press trade matters with his counterpart. It was only when Nakasone brought up the subject that a bilateral negotiating agenda was established.

In March 1985, with trade-oriented businesses feeling the squeeze of yet another rise in the dollar and with Congress alarmed at a global trade deficit that had topped $100 billion and was climbing, the White House acknowledged political reality by declaring it would not push the Trade Department proposal further "at this time." But this was followed, two days later, by the announced transfer of the presumed winner in that decision. Now that he had finally established himself as the administration's most respected and politically astute trade man, William Brock was to become secretary of Labor! What would this do to trade policymaking? There is no evidence that Reagan or his new chief of staff, Donald T. Regan, even asked this question. As *Washington Post*

---

24. Too often, the Reagan administration of 1981–84 failed to take the initiative in the early stages of an industry's trade-relief campaign. Rather than bringing in other interests in order to balance the political equation—using, for example, the industry advisory committees Strauss's STR had employed during the MTN—Reagan's trade leaders tended to wait until a powerful industry such as textiles or steel or autos had defined the issue. The question then became one not of whether to protect them, but of how much additional protection to provide.

columnist Hobart Rowen put it at the time, "The reality is that the White House seemed to have only one thing on its mind: the need to build new relationships with the labor movement. . . ."[25]

In that same March, the administration announced it would not seek renewal of the voluntary export restraint on autos; this decision, defensible in economic terms, was made without reckoning the congressional reaction. In August, Reagan said "no" to the escape clause petition of the shoe industry, a case championed by Danforth. He did this without any apparent recognition that denying relief through established channels to an industry that was clearly damaged by imports was bound to increase pressure for statutory solutions.

The administration appeared no more helpful to trade-embattled industries on what most considered the prime source of their problems: the sky-high dollar. Through the summer, the president and his chief of staff tended to speak of this as a good thing, yet another sign that "America was back." Business leaders who talked to the White House (outside the USTR) about the havoc this was wreaking in their markets found themselves rebuffed; some were told, in essence, that they were crybabies and should stop asking for government help against the workings of the marketplace. This made them angry and frustrated. They felt, like many others, that the prime cause of dollar strength was government policy, specifically the Reagan budget deficits. It was hard for these companies, through their own efforts, to offset an exchange rate estimated to give foreign competitors a 30 percent to 40 percent cost advantage! Lacking a hearing downtown, they descended with double strength on Capitol Hill.

In the spring and summer of 1985 Congress needed more executive branch help than ever, because of its own decentralization, and above all, because of the enormous trade deficit. It was getting just about none. In fact, the administration was doing the opposite of protecting Congress. It was diverting trade-restrictive pressures to Capitol Hill! Little wonder that the number of trade bills increased, as did their prominence and their progress through committees and onto the House and Senate floors. Not only were legislators genuinely concerned about the trade problem; not only did some of them see partisan advantage (or fear partisan disadvantage) in the issue; but they needed to shock the administration, to jar it back onto the activist track. As one aide to a Senate Republican involved in the spring's Japan bashing put it privately: "You don't understand. The target isn't the Japanese; it's the White House!" And rank-and-file administration trade officials were encouraging such congressional activity, since they too were trying to get the president's attention.

---

25. "Filling Bill Brock's Shoes," *Washington Post*, 28 March 1985. It took more than three months for Brock's successor, Clayton Yeutter, to be named, cleared by the administration, and confirmed by the Senate.

Reagan II: The Shift to Activism

Finally, in late September 1985, the administration unveiled a trade strategy. On Sunday the 22nd, Treasury Secretary James A. Baker III joined with the finance ministers of France, Germany, Japan, and the United Kingdom in a joint declaration calling for a weaker dollar (more precisely, for the "further orderly appreciation of the major nondollar currencies against the dollar"). The Group of Five indicated their intention to intervene in foreign-exchange markets to help bring this about. The dollar dropped sharply, particularly in Tokyo, where the Bank of Japan was a heavy buyer of yen.

The next day, Monday the 23rd, President Reagan gave a "fair trade" speech at the White House. He sounded his determination to fight for the rights of American producers in foreign markets, and announced an intent to press several unfair trade practice cases against Japan, the European Community, Korea, and Brazil.

This two-track strategy combined economic and political logic. Decline of the dollar would bring first the hope, then the reality, of improvement in the trade balance. Because of the J-curve effect, the impact on the nominal balance would be delayed, but the effect on the real balance—the volumes of exports and imports—would be greater than the dollar statistics showed. Since this real balance was important for trade politics, the administration could expect better days—if it could hold off pressures in the meantime. It would do so through its new aggressiveness in opening foreign markets to American exports. But it would resist the congressional push for trade legislation—at least until dollar decline could do its work.

Orchestrating the new administration strategy were Secretary of the Treasury Baker and his deputy, Richard G. Darman. They played a close hand on exchange rate matters, over which Baker had direct authority, and used the interagency Economic Policy Council, which Baker chaired, to develop the new strategy on trade policy. Responsibility for executing the new strategy was divided between Baldrige and the new USTR, Clayton Yeutter, but without the conflict that had characterized Reagan's first term. Baldrige had lost not only the battle for a Trade Department, but also his White House ally, Edwin Meese, who became attorney general, and the services of his aggressive under secretary, Lionel Olmer, who left government for private law practice. Much of the new trade strategy employed statutory authorities belonging to the USTR, and that office's congressional ties made it the main administration locutor on the specifics of the trade legislation. Moreover, with Baker there was now a clearer locus of decision-making power on international economic issues, unlike during the first Reagan administration. The USTR could use the Baker process to get the go-ahead to push more unfair-trade cases with foreign governments.

Yeutter came to the USTR job with prior trade policy experience, having served as assistant secretary of Agriculture and deputy STR in the Ford administration. So if he lacked his predecessors' close congressional ties and exceptional political talents, he knew a lot about trade. He also possessed seemingly boundless energy, which he employed to repair political fences. One tack he took was traditional. Following on the work of Brock and others, he chaired the cabinet-level US delegation to the September 1986 GATT ministerial talks at Punta del Este, which inaugurated the new "Uruguay Round" of multilateral talks on trade in goods and services. Working with Baldrige and Secretary of Agriculture Richard E. Lyng, Yeutter won agreement that the new round's agenda would include trade in agricultural products and services, subjects of particular American interest. In so doing, he demonstrated how the USTR leadership role can and should work within the executive branch.

But much of the USTR's energy was directed to what critics have labeled "aggressive unilateralism":[26] negotiations aimed at opening specific foreign markets under threat of closing our own. And the core authority they employed was Section 301 of the Trade Act of 1974.

Targeting the World: Section 301

Section 301 granted the president authority to take any of a broad range of retaliatory actions against a country that "maintains unjustifiable or unreasonable tariff or other import restrictions," or "subsidies . . . on its exports . . . which have the effect of substantially reducing sales of the competitive United States product . . ."[27] This was potentially a powerful club, but for its first decade it was generally kept in the closet. From 1975 through the summer of 1985, private firms filed 48 Section 301 petitions, on matters ranging from EC wheat flour export subsidies to Japanese import quotas on leather. These led typically to consultations, inside and outside the GATT. Some brought significant changes in foreign behavior; on others, GATT review dragged on for years. But prior to summer 1985, there were only two cases where the president took the retaliatory action that the law authorized.[28]

---

26. See, for example, Jagdish Bhagwati and Hugh T. Patrick, eds., *Aggressive Unilateralism: America's 301 Trade Policy and the World Trading System* (Ann Arbor: University of Michigan Press, 1990).

27. Section 252 of the Trade Expansion Act of 1962 had provided the president a more limited authority to act against "unjustifiable" or "unreasonable" foreign import restrictions.

28. Gary Clyde Hufbauer and Joanna Shelton Erb, *Subsidies in International Trade* (Washington: Institute for International Economics, 1984) 115; Thomas O. Bayard and Kim-

Congressional champions of Section 301 grew more and more unhappy. They had amended the law in 1979 and 1984: to establish timetables for action; to set specific criteria for judgment; to encourage the administration to initiate[29] cases on its own. But they found the response soft. In the words of Senator Danforth, the most persistent congressional champion of this authority, trade policy was "a failure" because no one ever saw "any possibility . . . that the United States [would] ever . . . retaliate."[30]

All this changed in September 1985. After an intensive internal review, the president ordered the USTR to recommend retaliation in several long-pending cases if resolutions were not reached by December. That same month, the USTR, for the first time initiated three Section 301 investigations on its own, without waiting for an industry petition—the targets were Brazilian informatics (computer and telecommunications) policy, Japanese import restrictions on tobacco, and Korean restraints on access to its insurance market. The USTR initiated one additional 301 case later in 1985, and six subsequent cases during the Reagan administration. Congress was not entirely satisfied, and its moves to toughen Section 301 were, to two senior USTR officials, "the heart of the 1988 Trade Act."[31] But one purpose may have been "to ensure that future administrations continue to apply this trade remedy in the vigorous manner of the Reagan administration from 1985 through 1988."[32]

Section 301 was "export politics" pursued by exceptionally aggressive means, a product of the egregious trade imbalance and frustration at foreign unfairness, real and perceived. And its most important single target was Japan. The administration worked, for policy and political reasons, to spread the pain among countries, but there was no doubt which country Congress had most in mind.

---

berly Ann Elliott, *Reciprocity and Retaliation in U.S. Trade Policy* (Washington: Institute for International Economics, 1994). The cases involved Argentina's breach of an export control agreement on hides and EC subsidies on wheat flour exports. In a third case, involving Canadian restrictions on US television broadcasting, the president recommended—and Congress adopted—mirror legislation. For a full list of Section 301 cases, see appendix D.

29. The word typically used in trade policy circles is "self-initiate," an expression that seems redundant and (to this ear) linguistically offensive.

30. Debate of 28 March 1985, *Congressional Record*, S35.

31. Judith Hippler Bello and Alan F. Holmer, "The Heart of the 1988 Trade Act: A Legislative History of the Amendments to Section 301," in Bhagwati and Patrick, eds., *Aggressive Unilateralism*, 49–89.

32. Ibid., 88.

Targeting Japan: From MOSS
to Semiconductor Sanctions

From the Strauss era, the US-Japan trade relationship had been the USTR's most challenging. The challenge grew through the 1980s, as the bilateral imbalance grew and the number of specific conflicts multiplied. In 1985, after Reagan discussed trade with Nakasone, the Market-Oriented, Sector-Specific (MOSS) talks were begun. These sought major Japanese concessions in four broad areas where US products seemed competitive but weren't selling: telecommunications, pharmaceuticals, microelectronics, and wood products. Hard negotiations led to significant Japanese concessions. The doubling of overall US sales to Japan between 1985 and 1989 was due mainly to the decline of the dollar, but the USTR's Advisory Committee concluded in early 1989 that in those product areas where the United States had pushed, sales had grown particularly fast.[33] There was also substantial negotiating achievement in agriculture and related products, with Japan agreeing to abandon beef and citrus quotas in 1988. The most dramatic and symbolic issue of the latter 1980s, however, was trade in semiconductors.

The semiconductor "chip" had been independently invented by two Americans in the late 1950s and had received a major early boost from official defense and space programs. US firms—based particularly in California's Silicon Valley—had led through the 1970s as hundreds, then thousands of electronic functions were crowded onto the tiny chips, which became indispensable to computers, telecommunications, and many other advanced industrial products.

But with government help and encouragement, Japan's integrated electronics firms began making major inroads into the semiconductor market in the late 1970s and early 1980s, particularly with the mass-produced, standardized dynamic random access memories (DRAMs). In 1983, the California-based Semiconductor Industry Association (SIA) published a report entitled *The Effect of Government Targeting on World Semiconductor Competition: A Case History of Japanese Industrial Strategy and Its Costs for America.* This report contrasted the rise in Japanese exports with the low and static share (around 11 percent) that US producers held in the Japanese market.

In July 1985, its members hit by growing Japanese competition and a severe slump in overall demand, SIA filed a Section 301 case claiming that this import resistance, encouraged by past government action, was an "unreasonable" barrier to US trade. In the months thereafter, anti-dumping cases were submitted by individual US firms and by the secre-

---

33. Advisory Committee for Trade Policy and Negotiations, *Analysis of the U.S.-Japan Trade Problem* (Washington: USTR, February 1989), chap. 6.

tary of Commerce. There were conflicting interests within the US industry, of course—major chip users, like the US computer industry, benefited from high-quality, low-cost Japanese inputs. Nonetheless, anxieties about erosion of US technological leadership, spreading from private industry to the Pentagon,[34] made support of the industry's case far broader than would have been received by a "low-tech" industry of comparable size.

There followed a year of complex—and fractious—negotiations, culminating in a unique "three-market" trade agreement announced in August 1986.[35] To halt dumping in the United States, the two governments adopted a system of minimum prices and reporting of sales by Japanese firms. There was also a somewhat looser system of price monitoring in third-country markets, aimed at protecting US exports against dumping there. Last but certainly not least was a commitment to increase US-based producers' share of the Japanese market, featuring a side letter from Japanese officials declaring, in the words of one US negotiator, that "they understood, welcomed, and would make efforts to assist the US companies in reaching their goal of a 20-percent market share within five years."[36]

The arrangement had political and economic logic. To act only against dumping in the US market would mean higher-priced chips here than elsewhere, undercutting producers of computers and other downstream products, such as IBM. Moreover, if the Japanese firms—NEC, Hitachi, Fujitsu, etc.—were able to restrict foreign access to their very large home market, it would be hard for US firms to hold their own globally. Nor did these firms wish for a two-market agreement that would encourage low-priced Japanese sales in the rest of the world. The deal completed was responsive to all of these concerns. But it was also internally contradictory. Specifically, the provisions aimed at dumping in the United States undercut the expansion of US market share in Japan and third countries.

The minimum (nondumping) prices in the United States were based on each Japanese firm's cost of production, and they were periodically updated. This procedure encouraged large production runs that brought down unit costs. But these large runs also brought oversupply and falling prices within Japan (the only market where the agreement did not

---

34. See US Department of Defense, Office of the Under Secretary for Acquisition, *Report of the Defense Science Board Task Force on Defense Semiconductor Dependency* (Washington: US Department of Defense, 1987).

35. For an extensive discussion of the semiconductor issue, see Laura D'Andrea Tyson, *Who's Bashing Whom? Trade Conflicts in High-Technology Industries* (Washington: Institute for International Economics, 1992), chap. 4.

36. Clyde V. Prestowitz Jr., *Trading Places: How We Allowed Japan to Take the Lead* (New York: Basic Books, 1988), 65.

set minimum prices). This undercut US firms' sales there. It led also to a "gray market" in third countries, as chips were flown out of Japan in suitcases for low-price resale. (The obvious way to combat this was for MITI to encourage the Japanese firms to limit production, but when the Japanese had suggested this during the negotiations, both SIA and the US government had opposed it—SIA because of concerns of its members about supply shortages, US officials because it was contrary to free market principles.)

By the end of 1986 SIA was complaining that both the Japanese and third-country market provisions of the agreement were being violated. US officials expressed growing concern to Tokyo and warned of retaliation. By early spring, MITI was pressing the Japanese firms to cut output, in order to drive the price up in Japan and take the profit out of the gray market. But before this could be effective, US patience ran out. Pressed by a Congress considering omnibus trade legislation, President Reagan announced in March 1987 that he would impose sanctions because of "Japan's inability to enforce" the agreement. In April, he imposed punitive (100 percent) tariffs against selected Japanese electronics imports[37] equivalent to the estimated sales lost to US firms in the Japanese market and in third countries.

These produced shock and headlines in Tokyo: "sanctions against an ally," the first such US action against Japan since World War II. Later that year, with the third-country dumping issue resolved, Reagan removed a portion of the penalties (and as discussed in chapter 7, US users of chips shortly found themselves facing sharp price *increases*, which they blamed on the agreement). But the major portion of the sanctions, retaliation for loss of anticipated US sales in Japan, continued through the decade—until the agreement was renegotiated and extended in 1991. Japanese dominance in the DRAM market continued through the decade as well. And as with the auto VERs earlier in the decade, the United States was forcing Japanese firms to increase their profits, and hence their longer-term competitive strength.

The semiconductor issue symbolized the complexity of modern trade issues: it was a high-technology production input sold by multinational firms in global markets. Trade policy was not an ideal instrument for addressing it, but it was the one most readily available. The USTR had to show toughness, to respond to semiconductor producers, but at the risk of damage to semiconductor users. And it had to keep one eye cocked toward that older political institution, the US Congress.

---

37. The tariffs were imposed not against semiconductors—this would have hit US users—but against selected "downstream" products that incorporated them: laptop and desktop computers, color TV sets, and power hand tools.

Working the Trade Bill: Damage Limitation

As discussed in chapter 4, the administration resisted trade legislation through 1986, then accepted it as inevitable and possibly desirable from 1987 on. One reason was the Democratic recapture of the Senate; another was that the USTR now needed extension of fast-track authority to complete the Uruguay Round. The USTR's can-do attitude toward the legislation was not universally shared in the administration: free market devotees at the Council of Economic Advisers and elsewhere felt that any bill passed by the Congress would be far too interventionist. When a senior trade official reported conference agreement, in early 1988, to remove a number of trade-restrictive provisions, one such economist responded that the USTR was "doing too well": now the president might actually sign the terrible thing!

But as that story illustrates, the game to the end was damage limitation: removal or modification of provisions that were clearly GATT-illegal, or that tied the executive's hands, or that tilted trade remedies further to the advantage of protection-seeking claimants. And notwithstanding his efforts, Yeutter did not possess in 1988 the congressional ties Brock had used to such advantage in 1984, and Strauss in 1979. He and his aides were thus excluded from some key conference-related meetings of the sort at which their predecessors had been included. Symbolic was the final bargaining of Subconference I on 31 March 1988. Senate Finance Chairman Lloyd Bentsen and House Ways and Means Chairman Dan Rostenkowski met in the Capitol, while Yeutter, Deputy USTR Alan Holmer, and General Counsel Judith Bello waited three hours in an adjacent room.[38] In contrast to the late 1970s, moreover, USTR people now found their best ties not with Senate Finance but with House Ways and Means, at both the member and the staff levels.

Nonetheless, their damage-limitation effort was at least a qualified success. In the most unfavorable trade-political climate since 1930, Yeutter and his aides had gotten the negotiating authority they needed, and had managed to neutralize—or modify—the most restrictive provisions. Retaliation was made "mandatory but not compulsory." And one issue on which the administration lost—congressional insistence on transferring some major trade authorities from the president to the USTR—represented a congressional vote of confidence for "its" executive broker. Rostenkowski had been particularly adamant in insisting on this transfer.

Taken as a whole, Reagan era trade policy represented a "strategic retreat"[39] for advocates of liberal trade. The president had granted "more

---

38. Bello and Holmer, "The Heart of the 1988 Trade Act," 56 (fn. 45).

39. William A. Niskanen, *Reaganomics: An Insider's Account of the Policies and the People* (New York: Oxford University Press, 1988), 137.

import relief" than any predecessor "in more than half a century,"[40] particularly during its first term. Damage had been limited during the second term, but the administration lost the trade initiative in 1985 and left office still struggling to regain it. Interestingly, Yeutter's successor would regain it. And she would do so, ironically, by exploiting the new authorities that Congress had forced on her reluctant predecessors.

Carla Hills and Super 301

Carla A. Hills came to the USTR post a seasoned Washington professional, a lawyer who had served as assistant attorney general and then secretary of Housing and Urban Development under President Gerald Ford. She had no special trade expertise, though she and her firm had represented international clients. Nor, unlike a number of her cabinet colleagues, did she enter office with close and long-standing ties to President George Bush. Secretary of Commerce Robert Mosbacher did possess such ties and used them to seize the initiative on a controversial agreement to codevelop the FSX fighter aircraft with Japan. For a while, it seemed possible that the Brock-Baldrige experience would be reenacted.

It wasn't. Hills proved competent, tough, and credible in her new role. The Bush administration rewarded such performance more reliably than had its predecessor. Mosbacher lost some luster when he ventured closer to advocating "industrial policy" than was safe in a free market, Republican administration, evoking the wrath of Budget Director Richard Darman and White House Chief of Staff John Sununu. And the new USTR benefited from the full negotiating agenda that Congress had left her.

Hills's most immediate challenge was the new amendments to Section 301. The 1988 Trade Act had transferred to the USTR from the president not only authority to determine whether foreign practices were unfair under that provision, but also to decide upon, and order, specific retaliatory action.[41] And it had added to Section 301's emphasis on specific trade practices a provision commonly known as "Super 301,"[42] a mandate that the USTR identify, by 31 May 1989, "priority foreign countries." These were to be named for the "number and pervasiveness" of

---

40. Remarks of Treasury Secretary James Baker at the Institute for International Economics, Washington, 14 September 1987.

41. To appease the administration, the phrase "subject to the specific direction, if any, of the President" was added to the USTR's action authority. Of course, the USTR would be subject to such direction in any case.

42. Actually, Section 310 of the Trade Act of 1974, as amended.

their "acts, policies or practices" that impeded US exports, and for the US export gains that might be anticipated from the removal of these impediments.

To the surprise and pleasure of the USTR (and Congress), two important US trading partners—Korea and Taiwan—were determined *not* to be so designated. To avoid this fate, they offered trade concessions they had previously resisted. The European Community and its Common Agricultural Policy would have met the statutory criteria nicely, but naming Europe was judged politically counterproductive. This left Japan—the prime congressional target of Super 301—and Brazil, with which the United States had been pressing a growing range of trade complaints. Also put on the list was India—a country with highly restrictive trading practices, to be sure, but not the sort of major US trading partner Congress had in mind. To soften the blow against these countries, the USTR limited its indictment to six very specific practices and markets, of the sort it had been pressing in any case. But to appease Congress, it proposed to Japan a separate negotiation outside the 301 framework on "structural impediments" to trade. The resulting Structural Impediments Initiative (SII) talks aimed at the sort of broader import resistance that Danforth and his colleagues had in mind, but the SII dialogue was to be two-way. Japanese could—and did—point to American structural problems as well.

Over the next year, Hills worked a range of trade problems, particularly vis-à-vis Japan, taking care to be responsive to both congressional and industry complaints. By April 1990, the second (and last) Super 301 deadline, she had built the political basis for a bolder approach. Stretching the language of the law to the limit—and perhaps beyond it—she declared that the United States' "top trade liberalization priority for 1990" was neither a specific product nor a particular country, but "the successful completion of the Uruguay Round of global trade talks by December."[43] As for specific countries, Brazil had moved to "dismantle its restrictive import licensing practices," and its new government, under President Fernando Collor de Mello, was "embracing market-driven reforms." According to Hills, Japan had "moved farther and faster than any of our other trading partners in the past twelve months. . . . Given our recent successes, we believe that the most effective way to achieve such results is through cooperation, not confrontation. Therefore, we think it would be counterproductive today to initiate new Super 301 cases against Japan."

She balanced this praise with a warning: "Japan is on notice: We expect maximum efforts that yield results." And because India had refused

---

43. This and subsequent quotations are from Hills's press statement of 24 April 1990, 1, 3 and 4.

to negotiate, it was renamed.[44] But no country was added to the Super 301 list. Members of Congress grumbled, but did nothing more:

> [I]n the week before the announcement [not to rename Japan], members had threatened to scuttle or hold hostage everything from trade agreements with the Soviet Union to the worldwide trade pact being negotiated through the General Agreement on Tariffs and Trade (GATT). . . . But after the announcement, the air seemed to have gone at least temporarily from the balloon.[45]

Geneva Versus Mexico City?

In her first 15 months in office, Hills had built enough credibility to be able to handle Super 301 on her own terms. But the way she did so increased her stakes in a successful Uruguay Round. This was consistent with her interests, and with the US trade policy tradition dating from Cordell Hull. And it made sense economically. Multilateral trade agreements would bring the greatest trade gains, with the partners of greatest importance to the United States. They would also constrain American protectionism and unilateralism. Finally, success in completing another major round would redound to the credit of the USTR.

But Hills inherited the central problem of the Uruguay Round: trade in agricultural products. This was the major area of economic activity least constrained by GATT rules, and the United States stood to gain (for many products) if markets were opened and subsidies reduced. This had been a US goal before, in the Kennedy Round of the 1960s and the Tokyo Round of the 1970s. Each began, in Dale Hathaway's words, "with a resounding declaration of the intent to reform agriculture . . . with the [United States] insisting on reform of the Common Agricultural Policy (CAP) and the Community refusing." In each, the "deadlock" was "finally broken by the United States abandoning its demands."[46] This time, it was declared US policy not to back down. Compounding the difficulty was the negotiating position initially adopted by the Reagan administration, which called for elimination of all trade-distorting measures in agriculture—tariffs, quotas, price supports, production and export subsidies—over a 10-year period. Whatever its substantive merit, this stance was counterproductive politically: it reinforced farmer resistance to concessions in

---

44. But 45 days later, Hills would determine "that India's insurance and investment practices are unreasonable and burden or restrict U.S. commerce, but that retaliation is inappropriate at this time given the ongoing negotiations on services and investments in the Uruguay Round of global trade talks." (USTR Press Release 90-39, 14 June 1990)

45. *Congressional Quarterly*, 5 May 1990, 1333.

46. Dale E. Hathaway, "Agriculture," in Jeffrey J. Schott, ed., *Completing the Uruguay Round: A Results-Oriented Approach to the GATT Trade Negotiations* (Washington: Institute for International Economics, 1990), 51.

Europe, and it postponed serious dialogue internationally and domestically about real-world priorities and possibilities.

Agriculture was but one of 15 Uruguay Round subjects, being addressed by negotiating groups whose settlement deadline was December 1990. And the Uruguay Round was not the only dance on the trade floor. For the Bush administration faced, to its south, a Mexican president, Carlos Salinas de Gortari, who was continuing and accelerating the trade liberalization policies begun by his predecessor, Miguel de la Madrid Hurtado. As noted in chapter 4, Salinas came to President Bush in June 1990 and asked that the United States negotiate a free trade agreement with Mexico, as it had with Canada in 1985–88. The USTR would just as soon have waited—the Uruguay Round was business enough—but Bush decided to move forward. Canada would soon seek to join the talks, and the aim became establishment of a North American Free Trade Area (NAFTA).

The Uruguay Round still had priority—the administration considered it far more important as a trade policy matter, and it was scheduled to conclude before the NAFTA talks could seriously begin. Bush had pressed the matter with colleagues at the seven-nation Houston economic summit that July, recognizing that his counterparts there—French President François Mitterrand, and above all Germany's Chancellor Helmut Kohl—held the key to an agriculture breakthrough. But notwithstanding the earnest efforts promised at that meeting, there was no significant movement in the EC position that fall.

The Brussels ministerial meeting of December 1990 produced a climax quite different from what the round's architects had intended. Carla Hills flew to Europe, accompanied by a large interagency supporting cast, observers from the Hill, and a strong delegation of US private-sector representatives. Also present in the European capital were thousands of angry European farmers. Kohl had just emerged victorious from a historic, all-German election, but his need for farmer support had trumped any commitment to trade compromise, leaving him in no position to return the kindness George Bush had shown in facilitating German reunification. So the talks failed. The agriculture negotiators could not even reach consensus on the framework for an agreement, with Korea and Japan joining the Community in casting crucial, negative votes. When Hills announced that without progress in agriculture the United States would not bargain on other issues, she won cheers from the assembled US private-sector representatives.

Broker in Need of a Breakthrough

As this response illustrated, Hills's tough stand at Brussels was helpful in Washington—for the time being. Senior members of Congress had expressed the view that she might have to "reject a bad agreement if she was to get a good agreement." And Hills had built herself a formidable reputation in the broader trade policy community. She knew the issues. She responded to specific problems raised by legislators, even when she could not offer satisfaction. Though she had never worked on Capitol Hill, she seemed to have an innate sense of what legislators wanted and needed, how much of what they demanded was real and how much was noise.

Her skill at congressional relations in-the-large was not matched by empathy in one-on-one dealings. She lacked the patience, and the personal inclination, to "schmooze" with senators and representatives as Strauss or Brock did. And when she testified at congressional hearings, she could not always mask her negative judgment on the quality of a question. These limitations created problems, according to several reports: for example, when it came time to line up votes for the renewal of the president's fast-track authority in the spring of 1991. Still, the general Washington view was that Hills was an exceptionally competent and effective USTR. Some hardened observers thought she was the best ever to hold the position.

But she needed a major negotiating success. And it had to be the Uruguay Round, on which she had staked so much. It was more than a little awkward for her that the NAFTA had replaced the round on center stage in the fast-track debate. And the possibility, widely reckoned through the summer of 1991, that the NAFTA might actually be completed first created serious policy and political problems. It was the multilateral GATT round that offered the big potential gains to mobilize export constituencies, and the broadest opportunity to advance US trade policy goals. But the demands on Hills compelled her to move wherever the trade opening was. So she and her senior deputy, veteran negotiator Julius Katz, found themselves giving major energy to the Mexico talks, a negotiation that was not central to US *trade* policy priorities, and one that evoked fears—particularly in Asia—of a US movement toward a three-bloc trading world. These fears would be useful if they made Japanese and Koreans readier to make concessions in Geneva. They would be counterproductive if they drove Asians to form their own trade bloc in response.

The ideal scenario for Hills and the United States remained a breakthrough in Brussels, and conclusion of the round by the new target of April 1992. Then, any NAFTA accord would be concluded in the context of a GATT that had a new injection of life. As 1992 began, this scenario looked difficult but possible, as the Germans and even the French showed some movement on CAP reform, and GATT Director General Arthur Dunkel put forward an ambitious, comprehensive compromise proposal for the round as a whole. But major differences persisted. The situation recalled the words of Franklin D. Roosevelt, uttered in very different circumstances a half-century earlier: "Never before have we had so little time in which to do so much."[47]

The USTR Enters Its Thirties

Before these negotiations were to conclude in December 1993, the Office of the United States Trade Representative celebrated its 30th birthday. Throughout its existence, the USTR's power base in the executive branch has proved intermittently difficult to maintain, particularly in the absence of an ongoing major trade negotiation. Presidential support has been anything but consistent. And even when a president backs the USTR's major enterprises—as George Bush generally did—his all-too-typical separation from day-to-day policy development can prove costly in other ways. It seems inconceivable, for example, that Bush would have made the series of policy and political blunders surrounding his January 1992 trip to Tokyo if he had worked as regularly with Carla Hills as he did with Secretary of State James Baker and national security assistant Brent Scowcroft, or if he had spent personally, on trade policy, even 10 percent of the time he spent on political-military matters.[48]

Still, the USTR office has shown renewed vitality time after time—in getting legislative authority for the Tokyo Round; in bringing that round to completion; in resisting trade protection in the 1980s; in launching and negotiating the Uruguay Round; in turning congressionally forced unilateralism to domestic and international advantage; and in winning continued delegation of congressional trade authority, particularly for major negotiations. The USTR entered the 1990s with a continuing—and in some ways strengthened—central role. On the majority of important trade issues, the buck clearly stops there.

But the forces at play seem ever more complex. So for a fuller picture of the problems faced by the USTR and the broader trade policy system, we must turn to other changes—in "the rules" under which trade-injured industries seek relief, and in the altered, more open national political circumstances within which trade policymakers now operate. These are the subjects of chapters 6 and 7.

---

47. Fireside chat of 23 February 1942.

48. For more on this disastrous episode, see chapter 8.

6

Changing the Rules: The Rise of Administrative Trade Remedies

Administrative remedy procedures—"the rules"—played a significant role in concept, and a growing role in practice, in postwar American trade policymaking.

In a manner consistent with Article XIX of the General Agreement on Tariffs and Trade (GATT)—the "escape clause"—US trade laws offered recourse to firms and workers injured by import competition. If they met the statutory criteria, the Tariff Commission could recommend and the president order temporary relief, including tariffs, quotas, or other import restraints.

In addition to such insurance, the rules also provided offsets to "unfair" advantages of foreign competitors, with the sanction of GATT Article VI. In accordance with a statute dating from 1897, if another government gave a "bounty or grant" to a particular industry or firm, the US government, on the petition of the American interests affected, was supposed to impose a countervailing duty (CVD) equivalent to the size of the foreign subsidy. It could impose a similar penalty on imports found to be "dumped," or sold in the US market at "less than fair value," or below the prices at which the good was sold in its home market.

Finally, there was a program to facilitate adjustment. Under the Trade Expansion Act of 1962, if firms were injured or workers lost jobs as a result of import competition, they were eligible for "trade adjustment assistance" (TAA), consisting of financial aid and retraining above and beyond normal unemployment benefits, designed to help them move into new, competitive lines of work.

Up through the early 1970s, however, US firms found it difficult to win relief under these statutes. Eligibility criteria for the escape clause and TAA were tightly drawn, and enforcement of the CVD law was at best a sometime thing. So import-competing interests lobbied successfully for changes in the rules that would broaden eligibility and tighten enforcement. Their success was reflected in the many more petitions for administrative import relief that they submitted in the 1980s, and the fact that, increasingly, they were winning those cases.

Champions of these quasi-judicial procedures defended them as a way to "depoliticize" trade issues, to "run trade on economic law."[1] They were seen as a way to keep trade decisions "out of politics," and petitioners off of legislators' backs, by establishing objective import relief rules that governed the strong and the weak alike. For major industries, however, this was not the actual result. As steel and textile producers moved increasingly to take advantage of these statutes, the effect—and often their clear intent—was not to lower the political temperature but to raise it. In the large cases, "the rules" changed from a means of diverting political pressure to a means of asserting it. Typically, the policy result was not the remedy specified in law but new "special case" protection for the claimants.

Still, changing the rules did succeed in reducing executive discretion and countering a range of "unfair" foreign practices. It made administrative trade relief available to a range of politically inconsequential plaintiffs. Indeed, successive amendments had so tilted the rules for calculating foreign and domestic prices that findings of dumping became nearly automatic!

□ □ □

The trade policy justification for the various quasi-judicial procedures was that they provided options for those damaged by the operation of the open system. The political rationale was that they offered an escape valve, a place for congressmen and executive branch leaders to refer complaints, thus easing the pressure to take immediate trade-restrictive action. There was also the promise of equity. Like other government regulatory procedures, the trade "rules" were supposed to take certain tariff and quota decisions out of the political arena, where benefits went to those with the greatest clout, and entrust them to institutions that would act "objectively," relating the rules to the facts of particular cases.

There was only one problem. In concept, such procedures appeared to give advantages to import-injured petitioners.[2] In practice, however,

---

1. Chairman Charles Vanik (D-OH), US Congress, House Ways and Means Committee, Subcommittee on Trade, *Trade With Japan*, 96th Cong., 2nd sess. (18 September 1980), 140.

2. J. Michael Finger et al. note that the "technical track" favors petitioners because it excludes from the review process those economic interests "who want access to foreign sources of supply." But they concluded that, through the 1970s, "this bias" toward pro-

through most of the postwar period, those who played by these rules tended to come out losers.

Through the Early 1970s: Little Relief

Under the escape clause, the Tariff Commission investigated 113 claims between 1948 and 1962 and recommended relief in 41 cases, but the president provided it in only 15.[3] Things grew worse for affected industries after the Trade Expansion Act of 1962 tightened relief requirements. The Tariff Commission considered 30 cases in the 12 years ended in 1974. It found injury justifying import relief in only four.[4]

Petitioners did not find the countervailing duty law much more helpful. In form, it required relief, as the Supreme Court had declared in 1919:

> A word of broader significance than "grant" could not have been used. . . . And if [a grant] be conferred by a country "upon the exportation of any article or merchandise" a countervailing duty is required. . . .[5]

But the practice proved very different. The law triggered 191 investigations between 1934 and 1968, but only 30 resulted in the imposition of CVDs. In 1968, just 13 CVD orders were in effect, with only 4 of them having been imposed in the 1960s: on canned tomato paste from France and on transmission towers, canned tomatoes, and wire mesh from Italy.[6] There were three more affirmative findings in 1969, and just eight more between 1971 and 1974.[7]

Trade relief was similarly elusive on antidumping cases. Out of 371 processed from 1955 through 1968, only 12 resulted in findings of dumping, although 89 more were concluded by revision in the price or termination of sales.[8]

---

tectionism was "not large": in 1975–79, "only 2.2 percent of US manufactured imports [were] granted relief under the [countervailing duty and antidumping] statutes, and only 3.8 percent under the escape clause." J. M. Finger, H. Keith Hall, and Douglas R. Nelson, "The Political Economy of Administered Protection," *American Economic Review* 72, no. 3 (June 1982): 454, 466.

3. Herbert G. Grubel, *International Economics* (Homewood, IL: Richard D. Irwin, 1981), 174.

4. Tariff Commission, *Annual Report*, Washington, various years.

5. As quoted in Shannon Stock Shuman and Charles Owen Verrill Jr., *Recent Developments in Countervailing Duty Law and Practice*, NBER Conference Report (Cambridge, MA: National Bureau of Economic Research, 1984), 105.

6. US Department of the Treasury, "Report of the Secretary of the Treasury," *Annual Report of the Department of the Treasury, 1968*, Washington, 416.

7. Ibid., Statistical Appendices.

8. Ibid., 416.

Finally, not a single petition for trade adjustment assistance for workers won favorable action in that program's first seven years, through fiscal 1969, even though TAA had been widely supported by liberal trade advocates as a constructive alternative to protection. The volume of petitions went up sharply in the early 1970s, but out of 110,640 workers seeking benefits by the end of 1974, only 48,314 received them.[9]

So in the first 30 postwar years, import-affected industries that played the trade policy game by the legal rules generally lost out.

The immediate effect was to make US markets more open than they otherwise would have been. The failure of these laws to grant meaningful import relief meant that less trade was being restricted. More important was the longer-term impact. Predominantly negative outcomes for petitioners discredited the trade-remedy procedures, discouraging their use and encouraging affected interests to seek direct help from Congress or the administration. This was, of course, exactly what "the rules" were intended to avoid.

As the Kennedy Round drew to a conclusion in 1967, executive branch trade leaders recognized that to restore the credibility of these statutes, they needed to have them amended so that the criteria were less forbidding. Legislators were even more committed to this goal. If the US trade policymaking system was to continue to provide "protection for Congress," other channels had to offer real relief alternatives. Otherwise, pressure on Congress to provide direct, product-specific protection could only increase. Indeed, such pressure built up rapidly in the late 1960s and early 1970s, as evidenced by the House vote in favor of general import quota legislation in 1970 and the introduction of the more restrictive, labor-endorsed Burke-Hartke quota bill the following year.

Twice during the decade of the 1970s, Congress responded to this pressure as one would have predicted: it changed the rules to make administrative trade relief easier for import-affected industries to obtain. It did so in 1974, as part of the Trade Act, authorizing US participation in the Tokyo Round trade negotiations. It did so again in 1979, in the Trade Agreements Act, which approved the round's results.

The Trade Act of 1974

The simplest and most straightforward action in 1974 was that governing the escape clause. The Trade Expansion Act of 1962 had toughened the earlier criterion for relief, by requiring that an industry prove that it had suffered serious injury, the "major cause" of which was imports due to US tariff concessions ("major cause" meant greater than all other fac-

---

9. US Department of Labor, "Labor Issues of American International Trade and Investment" (prepared for the National Manpower Administration Policy Task Force), *Policy Studies in Employment and Welfare*, no. 24, Washington, 1976, 52.

tors combined, a hard standard to meet). Section 201 of the Trade Act of 1974 lowered that threshold, requiring that imports be only a "substantial cause of serious injury, or the threat thereof" (this was defined as "not less than any other cause"). Section 201 also removed the proviso that such injury had to result from specific US tariff concessions.

Congress also sought to encourage favorable findings by increasing the independence of the Tariff Commission, which ruled on industry petitions. The terms of its members were lengthened from six to nine years, and it was renamed the US International Trade Commission (USITC) "because tariffs are no longer the major impediments to trade."[10] Moreover, in cases where the USITC recommended relief, the president was required to act on that recommendation within 60 days. If he did not grant the relief, Congress could override him and enforce the USITC recommendation by majority vote of both houses.[11]

As the 1974 legislation moved toward enactment, there was pressure on the Ford administration to commit itself, in advance, to grant escape clause relief in cases found deserving. To head off pressures from shoe interests for direct statutory benefits in December, Special Trade Representative William D. Eberle wrote a letter to Senator Thomas J. McIntyre (D-NH) declaring that "the escape clause provisions" of the pending Trade Act were "ideally suited for use by the American non-rubber footwear industry" and promising that "if the procedures suggested" that relief was needed, "you can be assured that the Administration would move expeditiously to provide it."[12]

On adjustment assistance, Congress insisted that the program be expanded and made easier to qualify for, notwithstanding organized labor's disillusionment with it and the Nixon administration's skepticism about the appropriateness of a special program for workers displaced by trade. One reason few workers had previously been eligible was that the criterion was essentially the same as those for tariffs or quotas: imports had to be the "major cause" of unemployment or underemployment. House Ways and Means Committee members thought trade adjustment assistance should be the easiest form of relief to obtain. So the law was changed to open it to workers for whom "increases of imports . . . con-

---

10. US Congress, Senate Committee on Finance, *Trade Reform Act of 1974*, 93rd Cong., 2nd sess. (26 November 1974), S. Rept. 93-1208, 25.

11. In *Immigration and Naturalization Service v. Chadha*, the US Supreme Court declared a similar legislative veto provision unconstitutional, on grounds that it did not provide for "presentment to the President," as in the normal legislative process. Congress responded, in the Trade and Tariff Act of 1984, by providing for a joint resolution congressional veto for presidential decisions under Section 201. Such a resolution is presented to the chief executive for his signature; should the president veto it, a two-thirds majority of both houses would be required to override.

12. Eberle to McIntyre, *Congressional Record*, 13 December 1974, 39813.

tributed importantly to loss of jobs." The magnitude and duration of benefits were also increased.

But the primary focus of efforts to "change the rules" in the early 1970s was the alleged foreign abuses covered by the CVD and antidumping statutes, addressed in a rather lengthy Trade Act title labeled "Relief from *Unfair* Trade Practices" (emphasis added).

This was a natural, even inevitable, emphasis, for the Kennedy Round's success in reducing industrial tariff levels had focused attention on nontariff barriers (NTBs) and other trade-distorting governmental practices. Among those thought to require regulation or discipline, subsidies were at the top of the list for American trade specialists. To some, in Gary Clyde Hufbauer's metaphor, subsidies were a "rising reef," increasingly granted in order to buttress favored industries and influence trade flows. Others concluded, more modestly, that it was the "falling water level" of reduced tariffs that had made the NTB reef more important, and certainly more visible.[13]

Joined with increased complaints about foreign subsidies was the sense that the United States was not doing much to combat them. Concerning the primary statute designed to counter such subsidies, the Senate Finance Committee expressed unhappiness "that the Treasury Department has used the absence of time limits to stretch out or even shelve countervailing duty investigations for reasons which have nothing to do with the clear and mandatory nature of the countervailing duty law."[14] This charge was not ungrounded, for at the administration end of Pennsylvania Avenue, particularly in the Treasury, there was a fairly widespread view that the law was archaic, with its old-fashioned language ("bounty or grant") and 19th century origins.

The increased attention to nontariff trade distortions, and above all to subsidies, reinforced the widespread Washington perception that other countries were taking advantage of the United States, that it was, in the words of Nixon White House aide Peter M. Flanigan, "more sinned against than sinning."[15] There was—and is currently—evidence to support this view. One study of overall Organization for Economic Cooperation and Development (OECD) data concludes that, among the seven major advanced industrial countries, "the United States has persistently exhibited the lowest ration of subsidies to GDP and, unlike [that of] other countries, the US ratio has declined since the late 1960s."[16] More-

---

13. Gary Clyde Hufbauer and Joanna Shelton Erb, *Subsidies in International Trade* (Washington: Institute for International Economics, 1984), 2.

14. US Congress, Senate Committee on Finance, *Trade Reform Act of 1974*, 93rd Cong., 2nd sess. (26 November 1974), 183.

15. Quoted in *National Journal*, 13 January 1973, 45.

16. Hufbauer and Shelton Erb, *Subsidies in International Trade*, 2.

over, the opaqueness of governments' nontariff policies affecting trade—
the difficulty in seeing and measuring them and determining their extent—made it hard to resist those who argued that such foreign practices were endemic and the United States needed to respond forcefully.[17]
The record on CVDs and dumping suggested that it had not been doing
so.

One way Congress addressed this problem was by making clear that
subsidies should be given priority in the upcoming Tokyo Round, in
which nontariff trade distortions were to be the central focus. The other
way was to tighten the remedy procedures. On countervailing duties,
the 1974 act added a requirement that final action be taken within a
year of receipt of a petition and made provision for judicial review of
decisions that denied relief. Such review was also provided for negative
antidumping decisions. One technical provision required the Treasury
Department to disregard certain low-cost home-market sales in determining the price against which export sales were compared to ascertain
whether dumping existed. This had the effect of favoring petitioners
and could even lead to findings of dumping in cases in which the average home and export prices were the same!

The Result: Slightly More Relief

The immediate response to the changing of the rules in 1974 was for
firms to file many more cases and for the government to move more
expeditiously in handling them. Petitions for escape clause relief, for
example, rose from 2 in 1973 (and none in 1974) to 13 in 1975. The
number of CVD investigations initiated shot up from 1 in 1973 (and 5 in
1974) to 38 in 1975, both because new claims were being submitted and
because the Treasury was moving faster on old ones under the new
timetable.[18]

But in terms of actual relief granted, industry petitioners were again
to be disappointed.

The new escape clause criteria established by Section 201 were affecting the US International Trade Commission, which was now finding
regularly in petitioners' favor. Between 1975 and 1990, the commission
conducted 62 investigations, which resulted in 30 affirmative determina-

---

17. For a perceptive discussion of how the opaqueness of nontax trade policy nourishes
perceptions of foreign "unfairness," see J. David Richardson, *Currents and Cross-Currents
in the Flow of U.S. Trade Policy*, NBER Conference Report (Cambridge, MA: National
Bureau of Economic Research, 1984), 2–3.

18. *International Economic Report of the President* (Washington: Government Printing Office, March 1976), 45.

tions. This 48 percent success rate at the USITC for those who sought relief contrasted sharply with the 13 percent rate (4 of 30) under the previous law. And the escape clause cases included important import-affected industries: carbon and specialty steel, shoes, color television sets, and, grandest of all, automobiles.

In the 1974 act, however, Congress had reluctantly retained the president's discretion to modify or reject a USITC relief recommendation, provided he determined that "provision of such relief is not in the national economic interest of the United States." This was a broader criterion than the industry-specific rules that governed the decisions of the commission. Applying this more comprehensive standard, presidents repeatedly rejected or modified the commission's escape clause recommendations.

In the 30 cases in which the USITC recommended import relief between 1975 and 1990, the president ordered tariffs or quotas in only 10 and denied all relief in 12. In five cases, he provided only adjustment assistance, and in the remaining three he initiated negotiations leading to orderly marketing agreements (OMAs) with the exporting nations to limit their sales. Congress complained that the law was not being implemented, but it never actually voted to override the president.

As it did prior to the 1974 Trade Act, this situation again yielded present gains for the liberal trade order.[19] But it piled up future costs, for the effect was to discredit the process, perhaps more than previously. Before, almost nobody got relief, but at least the rules were being followed. Now, industries were playing by the rules and winning in the USITC, only to have those decisions reversed by the president, who asserted his prerogative in an opaque White House decision-making process in which they had no established role. The footwear case of 1976 was a good example. The Ford administration's trade representative had promised favorable consideration of such a case when the Trade Act was before the Senate. But it reached the president for decision one month after he had granted relief to the specialty steel industry, and Ford was worried about the international repercussions of restricting trade twice in a row. So he rejected import relief, granting only adjustment assistance.[20]

The shoe case was in fact reconsidered, and the Carter administration negotiated export restraint agreements with Korea and Taiwan a year later. Nor was this unique. The producers of "bolts, nuts, and large

---

19. For a detailed analysis welcoming this result, see Walter Adams and Joel B. Dirlam, "Import Competition and the Trade Act of 1974: A Case Study of Section 201 and its Interpretation by the International Trade Commission," *Indiana Law Journal* 52, no. 3 (Spring 1977): 535–99.

20. See Roger Porter, *Presidential Decision Making: The Economic Policy Board* (Cambridge: Cambridge University Press, 1980), chap. 6.

screws," to cite another example from the latter 1970s, were denied relief by President Carter in 1978, only to be granted it the next year after strong congressional pressure led to reconsideration of their case.

These and other cases illustrate how, by easing the criteria but retaining presidential discretion, Congress had turned the political process on its head. The aim had been to take trade "out of politics." But once the USITC began regularly finding in petitioners' favor, product cases were thrown squarely into the political arena and resolved in a process governed by different "rules" entirely. The president had to weigh the demands of an injured industry, of trade politics, and sometimes of electoral support against the interests of the larger economy, the need to combat inflation, the demands of international economic leadership, etc. Industries had reason to fear that their legitimate cases would get lost in this larger shuffle.

The escape clause received a further blow in the automobile case of 1980, the most important and visible import issue ever addressed under the procedure. The American auto industry and its workers were suffering a severe drop in their production and sales, which was clearly exacerbated by record Japanese imports. Yet a three-to-two majority of USITC members found that the industry failed to meet the "substantial cause" criterion: factors other than imports were more important causes of the industry's plight—above all, the shift in market demand toward smaller cars brought about by the oil price increase of 1979. Thus, the USITC was unable to recommend relief.

The decision was defensible in terms of the law, and while the USITC might have found "threat of injury" from imports, the case for such a determination was not made effectively by the petitioners. Nonetheless, the result was to further discredit Section 201. The US political system found the negative outcome impossible to live with. House Trade Subcommittee Chairman Charles A. Vanik (D-OH) had argued repeatedly for running trade according to the rules, "depoliticizing" it. Yet when the "economic law" produced a negative outcome on autos, he was quick to call hearings to explore the need for alternative trade action.

In response to congressional pressure, and to a Reagan campaign commitment, the new administration ended up pressing—successfully—for Japanese voluntary restraint. As a result, the escape clause procedure was further discredited. In the three years after 1980, the USITC received only four escape clause petitions.

On countervailing duties—unlike the escape clause—there is no general presidential authority to override the procedure in the name of broader American interests. The basic law is mandatory: if a subsidy is found, a duty "shall be imposed." However, a special waiver authority was added for the Tokyo Round multilateral trade negotiations (MTN) of the 1970s, in which a primary US negotiating goal was to discipline trade-distorting subsidies.

The US government had something to give on this issue. Contrary to GATT rules, as Europeans had long complained, US law did not require that injury be found from dutiable imports before a CVD was imposed. Europeans were not about to negotiate if the United States simultaneously began enforcing a tough antisubsidy statute. So Congress reluctantly granted the secretary of the Treasury the authority to waive imposition of CVDs for four years if the foreign government was taking steps to reduce a subsidy's effect, and if the secretary found that imposition of a duty would "seriously jeopardize" completion of the MTN, including the desired subsidies code.

In practice, this waiver authority took away from affected industries much of the gain that the 1974 act provided. From 1976 through 1978, for example, the Treasury made a total of 35 affirmative CVD decisions, a marked increase from previous years. But the secretary then exercised the waiver in 19 of the cases. More than half of the time, then, "successful" petitioners were denied the full remedy that the law, in principle, provided.[21]

In contrast, the number of antidumping cases during this period remained at about the level of previous years. However, the filing of a large number of such cases by the steel industry in 1977 led the Carter administration to establish a price floor on imports with the trigger-price mechanism, which was enforced under the antidumping law.[22]

In summary, in the years after 1974, industries were getting only slightly more relief from administrative procedures than they had before—Trade Act changes notwithstanding. So unhappiness built up again about the remedy procedures. The House Ways and Means Committee reflected this in 1979, declaring that "both the countervailing duty and antidumping duty laws have been inadequately enforced in the past, including the lack of resources devoted to this important area of law."[23]

The Trade Agreements Act of 1979

The required approval of the MTN in 1979 gave Congress a new opportunity to act. The minimum need was legislation to implement the nontariff

---

21. US Department of the Treasury, *Annual Report*, Washington, various issues; US Congress, House Committee on Ways and Means, *Temporary Extension of Countervailing Duty Waiver Authority*, 96th Cong., 1st sess. (22 February 1979), H. Rept. 96-15. The latter describes the 19 waivers and their status as of the report date.

22. See Hideo Sato and Michael W. Hodin, "The U.S.-Japanese Steel Issue of 1977," in I. M. Destler and Hideo Sato, eds., *Coping With U.S.-Japanese Trade Conflicts* (Lexington, MA: Lexington Books, 1982), 27–72.

23. US Congress, House Committee on Ways and Means, *Trade Agreements Act of 1979*, 96th Cong., 1st sess. (3 July 1979), H. Rept. 96-317.

barrier codes completed early that year. Since the principal countries were unable to resolve their differences on escape clause issues, the intended safeguards code was not completed. So Section 201, the US law governing escape clause relief, was left unchanged.

The codes on subsidies and countervailing measures and on antidumping, however, were the MTN's centerpieces. The negotiation of the former had been fueled by a widely shared conviction, in the words of one leading authority, that "the current rules on subsidies and countervailing duties" were "woefully inadequate to cope with the pressures put upon importing economies by a myriad of subtle (and sometimes not so subtle) governmental aids to exports."[24] Now that the code was completed, legislation was necessary to make US law conform. The United States had to incorporate in its statutes the requirement that "material injury" be proven before countervailing duties were imposed on imports from countries adhering to the code. But nothing barred more extensive statutory changes as long as they were consistent with the codes and other US international obligations. So revision of these statutes became part of the bargaining process for MTN ratification.

In the 1974 act, Congress had committed itself to an expeditious, up-or-down vote on whatever implementing legislation the president submitted (see chapter 4). To ensure congressional support for this legislation, Special Trade Representative Robert S. Strauss, who led the Carter administration's negotiating enterprise at home as well as abroad, accepted the proposal of the Senate Finance Committee to have the bill designed and drafted on Capitol Hill, as a collaborative effort of the two branches. Key industries like steel, and concerned senators like John Heinz (R-PA), made it clear that their priority was the trade-remedy laws. They wanted to insure, this time, that they would provide petitioners effective and timely relief. And Strauss saw this as a tolerable price for their support.

The most visible change—a "material injury" test for all CVDs on products of countries adhering to the new code—had the formal effect of tightening the criteria relief-seeking firms had to meet. Here, the administration and the House Ways and Means Committee prevailed over a Senate Finance Committee proposal to soften the requirement to the single word, "injury." Lobbyists for the European Community actively supported the tougher standard. Still, "material injury" was defined as "harm which is not inconsequential, immaterial or unimportant"; this is significantly less demanding than the escape clause test that imports be "a substantial cause of serious injury." More important, perhaps, by bringing US law into conformity with GATT and international practice, the injury standard legitimized use of CVDs in future cases.

---

24. John H. Jackson, "The Crumbling Institutions of the Liberal Trade System," *Journal of World Trade Law* 12, no. 2 (March–April 1978): 95.

If the new injury test affected the criteria for obtaining relief, the Trade Agreements Act of 1979 employed a different means to aid petitioners—reforming the law's procedures and administration. Tighter time limits were mandated not just for CVD cases taken as a whole, but for their specific stages; for example, an investigation had to be initiated within 20 days, and only "clearly frivolous" petitions, or those lacking key information reasonably available to petitioners, were to be dismissed without any formal investigation. The overall timetable from initiation to final determination was compressed, in normal cases, from a year to seven months. This tended to favor petitioners, since foreign governments and firms had less time to develop the complicated countercases that were needed to rebut the data of those seeking relief. Moreover, if there was a preliminary finding of subsidy (and injury), importers would now have to post a deposit just three months (instead of a year) after a petition was submitted. Thus effective trade restraint could be obtained much sooner.

There were also a number of changes aimed at greater procedural openness. Administrative protective orders gave petitioners' counsel access to confidential business information supplied to the government by foreign exporters. Limits were imposed on private ex parte meetings between government officials and one party to a case; the substance of these meetings now had to be made public. Rights to public hearings and judicial review were also expanded. For example, labor unions and trade associations that had not initiated a case could now appeal. Parallel steps were taken on antidumping procedures to shorten time limits, advance the time when exporting firms had to pay or advance penalty duties, and promote openness and judicial review.

But in retrospect the most important single change was organizational, the shift of administrative responsibility for the unfair-trade remedies laws. This, although not an explicit provision of the Trade Agreements Act of 1979, was a not-so-subtle condition of its approval, as the Senate Finance Committee declined to bring that act to the floor until the president had submitted a comprehensive trade reorganization plan. In this plan, the power to enforce the rewritten CVD and antidumping laws was delegated not to the secretary of the Treasury—the responsible official under the law since 1897—but to the secretary of Commerce. Members of both key congressional committees were convinced that his department would take the job more seriously and be more sympathetic to industry concerns.

The Declining Use of the Escape Clause

How did the administrative trade remedies—"the rules" as amended—play out in practice after 1979? The most dramatic development was the

Figure 6.1 Escape clause investigations, 1979–94

Number of investigations

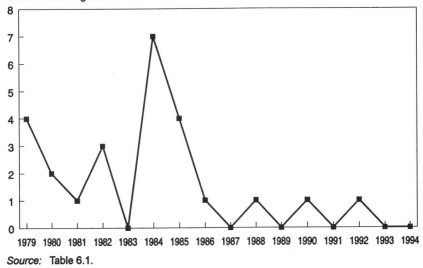

Source: Table 6.1.

Figure 6.2 Countervailing duty and antidumping investigations, 1979–94

Number of investigations

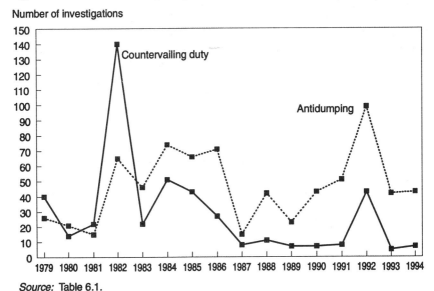

Source: Table 6.1.

contrast between the declining use of Section 201 and adjustment assistance and the upsurge in new petitions alleging unfair foreign trade practices. (See figures 6.1 and 6.2.)

The escape clause was used above all during the Reagan reelection campaign. The USITC ruled on just one case in 1981, one case in 1982, and two cases in 1983. January 1984, however, saw the carbon steel, shoe, copper, and table flatware industries all submitting petitions, in order to pressure the Reagan White House for sympathetic action at a time of maximum political vulnerability.[25] By March, the USITC suddenly found itself investigating no fewer than five escape clause cases. Section 201 had been transformed from a means of diverting political pressure into a device for asserting it. In two prominent cases—steel and copper—the USITC recommended protection, forcing presidential decisions in September, within two months of the general election. The president denied relief to the copper industry but ordered negotiation of export restraint agreements for steel, as spelled out later in this chapter.

The footwear industry was not so fortunate. In July 1984, the USITC made a unanimous negative finding on injury, because manufacturers' profits were high. At the initiative of Senator John C. Danforth (R-MO), Congress then changed the law so that profits could not be, by themselves, the decisive USITC criterion. The industry then resubmitted its case in December. Responding to the statutory change and a worsening of the industry's plight, the USITC now recommended stringent quotas. But now President Reagan said no, denying all import relief to the footwear industry in August 1985.

The rest of the decade saw only one more successful escape clause case—the petition of the wood shingles and shakes producers claiming injury from Canadian competition. Concerned about generating support for US-Canada free trade negotiations, President Reagan imposed in May 1986 a declining tariff with a peak of 35 percent. But there were only six more escape clause petitioners from that case through 1990, and none of them met the USITC's injury threshold.[26]

The Decline of Trade Adjustment Assistance

Also in decline over this period was that pressure-diverting program that had once seemed most promising and constructive: trade adjustment assistance for workers.

When such a program was originally proposed, the most sophisticated postwar study of trade policymaking lauded it as an approach that

---

25. In 1980, the United Auto Workers—in what was widely seen as a political blunder— did not submit its auto escape clause petition until June; as a result, the USITC did not reach its finding until after the November election.

26. The decline of the dollar made injury harder to establish, just as its rise had made it easier.

"could destroy the political basis of protectionism by giving the injured an alternative way out."[27] But because the injury threshold was originally set so high, it yielded little trade relief in the decade after its enactment in 1962. In the late 1970s, however, following the 1974 act's expansion of benefits and easing of eligibility criteria, this program began at last to be seriously tested. The explosion of TAA claims (mainly from laid-off auto workers), combined with the very generous financial benefits provided, drove the cost to $1.6 billion in fiscal year 1980, six times the previous peak.[28]

Jimmy Carter pointed to this expansion as a humane response to the workers' plight and a constructive alternative to protection. But Ronald Reagan came to power looking for programs to cut and predisposed against the economic interventionism that TAA exemplified. Since analytic studies indicated that TAA was not in practice fulfilling the goal of adjustment—helping workers move to other, more competitive industries—it was a vulnerable target for Reagan's new budget director, David A. Stockman, who was opposed to entitlement programs available only to certain groups of workers. Nor did the Reagan administration make this program a chosen instrument when it shifted to trade activism in the fall of 1985.[29]

So beginning with the Omnibus Budget Reconciliation Act of 1981, the level and duration of benefits were cut and total program funds were slashed. Stipends were limited to the level of regular unemployment insurance, whereas previously they had supplemented such benefits. Moreover, they were now available only after a worker's eligibility for unemployment benefits had been exhausted, and they were generally limited—by a 1988 amendment—to workers undergoing retraining. Congressional champions managed, through persistent effort, to keep TAA alive in statute. And a modest additional trade adjustment program was inaugurated in 1994 for workers displaced by NAFTA. But as of 1994, the overall TAA budget (including NAFTA)

---

27. Raymond A. Bauer, Ithiel de Sola Pool, and Lewis Anthony Dexter, *American Business and Public Policy: The Politics of Foreign Trade* (Chicago: Aldine-Atherton, second edition, 1972), 43.

28. C. Michael Aho and Thomas O. Bayard, "Costs and Benefits of Trade Adjustment Assistance," in Robert E. Baldwin and Anne O. Krueger, eds., *The Structure and Evolution of Recent US Trade Policy* (Chicago: University of Chicago Press, 1984), 184. For a comprehensive assessment of trade adjustment programs, see Gary Clyde Hufbauer and Howard F. Rosen, *Trade Policy for Troubled Industries*, POLICY ANALYSES IN INTERNATIONAL ECONOMICS 15 (Washington: Institute for International Economics, 1986).

29. Howard Rosen, "US Assistance for Trade-Related Workers: A Need for Better Coordination and Reform," statement before US Congress, House Committee on Ways and Means, Subcommittee on Trade (1 August 1991), processed, 8–12.

totaled only about $200 million annually, with just 65,000 workers eligible for benefits.

The Upsurge in "Unfair Trade" Cases

But if use of the escape clause has waned, and if TAA has barely survived, there has been a sharp increase in petitions under the unfair-trade practices statutes. The rise in the number of cases makes it clear that Congress succeeded in 1979 where it had failed in 1974. Many more cases are being submitted, covering a much greater volume of trade. And many more are being decided in petitioners' favor. For the first time, the process has been a serious one, with the responsible bureaucracy (the Commerce Department) making a strong effort to administer it according to its intended purposes. Reflecting on the experience of the 1980s, Gary Horlick and Geoffrey Oliver wrote that the "AD[antidumping]/CVD laws have become the usual first choice for industries seeking protection from imports into the U.S."[30]

There was an explosion in the volume of cases.[31] In response to industry petitions, Commerce initiated a total of 249 CVD investigations in the 1980–84 period, and 96 more in 1985–89. (This compares with one investigation initiated in 1973 and five in 1974.) Parallel antidumping investigation numbers were 221 for 1980–84 and 217 for 1985–89.

Moreover, when petitioners sought relief under these statutes, they more often than not obtained it. Of 258 CVD petitions carried through the full statutory process, 135, or 52 percent, won either imposition of duties or suspension of the offending foreign practice. The remaining 87 were withdrawn by petitioners, almost always because the source nation had promised to limit exports. On antidumping, the numbers were similar—out of 327 petitions carried to term, 173 (53 percent) resulted in duties or suspension agreements, and 111 more petitions were withdrawn, largely after agreement on voluntary export restraints.

Moreover, unlike relief under the escape clause—which is limited to a

---

30. Gary N. Horlick and Geoffrey D. Oliver, "Antidumping and Countervailing Duty Law Provisions of the Omnibus Trade and Competitiveness Act of 1988," *Journal of World Trade*, 23, no. 3 (June 1989): 5.

31. The numbers that follow are a compilation based on analysis and cross-checking of data from a range of documents, including Commerce Department reports submitted semiannually to the GATT; USTR Trade Action Monitoring System reports; USITC annual reports; congressional hearings; other Commerce, USTR, and USITC reports, and the *Federal Register*. These have been supplemented by direct communication with responsible officials to fill gaps and resolve contradictions. I am grateful to Diane T. Berliner for her persistent and painstaking work in putting these numbers together for the original edition, and to Paul W. Baker for his equally thorough and professional effort in reviewing and updating them in the second edition.

specified term—CVD and antidumping relief continues indefinitely, unless and until a Commerce Department review determines that circumstances no longer justify it. Thus, at the end of 1990 there were 72 countervailing duties still in effect, and 202 antidumping duties. This compares with 56 and 137, respectively, in effect in mid-1983.

The new industry success with the unfair-trade statutes was not accidental. There was now, for the first time, a serious enforcement operation: a core group of professionals organized to give priority to their implementation, determined to develop methods for the complex calculations required, and ready to decide cases on their merits as set forth in the law.[32]

A large volume of trade business is now being channeled through these procedures. So if the original political logic remained valid, both the petitioning industries and the supporters of liberal trade would be more or less satisfied. The former would be pleased because their cases are at last being judged on their merits, with trade relief the frequent outcome. The latter might be concerned about the increase in import restrictions, but comforted because they were being imposed by apolitical, quasi-judicial procedures that considered each case in isolation, protecting Congress and minimizing the risk of protectionist contagion.

In the real world, alas, almost no one seems happy with the result. Affected industries continue to protest the laws' inadequacy and seek their further elaboration and complication to cover imports that still escape their reach. But the same lack of executive branch discretion that keeps executive officials from denying or diluting relief also prevents them from tailoring it to an industry's needs, whether the goal be protection or adjustment.

Foreign interests are dismayed because the trade-remedy procedures seem arbitrary and unfair (and expensive) to them. (And liberal trade advocates are dismayed by one result of such frustrations—the increased use of the trade-remedy laws not to keep decisions "out of politics" but to raise their political prominence and force political solutions.) Foreigners are also unhappy because the US legal tradition clashes with their more discretionary ways of handling such issues. US laws are, for the most part, GATT-consistent, proper under the international trade rules that Americans have done so much to create. Indeed, elaborating these rules was one of the prime accomplishments of the Tokyo Round. But other peoples—Europeans, Japanese, Koreans, Brazilians—see "due process" for American domestic interests as a threat to their interests.

They (the Europeans above all) are anxious about the real trade ef-

---

32. See Shuman and Verrill, "Recent Developments." See also the candid testimony of former Deputy Assistant Secretary of Commerce Gary Horlick in US Congress, House Committee on Ways and Means, *Options to Improve the Trade Remedy Laws*, 98th Cong., 1st sess. (16 March 1983), part 2, 535–87.

fects of US legal decisions: their overall magnitude and how the pain will be distributed among foreign suppliers. They are unwilling to let their fates be determined by procedures that might seem objective and fair and nonpolitical to Americans, but which to foreign eyes appear both unpredictable and skewed in favor of the import-affected petitioner. And these cases inevitably involve "a host of arbitrary determinations":[33] calculating fair value, the full cost of production, the effect of different government programs on export prices, etc. Indeed, expert GATT panels began meeting after the Tokyo Round to try to establish common standards for such determinations, with negotiations continuing into the Uruguay Round. But progress has been hard to come by.

So it is not surprising that foreign firms and governments press for alternatives. If US processes are going to end up restricting their trade, they want to have a voice in how the pain is allocated.

Actually, the 1979 law did create one new procedure for negotiating an end to a trade-remedy case. In a major departure from previous trade laws, it authorizes "suspension of investigations" through agreements with foreign governments, or with "exporters representing substantially all of the imports of the merchandise"[34] covered by a case. But Congress sought to ensure that the purposes of the laws would not be subverted by conditioning such suspension on one of two forms of remedial action: elimination of subsidies or dumping (directly, or through imposition of an offset like an export tax), or elimination of their injurious effect. In other words, the point is to remove the subsidy, or at least its trade impact, not to bargain about market share.[35]

Typically, foreign firms and governments want more leeway than this. They may not agree with US legal determination of subsidy or "less-than-fair-value" (dumped) sales, and even if they do, they may have their own political or legal problems in complying. US firms have recognized and exploited this foreign vulnerability. Beginning with the steel antidumping petitions of 1977, they began to submit cases that seem aimed less at achieving the specific relief provided by statute than at creating an intolerable situation for foreign competitors, forcing them to come to the bargaining table and cut deals. Once a satisfactory arrangement is reached, the constraints of the law on suspension of investigations are circumvented by a simple device: the complaining industry

33. Robert W. Crandall, "The EEC-US Steel Trade Crisis," paper prepared for Symposium on Euro-American Relations and Global Economic Interdependence, College of Europe (Bruges, Belgium, 13 September 1984). Quoted with permission.

34. House Committee on Ways and Means, *Trade Agreements Act of 1979*, 54.

35. For a description and defense of Commerce Department administration of this provision through mid-1984, see Alan F. Holmer and Judith H. Bello, "U.S. Import Law and Policy Series: Suspension and Settlement Agreements in Unfair Trade Cases," *International Lawyer* 18, no. 3 (Summer 1984): 683–97.

withdraws its petition, and Commerce then terminates the investigation, as the law explicitly allows.

Forcing Political Solutions

A dramatic illustration came in the steel cases of 1982. There was little doubt that some foreigners were subsidizing steel that was being shipped to the US market: within Europe, the French and British were especially guilty.[36] So when on 11 January 1982, seven US steelmakers jointly delivered 494 boxes containing 3 million pages of documentation for 132 countervailing and antidumping petitions against foreign (mainly European Community) suppliers, this flood of litigation had real-world justification. And the remedy sought was the proper one provided under American law. Further petitions followed, bringing the total for 1982 to about 150.[37]

But there was little doubt also that pursuing these cases to their legal conclusion would be highly disruptive to the steel industries of individual European Community countries and to the network of political understandings among them. Inevitably, the Europeans sought to bargain. And US Secretary of Commerce Malcolm Baldrige was pushed into the position of brokering between foreign governments and domestic steel makers for a trade-restricting arrangement entirely outside established procedures. Under this arrangement the EC "voluntarily" restricted carbon steel exports to the United States to 5.44 percent of the US market. And while this overall limit corresponded roughly to what the outcome of enforcing US law would have been, the Europeans dis-

36. For one comprehensive effort to catalog such subsidies, see Bethlehem Steel Corporation and United States Steel Corporation, "Government Aid to the Steel Industry of the European Communities: Market Distortion in Europe and Its Impact on the U.S. Steel Industry," report prepared by Verner, Liipfert, Bernhard, McPherson, and Hand (Washington, 1984).

It does not follow, however, that foreign subsidies are the primary cause of US industry woes, or that their removal would bring substantial market relief. Robert W. Crandall argues, in fact, that while in an entirely private (nonsubsidized) European steel industry the worth of plants might be very much lower, "no one has presented any convincing evidence that capacity and output would be much lower under such a regime." And even if European output and exports did fall, "Brazil, Taiwan, Korea, and even Canada and Japan have the ability to expand their output and even their capacity substantially in response to any upward movement in export prices." See Crandall, "The EEC-US Steel Trade Crisis," 26.

37. US International Trade Commission, Annual Report, 1982, Washington, x; Office of the United States Trade Representative, *Twenty-sixth Annual Report of the President of the United States on the Trade Agreements Program, 1981–82*, Washington, November 1982, 114; Timothy B. Clark, "When Demand Is Down, Competition Up, That Spells Trouble for American Steel," *National Journal*, 7 January 1984, 9.

tributed the pain among themselves so that the efficient Germans ended up worse off than they would have been, and the inefficient British and French better off.[38]

In the fall of 1983 came another example of a major industry initiating an unfair-trade case in order to exert political pressure. This one involved China and textiles. Unhappy with the terms of a bilateral quota agreement concluded in August, the US textile industry retaliated with an innovative suit, alleging that China's dual exchange rate system constituted a subsidy under the CVD law.

This put US authorities in another bind. They had just reached a deal with a foreign government, but its substance was being threatened by a procedure over which they had little control in the short run. They feared that, to Beijing, the administration would appear either two-faced or impotent at a time when the president was preparing for a major state visit the following spring. And the Chinese government, choosing to treat the matter as an internal US problem, resisted supplying information to contest the suit.

The administration might have ridden the storm out internationally and domestically.[39] But senators from key textile states—Strom Thurmond (R-SC) and Jesse Helms (R-NC)—were up for reelection in 1984. They pressed the White House to do something for the industry. President Reagan, also up for reelection, saw personal political advantage in responding; moreover, in the 1980 campaign, he had made a general commitment to moderate the growth of textile imports. So in December 1983, against the overwhelming advice of his cabinet, he ordered a deal that gave the US textile industry tighter enforcement of existing quota arrangements, not particularly vis-à-vis mainland China but on East Asian imports generally. The industry then withdrew its suit at the last possible moment. Reagan had appeased the textile people without alienating Beijing, but at the cost of further compromise of both trade process and trade policy.

As 1984 began, the steel industry inaugurated a new round with the

---

38. It was primarily the Europeans who administered the restraint. However, to be on the safe side, the Commerce Department—with the aid of Senator Heinz and over the procedural protests of House Trade Subcommittee leaders—slipped through Congress an amendment to the Tariff Act of 1930 providing that "steel mill products" under arrangements entered into "prior to January 1, 1983" would be denied entry into the United States if they lacked proper foreign government documentation. (*Congressional Record*, 29 September 1982, S12474–75; *Congressional Record*, 1 October 1982, H8368–71, H8388–89.) With these "arrangements" completed, the industry petitioners withdrew their suits.

39. In May 1984, in fact, the Commerce Department would rule that the CVD law did not apply to imports from non-market-economy countries, and this position was later upheld in the Federal Circuit Court of Appeals. (Without a competitive market as a reference point, the word "subsidy" loses its meaning.)

same old tactics. With European sales fixed at about 5 percent of US consumption and the Japanese informally limiting themselves to about the same amount, the remaining threat was the newly industrializing countries: Brazil, Mexico, and Korea in particular. Again, there was a blizzard of paper, with multiple submissions of CVD and antidumping cases. This time no one tried very hard to conceal the political rationale. As David M. Roderick of United States Steel told a press breakfast in early February, US firms planned to file "a tremendous number" of unfair trade complaints, aiming to make the total impact so "burdensome" that the administration, and "all players of substance in the import game . . . would be very pleased to enter into quotas in a negotiated manner."[40]

The steel industry had been the prime force behind the legislative changes of 1979 and the prime user of the rules on unfair-trade practices since then. Now its explicit goal was "temporary" steel import quotas, however they might be achieved or implemented. The results would demonstrate that for trade also, in Justice Holmes's words, "great cases make bad law."[41]

Steel Wins Comprehensive Protection

What ended up forcing a decision was an action by United States Steel's principal rival, Bethlehem Steel, and their union, the United Steelworkers. Citing an increase in the market share taken by imports from 15 percent in 1979 to 25 percent in early 1984, at a time of decline in domestic production and a 200,000-person drop in steel employment, they submitted an escape clause petition in January 1984, seeking protection so that domestic firms could generate the cash flow to remain in business and finance modernization. (During this same time period, the industry in general was also pushing a quota bill to limit imports to 15 percent of the US market, as well as the flood of CVD and antidumping cases referred to earlier.)

The following July, the USITC found by a three-to-two vote that imports had been a substantial cause of serious injury in five of the nine major steel-import categories. For relief it recommended a mixture of tariffs, quotas, and tariff-rate quotas for five years on products in those five categories. This recommendation came in late July, and under the law the president had just 60 days to implement, modify, or reject it.

Ronald Reagan's response, in the midst of the general election cam-

---

40. *Washington Post*, 9 February 1984.

41. Oliver Wendell Holmes Jr., *Northern Securities Company v. United States*, 193 US 197, 400 (1904).

paign, was, in the words of one administration insider, "a masterpiece of blue smoke and mirrors."[42] He had his trade representative, William E. Brock, announce that the president was rejecting the USITC recommendation: "The President has clearly determined that protectionism is not in the national interest. It costs jobs, raises prices and undermines our ability to compete here and abroad."[43] But having hoisted the banner of free trade in the first paragraph, Brock's announcement then "noted," in the second paragraph, that American steel firms and workers faced an "unprecedented and unacceptable" surge of imported steel due both to "massive unfair trade practices" and "diversion of steel imports into the US markets due to quotas and import restraints in other nations."[44] Brock would therefore "consult with those nations responsible . . . with a view toward the elimination of such practices." Meanwhile, the government was "to vigorously enforce US fair trade laws."

So far, so good, perhaps. But after further bows to the need "to liberalize world trade" and not "put at risk the exports of our farmers and other workers in export industries," the statement reached the crux of the matter on its third page:

> The president's decision assumes the continuation of the US/European Community's arrangement on steel as well as voluntary agreements announced earlier by Mexico and South Africa . . . . in some instances the US Trade Representative could be instructed to negotiate voluntary restraint agreements with other countries. . . . Such restraint could cover products on which there was no injury determination. . . .

The statement concluded with an expression of "hope" that "this combination of actions, taken without protectionist intention or effect," would cause the market to "return to a more normal level of steel imports, or approximately 18 percent, excluding semi-finished steel."[45]

Brock insisted initially that this market-share figure was a target, not a

---

42. The announcement had both protectionists and antiprotectionists cheering—for a day! Then the latter figured out its real content. The insider was William A. Niskanen, then a member of Reagan's Council of Economic Advisers. See Niskanen, *Reaganomics: An Insider's Account of the Policies and the People* (New York: Oxford University Press, 1988), 143.

43. Office of the United States Trade Representative, press release, 18 September 1984, 1.

44. Such quotas and import restraints were indeed rife abroad, but the case linking them to diversion of steel here was weak. Were that the case, prices in the US market would have been below those in, say, Japan. In fact, they were higher. The prime cause of increased imports was, rather, the growing competitive disadvantage of US firms in many product lines, which was exacerbated by the strong dollar.

45. This translated into an import-share figure of 20.2 percent when semifinished products were added.

binding commitment, but steelmen who had just met with the president clearly felt otherwise, and they expressed their gratification with the decision. And little wonder: the events of the remainder of 1984 made it clear that the president's "national policy for the steel industry," as it came to be labeled, was a lot more protectionist than the USITC program he rejected. Asked, as in 1982, to provide backup enforcement authority for foreign export restraints, Congress did this and more. It put into statute a target for fair import share: 17 percent to 20.2 percent of the US market, declaring further that in the absence of "satisfactory results within a reasonable period of time, the Congress will consider taking further legislative action."[46]

In the months that followed, agreements were negotiated or reaffirmed with every major foreign seller, whether or not the seller in question subsidized sales, and whether or not the USITC had found injury from imports of the seller's products. What all this amounted to was systematic circumvention of the rules for enforcing fair trade, for creating a level playing field, to which the administration, and Congress, claimed to give highest priority!

Five years later, Ronald Reagan's successor, George Bush, followed a similar course. The Reagan VERs lasted five years, through 30 September 1989. Having committed himself to extending them during the 1988 election campaign, Bush now needed to decide how. The circumstances clearly favored some relaxation of the system: over the original quota period, the dollar had plummeted and the US steel industry had undergone major restructuring. As a result, according to the USITC, "nearly all of the VRA countries exported less steel to the United States in 1988 than they were allowed."[47] After an intense debate among competing interests, Bush announced on 23 July a "Steel Trade Liberalization Program," with the declared objective "to phase out in a responsible and orderly manner the voluntary restraint arrangements . . . and to negotiate an international consensus to remove unfair trade practices."[48] In the meantime, however, Bush basically kept the quotas in place, though country ceiling levels were raised slightly. The phase-out period was set for two and a half years, so quotas would come off early in the election year of

---

46. Quotations taken from the Trade and Tariff Act of 1984, sec. 803, and US Congress, House, "Joint Explanatory Statement of the Committee of Conference," *Trade and Tariff Act of 1984*, 98th Cong., 2nd sess. (5 October 1984), H. Rept. 98-1156, 197–98.

47. US International Trade Commission, *The Effects of the Steel Voluntary Restraint Agreements on U.S. Steel-Consuming Industries*, Report to the Subcommittee on Trade of the House Committee on Ways and Means on Investigation No. 332-270 Under Section 332 of the Tariff Act of 1930, USITC Pub. 2182, Washington, May 1989.

48. Letter from USTR Carla A. Hills to Anne Brunsdale, chairman, USITC, in *Steel Industry Annual Report*, Report to the President on Investigation No. 332-289 Under Section 332 of the Tariff Act of 1930, USITC Pub. 2316, Washington, September 1990, A-2.

1992.[49] And when Bush delivered on his pledge to phase out the quotas, the industry responded with a barrage of new CVD and antidumping cases (see chapter 9).

In the United States, this tendency to exploit unfair-trade laws to gain favorable trade-restricting deals left liberal traders and procedural purists isolated and vulnerable. It also put executive officials in a bind. It is hard for them to resist cutting a deal when producing interests on both sides of the border want one—foreign exporters seeking market stability (and quota rents) and home firms pressing for import constraint.

Trade-Remedies Reform: The Gibbons Bill

Even as steel and other industries were exploiting existing laws to force negotiated protection, other parties were seeking further amendment of these laws. Foremost among these were industries pointing to alleged abuses the laws did not cover, but also seeking change were persons who opposed political fixes and wanted to make it harder for industries to use the laws to this end. An early leader in this movement was a man with a foot in both camps, Chairman of the House Ways and Means Subcommittee on Trade Sam M. Gibbons.

The Florida Democrat opposed quotas and trade restrictions generally, but supported those designed to counter unfair foreign trade practices. Gibbons believed the latter were substantively proper and politically useful, channeling relief claimants into objective, fact-finding procedures and thus diverting pressures for direct congressional action. Gibbons did not think it proper, however, that the trade-remedy laws be circumvented through negotiation of quota arrangements.

Gibbons also had problems that were specific to his personal situation in the House. As a labeled free trader, he was vulnerable to the charge that he no longer reflected the prevailing view of House members in general, and House Democrats in particular. This charge threatened the trade leverage of his subcommittee, and of Ways and Means as a whole, at a time of fierce jurisdictional conflict with Energy and Commerce under the aggressive leadership of John D. Dingell (D-MI) (see chapter 4). Gibbons therefore needed to show that he too could be tough about trade, but in a way that did not undercut the liberal system to which he was devoted.

So he held comprehensive hearings on the trade-remedy laws in the spring of 1983, declaring "our concern that US law does not operate as

---

49. One other set of major antidumping cases led to a comprehensive political settlement in the 1980s—those concerning semiconductors from Japan. One of the elements of this settlement was a set of minimum prices in the US market. See chapter 5.

effectively as it should to insure the fair conduct of international trade and the competitiveness of US industries."[50] And his subcommittee proposed a "Trade Remedies Reform Act" in early 1984 that would extend the CVD law to two previously uncovered foreign practices that industry petitioners saw as damaging subsidies. One of these was *export targeting*, defined broadly as "any government plan or scheme . . . the effect of which is to assist the beneficiary to become more competitive in the export of any class or kind of merchandise."[51] The object of concern was Japan. The semiconductor[52] and Houdaille[53] machine-tool cases had brought to prominence the claim that "industrial targeting," or the singling out of specific industrial sectors for government favor to enhance their future export prospects, had been a prime cause of Japanese economic success. The second of these practices was *natural resource subsidies*: a government such as Mexico would keep the domestic price of, say, oil or natural gas, below international market levels, conveying a cost advantage to producers of an energy-intensive product like fertilizer. So US ammonia producers sought relief.[54]

But as it emerged from the subcommittee the bill balanced these potentially trade-restrictive steps with an effort to protect the integrity of the rules. It required that the president, not the secretary of Commerce, make all decisions to suspend or terminate CVD or antidumping investigations, and it provided that any resulting export restraint agreement could not "have an effect on US consumers more adverse"

---

50. House Committee on Ways and Means, *Options*, 3.

51. US Congress, House Committee on Ways and Means, *Trade Remedies Reform Act of 1984*, 98th Cong., 2nd sess. (1 May 1984), H. Rept. 98-725, 26.

52. Semiconductor Industry Association, *The Effect of Government Targeting on World Semiconductor Competition: A Case History of Japanese Industrial Strategy and Its Costs for America*, report prepared by Verner, Liipfert, Bernhard, and McPherson under the direction of Alan Wm. Wolff (Washington, 1983).

53. An enterprising Washington attorney, Richard Copaken, developed an ingenious argument for a once-obscure Florida machine-tool firm, alleging that Japanese subsidies of its industry derived (in part) from proceeds of community bicycle races. This case was, in the end, rejected by the Reagan White House in the spring of 1983, but in the meantime Copaken made the "Houdaille case" a household word among trade cognoscenti and a preoccupation within the executive branch for the better part of a year.

54. Such subsidies had not been countervailable under US and international practice because they did not meet the specificity test: they were not provided selectively to particular firms or industries, but were available on an economywide basis. For detailed treatment of these issues by two lawyers who addressed them in the Department of Commerce, see Alan F. Holmer and Judith Hippler Bello, "The Trade and Tariff Act of 1984: The Road to Enactment," *International Lawyer* 19, no. 1 (Winter 1985): 287–320; and Bello and Holmer, "Subsidies and Natural Resources: Congress Rejects a Lateral Attack on the Specificity Test," *George Washington Journal of International Law and Economics* 18, no. 2 (1984): 297–329.

than the imposition of penalty duties through normal operation of the law.[55]

As trade law, the Gibbons bill presented serious problems. For one thing, it represented unilateral American efforts to extend the scope of countervailable trade practices well beyond that which commanded international agreement. Moreover, if such rules became the international norm, US exports could become vulnerable—computers as beneficiaries of Pentagon targeting, farm exports because of government-subsidized irrigation. Nevertheless, the trade-remedies bill was a sincere effort, by a protrade congressman, to deal constructively with complex problems under most unfavorable political conditions.

But step by legislative step, the Gibbons package came apart in 1984. In the spring, the full Ways and Means Committee, in a 22-to-12 vote, gutted the section of the bill that sought to prevent circumvention of the rules through VERs. By late June, prior to action by the full House, a coalition of labor, industry, and agricultural interests forced Gibbons to jettison the export-targeting section. The natural-resource subsidy provision did pass the House and went to conference that fall as part of the 1984 trade package. But despite the strong backing of ranking Finance Democrat Russell B. Long of Louisiana, Senate conferees—responding to strong administration opposition—rejected it by a four-to-three, party-line vote. So it, too, was dropped.

But the effort did not die in 1984. In fact, trade-remedy reform became a central issue in the omnibus trade legislation that began in the House in 1986, and became law in 1988.

The Omnibus Legislation of 1986–88

Changing the rules might not take specific trade decisions out of politics, but it continued to perform two other important functions. For members of Congress, it offered continued political protection: it was a way for them to respond to industry pressures while pushing the individual case responsibility elsewhere. For private interests, additional elaboration of the trade rules could further tilt the political and policy balance, increasing their odds for obtaining some form of import relief, either within the rules or outside them.

---

55. US Congress, House Committee on Ways and Means, Subcommittee on Trade, "Description of H.R. 4784, the Trade Remedies Reform Act, as Ordered Reported" (29 February 1984), processed, 2. As the full committee later explained the concern, "the antidumping and countervailing duty laws have been used as a device to implement quantitative import restrictions, including voluntary restraints, without sufficient consideration of their economic consequences, and contrary to Congressional intent that the primary remedy be offsetting duties." Committee on Ways and Means, *Trade Remedies Reform Act*, 17–18.

So Ways and Means trade-remedy proposals were an important component of HR 4800, the omnibus measure approved by a 295-to-115 House vote in May 1986. "Resource input subsidies" were made actionable under the CVD law and "export targeting" was listed as an "unreasonable or unjustifiable" foreign practice under Section 301. The escape clause was amended to allow emergency relief for producers of perishable products, and to transfer final decision-making authority from the president to the US trade representative.[56] Indeed, though the bill contained a broad range of provisions, its main thrust was to add to the already formidable list of legal rights that US producers could invoke against foreign products or foreign governments and to reduce executive flexibility in responding to assertions of these rights. The end result, critics argued, might not be another Smoot-Hawley, but it would be import barriers all the same, won through what they came to label "process protectionism."

The 1986 bill died in the Senate, as chronicled in chapter 4. But such provisions were dusted off and reincluded in the legislation of 1987 and 1988. The House bill contained "several amendments sought by coalitions of import-competing U.S. industry seeking more restrictive AD/CVD laws." These were "greatly changed in the Senate, following sustained lobbying by the Administration and by export-oriented large U.S. businesses," but that body added several additional AD/CVD amendments, "none of which were in the House bill."[57] Most prominent, once again, was the natural-resources provision. Others featured such lawyerish labels as "diversionary input dumping," or addressed thorny technical problems like "non-market-economy dumping."

Because problem provisions were split between the two bills, and because the administration (and some export-oriented businesses) fought hard against them, the conference negotiations "led to the rejection or dilution of nearly all the 'restrictive' AD/CVD amendments."[58] There was a modest clarification of the "specificity test" for subsidies—Commerce was to consider not just whether a subsidy was de jure available to all producers within a country, but whether it was de facto widely used. If it was not widely used, then it would meet the specificity test and be countervailable under US law.[59]

The experience of the 1980s underscored the impossibility of managing

---

56. See US Congress, House Committee on Ways and Means, *Comprehensive Trade Policy Reform Act of 1986*, 99th Cong., 2nd sess. (6 May 1986), H. Rept. 99-581, part 1.

57. Horlick and Oliver, "Antidumping and CVD Law Provisions," 6.

58. Ibid.

59. In fact, Commerce had been applying the test in this way for several years, but the statutory language cleared up the confusion created by several Court of International Trade decisions.

Table 6.1   Antidumping, countervailing duty, and Section 201 investigations initiated, 1979–94

Year	Antidumping cases	Countervailing duty cases	Section 201 cases
1979	26	40	4
1980	21	14	2
1981	15	22	1
1982	65	140	3
1983	46	22	0
1984	74	51	7
1985	66	43	4
1986	71	27	1
1987	15	8	0
1988	42	11	1
1989	23	7	0
1990	43	7	1
1991	51	8	0
1992	99	43	1
1993	42	5	0
1994	43	7	0
Total	742	455	25

Sources: Author's calculations, based on case tallies from USITC, ALLAD-Casis and ALLCVD-Casis databases, and *Federal Register*, various issues.

volatile trade issues primarily through the elaboration of quasi-judicial procedures. One could not make the laws reach potential, borderline subsidies without extending them into uncertain and controversial new areas supported by neither domestic nor international consensus. It is hard to avoid seeing the trade-remedy reform movement as a new pursuit of an old illusion—that major trade cases, the really "hot" ones, could somehow be diverted from the political arena—that the United States could, in the words of Gibbons's predecessor, "run trade on economic law."

In the end, the movement to further tighten trade-remedy legislation had only modest impact in the 1980s. What did have effect, however, were the changes enacted in the 1970s. In addition to facilitating the political fixes treated at some length above, they led to many more specific impositions of countervailing and antidumping duties. And the threat of their imposition had an additional trade-deterring effect.

Administrative Remedies: A Balance Sheet on the 1980s

In the course of the 1980s, there were 345 countervailing duty and 438 antidumping investigations initiated in response to specific petitions. Table 6.1 shows their distribution by year. And it shows clearly contrasting patterns.

Countervailing duty cases surged in the first half of the decade, peaking in 1982 and 1984 and dropping precipitously after 1986. This suggests what our earlier discussion makes clear—that a very large share were steel cases, intended mainly to force political settlements, which fell to a fraction of their former level once this goal had been achieved. Outside of steel, government subsidies were harder to prove—and their use probably declined through the decade as more and more countries adopted market-oriented economic strategies. By the end of the decade, new CVD investigations were down to seven a year, below the level of the mid-1970s.

In contrast, antidumping cases persisted. They peaked in 1984 and 1986, to be sure, and no annual total between 1987 and 1990 was as high as any for 1982 through 1986. One important reason, apparently, was the decline of the dollar, which cut into the growth of imports and made it harder for firms to prove injury. Nonetheless, there were more antidumping cases in 1988–90 than in 1980–82, whereas there were only one-seventh as many CVD cases. And antidumping petitions increased further after 1990.[60]

What were the outcomes of antidumping cases in the 1980s? There was one piece of "good news" for liberal traders and procedural purists: resolution through negotiated VERs dropped sharply. As shown in table 6.2, 1980–85 featured many occasions where plaintiffs withdrew their petitions, predominantly because they had forced political solutions. But there were only four antidumping petitions withdrawn in 1987 through 1989 (and only one CVD case).

The other side of the coin, however, was a rising success rate in winning relief under the antidumping statute itself. In the first half of the decade, 41 percent (56 of 137) of petitions carried to completion led to either antidumping duties or suspension agreements. In the second half, 63 percent (119 of 190) were successful.

When petitioners were unsuccessful, moreover, it was rarely because they were unable to meet the statutory criterion for dumping. Only 23 of 327 petitions (7 percent) failed for this reason, and only 8 of 190 (4 percent) in 1985–89. In contrast, 40 percent (131 of 327) failed because the USITC did not find "material injury" to the producer from the imports alleged to be dumped.[61]

Clearly by the late 1980s petitioners were finding relief. Indeed, the numbers suggest that unfair trade must be rampant, since the Depart-

---

60. For analysis of the 1990s, see Chapter 9.

61. For a comprehensive count of 1980–88 cases that reaches similar conclusions, see J. Michael Finger and Tracy Murray, *Policing Unfair Imports: The U.S. Example*, Working Paper 401 (Washington: World Bank, Country Economics Department, March 1990). Finger and Murray also offer interesting information on which countries are most likely to be targeted with unfair-trade petitions. For a broader analysis treating specific cases in detail, see Finger and Nellie T. Artis, *How Antidumping Works and Who Gets Hurt*, (Ann Arbor: University of Michigan Press, 1993).

Table 6.2 Antidumping cases and results, 1980–93

Year	Total[a]	Cases withdrawn[b]	Cases completed[c]	Cases affirmed[d] Number	Percentage[e]	Negative dumping[f] Number	Percentage[e]	No injury[g] Number	Percentage[e]
1980	21	9	12	3	25	1	8	8	67
1981	15	4	11	7	64	1	9	3	27
1982	65	24	41	14	34	3	7	24	59
1983	46	5	41	19	46	5	12	17	41
1984	74	42	32	12	38	5	16	15	47
1985	66	16	50	29	58	2	4	19	38
1986	71	7	64	44	69	3	5	17	27
1987	15	1	14	9	64	0	0	5	36
1988	42	0	42	22	52	3	7	17	40
1989	23	3	20	14	70	0	0	6	30
1990	43	2	41	19	46	0	0	22	54
1991	51	4	47	24	51	1	2	22	47
1992	99	11	88	44	50	1	1	43	49
1993	42	6	36	18	50	2	6	16	44
Total	673	134	539	278	52	27	5	234	43

a. Total number of petitions submitted during the year.
b. Cases terminated by withdrawal of petition.
c. Cases followed through to an official finding.
d. Cases resulting in an antidumping action.
e. Of cases completed.
f. Cases ending with finding of no dumping.
g. Cases ending with finding of no injury to petitioner.

ment of Commerce has been finding dumping on the overwhelming majority of petitions submitted. There is substantial evidence, however, that the enforcement of the unfair-trade laws has become sharply skewed in favor of petitioners and against their foreign competitors. The basic premise of the law is consistent with GATT Article VI: that US producers should not be undercut by foreign competitors who sell at lower prices in the US market than in theirs.[62] However, the way US law is written and implemented tilts the playing field in favor of the petitioner—and thus against the foreign producer *and* the US users of its products, through "practices and procedures which tend to systematically favor higher rather than lower dumping and CVD 'margins.' "[63] Specifically, the law encourages the Commerce Department to exclude from the calculation of the "foreign market value" of a product (the foreign producer's home-market average price) any sales that are below his average costs and to ignore in the calculation of the average price at which he sells in the United States any sales that are above the foreign market value. And when data on the accused producer's production costs are judged insufficient, Commerce substitutes a "constructed value" based on estimated average cost of production plus overhead plus profit. Since it is standard business practice to sell below average total cost of production on a variety of occasions—and by definition profitable, at the margin, to sell at any price above marginal costs—this means that the only way a producer can avoid being found guilty of dumping is to sell in the US market at prices well above those at home!

It is no wonder that escape clause cases had virtually disappeared by 1990, for if a finding of dumping is quasi-automatic, the antidumping procedure has the advantage of a lower injury threshold, no presidential power to overturn an affirmative decision, and indefinite duration for any import relief imposed—unless the foreign producer wins revocation of the duty by raising prices, which has the same net benefit for the US producer. The only question is why the number of antidumping cases did not continue to increase in the latter part of the 1980s![64]

---

62. Even this principle does not go uncontested. Carried to extremes, "dumping" amounts to the predatory pricing for which remedy is available against competing *domestic* firms. But as typically carried out, it is similar to the market discrimination, setting different prices for different customers or in different economic circumstances, which is common and indeed necessary business practice *within* national boundaries.

63. Richard Boltuck and Robert E. Litan, *Down in the Dumps: Administration of the Unfair Trade Laws* (Washington: Brookings Institution, 1991), 13. The remainder of this paragraph draws upon their analysis.

64. When one asks this question to trade officials and lawyers, the answers include the cost of legal assistance for filing cases, the decline of the dollar (which made it harder to prove injury in the latter 1980s), the fact that many potential claimants are already protected by antidumping orders (or other forms of trade protection), and the fact that the level and form of protection cannot be tailored to the plaintiff's needs.

The Limits of Administrative Remedies

"The rules" have come full circle. For decades they had been a sideshow on an obscure bureaucratic stage; now they are prominently affecting—and impeding—trade flows. For years they were properly denounced as ineffective; by 1992 they were, with equal accuracy, attacked as tilted in favor of US producers. And the debate continues, much as it has in the past.

Advocates of strengthening the unfair-trade laws have long pointed to examples like the endless Zenith television case: despite a finding in 1971 of dumping of television sets by Japanese manufacturers, in collaboration with American importers, specific duties were not set until 1978, and the administrative and legal processes on this and related suits continued endlessly thereafter. Efforts to set and collect the duties have been subject to "an extraordinary number of claims and counterclaims," during which litigation "the complexion of the American consumer electronics industry changed irreversibly," as US firms moved offshore and Japanese firms built American plants.[65]

A comprehensive study by the Office of Technology Assessment concludes that this was a case in which "American manufacturers of TVs have been entitled to trade protection but have not yet received it."[66] Hence the case was fuel for those seeking to tighten the trade-remedy laws to provide surer relief, and it underscored even more the difficulty of providing definitive resolutions in such cases.

But the same case was also fuel for critics who saw the procedures as promoting "multiple harassment" of importers. Even as the dumping case was proceeding, US television manufacturers were also pressing, with mixed results, parallel claims against their Japanese counterparts under the antitrust laws, the countervailing duty law, Section 337 of the Tariff Act of 1930 governing unfair practices in import trade, and the escape clause. Critics called this "legal protectionism," suggesting that the trade-remedy procedures, taken as a whole, constituted a substantial US nontariff barrier.[67] As one panel summarized the argument (without explicitly endorsing it), "there is an incentive for domestic industries to use first one then another statute, seeking relief from different government agencies and harassing their competition. Even if they are unsuc-

---

65. US Congress, Office of Technology Assessment, *International Competitiveness in Electronics* (November 1983), Rept. OTA-ISC-200, 440–41.

66. Ibid., 441.

67. See Carl J. Green, "Legal Protectionism in the United States and Its Impact on United States-Japan Economic Relations," in *Appendix to the Report of the Japan–United States Economic Relations Group* (Washington, April 1981), 262–312.

cessful in securing relief, they may well impose heavy legal costs upon the future entry into the American market."[68]

The seeming irrationality of the procedures, and their strange legal-political effects, has led many reformers to argue that the United States has overemphasized the unfair-trade remedies as a response to import competition. They therefore look for means to reduce the relative attractiveness of these statutes: by making it harder to get relief under these statutes, and perhaps easier under Section 201.[69] One could do this within the structure of the current trade-remedy laws—as Hufbauer and Rosen propose—or by an approach that gives the president and the USTR greater discretion in applying all trade remedies. The political disadvantage of granting such discretion could be considerable, of course. One reason why "the rules" have been an attractive means of handling trade pressures is that they deny executive branch as well as congressional politicians the power to say yes to industry petitions unless regulators first approve.

Such considerations encourage other experts of liberal trade persuasion to argue that it is better to live with the quasi-judicial trade-remedy system. Included among them is one of America's foremost trade law authorities, John H. Jackson, University of Michigan professor and former STR general counsel. After reviewing the trade cases of several decades through the early 1980s, he finds "few instances" of actual multiple harassment, though he recognizes that "even the threat of such activity . . . may itself be somewhat inhibiting to foreign exporters." After considering a range of other costs and benefits, Jackson concludes with a cautious affirmative: the system is better than likely alternatives "if we can believe . . . that the US legalistic system—cumbersome, rigid, and costly as it is—in fact provides for an economy more open to imports than virtually any other major industrial economy in the world."[70]

This may still be true, in relative terms, but others counter by underscoring the rules' broad trade-deterring effects, particularly those of the antidumping law. A study by the Secretariat of the United Nations Conference on Trade and Development (UNCTAD) concludes that investiga-

---

68. *Report of the Japan-United States Economic Relations Group,* January 1981, 92.

69. Hufbauer and Rosen, for example, would require the president to provide limited-duration import relief in Section 201 cases, conditioned on the industry's following a "downsizing" adjustment plan to restore its competitiveness. See *Trade Policy for Troubled Industries.*

70. John H. Jackson, "Perspectives on the Jurisprudence of International Trade: Costs and Benefits of Legal Procedures in the United States," *Michigan Law Review* 82, no. 6 (April-May 1984): 1579–80, 1582.

Jackson recognizes, however, that as discussed in earlier pages, for "very big cases . . . the system breaks down and in fact returns, by one subterfuge or another, to a 'non-rule system' of extensive executive discretion and 'back-room bargaining.'" Ibid., 1580–81.

tions of unfair-trade practices often cut back trade without a final legal resolution.[71] A more recent analysis by a World Bank scholar finds that "import prices increased by as much as 10 percent for some manufacturing sectors (such as garments) during an investigation," before official action is even taken.[72]

To ignore the trade sins these laws were designed to counter would be inconsistent with GATT rules and politically counterproductive. To be obsessed with them, however, exaggerates their marginal contribution to overall American trade woes, fueling the growing, rather self-indulgent conviction among business people and politicians that the international trade game is systematically rigged against the United States. The lack of transparency of nontariff trade barriers and the welter of conflicting and confusing evidence allowed great leeway for the eyes of beholders inclined to see how other governments interfere with trade while ignoring how the United States does so. This has weakened the policy tolerance that was central to the international trade system's effective functioning.[73]

The moral cast of this ongoing debate not only favors domestic plaintiffs over foreign producer interests, but it also disadvantages the domestic users of the products subject to trade sanctions. Their interests have no special standing in the litigation over unfair-trade laws, but they suffer if prices of steel, for example, are increased as a result of the outcomes of unfair-trade cases. Gradually, these users have begun to mobilize in response. When the price understandings in the US-Japan semiconductor agreement of 1986, reached pursuant to antidumping petitions, led to a doubling of the price of chips in the US market, IBM and other computer makers protested and forced a modification of the antidumping provisions in the follow-on agreement reached in 1991. A similar reaction followed antidumping duties imposed on ball bearings, an important input to many manufacturers, in 1989. And in the summer of 1991, users rose up in arms when a small American producer of flat-panel display screens for laptop computers succeeded in winning huge antidumping duties against the Japanese imports that dominate the US market. Such a determination, Apple and Compaq and IBM declared, would render it uneconomic to produce their next-generation laptops in the United States and force a transfer of production to overseas plants.

---

71. United Nations Conference on Trade and Development, "Protectionism and Structural Adjustment: Anti-Dumping and Countervailing Duty Practices," draft note by the UNCTAD Secretariat (Geneva, 4 January 1984), processed, 9.

72. Ann Harrison, "The New Trade Protection: Price Effects of Anti-Dumping and Countervailing Measures in the United States" (Washington: World Bank, April 1991), processed, 32.

73. Richardson, "Currents and Cross-Currents," 2–3.

These users were among those backing an important (though unsuccessful) effort under the Emergency Committee for American Trade (ECAT) at decade's end to modify GATT trade-remedy laws to take account of their interests, and those of others adversely affected by antidumping duties. Their increased activity is part of a more complex interplay among trade interest groups, a pattern addressed in greater detail in chapter 7. But it is an uphill political struggle, ever vulnerable to the charge of "weakening the unfair-trade laws" or aligning with foreign adversaries. The fact that foreign governments are increasingly invoking similar dumping laws against US exporters has not yet provoked a strong Washington response. For unfair-trade laws remain politically popular, and they have become—at long last—economically successful for their users. They have become, to repeat a phrase quoted earlier, "the usual first choice for industries seeking protection from imports into the U.S."[74] And for members of Congress pressed by trade-affected constituents, predisposed to see unfairness in foreign competition, and reluctant to take action directly, they seem to offer the best of all worlds: a chance to occupy the moral high ground of backing "free but fair trade."

---

74. Horlick and Oliver, "Antidumping and CVD Law Provisions," 5.

7

The National Arena: More Open, More Partisan

Through most of the postwar period, the American trade policymaking system operated within a national political environment that was unusually conducive to liberal policies. There were four basic reasons.

First and foremost, foreign trade was not a major partisan issue. There was competition between Democrats and Republicans for the favor of specific interest groups, but neither party used trade policy as a major means of defining its differences with the other. This both reflected and reinforced a second condition: there was an overwhelming elite consensus in favor of market openness and trade expansion. Given limited interest among the relatively protectionist mass public, this bolstered governmental leaders in their liberal inclinations.

Third, the issue posed by interests seeking import relief was typically a straightforward one—whether to insulate a particular industry's firms and workers from international competition or to make them take their market medicine. This made it easy to label these interests "protectionist," placing them very much on the defensive in the postwar policy environment. Fourth and finally, interest-group initiative was limited and usually followed a simple pattern. A relatively small number of industries sought protection, each on its own track—textiles, shoes, steel, and smaller ones like watchmakers. Other manufacturing and labor interests were typically inactive on trade issues, but many were on call to be mobilized for major liberalizing initiatives.

All four of these conditions made trade policy relatively manageable, facilitating the liberal policies that government leaders wished to pursue. And all four conditions changed markedly in the 1970s and 1980s.

Trade politics grew more partisan, as a number of prominent Democrats began to see electoral opportunities in assuming a trade-restrictive posture, and as some Republicans reacted by toughening their trade stances. Elite leaders, particularly those in business, grew weaker and more qualified in their commitment to liberal trade. New trade-related issues entered the policy debate—industrial and "competitiveness" policy, misaligned exchange rates. These issues weakened the notion that, on international economic matters, government was best when it intervened least. And they offered broad national-interest rationales for certain trade-restrictive proposals. Finally, interest-group politics became more complex. The AFL-CIO became an across-the-board backer of trade restrictions, and a much larger range of interests sought government trade action, including segments of frontier, high-technology industries like semiconductors. But the protectionist forces were being countered by a new antiprotectionist activism among certain exporters, importers, and industrial consumers. And there seemed to be some erosion in the effectiveness of the mainstays of traditional protectionism, the textile-apparel coalition in particular.

These changes are still in process, and their ultimate import remains unclear. But many of them have tended to make the maintenance of open trade policies more difficult. Together with the developments addressed in previous chapters, they have undercut time-tested methods of managing trade issues without substituting reliable new ones.

□ □ □

In 1962, in the key House vote on John F. Kennedy's Trade Expansion Act, Democrats voted 210 to 44 in support; Republicans lined up 127 to 43 behind a motion to "recommit" (kill) the bill. This was consistent with the basic political alignment of the three prior decades, beginning with Smoot-Hawley in 1930 and the Reciprocal Trade Agreements Act of 1934. Democrats backed liberal trade and lower tariffs; Republicans sought to maintain or increase protection for domestic industry.

But little more than a decade after President Kennedy's landmark legislative victory, a new alignment seemed to be developing. When authorizing legislation for a new major trade round came before the House in 1973, it was the Democrats who voted 121 to 112 against, while Republicans were almost unanimous, 160 to 19, in favor. For northern Democrats, the turnabout was even greater: 141 to 7 "yea" in 1962; 101 to 52 "nay" in 1973.

An "Amazing Political Reversal"?

At the time, this shift attracted little attention. Trade had not been a prominent source of partisan contention since the 1930s. There was, of course, tactical competition for the support of specific constituencies. President Kennedy, for example, promised comprehensive protection for cotton textiles in 1960, strengthening his position in New England and the southern coastal states. Richard M. Nixon, not to be twice outdone, made an even stronger textile promise eight years later. But although these pledges (Nixon's in particular) did have important policy consequences, neither was rooted in a broader trade stance that distinguished one party from its rival. And neither was directed at the national electorate. Similarly, Republicans who voted "protectionist" in 1962 (and Democrats who did so in 1973) were not inclined to advertise that fact. Advocacy of trade restrictions might win plaudits from trade-affected interests, but the mass public was indifferent and opinion leaders were hostile.

Some of the difference between 1962 and 1973, moreover, could be explained by the fact that members were voting on the program of a Democratic President (Kennedy) in the first instance and a Republican (Nixon) in the second. On almost any issue, partisan loyalties pull members toward support of an administration initiative when the White House is occupied by one of their own.

But deeper forces were at work, forces that had been developing for many years. Most important was the shift in the geographic bases of the two political parties. In the first half of the 20th century, the Republican heartland was the industrial Northeast and Midwest: Herbert C. Hoover carried Pennsylvania in 1932, but not a single state farther west (and no state south of Delaware). Indeed, from the first Lincoln election until the reign of Franklin D. Roosevelt, not a single Democratic presidential candidate carried either Pennsylvania or Michigan. This general pattern persisted as late as 1948: Harry S Truman scored his upset reelection victory even though his favored Republican rival, Thomas E. Dewey, carried those two states, and New York and New Jersey as well. But the Kennedy-Nixon election of 1960 reversed the pattern. JFK won 303 electoral votes, exactly the same number as Truman. But unlike Truman, he lost badly in the West but won Michigan, Pennsylvania, New York, and New Jersey. Since that time, the Northeast has become the Democratic heartland, while the GOP has flourished in the sunbelt—the West and, increasingly, the South.

This shift reduced Republican dependence on historically protectionist northeastern and midwestern industrialists. In contrast, the Democrats' new heartland was where organized labor was the strongest. It was therefore natural to expect some adjustment of the parties' dominant positions on trade, and in fact Raymond A. Bauer and his colleagues detected signs of an "amazing political reversal" as early as 1953. Closely analyzing a Roper poll taken that year, and looking particularly at respondents with the most polar views, they found that "ultrafree-traders" were "strongly Republican," whereas "ultraprotectionists" tended to be

Democrats. And important among the group most committed to trade restrictions were "industrial workers who see a threat to their jobs."[1]

Through the 1950s and 1960s, the major national labor organizations still held to a free trade position, although the textile unions were an important exception. The AFL-CIO endorsed the Trade Expansion Act of 1962, in part because of its new provisions for trade adjustment assistance to workers. A decade later, however, labor leaders were deriding that program as "burial insurance," and AFL-CIO President George Meany was singing a decidedly different trade tune. Urban Democrats followed him from support to opposition of liberal trade, particularly in the House of Representatives. But with a few iconoclastic exceptions, like Senator Vance Hartke (D-IN) of Burke-Hartke fame, they did so quietly. In the Senate, in fact, liberal activists like Walter F. Mondale (D-MN) fought the House-passed quota bill of 1970 and backed the Nixon-Ford trade act when it came before them four years later.

It was a Republican, John B. Connally, who was the first postwar presidential aspirant to make trade a prominent issue in the quest for his party's nomination. He won cheers on the campaign circuit in 1979 with his threat to leave Japanese Toyotas rusting on the docks. But his bottom line—exactly one convention delegate in 1980—did not inspire emulation.

By 1982, however, Democrats began to sniff major political opportunity. They were again outsiders in the White House and newly a minority in the Senate as well. The economy was suffering its deepest and longest recession in more than 40 years. The rust belt industrial heartland states like Pennsylvania, Ohio, and Michigan were particularly hard hit, as were their key industries like autos and steel. And US trade was moving deeper into deficit. Mondale was now seeking the Democratic presidential nomination, and the AFL-CIO had decided, for the first time, to endorse a candidate before the primaries. Mondale needed that endorsement; he also needed an issue on which he could take a "tougher" stand than the president. He fastened upon trade. He did not neglect the broader macroeconomic causes of America's distress. But to labor audiences in particular, he went after the Japanese and unfair-trade practices, and denounced the Reagan regime for failing to combat them. The United States needed to get tough on trade, he argued, lest job opportunities for its youth be limited to working at McDonald's or sweeping up around Japanese computers.

For the most part, Mondale avoided concrete commitments to trade protection; he remained at heart an internationalist, who would rather open foreign markets than close American ones. Nevertheless, the United Auto Workers had made its highly restrictive domestic-content

---

1. Raymond A. Bauer, Ithiel de Sola Pool, and Lewis Anthony Dexter, *American Business and Public Policy: The Politics of Foreign Trade* (Chicago: Aldine-Atherton, 1972), 91–92.

bill a litmus test for labor Democrats, and Mondale endorsed it. So did the Democratic-controlled House of Representatives in 1982, and again in 1983. In the latter year, only two Democrats from the Northeast and industrial Midwest voted "no" on final passage. Thus, as the nation approached the 50th anniversary of the Reciprocal Trade Agreements Act of 1934, it seemed to be witnessing the reemergence of trade as a highly visible partisan issue, but with the two major parties having switched positions. Senator John H. Chafee (R-RI) remarked, seemingly with some relief, that here was one issue on which the Republicans were wearing "the white hats."

The new advocacy of trade restrictions by certain Democrats was not without its logic. Ever since the New Deal, theirs had been the party favoring an active government to redress the imbalances and inequities of the marketplace. Republicans, by contrast, had been critics of government intrusion in business. On trade, however, these positions had been reversed. Would not a new trade realignment make more intellectual sense, then, with the domestic interventionists becoming international interventionists as well?

For all of these reasons, it seemed very possible in the 1980s that trade would become, as in the years before 1930, one of the prime issues dividing and defining the two major political parties. But this did not happen: the "realignment" remained incomplete. Democrats hedged their bets; Republicans did also.

Mondale found that the "protectionist" label retained its sting, as editorial writers and internationalist Democrats reacted with dismay.[2] So the Democratic challenger backpedaled adroitly. He did not change any specific stand, but from early 1983 onward he deemphasized trade restrictions and highlighted the macroeconomic causes of the trade imbalance.[3]

Meanwhile, Ronald Reagan was looking more protectionist. The president remained a free trader in principle, but as noted in chapter 5, he was protecting his political flanks in practice, approving new restraints on heavyweight motorcycles, textiles, and specialty steel, a fourth year of Japanese auto export limits; and—in the middle of the election campaign—a network of voluntary restraint agreements on carbon steel aimed

---

2. Moreover, once Senator Edward M. Kennedy (D-MA) withdrew from the contest, Mondale no longer had serious competition for the labor endorsement.

3. The Democratic party platform negotiated by Mondale's aides actually attacked the Reagan administration from the internationalist side, citing as the administration's "most fundamental" mistake its acting "as if the United States were an economic island unto itself." The platform's only specific reference to trade relief employed the modifier "temporary," and called for a quid pro quo in the form of industry commitment to "a realistic, hardheaded modernization plan which will restore competitiveness." Reprinted in *Congressional Quarterly*, 21 July 1984, 1748, 1760.

at limiting imports to 20.2 percent of domestic production.[4] So, contrary to widespread expectations, trade did not become a major issue in the 1984 general election.

But trade reemerged as a partisan issue in 1985 and 1986. Democrats, staggering from Reagan's 49-state electoral sweep, needed to counter the administration in its two areas of electoral strength—economic recovery at home and "standing tall" in the world. To Representative Tony Coelho of California, chairman of the House Democratic Campaign Committee, trade met both needs perfectly: it was the "Democratic macho issue."[5] By targeting the unparalleled trade deficit, Democrats could spotlight the underside of Reaganomics and attack White House softness toward trade competitors.

Thus partisan interest was one force driving the congressional upsurge chronicled in chapter 4: the Bentsen-Rostenkowski-Gephardt bill taxing imports from countries running large trade surpluses; House Speaker Thomas P. "Tip" O'Neill's declaration about trade having become the "number one" issue on Capitol Hill;[6] the omnibus trade bill with a decidedly protectionist tilt that O'Neill and other Democratic leaders pushed through the House the following spring. When Democrats regained control of the Senate in the mid-term election of 1986, trade was the issue they chose to show that their party could legislate. When Richard A. Gephardt (D-MO) decided to run for president in 1988, an aggressive trade posture helped him win the Iowa caucuses.[7] When the Bush administration initiated negotiations toward a North American Free Trade Agreement (NAFTA), a majority of Democrats voted against extending fast-track authority in 1991, driven importantly by the AFL-CIO campaign against it. And though they lost the vote on Capitol Hill, they won one that fall in Pennsylvania, with NAFTA reasonably prominent among the issues in Democratic Senator Harris Wofford's surprise special election victory over former Bush administration Attorney General Richard Thornburgh.

---

4. Reagan's stand was less restrictive than that of Mondale, who called for a 17 percent import share, but the Democrat conditioned his proposal on the industry's commitments to adjust. Not to be outdone, Congress incorporated elements of both candidates' positions—and a modified industry adjustment requirement—into the Trade and Tariff Act of 1984.

5. Quoted in Pietro Nivola, "Trade Policy: Refereeing the Playing Field," in Thomas E. Mann, ed., *A Question of Balance: The President, Congress and Foreign Policy* (Washington: Brookings Institution, 1990), 235.

6. "President Reagan," he intoned, "seems willing to preside over the de-industrialization of America. We in Congress are not." Quoted in *Washington Post*, 20 September 1985.

7. Important in Gephardt's narrow plurality, by most accounts, was a television spot attacking the unfairness of Korean import restrictions against American-made automobiles.

Yet trade remained, for Democrats, a two-edged sword. Mondale and Gephardt found their "protectionism" attacked by editorialists and by Democratic primary competitors. Other Democrats, like Ways and Means Chairman Dan Rostenkowski (D-IL) in the House and Bill Bradley (D-NJ) in the Senate, were unwilling to abandon the legacy of Cordell Hull, however much they might criticize the administration's passivity on trade and related issues. Rostenkowski and Finance Chairman Lloyd Bentsen (D-TX) both supported fast-track for NAFTA, as did the House and Senate democratic leadership. As long as Democrats were deeply divided on whether to move in a protectionist direction, the issue could not be a good one for mobilizing and unifying the party against the opposition. Their ambivalence was underscored when Gephardt, in his new role of House majority leader, voted in favor of fast-track for NAFTA in the spring of 1991, and then rebalanced his position by introducing a new Gephardt amendment targeting Japan in the fall.

Nor were Republicans prepared to stand still while Democrats decided whether to attack. Just as Reagan had made protectionist concessions in 1984, Senate Finance Republicans led the campaign against Japanese trade practices in 1985. Fifty-nine House Republicans joined 236 House Democrats in supporting the omnibus legislation in 1986, and *their* need to balance their positions pushed the Reagan administration toward trade compromise in 1988. Patrick Buchanan took a blatantly protectionist stance in his "conservative" challenge to President George Bush's renomination in 1992.

Still, there had developed in the 1970s and 1980s the potential for sharp interparty division on trade in the years to come. And if a future Democratic president were to come to power on a truly protectionist platform, this would remove from the American trade policymaking system the most crucial pillar of support for open policies—the liberal-leaning leadership of the executive branch.

A Newly Ambivalent Elite

A related development was the weakening of support for liberal trade policies within the American leadership community. As spelled out in chapter 2, open trade policies had never won overwhelming backing from the mass public. Rather, they were sustainable because of mass indifference, combined with strong support from leadership groups. These conditions helped keep trade issues out of the larger public arena, so that specific pressures could be diverted or accommodated by special deals.

Between the 1930s and the 1960s, elite support of liberal trade increased. Postwar prosperity served to confirm the rightness of open trade policy just as the Great Depression had discredited the Smoot-Hawley alternative. Thus, as Judith L. Goldstein has written, liberalism became the dominant ideology because it was associated with the unparalleled prosperity of the years after 1945.[8]

But just as the Munich lesson for security policy was supplanted by Vietnam, the connection between Smoot-Hawley, global depression, and World War II faded also. One reason was time. Another was the afflictions chronicled in chapter 3: increased trade exposure, the American "decline," the rise of new competitors, the erosion of the General Agreement on Tariffs and Trade (GATT), stagflation, and the misaligned dollar. Substantial—if not entirely conclusive—evidence from opinion polls tends to confirm what the tone of the recent American trade debate suggests: that leadership backing for liberal trade has weakened significantly since the 1960s. At the same time, the mass public, which has always been somewhat inclined toward protection, may have grown stronger in this inclination.

Available indicators from the murky world of opinion polls offer no single, simple answers. The Roper organization acknowledged as much when it circulated a June 1981 report regarding international economic issues under the heading "Foreign Trade: A Confused View." Similarly, the most thorough analysis of the 1950s underscored "the degree to which apparent expressions of opinion vary according to the way the issue is posed."[9]

Other polling organizations have not always been as careful as Roper in heeding the consequent admonition of Bauer, Pool, and Dexter "to exercise extreme caution in interpreting the poll results."[10] The Harris Survey, for example, used the following headings to report virtually identical public opinion findings: "More Restrictions on Imports Favored Over Traditional US Policy of Free Trade" (15 March 1979); "Americans Favor Restricting Foreign Car Imports" (10 March 1983); and "Americans Want Free, Balanced Trade" (14 March 1983).

Analysis of public opinion is impeded more fundamentally by the lack of any staple questions that were posed consistently by pollsters throughout the postwar period. Gallup asked regularly, during the 1940s and 1950s, whether people favored higher or lower tariffs, and got consistent pluralities for the latter. It also got a consistently positive response to questions about whether people supported continuation of the reciprocal trade agreements program. But these questions are no longer put to the public.

When questions have been posed in terms of jobs or the desirability of imports per se, mass opinion has shown a consistently protectionist tilt. In

---

8. Judith L. Goldstein, "Ideas, Institutions, and American Trade Policy," *International Organization* 42, no. 1 (Winter 1988): esp. 187–88.

9. Bauer, Pool, and Dexter, *American Business and Public Policy*, 84.

10. Ibid., 85–86.

1953, Roper asked, "Would you rather see this country import more goods from foreign countries than we do now, or put more restrictions on goods imported into this country from abroad?" Of those willing to take a position, 37 percent favored restrictions, and 26 percent favored imports.[11]

Recent surveys suggest a stronger leaning in the restrictive direction. When, between 1977 and 1983, Gallup asked virtually the same question as Roper in 1953—posing a choice between more imports and more restrictions—imports won just 12 percent to 15 percent support, as against 68 percent to 75 percent for restrictions.[12] And most Americans see a direct connection between imports and the loss of jobs. A 10 March 1983 Harris survey found that a 75 to 21 percent majority of respondents were convinced that import competition from abroad was harmful to American labor. There is also evidence that public sentiment is moved by both the trade balance and the state of the US economy. The percentage of Americans saying that "restrictions" were necessary to protect domestic industries fell from 56 percent in 1988 to 51 percent in 1990, then jumped to 63 percent in the recession year of 1991. Conversely, those willing to "allow free trade even if domestic industries are hurt" rose from 34 to 39 percent, and then dropped to 27 percent.[13]

Yet ambivalence remains, and so too does relative lack of interest. Presented in 1983 with the proposition that "we have to produce better products with more efficiency to compete in the world rather than depend on artificial trade barriers, such as tariffs," Americans agreed by 90 percent to 7 percent![14] One expert writing during the congressional trade storm in the spring of 1985 found "not much evidence" of "surging public resentment over our imbalance of trade."[15] A New York Times/CBS News poll three months later found "foreign trade" dead last in importance among five listed issues "that people are concerned about,"[16]

---

11. Ibid., 85.

12. Gallup Report International, October 1983. Roper asked, from 1973 to 1984: "Generally speaking, do you think the government should or should not place restrictions on imports of goods from other countries that are priced lower than American-made goods of the same kind?" Responses fluctuated narrowly, with 61 percent to 68 percent pro-restriction and 21 percent to 31 percent against. The 68 percent pro came in late 1979 and early 1983; the 31 percent against in late 1981. See William Schneider, "Protectionist Push is Coming from the Top," *National Journal*, 27 April 1985, 932.

13. New York Times/CBS News Poll, June Survey, 3–6 June 1991, processed, 4.

14. "The Harris Survey," 14 March 1983.

15. Schneider, "Protectionist Push," 932.

16. "Here are five things that people are concerned about—arms control, foreign trade problems, tax reform, the budget deficit and war in Central America. Which of these is most important right now . . ." Answers: arms control (19 percent); foreign trade (9 percent); tax reform (19 percent); budget deficit (29 percent); war in Central America (19 percent). July 1985 Survey, 3.

even though the subject had been in the news more prominently than at any time in postwar memory.[17]

There is, however, increasing public concern about Japan. In the 1990 Chicago Council on Foreign Relations poll, that nation tied for third place (and tied for first among the leadership sample) among countries Americans considered most important to the United States, but 60 percent of the public saw "the economic power of Japan" as "a critical threat . . . to the vital interest of the United States in the next 10 years." An overwhelming 71 percent of Americans agreed with the general statement that Japan practiced "unfair trade with the United States," compared with 40 percent believing the European Community was unfair. And on the Chicago Council's "feeling thermometer" charting Americans' attitudes toward specific countries, Japan dropped from an exceptionally high level of 61 percent in 1986 to 52 percent in 1990.[18]

But if mass opinion shows limited change, there is evidence of emerging divisions within leadership groups. The Chicago Council polls found that "top figures in business, labor, government, the media, religion and education" were 75 percent in favor of eliminating tariffs in 1978 but only 64 percent in favor in 1990. "Among labor leaders, the change was quite sharp," from 53 percent favoring tariffs in 1978 to 75 percent in 1990. Earlier indicators of such trends led William Schneider, a leading public opinion analyst, to conclude in 1983 that "trade protectionism is growing from the top down."[19] Lending further credence to Schneider's view was a 1983 survey of "opinion leaders" by the Opinion Research Corporation (ORC). It found 75 percent to 20 percent support for "industrial modernization agreements," which might include short-term relief from imports in exchange for management and labor commitments to improve efficiency.[20]

Doubtless the recession of 1982 and the strong dollar of 1980–85 influenced these polls. Conversely, business support for eliminating tariffs rose from 71 percent to 78 percent between 1986 and 1990, reflecting—

---

17. However, the 1990 poll of the Chicago Council on Foreign Relations found "Protecting the jobs of American workers" and "Protecting the interests of American business abroad" ranked no. 1 and no. 2 by the general public (though not by its leadership sample) among "a list of possible foreign policy goals that the United States should have." John E. Rielly, ed., *American Public Opinion and U.S. Foreign Policy 1991* (Chicago: Chicago Council on Foreign Relations, 1991), 15.

18. Ibid., 20–22, 28. By comparison, the "temperature" was 58 in 1986 and 56 in 1990 for France, 53 and 45 for China, and 62 in both years for Germany.

19. Schneider, "Trade Protectionism is Growing From the Top Down," *National Journal*, 29 January 1983, 240–41. Figures earlier in this paragraph come from Schneider and from Rielly, *American Public Opinion 1991*, 26–27.

20. LTV Corporation, "The Future of America's Basic Industries: A Survey of Opinion Leaders," conducted by Opinion Research Corporation, 1983.

presumably—the late 1980s' export boom. Still, it is clear that elite support for liberal trade has eroded, though it remains substantial.

Challenges to Laissez-Faire Trade Doctrine

Both reflecting and contributing to elite ambivalence was the increased questioning of liberal trade ideology, not just in the Washington policy community but at leading intellectual centers. Just as the Great Depression and postwar prosperity had discredited "protectionism," the relative decline of the United States weakened support for "free trade." The audience was growing for perspectives that held free trade ideology to be flawed or incomplete. The new challenges were of two basic sorts. The first, focusing on specific firms and industries, argued that the free trade-protectionist distinction was obsolete in a world characterized by pervasive government intervention in the marketplace. The second, which rose and fell with the trade imbalances, questioned the compatibility of open market policies with exchange rate misalignments that saddled producers with enormous competitive burdens not of their own making.

At the broadest level, proponents of the first school argued that the actual world economy was not at all like that posited by Adam Smith. The United States did not have autonomous firms jousting for business on their own, with rewards to the most efficient. Rather, other governments rigged the game through a range of actions—subsidies, product standards, procurement regulations—that favored their national producers at the expense of foreign competitors. American firms thus operated not on a level playing field, but on one tilted against them.

For some critics, the challenge was economywide. The Labor-Industry Coalition for International Trade (LICIT), comprising 8 firms and 11 labor organizations, found in 1983 that "our nation's industrial base has been weakened across a spectrum ranging from basic industries to the most technologically advanced." It placed much of the blame on "the widening gap between specific industry support efforts in other countries and the absence of such policies and programs in the United States." It argued that the "resulting 'industrial policy gap' has put American industry at a systematic disadvantage." To close the gap, LICIT recommended a range of policy changes aimed at both offsetting the effects of foreign industrial subsidies and providing broader government support to American industrial enterprise.[21]

In essence, the argument was that because other nations subsidize and protect their industries, the United States must do so, lest it fall

---

21. Labor-Industry Coalition for International Trade, *International Trade, Industrial Policies, and the Future of American Industry* (Washington: Labor-Industry Coalition for International Trade, 1983), iii, iv, 57–66.

behind. But the very comprehensiveness that made the LICIT line attractive for coalition-building purposes made it relatively easy for trade traditionalists to refute. For what made products move in international commerce was *comparative* advantage. No country could gain an across-the-board trade supremacy, since one had to import in order to export, and vice versa. A foreign government that subsidized its industries in general would not help any particular one and would probably contribute to overall inefficiency. Or if it subsidized a particular industry, like steel, costs would be borne by other sectors of its economy, and benefits would accrue to consumers of its steel, importers included. For the United States, the choice was then a simple one: accept the foreign subsidy in the form of cheaper steel (which would harm US steel makers but help steel users), or offset it with a countervailing duty. In this case also, no comprehensive policy response was required.

But what if a nation could prepare the way for market success tomorrow by helping an industry today? Many critics correctly argued that trade theory rested on "static comparative advantage." Trade flowed according to current prices, reflecting current production costs. But the process by which producers achieved international competitiveness was a dynamic one, subject to influence by national policies.[22] Governments might, by targeting growth sectors, create comparative advantage: they could aid and protect industries that would one day become strong enough to conquer world markets. Japan had done so persistently and successfully, argued scholars such as Ezra Vogel of Harvard and Chalmers Johnson of the University of California, Berkeley, creating what Johnson labeled the "developmental state."[23]

---

22. Classical trade theory did focus on static comparative advantage, but it does not necessarily follow that a longer-term perspective undercuts the liberal trade case. Indeed, a central theme in Mancur Olson's analysis is the opposite: that the "gains from trade" are much larger than traditional models specify because of the pressure that competition generates for technological innovation and ongoing resource reallocation. See Olson, *The Rise and Decline of Nations* (New Haven, CT: Yale University Press, 1982).

23. Ezra Vogel, *Japan as Number One: Lessons for Americans* (Cambridge, MA: Harvard University Press, 1979); Chalmers Johnson, *MITI and the Japanese Miracle: The Growth of Industrial Policy, 1925–1975* (Stanford, CA: Stanford University Press, 1982). On the critical side, Philip H. Trezise countered that such "models of Japan's postwar economic development are subject to so substantial a discount as to make them largely valueless as guides to understanding. . . . To suppose . . . that politicians and officials in league with businessmen were able to plan and guide Japan's explosive economic growth in detail is neither credible in the abstract nor (as will be seen) supported by the realities." See Trezise, "Politics, Government, and Economic Growth in Japan," in Hugh Patrick and Henry Rosovsky, eds., *Asia's New Giant: How the Japanese Economy Works* (Washington: Brookings Institution, 1976), 753–811. Marcus Noland finds that "while in some cases Japanese industrial policy may have successfully targeted industries, welfare-enhancing interventions have been the exception, not the rule." See Noland, "The Impact of Industrial Policy on Japan's Trade Specialization," *Review of Economics and Statistics* 75,

This raised the question of whether, for certain products in certain types of markets, industry-specific trade policy intervention might promote broader national interests, not just those of the specific workers and firms involved. The National Bureau of Economic Research (NBER) inaugurated a major project examining possible economic rationales for interventionist trade policies, export subsidies as well as import barriers, drawing upon oligopoly models of "imperfect" interfirm competition. In a world with a limited number of firms, some drawing support from home governments, the NBER analysts hypothesized, laissez-faire might not always be the best policy. In certain oligopolistic industries with increasing returns to scale, timely government intervention could enable American firms to gain a greater share of "supernormal profits," bringing gains to the nation greater than the cost of the subsidy provided.[24]

The conclusions of the NBER-sponsored analyses were tentative and cautious, recognizing the real-world difficulty of determining, in advance, when to intervene, in which industries, through what instruments. Centers of political analysis like the Berkeley Roundtable on the International Economy (BRIE) at the University of California, led by John Zysman and Stephen S. Cohen, were less hesitant in setting forth conceptual rationales for government intervention, which they viewed as essential to meet the Japanese challenge and guide the United States toward a competitive future industrial structure.[25] Meanwhile, on the East Coast, Bruce R. Scott and George C. Lodge were making a case for activist government industrial policy at the Harvard Business School.[26] And be-

---

no. 2 (May): 241–48. For other critical evaluations of the contribution of industry-specific policies to Japan's economic miracle, see Edward J. Lincoln, "Japan's Industrial Policy," prepared for the Japan Economic Institute of America (Washington, April 1984); and Gary R. Saxonhouse, "What Is All This about 'Industrial Targeting' in Japan?" *World Economy*, 6, no. 3 (September 1983): 253–73.

24. See Paul R. Krugman, ed., *Strategic Trade Policy and the New International Economics* (Cambridge, MA: MIT Press, 1986), esp. the articles by advocates James A. Brander and Barbara J. Spencer and by critic Gene M. Grossman. For a comprehensive critique of this literature, see J. David Richardson, "The Political Economy of Strategic Trade Policy," *International Organization* 44, no. 1 (Winter 1990): 107–35.

Of course, oligopoly has multiple effects, and in another essay Richardson cited empirical work showing "that the gains from trade were *larger* under imperfect competition than they would have been with perfectly competitive markets" (emphasis added). The quote is a paraphrase by Anne O. Krueger in Robert Z. Lawrence and Charles L. Schultze, eds., *An American Trade Strategy: Options for the 1990s* (Washington: Brookings Institution, 1990), 84n. The Richardson work is "Empirical Research on Trade Liberalization with Imperfect Competition: A Survey," *OECD Economic Studies*, no. 12 (Washington: Organization for Economic Cooperation and Development, Spring 1989): 8–44.

25. Stephen S. Cohen and John Zysman, *Manufacturing Matters: The Myth of the Post-Industrial Economy* (New York: Basic Books [for the Council on Foreign Relations], 1987).

26. See Bruce R. Scott and George C. Lodge, eds., *U.S. Competitiveness in the World Economy* (Boston: Harvard Business School Press, 1985).

fore the end of the Reagan administration, one of its battle-scarred trade negotiators, Clyde V. Prestowitz Jr., had resigned and written a book entitled *Changing Places: How We Allowed Japan to Take the Lead*. In it he documented, relentlessly, his argument that the divided, disorganized, multipurpose US government was no match for centrally orchestrated Japanese industrial policies. Hence we were "losing the chips,"[27] and many other industries besides.

Prescriptions varied as to how Americans should respond to government-created comparative advantage. Indeed, even critics like Prestowitz were not immune from the tendency to follow sweeping critiques with proposals for marginal policy change. No one in this school called for protection per se; in fact, all warned that a simple defensive response would only make things worse for the United States. But most were inclined toward some form of selective intervention, although their purposes varied. One arresting formulation was that of Robert B. Reich, who saw a need for the United States to move "beyond free trade." He argued that trade-related US policy should not be laissez-faire but pro-adjustment. The US goal should be one of "promoting the rapid transformation of all nations' industrial bases [especially that of the United States] toward higher-value production." Existing US trade policies had, in Reich's view, "just the opposite effect."[28]

The case for activist industrial policy rested on the conviction that the United States faced a deep and pervasive industrial competitiveness problem. As summarized by a trenchant skeptic, Charles L. Schultze, the cases of most proponents in the early 1980s were built on four premises: first, the United States had been "deindustrializing" and was suffering substantial losses (absolute or relative) in its manufacturing capacity; second, without assistance, US management and labor might not be capable of making the transition from old heavy to new high-technology industries; third, the United States was losing its edge in world export markets, with a consequent threat to its global leadership position; and fourth, other countries, and Japan in particular, had been successful in pursuing industrial policies, "selecting potential winners in the technological race" and nurturing them through a range of policy devices.[29]

If these four premises were correct, the conclusion followed clearly: the United States needed an aggressive industrial policy to manage the transition to a new industrial era, to move resources from declining industries into growth industries, to defend itself in a mercantilist world.

---

27. This was the title of Prestowitz's second chapter, on the semiconductor industry. See Prestowitz, *Changing Places* (New York: Basic Books, 1988).

28. Robert B. Reich, "Beyond Free Trade," *Foreign Affairs*, 61 no. 4 (Spring 1983): 790.

29. Charles L. Schultze, "Industrial Policy: A Solution in Search of a Problem," *California Management Review* 24, no. 4 (Summer 1983): 5–6.

Otherwise, this school suggested, the US economy might end up a sort of residual comprised of those industries that were left after more purposive nations had chosen theirs.

Schultze found this case unpersuasive: the evolution of international trade in the 1970s did not, on balance, support any of the four premises of the "industrial policy" critique. In fact, the US balance of trade in manufactured goods improved markedly during this period.[30] In addition, advocates of activist, industry-specific policy intervention carried a political burden. Such policy was far easier to prescribe than to pursue. Was the United States capable of selective mercantilism? Could its political system tilt in favor of industries with future potential and allocate resources to them? Or would political pressure from those currently feeling trade pain inevitably channel public resources to the entrenched, embattled industrial "losers"? Alternatively, if economywide industrial policy were attempted along LICIT-recommended lines, would not this build up, within the US government, strong bureaucratic interests in the welfare of specific industrial sectors, interests that would impede economywide adjustment and slow down growth for the nation as a whole?[31]

Industrial policy proposals flourished particularly in 1981–82, when the US economy suffered a severe cyclical downturn. They withered in the years thereafter, as the economy recovered and *domestic* laissez-faire gained backing inside and outside the administration. But if "industrial policy" became a label for policy packagers to avoid, the same was not true of "critical technologies," or "high-tech industries."[32] These phrases evoked a response: from many in the business community worried about future economic competitiveness, and from many in the defense community who saw loss of technological leadership as a threat to military preparedness.[33] There was particular anxiety about dependence on Japanese suppliers, and lively debate over whether and how the United States should respond. Congress enacted the Exon-Florio amendment to the 1988 Trade Act authorizing the president to block foreign takeovers of US firms on national security grounds, and a prominent 1991 proposal—

---

30. See Robert Z. Lawrence, *Can America Compete?* (Washington: Brookings Institution, 1984).

31. For a comprehensive argument linking the rise of "distributional coalitions" seeking maximum income for their members to slowdowns in national economic growth, see Olson, *The Rise and Decline of Nations.*

32. For an analysis by a "cautious activist," see Laura D'Andrea Tyson, *Who's Bashing Whom? Trade Conflicts in High-Technology Industries* (Washington: Institute for International Economics, 1992).

33. See Defense Science Board, *Defense Semiconductor Dependency* (Washington: Defense Science Board Task Force, Department of Defense, Office of the Under Secretary for Acquisition, February 1987).

the Collins-Gephardt bill—aimed to broaden the Exon-Florio review process to encompass threats to US technology.[34]

As these examples illustrate, Capitol Hill was a ready market for such ideas. Especially receptive were those who would challenge existing centers of trade leadership. This was part of the broader flowering of "issue politics." With decentralization in the Congress and electoral entrepreneurship in individual districts, members sought press attention by espousing "new ideas" that differentiated them from their political rivals. Both the internationalization of the US economy and the new forms of (fair and unfair) foreign competition provided ample sources of such ideas, particularly among activist Democrats. And the ideas of Cordell Hull were no longer at the intellectual cutting edge.

And even as the industrial-policy school was losing its audience, the American industrial trade balance was turning enormously negative. The prime cause was another phenomenon that highlighted the limits of laissez-faire trade doctrine—the incredible, unanticipated surge of the dollar (see chapter 3). By early 1985 the massive international capital inflows that were needed to finance record US budget deficits had driven the dollar to roughly 40 percent above the level that would have brought balance to the US international current (trade and services) account. This meant that in competition with foreign producers, American firms faced the equivalent of a 40 percent tax on their exports and a 40 percent subsidy on competing imports.[35]

As the French economist Albert Bressand put it, the United States seemed afflicted with " 'good things' that do not go together," a free-market currency regime that wreaked havoc on the free market in trade.[36] And, as C. Fred Bergsten noted as early as 1981, the trade imbalance produced by a strong dollar was bound to generate enormous pressure for trade restrictions as it expanded the ranks of the "trade losers" in the American industrial economy.[37] At the urging of such international economic policy analysts, organizations like the Business Roundtable began to make the overvalued dollar (and the undervalued yen) one of their chief "trade" policy priorities.

---

34. Edward M. Graham and Paul R. Krugman, *Foreign Direct Investment in the United States* (Washington: Institute for International Economics, second edition, 1991), 121–28.

35. John Williamson, *The Exchange Rate System*, POLICY ANALYSES IN INTERNATIONAL ECONOMICS 5 (Washington: Institute for International Economics, second edition, 1985); Stephen Marris, *Deficits and the Dollar: The World Economy at Risk*, POLICY ANALYSES IN INTERNATIONAL ECONOMICS 14 (Washington: Institute for International Economics, second edition, 1987).

36. Albert Bressand, "Mastering the 'Worldeconomy,'" *Foreign Affairs* 61, no. 4 (Spring 1983): 762.

37. C. Fred Bergsten, "The Costs of Reaganomics," *Foreign Policy*, no. 44 (Fall 1981): 24–36.

As in the case of industrial malaise, a focus on the exchange rate did not yield a persuasive, broadly supported, general-interest alternative for US trade policy. On the contrary, its message was that the required measures lay outside the trade sphere: such as the Group of Five initiative of September 1985, which helped move the dollar down, and like the continuing need to reduce the federal budget deficit. Explicators of macroeconomic causes and cures, in fact, performed a singular service to American trade politics in the mid-1980s, muting protectionist responses by exposing their irrelevance to the trade imbalance.[38] But then, after the dollar went down, the trade deficit continued to rise—for a year longer than most experts had expected.[39] A new skepticism emerged, built upon the seeming limits of exchange rate adjustment—especially vis-à-vis Japan—or on its costs in making US assets cheap to foreign investors.

In due course, the trade balance did improve, with manufactured products sharing disproportionately in the gains. Rust belt areas devastated by the 1981–82 recession were less affected by the recession of 1990–91. Still, US manufacturing employment remained below its spring 1979 record of 21.1 million workers. When it reached another prerecession peak a decade later, the total was just 19.6 million.

Moreover, years of misaligned exchange rates, together with intensified industrial competition, have spawned an intellectual challenge that puts free market purists on the ideological defensive. Liberal values continue, of course, to be widely held; no competing doctrine for trade policy has yet won comparable acceptance. Still, recent challenges have muted the liberal-protectionist dichotomy that served as an enormous political advantage to trade expanders throughout the postwar period. Thus, intellectually as well as politically and procedurally, the trade policy game has become more open, and this has added to the unpredictability of policy outcomes.

New Patterns of Interest-Group Politics

Finally, there were significant shifts from the pattern of trade politics that predominated in the early postwar period. During that time, a modest

---

38. Thus one contemporary analysis on the 1988 trade legislation noted that "the economic sophistication of Congress" had "improved greatly." "Most members of Congress recognize that foreign protection is not the cause of the trade deficit." Raymond J. Ahearn and Alfred Reifman, "Trade Legislation in 1987: Congress Takes Charge," in Robert E. Baldwin and J. David Richardson, eds., *Issues in the Uruguay Round* (Cambridge, MA: National Bureau of Economic Research, 1988), 80.

39. The common prognosis, reflected in the first edition of this book, was that dollar decline beginning in 1985 would lead to decline in the annual trade deficit by 1987. In fact, this did not arrive until 1988.

number of industries typically sought protection, each more or less on its own. Executive and congressional leaders encouraged each to go it alone, in order to avert logrolling of the Smoot-Hawley variety. They pointed the smaller industries toward the Tariff Commission (now the US International Trade Commission) and the quasi-judicial trade-remedy procedures. Larger industries, mainly textiles, cut separate deals for themselves, part of which involved promises not to obstruct broader trade-liberalizing initiatives like the Kennedy and Tokyo Rounds. No important groups took across-the-board protectionist stances.

Nor was there much self-initiated interest-group activism on the liberal trade side. National business and labor organizations were generally on call to endorse major new trade-expanding initiatives; yet once particular legislative battles were fought and won, the coalitions supporting them faded away. Nor were those who benefited specifically from open trade—importers, industrial consumers, and retail consumers—inclined to enter the political fray.[40]

The 1970s and 1980s have brought four significant changes in this pattern.

First and most important, the number and range of industries seeking governmental trade action have increased. Substantial protection has been achieved not just by the textile-apparel coalition, but by other mature industries such as steel and automobiles. Nor is pressure on trade policy any longer limited to those who are clearly current trade losers: the low-technology sectors whose manufacturing processes can be widely replicated around the world. The old rule was that losers enter trade politics while winners stick to business. But beginning in the late 1970s, producers of high-technology products like semiconductors, telecommunications, and machine tools were beginning to press for governmental action.

The Semiconductor Industry Association went to Capitol Hill with its concerns about Japanese competition. Executives of Corning, a leader in fiber optics, expressed concern that Japanese industrial targeting was making international trade a losing proposition for them. An important electronics firm, Motorola, began in 1982 to place a series of 20 full-page advertisements in the *Wall Street Journal* under the heading, "Meeting Japan's Challenge." And in early 1985, even David Packard, chairman of the board of the successful high-tech Hewlett-Packard Co. and cochair of

---

40. Those whose overall interests tilted toward open trade but who might at some point want protection for certain products were influenced by the long-established practice of "reciprocal noninterference," which induced them, in the words of E. E. Schattschneider, "to accept the incidental burdens" of others' protection without protest. See Schattschneider, *Politics, Pressures and the Tariff* (New York: Prentice-Hall, 1935), 284. Those actively involved in the import business felt disadvantaged in the political arena, since they could be charged with helping foreign interests take away American jobs. In both cases, abstention from politics therefore seemed the wisest course.

a binational US-Japan Advisory Commission, suggested that the United States consider imposing temporary quotas to "decrease the growth of Japan's exports to the U.S."[41]

What moved Motorola and other firms in technology-intensive industries was a new mix of export-market interest and import-market anxiety. As a group, they had done very well in the international marketplace; as noted in chapter 3, they were disproportionately responsible for the explosion of US exports in the 1970s. But they had suffered trade losses also, particularly in 1982–86, and they worried about competing, as solitary private actors, against what they feared was a government-industry combine headquartered in Tokyo. They contrasted the inroads Japanese producers were making in American markets with their own problems in selling across the Pacific. Their call was seldom for out-and-out protection (although the machine-tool industry did win import limits in 1986 on grounds of national security interests). Rather, they became advocates of what trade specialists call "sectoral reciprocity."[42] If, by hard negotiations, the US government could not persuade other nations—above all Japan—to open up their markets to US products, to establish a level playing field for trade, then the United States should take protective action in return.[43]

By and large, trade-afflicted firms still pursued their campaigns separately, on behalf of their particular industry groupings, though (as noted in chapter 6) they did join in coalitions seeking revision of the general trade-remedy laws. A textile-shoe alliance was formed in 1970—and again in 1985—to win statutory import quotas, but it faded as soon as the textile firms won new protection by traditional (executive-negotiated) means. At the same time, there did emerge in the 1970s and 1980s a major national, cross-industry organization—a coalition, more accurately—that took an across-the-board trade-restrictive stance. That was, of course, organized labor, whose shift from early postwar trade liberalism was the second major development in interest-group politics.

In its direct impact on trade legislation, labor's new protectionism was limited. After two decades, it had virtually nothing in statute to show for its major trade stands: for the Burke-Hartke quota bill of 1971, against the Nixon-Ford trade bill in 1973–74, for domestic-content legislation for

41. Letter from Packard to Stephen R. Levy, chairman, International Committee, American Electronics Association, 5 March 1985, released by AEA, Washington.

42. For an academic defense of this position, see Stephen D. Krasner, *Asymmetries in Japanese-American Trade: The Case for Specific Reciprocity*, Policy Papers in International Affairs 32 (Berkeley: University of California, Institute of International Studies, 1987).

43. For a sophisticated comparative analysis of the extent to which high-technology industries embraced the new "strategic trade" gospel, see Helen V. Milner and David B. Yoffie, "Between Free Trade and Protectionism: Strategic Trade Policy and a Theory of Corporate Trade Demands," *International Organization*, 43, no. 2 (Spring 1989): 239–72.

autos in 1981–84, and against extension of trade preferences to advanced developing countries in 1974 and 1984. An older labor priority, trade adjustment assistance for workers, was inaugurated in 1962 and expanded in 1974, but was gutted in 1981. Steel unions were able to obtain in the trade bill of 1984 a provision requiring firms to reinvest net cash flow in steel facilities and worker training. But as discussed in chapter 4, labor failed to exploit the vulnerability of that bill to extract concessions on any of a number of its long-standing concerns. Labor did score a major symbolic victory in the legislative drama of 1988: first, attaching to the omnibus legislation a requirement that workers be prenotified of plant closings; and then, after the president vetoed the bill because of this measure, forcing Reagan to swallow a separate bill with the identical requirement. Labor was, moreover, fast off the mark in 1991 in mobilizing opposition to granting fast-track authority for a free trade agreement with Mexico. But labor ended up losing this one, too, as it generally did on major trade issues.

What labor did achieve was indirect: it neutralized important potential supporters of liberal trade. The hearts and minds of many Democrats who voted for the domestic-content bills were elsewhere, but House members who were unwilling to buck the United Auto Workers (UAW) on a proposal that had so little other support were not going to be spear carriers for trade liberalization more generally. Instead, they would either look for issues on which they could take a trade-restrictive stance or confine their activism to other policy areas. Similarly, organizations like the Consumer Federation of America (CFA), an umbrella group that counted the UAW among its members, found the union "calling in some old debts" to extract an endorsement of domestic content. "On the surface, this might appear to go against consumer interests" in lower prices and in variety and quality of products, admitted the CFA's executive director to the *Wall Street Journal*. But "we appreciate all the work for consumer issues that the UAW has done over the years."[44]

More generally, consumers did not fulfill the hopes of liberal traders who saw them as a natural domestic constituency for international openness. Consumers Union did file a suit that contributed to temporary abandonment of US-EC-Japanese steel export restraint in the early 1970s. But the more politically activist consumer advocates like Ralph Nader did not play, lest labor be offended. (A symptom of this difficulty is the fact that Consumers for World Trade, a dedicated antiprotectionist lobbying group in Washington, has a board of directors that is impressive in its international economics and business expertise but limited in its connections to the domestic US consumer movement.)

There did emerge, however, an activist group on the trade-expanding side: the Emergency Committee for American Trade (ECAT), created in

---

44. *Wall Street Journal*, 3 September 1982.

1967. Unlike labor, this organization representing major multinational firms kept a relatively low profile but cultivated congressional power centers skillfully, supplying needed analysis and argumentation and staying alert to the timing of trade action (as labor often was not). Also active were general-purpose industry organizations like the Business Roundtable, the Chamber of Commerce, and the National Association of Manufacturers. In the mid-1980s, such general business groups became subject to cross-pressures within their memberships, as a result of increased US trade exposure and the record trade deficit.[45] But they recovered some of their unity and energy in the final stages of the omnibus legislation battle in 1988, and put forward a strong, unified effort to win extension of fast-track authority in 1991.

The third new development in interest-group politics was the emergence of "special interests" who benefited from exports or imports and were driven, by the prospect of economic losses, to do direct battle against seekers of protection.[46]

One example came in mid-1983. The Reagan administration, unable to win Chinese adherence to stringent textile restraints, imposed quotas unilaterally. The government in Beijing, urged on by Washington-based liberal trade advocates, retaliated by withholding purchases of American grain. This brought farm organizations—and Senate Finance Committee Chairman Robert J. Dole (R-KS)—into the fray in a campaign to soften the administration's stance.

In mid-1984, again under industry pressure, the administration moved to tighten enforcement of country-of-origin rules under the textile quota regime. Importers and retailers charged that this would "steal Christmas" by making them unable to fill their orders for the holiday season. The Retail Trade Action Coalition (RITAC), representing major chain stores and trade associations, raised such a howl that the administration first deferred implementation of the new rules and then adjusted them to ease their impact.

In that same summer, after the USITC found that imports had injured the US copper industry, fabricators of wire and other copper products protested that this would simply lead to increased import competition for them without giving the producers more than temporary relief. They made it clear to the White House, facing decision in the midst of the election campaign, that they had more workers than did the copper mines, and that their workers were more strategically placed insofar as electoral college votes were concerned. Their argument was a factor in the president's decision not to grant protection to the copper producers.

---

45. See I. M. Destler and John S. Odell, assisted by Kimberly Ann Elliott, *Anti-Protection: Changing Forces in United States Trade Politics*, POLICY ANALYSES IN INTERNATIONAL ECONOMICS 21 (Washington: Institute for International Economics, 1987), chap. 6.

46. Ibid.

A year later, shoe retailers mobilized against a USITC recommendation for footwear import quotas, getting 19 Republican senators to sign a letter in opposition. Reagan said no to shoe protection as well. The new activism of apparel retailers was visible in resistance to textile quota bills of 1985, 1988, and 1990. Users of steel worked against the renewal of negotiated quotas in 1989 and may have influenced President Bush's commitment to phase out protection in two and a half years. Stung by the Commerce Department's imposition in 1989 of antidumping duties on ball bearings, a broadly used industrial input, firms began mobilizing for reform of the dumping laws. And when the Semiconductor Industry Association sought renewal, in 1991, of the trade agreement with Japan, it had to deal with chip users burned by the sharp price rises that the agreement had precipitated in 1987 and 1988.[47] They insisted that the renewal pact include softer constraints on pricing in the US market. SIA acceded, since it needed the users' backing in order to persuade the lukewarm Bush administration to back a renewal.

Such antiprotectionist groups often worked in parallel with foreign interests: auto retailers worked with Japan-based companies; on copper, the National Electrical Manufacturers Association played an up-front role, with the government of Chile (the principal copper exporter) very active in the background. And while Toshiba spent millions to block a statutory embargo on its products—an initiative provoked when a Toshiba subsidiary sold sensitive equipment to the Soviet Union—the decisive pressure came, by several accounts, from US firms that feared the disruptive costs of being cut off from Toshiba inputs.[48] Taken together, the activity of domestic and foreign antiprotection interests provided a welcome—if hardly equal—balance to the activity of protection seekers. It communicated one important political point. As firms seeking trade relief escalated their demands, they could no longer be assured that adversely affected business interests would stay on the sidelines. Politicians were likely to feel pressure from more than one direction.

And if some saw the foreign element in this lobbying as nefarious, others viewed it as a normal consequence of internationalization. In a world of multinational firms, Kenichi Ohmae preached the pervasiveness of interdependence,[49] and Robert Reich asked the gut question, "Who

47. Laura D'Andrea Tyson, *Who's Bashing Whom?* chap. 4.

48. For a sweeping and thoroughly unconvincing picture of omnipresent, ever-winning lobbyists for Japanese interests, see Pat Choate, *Agents of Influence: How Japan's Lobbyists in the United States Manipulate America's Political and Economic System* (New York: Alfred A. Knopf, 1990).

49. Kenichi Ohmae, *Triad Power: The Coming Shape of Global Competition* (New York: Free Press, 1985).

Is Us?"[50] If, in certain industries, it was the foreign-owned firms that were producing high-value-added products on American soil, should not US policy be supporting them rather than the Asia-based production of American-owned electronics firms?

The fourth interesting development in interest-group politics was the apparent erosion in the strength and political astuteness of the oldest supporters of protection. The steel industry was one apparent case. More significant, at least potentially, was the textile-apparel coalition.

Throughout the postwar era, textile industry leaders had dealt effectively with both branches of government. They would win action commitments from presidential candidates of both political parties: John F. Kennedy in 1960, Richard M. Nixon and Hubert H. Humphrey in 1968, Ronald Reagan in 1980. They would show, on Capitol Hill, a capacity to block or threaten trade liberalizing legislation—from the Eisenhower administration in the late 1950s to the Carter administration in the late 1970s. They seemed to understand that Congress would not, in the end, enact a bill restricting textile imports: that was outside the rules of the postwar policy game. But by working both ends of Pennsylvania Avenue, the textile executives repeatedly won new increments in *negotiated* textile protection.

In the mid-1980s, the industry began by employing a similar strategy. Imports were now a really serious problem: after slow growth in the 1960s and 1970s, the import-consumption ratio for textiles and apparel rose from 12.1 percent in 1980 to 22 percent in 1986, and from 18.4 percent to 31.1 percent for apparel alone.[51] In response the industry put forward a bill, proposed by Ed Jenkins (D-GA), whose formal aim was to impose statutory quotas on textile imports but whose effect was to toughen the US position in negotiations for renewal of the Multi-Fiber Arrangement (MFA). After favorable House and Senate action and the expected Reagan veto in December 1985, the industry's House backers developed a new twist. Rather than following the standard practice of going for an override vote as soon as possible after the bill was returned, they arranged for such a vote to be scheduled eight months later, when the MFA talks were to be concluded. This kept the heat on USTR negotiators, and achieved at least a marginal stiffening of the US position.

But in the years thereafter the industry overreached, abandoning its hitherto winning formula. Intoxicated perhaps by coming so close to enacting a quota bill—the House override vote in 1986 was eight votes shy of the two-thirds required—textile executives overrode the cautions of their Washington representatives and made enactment of stiff quota

50. This was the title of a widely read article in the January–February 1990 *Harvard Business Review*, 53–64.

51. William R. Cline, *The Future of World Trade in Textiles and Apparel* (Washington: Institute for International Economics, revised edition, 1990), 49.

legislation their overarching political goal. Previously they might have held an omnibus bill hostage; now they allowed the legislation of 1987-88 to move forward, in exchange for the promise of smooth procedural sailing for their separate bill.[52] Both the House Ways and Means and Senate Finance committees kept the promise, reporting the industry bill for floor action without recommendation, but the Senate did not pass it until September 1988. Reagan promptly vetoed it, and the House override failed by 11 votes. In 1990, the ritual was repeated, with George Bush casting the veto this time and the industry losing the override by 10 votes.

Neither vote yielded anything discernible for the industry, though both allowed strong (slightly under two-thirds) majorities in both chambers to go on record for textile protection, secure in the expectation that the bill would fail. In the meantime, textile representatives reportedly alienated USTR Carla Hills with both the style and substance of their uncompromising position on the Uruguay Round textile talks. This increased the risk of a negotiated phaseout of the MFA, which developing countries were demanding.

At a minimum, the industry seemed guilty of serious tactical miscalculation. Its failure also reinforced a growing feeling that its trade policy power had peaked, an impression reinforced by evidence of strains in the coalition between cloth and apparel makers. The industry remained one, of course, that no trade policy leader could ignore. But in contrast to previous decades, the industry was now presenting to executive and congressional leaders both the incentive and the opportunity to confront and beat it politically, rather than join in negotiating trade-restrictive compromises.

Conclusions

Trade politics has become more partisan. The elite has grown less committed to liberal trade. Intellectual challenges to open-market policies have grown. Patterns of trade politics have become more complex. All these changes have weakened the old system for diverting and managing trade policy pressures, and most have increased the political weight of those backing trade restrictions.

The greatest risk, at least potentially, is that posed by the *threat* of a new interparty competition on trade policy. If the Democrats were in fact to become an out-and-out protectionist party, this would risk for

---

52. In the House they had no choice: Speaker Jim Wright (D-TX) insisted on keeping product-specific measures out of the omnibus trade bill. In the Senate, however, industry leaders could have exploited the chamber's more open rules by seeking to attach their bill as a rider to the omnibus legislation.

trade policy the fate that befell policy toward the Soviet Union and arms control in the 1970s and early 1980s. A new president would represent not continuity but drastic change. And this would remove the strongest anchor of the old trade-management system—the liberal-leaning executive branch.

Most of the other changes point not toward protectionism in the traditional sense, but toward greater negotiating activism, more confrontation with trading partners, stronger emphasis on unfair-trade statutes, and increased readiness to brandish the *threat* of protection at home to pry open markets abroad. Super 301 was a natural response to these pressures.

At a minimum, these changes have combined with changes in the congressional, executive, and regulatory domains to make trade politics a much more open, unpredictable game. Possible consequences are considered in chapter 8; what the United States might do about it is addressed thereafter.

III

SUMMATION AND PRESCRIPTION

8

Summing Up: The System Held, But Stay Tuned

"Taken together, the four previous chapters depict an American trade policymaking system that shows serious erosion."[1] So concluded the first edition of this book, published in the white heat of still-rising trade deficits and the unprecedented congressional activism of the mid-1980s. Record import penetration generated record pressure on legislators. They were less protected from such pressure than before because of their own internal reforms, and because the Reagan administration had been slow to provide needed leadership. Thus as Congress was driving to enact strong, and potentially very restrictive, trade legislation, the executive had lost the initiative and was struggling to regain it.

Compounding these problems was the transformation of the trade-remedy laws, from instruments for diverting pressure to vehicles for attaining it, often by forcing voluntary export restraints like those won by the steel industry from the Reagan administration. Congressional Democrats were on the march, and trade was displayed prominently on the banners they unfurled. Belief in the virtues of liberal trade was waning, particularly among elites. And American trade protection was growing. Thus, the weakened US trade policymaking system faced "some bleak prospects":[2] a new ideological debate on trade, a further surge of process protectionism through the trade-remedy laws, or perhaps even a return to legislated protectionism à la Smoot-Hawley.

---

1. *American Trade Politics: System Under Stress* (Washington: Institute for International Economics and New York: Twentieth Century Fund, 1986), 165.

2. Ibid., 172–75.

It is clear that the United States has avoided the worst among *those* outcomes. The system has, in essence, held. But it has sustained further damage in the process. Moreover, as of early 1992 it confronted:

- a persistent US recession, combined with deepening pessimism about longer-term US growth prospects;

- continuing stalemate and possible breakdown in the global (Uruguay Round) trade negotiations;

- a new, more intense round of Japan bashing in the United States, accompanied this time by America bashing across the Pacific;

- the end of the Cold War, indeed the disintegration of the Soviet adversary, removing one strong force for economic cooperation in a newly tripolar world.

At once victim and catalyst of this volatile new brew was President George Bush, whose disastrous January 1992 trip to Tokyo threw American trade politics into disarray and undercut the president's capacity to play his essential, stabilizing role. Meanwhile, the presidential election campaign was heating up, with Pat Buchanan's protectionist, "America First" campaign challenging Bush from the Republican right and Democrats on his left jousting over how to turn the new situation to advantage. This chapter summarizes the situation as of that time; chapter 9 brings the story through 1994.

First, Some Good News

In the mid-1980s, even as the trade-politics steamroller seemed to gather speed, the economics were changing direction. The dollar peaked in late February 1985, and dollar depreciation became the declared objective of the advanced industrial countries at the Plaza the following September. By the last quarter of 1986, the *constant-dollar* trade deficit (reflecting all-important volumes of goods) began to decline. A year later, the *nominal* deficit followed. American exports surged. Between 1986 and 1990, they rose 74 percent overall, 90 percent for manufactured goods, and 81 percent to Japan. Not until 1991 would the total deficit fall below the magic number of $100 billion, to $74.1 billion, but the ratio of imports to exports dropped over this period from 1.65 in 1986 to 1.18 in 1991.

During 1980–85, the trend had been quite the opposite. The trade deficit shot up from $25 billion to $122 billion, dwarfing the previous peak deficits of $6.5 billion in 1972 and $34 billion in 1978. Of course, the dollar value of US trade had grown almost sixfold between 1970 and 1980, and so it was not surprising that the trade deficits of the 1980s were larger. Indeed, due largely to inflation, virtually all US economic aggregates—gross national product, government spending, etc.—had ballooned during the 1980s beyond previous comprehension. What was alarming was that the US imbalance was proportionately greater with each cycle. US merchandise imports were 113 percent of exports in 1972, 124 percent in 1978, and 157 percent in 1985.

Not only was this imbalance unprecedented for modern America; it was the worst imbalance experience by any advanced industrial nation since the 1940s. To finance the trade deficit—and the related federal budget deficit—the United States was "going into debt faster than any major developed country since World War II, and faster than the average of the seven major developing-country debtors on the eve of the debt crisis."[3]

For the early and mid-1980s, moreover, the current-dollar trade figures understated the real changes in product flows, and hence trade's impact on US producers, because the super-strong dollar depressed the prices of imports as denominated in the US currency. Measured on a price-deflated basis, total merchandise imports rose from 18.9 percent to 25.8 percent of US goods production between 1980 and 1986. And between 1980 and 1984, exports plunged as a share of goods production from 18.0 percent to 14.8 percent,[4] a drop nearly as great as that precipitated 50 years earlier by the Great Depression and the Smoot-Hawley act.[5]

Thus American producer interests that normally had the strongest stakes in trade expansion found themselves at a serious disadvantage in overseas markets, even as foreign products surged into US markets. So, even as many more industries hurt by imports sought trade protection, the political counterweight weakened as exporters lost market share and grew demoralized.

---

3. Stephen Marris, *Deficits and the Dollar: The World Economy at Risk*, POLICY ANALYSES IN INTERNATIONAL ECONOMICS 14 (Washington: Institute for International Economics, first edition, 1985), 94.

4. These percentages are based on production and trade in 1982 dollars, as reported by the Bureau of Economic Analysis, Department of Commerce. See *Economic Report of the President*, February 1991, tables B-7 and B-21. The careful reader may notice that these figures differ from those in the first edition, which were calculated using the 1972 dollar data then available.

The pattern between 1970 and 1980, by contrast, was of a significant increase in the proportion of *both* imports and exports: the former rose from 14.7 percent to 18.9 percent of US goods production, and the latter surged from 11.7 percent to 18.0 percent. This growth was part of an enormous expansion in the volume of trade worldwide.

5. Between 1929 and 1933, price-deflated merchandise exports dropped from roughly 9.6 percent to 7.6 percent, or by 21 percent, as a share of US goods production. Between 1980 and 1984 they dropped by 18 percent. Percentages are computed from data in 1982 dollars. See *Economic Report of the President*, February 1991, tables B-7 and B-21.

Procedural norms and pressure-diverting devices could not be expected to survive overwhelming political assault. They are useful at the margins, for calling in counterforces, for muting certain influences, and for encouraging others. They are helpful for riding out tough economic and political periods. But if the circumstances of the mid-1980s had continued, driving both export and import-competing interests to question whether open international trade served their interests, it is most unlikely that the system could have held.

Fortunately, in late 1986, the trade numbers began to improve: the constant-dollar ratio of exports to goods production rebounded to 15.2 percent in 1986, 19.4 percent in 1988, and 23.2 percent in 1990.[6] And as the trade balance improved, the political balance did likewise. The number of administrative trade cases leveled off in 1985–86 and fell significantly beginning in 1987. The number of trade bills did not decline, but seasoned Capitol Hill observers noted a sharp fall-off in the number of *new* trade-impacted industry claimants. Thus the Reagan administration, which had granted much import relief in its first term, gave surprisingly little in its second. And American exporters reentered the political fray to support liberalization and fight proposed laws that might impede open trade. Their boom was beginning, and they wanted it to continue.

Even at the peak of their activism, congressional leaders were reluctant to reclaim direct, product-specific authority over trade policy. They failed to override a presidential veto of textile quotas in 1986, as well as in 1988 and in 1990. They did initiate, and push to fruition, the Omnibus Trade and Competitiveness Act of 1988, the first major trade bill *not* originating with the executive since the days before Smoot-Hawley. But Congress excluded product-specific measures from that law, and watered down measures aimed at further tilting the trade-remedy laws. The act's main theme was not protectionism on imports but aggressiveness on exports. And though the prime vehicle of this approach, Section 301, has been widely and bitterly denounced abroad, it appears to have had a net liberalizing effect on world trade, and to have been tolerated by America's trading partners.[7]

The years since mid-decade have also seen a reassertion of executive branch trade leadership. This began on 23 September 1985, the day after the Plaza Agreement, with President Ronald Reagan's White House speech calling for "fair trade" and announcing that the administration would, for the first time, initiate unfair-trade cases against foreign firms and

---

6. The parallel imports-production ratio also kept rising, albeit at a slower pace, from 25.8 percent in 1986 to 28.2 percent in 1990.

7. Thomas O. Bayard and Kimberly Ann Elliott, *Reciprocity and Retaliation in U.S. Trade Policy* (Washington: Institute for International Economics, 1994).

governments. And if, under the circumstances, US Trade Representative (USTR) Clayton Yeutter was inevitably in a defensive posture, his successor—Carla Hills—was able to take the offensive. Turning statutory mandates into opportunities, she pressed specific trade cases with Japan and other nations, even as she softened the hard edges of "Super 301." Consulting assiduously with Congress in general, and the trade committees in particular, she could declare the Uruguay Round her "top trade liberalization priority" and subsequently win plaudits on Capitol Hill for her willingness to walk away from the negotiating table when the requisite deal did not materialize.

Hills's enhanced credibility helped make possible the extension of fast-track authority in the spring of 1991, as Congress renewed one more time its delegation of negotiating power. Thus was extended the notable, interbranch political innovation of the 1970s, which made it possible for the United States to negotiate and implement nontariff trade agreements. Extension of fast-track renewed the possibility of constructive US leadership in the Uruguay Round, just as the procedure had made possible the completion of the Tokyo Round. The vote of confidence was all the more impressive given the stalemate at Geneva and the new issues raised by the proposal by President Bush and Mexican President Carlos Salinas de Gortari for a free trade agreement between the United States and Mexico.

So the system held. Congress pressed its priorities—its predisposition toward toughness—but Congress refrained from reclaiming, directly, the primary trade power granted by the Constitution.[8] Pro-trade interests rose to counter the forces for restriction. The USTR, armed with new statutory powers, had once again vindicated its anomalous, but critical, brokering role.

But the Bush administration incumbent, Carla Hills, had used the prospect of a Uruguay Round breakthrough to hold it all together. Even if she proved successful on that front, and won approval of the implementing bill to follow, difficulties would remain. Moreover, President Bush—who supported Hills on many specific occasions—showed astonishing incompetence in the way in which he raised trade issues during his star-crossed trip to Tokyo in January 1992. This trip reflected a broader weakness: that of a president (and a policymaking system) that separated political-strategic from economic issues and blundered badly when the fractious economic relationship with Japan emerged as central to the new high politics of the post–Cold War era.

---

8. For an extended discussion of why such restraint may serve legislators' political interests, see my "Delegating Trade Policy," in Paul E. Peterson, ed., *The President, the Congress, and the Making of Foreign Policy,* (Norman: University of Oklahoma Press, 1994).

Next, The Bad News

Notwithstanding the good news on several fronts, liberal trade policy remained on the defensive in the early 1990s. Trade deficits compounded frustration over trade with specific countries and in specific products to fuel new initiatives, such as the bill introduced in November 1991 by Representatives Richard A. Gephardt (D-MO) and Sander Levin (D-MI) to extend Super 301 and "give it teeth."[9]

Imports continued to exceed exports, albeit less egregiously. The imbalance for 1991 was down to $74.1 billion (table 3.1), after seven years of 12-digit figures, and the deficit with Japan held at just over $40 billion. This was down from the peak of $56 billion in 1987; in fact, for each of the years 1988 through 1990, Japan's sales to the United States grew less rapidly than total US imports, and Japanese purchases from the United States grew more rapidly than total US exports. But because the proportionate imbalance had been so great, the deficit receded but slowly.[10]

So the trade imbalance remained one burden that trade policy had to bear, and one very likely to continue until Americans took strong further action on the fiscal front. A second burden was the continuing American competitive decline, relative to East Asian trading partners in particular, and the two-decade-old stagnation of American living standards. Both were exacerbated—and made visible—by the slow growth and recession of the first years of the Bush administration.[11] Economic unhap-

---

9. Statement of 4 November 1991 by Richard A. Gephardt, as released that day by his office. The bill was drafted to force attention to Japan in general and trade in auto parts in particular. The deficit in auto parts trade was growing because of foreign purchases by "Japanese transplant" factories in the United States.

10. In 1985–87, US imports from Japan were triple the level of US exports to that country. This meant that, for the bilateral deficit to decline, US exports had to grow at more than three times the rate of import growth. In fact, they grew 12 times as fast between 1987 and 1990, reducing the total imbalance and bringing the ratio of US imports to exports down below 2-to-1 by 1990. But while this was economically and statistically significant, the fact that Japan now sold to the United States "only" about double what it bought from the US was hardly the sort of change that could transform the political arena.

Moreover, the US-Japan imbalance rose from $41.1 billion in 1990 to $43.4 billion in 1991, just as the US global imbalance was showing sharp improvement. This fueled charges that the American trade problem was now primarily with Japan. In arguing for a new Super 301 targeted at Japan, Representative Richard Gephardt noted that "with Japan we continue to have a $40 billion trade deficit out of a total of a $60 billion trade deficit," and argued that this reflected an "incompatibility" between Japan and the rest of the world. Address of 10 September 1991, at the Institute for International Economics, Washington, Reuter transcript, processed, 10.

11. Real US economic growth averaged under 1 percent for the first three years of President Bush's term, the worst for any president since the postwar readjustment under President Harry S Truman. Ironically, the recession made the US trade deficit lower than it would otherwise have been, because it reduced demand for imports.

piness helped fuel perceptions of "unfairness"—in the trading system as a whole and in trade with Japan in particular. It was not that Americans simply exported the blame for their troubles: in fact, their main targets seemed to be themselves (for loss of moral fiber[12]) and the politicians in Washington, particularly those on Capitol Hill. And when President Bush took the Big Three auto executives to Tokyo with him in January 1992, they became targets also—for drawing salaries several times those of their Japanese counterparts even as their firms were losing money and market share. But resentment of the Japanese grew also. And frustration with economic circumstances continued to eat away at prevailing policies and institutions—liberal trade, the GATT—just as postwar economic success had served to strengthened them.

Moreover, changes in American trade law had created powerful incentives for business and labor to define their trade problems as involving "unfair" foreign practices. As noted in chapter 6, the 1988 act ended up making few consequential changes in the trade-remedy laws. But the rewriting of these laws in the 1970s transformed the system from one under which relief was almost never granted to one where it was widely available.

The change was particularly striking in the flow of antidumping cases. During the course of the 1980s, only 7 percent of the cases carried to completion were rejected due to a failure to prove dumping. An additional 40 percent, it is true, fell through a failure to prove injury, but it remained far easier for firms to show "material injury" under the antidumping statute than to establish that imports were a "substantial cause of serious injury," as required under the escape clause (Section 201). And antidumping relief was automatic once the dumping and injury tests were met, whereas the president could overrule the recommendation of the US International Trade Commission in cases brought under Section 201.

The result was a skewed trade-remedy system, with the antidumping statute serving de facto as the United States' escape clause and Section 201 being virtually ignored. In the early 1980s, the antidumping and countervailing duty laws were used primarily to generate pressure for political fixes, culminating in the steel voluntary export restraints (VERs) negotiated by the Reagan administration in 1984–85 (and extended by President Bush in 1989). More recently, relief has typically been granted

---

12. "The public . . . sees the economy not in terms of new technology, productivity and a more technically skilled work force but mainly in terms of consumption and 'moral fiber'. . . . In the economy, people see the United States as producing shoddy and disposable products that do not match the high quality of Japanese goods. In education, people see permissiveness, drugs, and lack of discipline." Daniel Yankelovich, *Coming to Public Judgment: Making Democracy Work in a Complex World* (Syracuse: Syracuse University Press, 1991), 102.

within the rules of the antidumping statute—rules that tilt the playing field significantly in favor of the petitioning industry. But whatever the specific path to protection, the fact that this statute attacks allegedly "unfair" foreign practices makes support for balancing amendments hard to mobilize in the American political arena. It also undercuts opposition to trade restrictions in specific cases.[13]

There was other movement toward new protection of the American market. The early 1980s brought acceleration of a well-established postwar pattern: pressure for trade restrictions led not to statutory protection but to a growing number of "special deals" for "special cases," arranged by the executive branch. Automobiles, the largest and long the proudest of US manufacturing industries, sought and won protection in 1981, as Japan enforced VERs at the Reagan administration's behest. Sugar import quotas were reimposed in 1982. Carbon steel restraints were negotiated with the European Community in 1982 and with other major exporters two years later. Meanwhile, producers of motorcycles, specialty steel, and wood shingles gained temporary protection through escape clause proceedings, machine-tool makers won a presidential import-relief decision on national security grounds, and the textile industry won several tightenings of the rules for enforcing quota restrictions.

Taken together these cases meant a substantial expansion of the proportion of the US market governed by "managed trade." Bela and Carol Balassa found just 6.2 percent of US manufactured imports subject to visible quantitative restrictions in 1980; in 1981–83, an additional 6.52 percent of US imports came under such restraints.[14] Gary Clyde Hufbauer and his colleagues calculated that "US imports covered by special protection," including high tariffs as well as quantitative restraints, rose from 12 percent of total imports in 1980 to 21 percent in 1984.[15]

The Balassa and Hufbauer estimates seem, at first glance, to indicate very substantial increases in US protection during the early 1980s: more

---

13. In a study of 14 product episodes, John S. Odell and I concluded—on the basis of quantitative and qualitative evidence—that "the growing tendency of US petitioners and politicians to seek import relief by alleging unfair foreign practices clearly suppresses anti-protection political activity, whether the claim is legitimate in a given case or not." See Destler and Odell, assisted by Kimberly Ann Elliott, *Anti-Protection: Changing Forces in United States Trade Politics*, POLICY ANALYSES IN INTERNATIONAL ECONOMICS 21 (Washington: Institute for International Economics, 1987), 135; see also 73–74 and appendix C.

14. Bela and Carol Balassa, "Industrial Protection in the Developed Countries," *World Economy* (June 1984): 187. For the product breakdown, see their "Levels of Protection on Manufactured Goods: The U.S., EC, Canada, Japan," 1984, processed.

15. Gary Clyde Hufbauer, Diane T. Berliner, and Kimberly Ann Elliott, *Trade Protection in the United States: 31 Case Studies* (Washington: Institute for International Economics, 1986), 21.

than a doubling by the first measure. And a broader econometric analysis by two World Bank economists reaches an even stronger conclusion. Examining the total welfare costs to the US economy in 1984 of VERs in the auto, textile, and steel sectors, Jaime de Melo and David Tarr found that it was equivalent to imposing an average tariff level of 23.4 percent on *all* US products. They concluded, therefore, that "Qrs [quantitative restraints] have taken us back to pre–World War II levels" in terms of the total costs of protection to the United States.[16]

Such evidence seems to vindicate the conclusion of many contemporary observers, in the words of a 1985 *New York Times* editorial, that "industry by industry, the battle to maintain open markets is being lost."[17] But on closer examination, the numbers cited above tend to exaggerate the actual protection provided by US import restraints. The de Melo-Tarr analysis finds "about two-thirds of welfare costs are due to the rent transfer component"—the fact that VERs make it possible for foreign suppliers to raise their prices and thereby increase their profits.[18] And the increase found by the Balassas and the Hufbauer study is due almost entirely to a single—albeit important—trade policy action, the Japanese VER imposed in 1981 on auto exports to the US market. Without the $29 billion in imports covered under this VER in 1984, the Hufbauer measure would have remained at 12 percent, and the Balassas' measure of the increase in US protection would have been under 1 percent. (The auto VERs have similar impact, proportionately, in the de Melo-Tarr analysis.)

The auto restraints remained technically in force throughout the decade, but they had lost their bite by the late 1980s. Quotas were enlarged by 24 percent in 1985, and the combination of the weaker dollar

---

16. Jaime de Melo and David Tarr, *A General Equilibrium Analysis of United States Foreign Trade Policy* (Cambridge, MA: MIT Press, 1992), chap. 9, 15. See also the authors' "Welfare Costs of U.S. Quotas in Textiles, Steel and Autos," *Review of Economics and Statistics* 72, no. 3 (August 1990).

17. "Even Out the Free Trade Pain," *New York Times*, 14 January 1985. Even then, of course, the increased imposition of legal impediments to imports represented in part a rear-guard, defensive reaction to the ongoing internationalization of the US economy. In this sense, it was perhaps a testimony to the success of liberal policies rather than a harbinger of their failure. A related interpretation is that of Charles Lipson, who asked in 1982 why "world trade has continued to grow while trade restraints have been tightened." He concluded that the new barriers were in mature, basic industries, while trade expansion had come mainly in growth sectors where industries have differentiated products and high R&D expenditure. See Lipson, "The Transformation of Trade: The Sources and Effects of Regime Change," *International Organization* 36, no. 2 (Spring 1982): 417–55.

18. de Melo and Tarr, *A General Equilibrium Analysis*, chap. 9, 4. For a comprehensive analysis of the costs of "quota rents" reaped by foreign producers, leading to an argument for the elimination of VERs, see C. Fred Bergsten et al., *Auction Quotas and United States Trade Policy*, POLICY ANALYSES IN INTERNATIONAL ECONOMICS 19 (Washington: Institute for International Economics, 1987).

and increased car production by Japanese firms on American soil made it increasingly difficult for Toyota and its rivals to fill the quotas in the years thereafter: imports dropped below 2 million vehicles a year, whereas the VER allowed 2.3 million. Japan's Ministry for International Trade and Industry (MITI) kept extending the auto VER, to avoid the political storm that might follow its removal, but it had become all symbol, no substance.[19]

Restraints on textiles retained their bite, of course, notwithstanding the failure of the industry to win statutory protection, and notwithstanding the Uruguay Round prospects for liberalizing or terminating the Multi-Fiber Arrangement (MFA).[20] And the number of products subject to countervailing or antidumping duties rose 42 percent between mid-1983 and the end of 1990. There was also, as discussed in chapters 5 and 7, a new precedent for managed trade in semiconductors—under the US-Japan agreement reached in 1986 and renewed in 1991. In summary, however, the most reasonable conclusion is that American trade protection increased sharply in the early 1980s but receded somewhat thereafter. The net increase over the decade was less than one might have expected given the pressures at play.

Recent years have also brought a modest shift in the focus of trade-liberalizing energies: from multilateral to bilateral and regional negotiations. The former continued to have top priority for the USTR—and, when pressed, for Presidents Ronald Reagan and George Bush as well. Yet the US negotiations with Canada and Mexico signaled an American willingness to pursue preferential arrangements close to home, and Bush's Enterprise for the Americas Initiative invited other Latin American nations to come forward with their own liberalization proposals.[21]

A further cause for concern in the early 1990s was the new vulnerability of the fast-track process. This expedited-vote, no-amendment procedure for implementing trade agreements was born in the Trade Act of 1974, extended for eight years in the Trade Agreements Act of 1979, broadened to encompass bilateral deals in the Trade and Tariff Act of 1984, extended with modest amendments in the Omnibus Trade and

---

19. Thus, a subsequent study by Hufbauer and Elliott finds that the "share of total US exports affected by trade barriers dropped from 21.5 percent of all imports in 1984 to only 10.4 percent in 1990." See their *Measuring the Costs of Trade Protection in the United States* (Washington: Institute for International Economics, 1994), 14.

20. Imports of textiles and apparel rose sharply in the 1980s, the MFA notwithstanding. For detail on that trade, the costs of textile and apparel protection, and Uruguay Round alternatives, see William R. Cline, *The Future of World Trade in Textiles and Apparel* (Washington: Institute for International Economics, second edition, 1990).

21. J. David Richardson labels this approach "minilateralism," a readiness to pursue liberalization in smaller groupings when multilateral opportunities appear limited or blocked. See "U.S. Trade Policy in the 1980s: Turns—and Roads Not Taken," Working Paper 3725 (Cambridge, MA: National Bureau of Economic Research, 1991).

Competitiveness Act of 1988, and extended once again by Congress in the spring of 1991. Thus it had received five votes of confidence from the Congress in a span of 15 years.

But en route to the last of these, something new happened: fast-track became a public issue. On all previous occasions, it was worked out quietly between the USTR and the committees of primary jurisdiction. And this was understandable, since in addition to promoting efficiency in trade policy the arrangement suited these actors' institutional interests. But in 1991 the process "came out in the open" for the first time, with fast-track itself becoming the specific, central subject of debate and votes on the House and Senate floors. Members of Congress not on House Ways and Means or Senate Finance were sensitized to the cost of these procedures in terms of their political and policy interests. There was little they could do about this in 1991, since the rules governing *that* extension favored the proponents: amendments were not in order, and a negative House or Senate vote would have brought major US trade negotiations, multilateral and bilateral, to a crashing halt. But next time it would take affirmative legislation to extend fast-track. This would at a minimum involve a major debate, and the legislation would presumably be open to the normal legislative weapons of amendment and delay.[22]

Last, but assuredly not least, was trade's reemergence as a front-burner political issue in the fall and winter 1991–92. The immediate causes were the unexpected persistence of recession and President Bush's remarkable vulnerability on economic issues. Through most of 1991, economists predicted that recovery would come soon. It did not. Through most of 1991, in the afterglow of the Persian Gulf War, Bush's public approval rating remained above 70 percent—higher than Ronald Reagan's had ever been—and the president was expected to enter the 1992 elections in a commanding political position. He did not. As the economy stagnated and unemployment grew, he increasingly came under attack for his international preoccupations: by September, no less than 66 percent of Americans felt their president was spending "too much time on foreign problems" and not enough on domestic.[23] Two months later, in economically depressed (and traditionally protectionist) Pennsylvania, Democrat Harris Wofford won an upset Senate victory over former Bush administration Attorney General Richard Thornburgh on the slogan that Americans should "take care of our own."

The president responded with what can only be described as panic,

---

22. Technically, fast-track extension could be included in implementing legislation for the Uruguay Round, as done in 1979 for the Tokyo Round, with action thereon again constrained by fast-track rules. But given the procedures' new visibility, such a step would risk undermining prospects for congressional approval of the results of the Uruguay Round.

23. ABC News poll, reported in *National Journal*, 12 October 1991, 2510.

abandoning the international leadership that had hitherto been his forte. He made decision after disastrous decision, each as ill-conceived substantively as it was disastrous for him politically. First Bush canceled (without credible reason) a once-postponed trip to Tokyo and the Far East, which the Japanese government had been counting on to buttress the post–Cold War alliance and give a positive twist to Pearl Harbor's 50th anniversary. He then rescheduled the visit and recast it as an export-sales mission—in search of "jobs, jobs, jobs"—without time for the advance preparation that success would require. He invited 21 business leaders to join him, thus making the enterprise hostage to what *they* said and did. And as icing on the cake, he included among them the embattled leaders of the Big Three auto companies, men for whom no conceivable breakthroughs in the Japanese market could provide the short-term relief they so badly needed, and who indeed needed for the mission to be *unsuccessful* in order to build support for protectionist action at home.

The trip proved a disaster, made forever memorable by the president's sudden stomach ailment at a Japanese state dinner. It unleashed a torrent of Japan bashing (and America bashing) in the days and weeks that followed, together with a grassroots "buy America" campaign.[24] Suddenly, US trade policy seemed again up for grabs. The multilateral Uruguay Round was again stalemated, after progress the previous fall. The president had both legitimized attacks on Japan and undercut his capacity to counter them. And victory in the Cold War had removed the protection that military alliance had heretofore provided for trilateral economic relations: there was no longer a common enemy against which America, Europe, and Japan needed to unite.

Looking Ahead

Of the "bleak prospects" set forth in this book's first edition, one has clearly receded. That is the tried-and-true bogeyman of the liberal trade community, a return to legislative protectionism à la Smoot-Hawley. It seemed possible in 1986, albeit unlikely, that the combination of much stronger trade pressures and weaker congressional resistance could bring an end to the half century of "voluntary legislative restraint" on trade matters. House members had twice endorsed the UAW-backed domestic-content bill for automobiles. Both houses had backed enforcement of steel protection in the Trade and Tariff Act of 1984, and had

---

24. One feature was employers giving bonuses to workers for purchasing US-made automobiles. Americans soon discovered that it was not easy to determine what was an "American car": many models with Big Three nameplates were in fact assembled in Canada or Mexico or across the Pacific, whereas a growing number of Toyotas and Hondas and Nissans were "made in USA."

mustered strong majorities for the bill sponsored by Representative Ed Jenkins (D-GA) to roll back textile imports. But none of these initiatives has gained ground since, and the 1988 act, by excluding product-specific protection, set another clear precedent against it. Then and subsequently, legislators have given renewed evidence of their preference to delegate product-specific trade responsibility. Moreover, as discussed in chapter 7, the internationalization of the US economy has multiplied the number of business interests that depend on trade and suffer from its restriction—even as it multiplies the number of trade disputes US officials must address. And the power and effectiveness of the textile industry—the indispensable core for any logrolling protectionist coalition—appears to be receding.

Thus the likelihood of direct, full-blown statutory protectionism is now very low—global interdependence has seen to that. The same cannot be said, however, of what has been labeled "process protectionism": an expansion of opportunities for import relief under the trade-remedy laws, particularly the "unfair trade" statutes, and a further reduction of executive branch discretion in resolving such cases. This approach is attractive to legislators because it allows them to be responsive to petitioners while keeping the final responsibility off their backs—the specific protection is worked out elsewhere. And to some degree, this is what has come about in recent years. Congress did not add much in the 1988 act to petitioners' rights and opportunities under the trade-remedy laws, and the campaign to further tighten these laws has lost some of its steam. But they had already been tilted significantly in petitioners' favor, with results amply reported in chapter 6 and summarized above.

In some instances, the trade-remedy laws have been exploited to bring about special deals for special cases, as with the steel VERs of 1984. Such deals have not always been bad for trade policy: they have sometimes bought needed support for, or tolerance of, major trade-liberalization initiatives. But without such major offsets, "special deals for special cases" are transformed from a means of shielding an expanding liberal trade-policy regime to a threat to that regime's core purpose.

Seeking to limit such US trade restrictions, to retain some room for maneuver, liberal-minded administration and congressional leaders repeatedly focus their attention on attacking other governments' import barriers and export subsidies. In this way also they are walking in the footsteps of their predecessors: since the 1930s, government leaders have found the pursuit of expanded markets abroad a principal means of fighting protection at home. The 1980s brought a major toughening of US tactics, as illustrated by the Reagan administration's "new" trade policy of 1985 and later by congressional enactment of Super 301.

Such tactics can sometimes be very useful in international trade bargaining. Under current circumstances, they remain critical to the administration's domestic credibility. In this sense, Section 301—even Super 301—is a logical descendent of the "bargaining tariff." The problem is one of policy balance. One needs carrots, not just sticks, in negotiations with other countries. If the domestic political situation forces US leaders to demand the moon without offering much earthly value in return, Americans should not be astonished if the response of foreign governments is increasingly limited and grudging. And while the results of US unilateralism to date have been mainly constructive, a sharp accentuation of Section 301–style demands could prove more than the international trading system could bear.

The final threat posed in this book's first edition, treated here in chapter 7, is that of a new ideological debate on trade, featuring a philosophical division between the two political parties not seen on this issue since the 1940s. Republicans would hold to free market policies in principle, as an extension of their stance against industry-specific government intervention. Democrats—under pressure from organized labor and seeking to renew their party tradition of active government engagement in the economy—would be disposed to employ trade protection as one of several tools to nurture and strengthen US competitiveness.

So far, Democratic "protectionism" has in fact been muted and has receded from its recent peak. And the insurgent presidential candidacy of Pat Buchanan suggests that Republicans may also find tough trade talk tempting—as did John Connally three campaigns before. But if the two parties were to coalesce around competing trade policy positions, then shifts in party control of the White House would likely bring the sort of oscillation in US trade policy that occurred on defense and arms control in the last decades of the Cold War. And if a future president of either party were to come to office on a trade-restrictive platform, the system of trade politics would lose its most critical pillar, the liberal-leaning executive.

This threat—and that of across-the-board protectionism—seems to have receded since the mid-1980s. But others have risen to take their place. The global geopolitical transformation has left three economic power centers—America, Europe, Japan—with no common adversary to bind them. This does not necessarily make them enemies to one another—indeed, continued global well-being depends on their continued cooperation. But the security imperative no longer constrains them; the United States is no longer motivated to mute its economic demands to strengthen its alliances, and US allies are no longer driven to yield economically because they are dependent militarily.

In this new global context, the Bush and Clinton administrations were called upon to complete two complex negotiations, NAFTA and the Uruguay Round, and to win congressional enactment of implementing legislation. The story of how they did so is told in chapter 9. Chapter 10 follows with prescriptions for further strengthening of US trade policy and the institutions that shape it.

9

1992–94: Missions Accomplished?

The years 1992–94 were big years for American trade policy. Two land-mark agreements were completed, and were implemented by Congress. One of them—the North American Free Trade Agreement (NAFTA)—set off the most prominent and contentious domestic debate on trade since the Smoot-Hawley Tariff Act of 1930. The second—the Uruguay Round under the GATT—broke new ground in three major ways: the comprehensiveness of its coverage; the number of countries signing onto its main obligations; and the creation, at long last, of a World Trade Organization (WTO) with strengthened dispute settlement procedures.

The same three years featured other important trade action. There were contentious talks with China: first over human rights improvements as a condition for extending most-favored nation (MFN) treatment, then over Chinese violations of international norms of intellectual property. The latter dispute carried over into 1995 and thwarted Beijing's desire to be a founding member of the WTO. The Clinton administration also took an aggressive new tack on economic issues with Japan, generating new conflict and modest results. However, it balanced this bilateral aggressiveness with an active consensus-building role in the Asia Pacific Economic Cooperation (APEC) forum, whose 18 members committed themselves to achieving free trade by the second decade of the 21st century. Western Hemisphere nations followed by establishing 2005 as their target date for completing a NAFTA-type arrangement among themselves.

The evolution of trade policy was not entirely in the liberal direction.

Antidumping laws, for example, survived a major international reform effort without significant change in their net impact. But taken as a whole, the period was one of major policy and political victories for advocates of trade expansion. Protectionists were unusually vocal and visible, but they ended up losers.

But US free traders could not rest easy. Looking back, they knew that a strong opposing coalition—organized labor, Ross Perot, Ralph Nader, Pat Buchanan—had more than once dominated the public debate and driven them onto the defensive. Looking ahead, they faced the problem of maintaining interbranch cooperation between an embattled Democratic president and a resurgent Republican Congress. In particular, they needed to find a formula for Congress to provide "fast-track" authority for new negotiations whose substance was, in many cases, just beginning to be defined.

From Bush to Clinton

The Bush administration entered 1992 engaged in two major trade negotiations. Most visible and controversial was the NAFTA negotiation with Mexico and Canada. Most consequential in its potential economic impact was the Uruguay Round/GATT negotiation. For both, Congress had voted to extend the deadline to 1 June 1993.[1] 1992 was, of course, an election year, and President George Bush—under attack for neglecting the home front—was atypically inactive on most international issues. But trade was different. Here he wanted results, for their own sake and for their use in the presidential campaign.

The Uruguay Round was the administration's top trade priority and had been for four years—particularly for Carla Hills and her Office of the US Trade Representative (USTR). But NAFTA moved faster. One reason was the personal commitment of Mexican President Carlos Salinas de Gortari, whose legacy would depend on success in the talks. Another was that the prime interlocutor on the GATT, the European Community, seemed only able to negotiate during the final three months of each year. The other nine months the Europeans spent getting their internal act together, particularly on agriculture.

On NAFTA, there was no such problem, and USTR sought to complete a deal in the spring for presentation to Congress in the summer

---

1. This meant that agreements signed by that date would receive "fast-track" congressional consideration: action on the implementing legislation within 90 days, with no amendments permitted. Chapter 4 treats the origins of the fast-track authority and its extension in 1991.

and action before the November elections. This proved impractical. The pace of NAFTA negotiations did accelerate in the first nine months of 1992, however, and the three nations reached agreement in August. After the required period for notification and consultation with Congress and affected industry groups, the North American Free Trade Agreement was signed on 17 December 1992. It provided for phased elimination of tariff and most nontariff barriers, most of them within 10 years. NAFTA also contained important measures for liberalization of investment. And its nearly 2,000 pages included detailed provisions defining "North American content" for autos and textiles, designed to give competitive advantages to North American companies. On balance, the United States gained much more than it gave, winning major Mexican tariff reductions and changes in many restrictive procedures.[2]

Republicans were overwhelmingly positive about the NAFTA negotiations; Clinton's party was divided but leaning against, as had been earlier reflected in House Democrats' 170–91 vote against fast-track renewal in May 1991. Thus, once agreement was reached, Bush pushed candidate Bill Clinton to take a stand one way or the other (and thereby alienate part of his party). In October 1992, Clinton responded with a major speech endorsing NAFTA, rejecting the idea of renegotiating the text but declaring it insufficient in dealing with three issues: the environment, worker standards, and the threat of sudden import surges. He called for negotiation of side agreements for each of these three. Through this politically adroit response, which gave something to both sides, Clinton solved his campaign problem. But the cost would prove dear once he entered office, for the speech encouraged NAFTA opponents to believe that he might reconsider his support, since he could always declare that satisfactory side agreements were proving unattainable.

The GATT negotiations continued through the November election. In fact, one important meeting was held on election day in Chicago, and when it stretched on too long, Deputy USTR Julius Katz was unable to get back home in time to vote. The central issue remained agriculture, as it had been since the talks started. A long-festering US-EC dispute over EC subsidies for oilseeds producers provided the catalyst, with a threat of US retaliation against a billion dollars of EC exports bringing new urgency to the broader farm issue.[3] Finally, the trade and agriculture

---

2. For an overview and assessment, see Gary Clyde Hufbauer and Jeffrey J. Schott, *NAFTA: An Assessment*, revised edition, October 1993.

3. For details on this dispute and its relation to the Uruguay Round, see Charles Iceland, "European Union: Oilseeds," 209–32, in Thomas O. Bayard and Kimberly Ann Elliott, *Reciprocity and Retaliation in U.S. Trade Policy*, Institute for International Economics 1994.

ministers of the United States and the European Community met at Blair House, across Pennsylvania Avenue from the White House. They reached a compromise deal on 20 November imposing significant limits on European export subsidies and modest ones on domestic support levels. Bush administration officials then pressed an eleventh-hour campaign to complete the entire Uruguay Round agreement during the November-to-January presidential transition. Without such an effort, they argued, fast-track authority for the talks would expire before the new administration could get its trade team operating effectively. And the talks received an eleventh-hour shot in the arm when the purposive Leon Brittan became negotiator for the European Community, replacing the oft-ineffective Frans Andriessen.

Clinton supported the effort publicly: "America has only one president at a time," he said the day after the election, and talks on arms control and trade should go on. But signals from his Little Rock transition team were mixed as time went on: one Bush negotiator recalls a deadly "no comment" about a story that Clinton's advisers wanted the negotiation put on hold until Inauguration Day.[4] It was arguably in the Clinton administration's interest to have Bush people close the deal: it would grease the skids for implementation and reduce the amount of old business the new team would have to address. But the credibility of the old team would have been hard to maintain in any event, even if there had been perfect confidence and coordination between them and the Clinton people. And as illustrated above, there was not. So though talks continued into January, time ran out for the Bush negotiators. Shortly thereafter, fast-track authority for the round expired.

So Bill Clinton entered office with two major pieces of unfinished trade business: NAFTA to get implemented, assuming suitable agreements could be reached on labor and the environment, and the Uruguay Round to complete. He had not, in his campaign, given special attention to trade policy, but he had given top billing to the economy: to the weak recovery from the Bush recession, and to the longer-term problem of stagnation in middle-class incomes. He had signaled, moreover, that he intended to elevate the weight given to economic interests in US international relationships.

Charged with the task of bringing NAFTA and GATT to fruition was Clinton's National Campaign Chair (and Democratic party activist) Mickey Kantor. Kantor was smart, experienced as a bargainer in his legal and political careers, and a *tabula rasa* on trade. In choosing such a person for US trade representative, Clinton was emulating his three predecessors. None of their initial designees—Robert Strauss, William Brock, Carla Hills—

---

4. Personal interview. *The New York Times* reported on 8 December 1992 that the Clinton transition team had "been reviewing whether to try to rein in the negotiations but had reached no conclusions."

had been identified with trade policy before being chosen for the post. And in so acting, Clinton passed over trade policy veterans clearly associated with the free trade and protectionist camps. Both continuity and trade expertise, however, were provided by the designation of Rufus Yerxa as deputy USTR with prime Washington responsibility for the Uruguay Round. (Yerxa had served as the Geneva deputy during the Bush administration and prior to that as senior staff aide to the House Ways and Means Committee.)

In its initial months, his administration sent off mixed signals, both substantive and organizational. The president gave a free trade speech in February but appeared to be supporting in March a steep rise in tariffs on minivans[5] and became identified—beginning in April—with a "managed trade" stance in negotiations with Japan. He gave Kantor the principal mandate for trade policy implementation but created a National Economic Council (NEC), parallel to the National Security Council (NSC), to raise the priority to overall economic policy, international as well as domestic. The NEC's trade role was distinct from USTR's in theory—coordination and oversight, not negotiations—but it overlapped in practice. Clinton appointed a "cautious trade activist," Laura Tyson, as chair of his Council of Economic Advisers, a move widely interpreted as a break with the normal practice of placing a vintage free trader in that position.[6] He did seek, and win, legislation extending to 15 December 1993, the deadline for concluding the Uruguay Round.[7] But on NAFTA there was mostly silence, as Kantor moved to negotiate the labor and environment side agreements.

---

5. Technically, the question was whether minivans should be classified for tariff purposes as passenger cars or light trucks. Established practice was to treat them as cars, since they had, in practice, replaced station wagons in the US market. This meant a tariff of 2.5 percent. If reclassified as trucks, they would be subject to the 25 percent duty established in the 1960s in retaliation for new EC trade restrictions. In the 1990s, of course, this tariff bore principally on Japanese light trucks, and Japan was the principal source of imported minivans as well. The import share of the minivan market was modest, however.

In the end, the administration did *not* take this step, which would certainly have been challenged as a violation of US commitments in prior trade negotiations.

6. The quotation is from the title of chapter 1 of her book, *Who's Bashing Whom?* (Institute for International Economics 1992), published just before her designation as CEA chair. In fact, Tyson generally supported liberal trade—spiced with some aggressive export bargaining—and she proved a "free trade" stalwart within the Clinton administration.

7. Technically, the deadline was 16 April 1994, but the president had to notify Congress of his intent to enter the agreement no later than 15 December, and this notification had to contain details on the expected substance of the agreement. Advisory committee reports were due 30 days thereafter. If these target dates were not met, the fast-track procedures would not apply to the Uruguay Round implementing legislation.

The NAFTA Debate: Clinton Cedes the Field to the Critics

This silence made some tactical sense. If the president were to deliver on his campaign promise, he needed to withhold final endorsement of NAFTA until the side agreements were completed and he could declare the overall package improved and worthy of his endorsement. Moreover, the president was centering his attention on his budget and tax package, a serious (and politically courageous) attack on the federal deficit. Winning its enactment (in modified form) took until early August, and the margins were razor-thin: 218–216 in the House and 51–50 (with Vice President Albert Gore's tiebreaker) in the Senate.

But the president not only withheld the final go-ahead on NAFTA, he allowed White House aides to fight one another more or less publicly over it through the spring and into the summer. Nor did the White House press congressional Democrats to remain neutral until the side agreements were negotiated.[8] All this had the effect of fueling doubts as to whether Clinton would *really* support NAFTA in the end, much less make the all-out push that congressional approval would require. These doubts extended to NAFTA supporters inside the administration: Secretary of the Treasury Lloyd Bentsen, by Bob Woodward's account, "felt that the odds were that Clinton would abandon NAFTA because the labor groups in the party opposed it,"[9] and Mickey Kantor reportedly offered as late as mid-summer to "blow up" the negotiations over the side agreements if the president so wished.[10] With the administration divided and ineffective for a full half year, NAFTA opponents had a field day. They won the ear of the public, and votes on Capitol Hill.

Most visible among these opponents was Ross Perot. In his self-financed independent campaign for president in 1992, Perot had attacked NAFTA (though he gave much more prominence to the fiscal deficit). But in 1993, he made NAFTA his central issue—with frequent speeches, with a widely circulated book (coauthored with Pat Choate) entitled *Save*

---

8. Carter administration officials had done this on the Panama Canal treaties in 1977, persuading a number of senators not to cosponsor an opposition resolution but hold off until negotiations were completed. Pro-NAFTA Congressman Robert Matsui (D-CA) had asked that at least the freshmen be brought to the White House so the president could suggest to them that they remain neutral, but this proposal fell victim to the internal White House fight.

9. *The Agenda: Inside the Clinton White House* (Simon and Schuster, 1994), 317–18.

10. Elizabeth Drew, *On the Edge: The Clinton Presidency* (Simon and Schuster, 1994), 288–89. Kantor argued at the same time, however, "that if Clinton fought for congressional approval of the treaty and won despite the opposition of labor and some of the House leadership, it would be a big win and a big plus for him. He would have stood up to the unions and fought a bipartisan fight. . . ." (289)

Your Job, Save Our Country: Why NAFTA Must be Stopped—Now! He wrote (and spoke) "of a giant sucking sound": NAFTA would mean "the loss of millions of jobs" pulled southward by low Mexican wages, with no less than one-third of US manufacturing jobs (6 million out of 18 million) "at risk."[11]

These arguments had real resonance in a nation where middle-class incomes had been stagnant for 20 years and whose industrial heartland had faced fierce foreign competition. They established "jobs" indelibly as the central NAFTA issue, with the public disposed to see the agreement as a job loser.[12] And if Perot supplied the most visible opposition, organized labor provided the muscle. With membership declining and wages being squeezed, its rank-and-file members saw competition from low-wage Mexican workers as a serious threat. So the AFL-CIO and its member unions went to their many Democratic friends in Congress, making it clear that labor considered NAFTA to be *the* test of fidelity to the workers' cause. Their hope, of course, was to confront the president with such overwhelming opposition within his own party that he would decide not to press ahead. Many members signed up—enough so that Clinton's budget director, former Congressman Leon Panetta, declared NAFTA "dead in the water" that spring.

Not only was labor aroused, environmental groups were upset as well. They had at least three concerns. First, they saw trade as spurring industrial development, which produced environmental degradation—unless it was carefully regulated. Terrible conditions on the US-Mexico border made this more than a theoretical concern. Second, they saw lower developing-country environmental standards as an incentive for industries to leave the United States, thus putting pressure on the United States to ease its standards in order to prevent the flight of US manufacturing. Last but not least, in some circumstances environmentalists wished to employ trade sanctions in support of environmental goals: the Marine Mammal Protection Act of 1972, for example, provided that tuna harvested by foreign fleets be barred from the United States if the methods used killed too large a number of dolphins. When this resulted in blocking imports of tuna from Mexico, the Mexicans appealed to the GATT. USTR lawyers defended the US position in Geneva, but a GATT panel ruled in the Mexicans' favor. Environmentalists hit the roof.

It was assumed throughout that the main NAFTA battle would be in the House, just as had been the case with fast-track extension in 1991.

---

11. Ross Perot (with Pat Choate), *Save Your Job, Save Our Country: Why NAFTA Must Be Stopped—Now!* (New York: Hyperion [for United We Stand America], 1993), esp. 41–57.

12. A Yankelovich poll published in *Time* on 7 June asked, "Do you agree with Clinton's view that the free trade agreement with create US jobs, or with Perot's view that it will cost US jobs?" Twenty-five percent sided with Clinton, 63 percent with Perot! (Some polls conducted in the fall showed less lopsided results.)

And the Democratic leadership was divided: Speaker Tom Foley (D-WA) was supportive, but Majority Leader Dick Gephardt (D-MO) was leaning against and the number three Democrat, David Bonior (D-MI), was leading the opposition. To lead the pro-NAFTA forces, the White House initially looked to Bill Richardson (D-NM), a Hispanic-American (surname notwithstanding) who had received prominent consideration for a Cabinet post. But Ways and Means Chairman Dan Rostenkowski demurred. He felt he and his committee should be calling the shots, and he insisted on a senior Ways and Means colleague, Robert Matsui (D-CA), a focused, effective legislator (who happened to be a Japanese-American). The presumption was that NAFTA would need overwhelming Republican support. But unless Democrats could deliver a substantial number of their own, it was not clear that Minority Whip Newt Gingrich (R-GA) would play ball. And Gingrich was clearly *the* rising force on the Republican side of the aisle.

Clinton Recovers, and Wins Big

In August, the labor and environmental side agreements were completed. Clinton approved them, had more than one "last" meeting among his advisers, and came down strongly, at last, in NAFTA's favor.[13] The side agreements did nothing to soften labor opposition, but the results were much better on the environment: NAFTA now won support from most of the mainstream environmental organizations.[14] Environmental issues, very prominent during the NAFTA negotiations, now receded to the periphery in the congressional battle, particularly after the administration won its appeal of a 30 June decision in Washington, D.C., District Court that NAFTA required submission of a comprehensive "environmental impact statement."[15]

Progress with environmentalists notwithstanding, NAFTA still faced

13. Drew, *On the Edge*, p. 290. As Drew notes, Clinton was so open to discussing and rediscussing issues that his staff didn't always treat matters as decided even when the president thought he had decided them.

14. NAFTA was endorsed on 14 September 1993 by six major groups, including the National Wildlife Federation, the Environmental Defense Fund, and the Natural Resources Defense Council. They called it "an unprecedented tool for reconciling ecological and economic objectives." Grass-roots oriented organizations like Friends of the Earth and the Sierra Club opposed the pact, aligning with the Citizens Trade Campaign to denounce it as "ravaging" the North American environment. For a more detailed discussion, see Daniel C. Esty, *Greening the GATT: Trade, Environment, and the Future* (Institute for International Economics, 1994), esp. 27ff.

15. The case was filed by Public Citizen, Sierra Club, and Friends of the Earth. The requirement was routinely applied to domestic legislation but had never been imposed on an international agreement.

an uphill struggle. The White House congressional relations chief Howard Paster feared that the votes were not there and that the administration had spent all its political chips in the budget fight. But once the decision was made, the administration knew it had to go all out. The president recruited William Daley of Chicago (brother of the mayor, and another loser in the cabinet sweepstakes) to coordinate the pro-NAFTA congressional campaign. Republicans asked for their own representative on the White House team, and after consulting with them Clinton named William Frenzel, a Minnesotan recently retired from 20 years of congressional service. Frenzel took the job after asking for, and receiving, face-to-face assurance from the president that "you're going to work your head off on this." Frenzel then set out to "sell Republicans," stationing himself in the minority staff office of the House Ways and Means Committee.

With Daley as overall coordinator and Kantor handling the substance, the campaign began in earnest after Labor Day, in the expectation of a vote before Congress adjourned for the year. President Clinton invited three former presidents to the East Room of the White House on 14 September to dramatize their united, bipartisan support. In a stirring speech, he pointed to the global changes that were revolutionizing the US marketplace, NAFTA or no NAFTA, and defined "the debate about NAFTA" as centering on "whether we will embrace these changes and create the jobs of tomorrow, or try to resist these changes, hoping we can preserve the economic structures of yesterday."[16] His governmental team worked in tandem with USA-NAFTA, the corporate support coalition. With a widely circulated survey finding the sentiment in the House still moving the wrong way, the first need was to stop further erosion in support.[17] Fence-sitting Democrats were feeling heat from labor; Republicans were worried about Ross Perot, with whose local organizations many of them had allied in the budget fight.

One immediate need was to firm up support in the elite media—the editorial writers traditionally disposed toward free trade. This was done expeditiously: administration officials pulled together the economic case, stressing that NAFTA would create US jobs and buttress global US competitiveness. This campaign was aided by careful outside analyses.[18] It was also aided unwittingly by Ross Perot. The arguments in his book

16. Transcript released by White House Press Office, 14 September 1994. Speaking after the president, George Bush declared that after hearing Clinton's "very eloquent statement . . . now I understand why he's inside looking out and I'm outside looking in."

17. A USA-NAFTA poll found that, as of 20 September, 47 Democrats and 114 Republicans were in favor (strongly or leaning), with 159 Democrats and 31 Republicans against. The remainder were undecided or their views were unknown. (*Inside US Trade*, Special Report, 1 October 1994) This was a decline in support from a survey taken in August.

18. See, for example, Hufbauer and Schott, *NAFTA: An Assessment*.

were illogical, extreme, and easy to refute, and they drew attention away from more moderate anti-NAFTA arguments.

When the campaign began, members' mail was running overwhelmingly against NAFTA. USA-NAFTA set out to turn it around, and by November "the mail bags were balanced," in the words of one active participant. And while this involved mainly working with pro-NAFTA business interests, the fall also brought a significant rise in public support: from 42 percent in September to 53 percent in November.[19] Republicans were reluctant to commit unless Democrats did their share; they insisted on a minimum of 100 votes. (Ninety-one Democrats had backed fast-track extension in 1991.) So targets were agreed to: 100 Democrats, 120 Republicans. The president was phoning Democrats and finding the going hard—the price of his earlier neglect. Members expressed sympathy substantively and politically but declared they were committed. At one point, this drove Clinton to frank, public criticism of labor, and this helped with Republicans by showing he was really serious. Also, of course, Republicans took satisfaction in the strains that NAFTA was imposing on the Democrats' support coalition.

Early in the year, NAFTA supporters saw Majority Leader Gephardt as key: he had backed fast-track in 1991 after extracting commitments on labor and the environment. But he was increasingly critical of NAFTA, and soon came out in opposition. White House Chief of Staff Mac McLarty stayed in touch, but it was increasingly clear that the battle would need to be won without Gephardt's help. And the number three Democrat, David Bonior of Michigan, was leading the fight against. So neither supporters nor opponents could use the regular House organization to line up votes. Matsui played a central role among the Democrats in mobilizing support, and Richardson proved important as well. The most energetic and effective Republicans included two members not on Ways and Means: Jim Kolbe of Arizona and David Dreier of California. In the end, however, the single most effective Republican was Minority Whip Gingrich, who was particularly helpful in negotiating agreement on how to replace the tariff revenues that NAFTA would cost the US Treasury.[20]

The battle remained uphill through October and into November, driving the administration into policy bargaining as well. An October promise to create a North American Development Bank, aimed at Hispanic legislators, netted at first only the idea's originator, Rep. Esteban Torres (D-CA). "One bank, one vote," concluded skeptics. But attention soon

---

19. NBC News/*Wall Street Journal* polls of September and November 1993, cited in Eric M. Uslaner, "Trade Winds: NAFTA, the Rational Public, and the Responsive Congress," draft paper 1994.

20. The budget law required that any measure that reduced revenues must contain provisions to offset this loss.

moved to product areas directly affected by the agreement. Two key industries, automobiles and textiles, had done their policy bargaining during the negotiations. The Big Three automakers won a 62.5 percent "North American content" requirement, making it harder for Japanese firms to produce in Mexico and export tariff-free to the United States. Textiles won a "triple transformation test": to benefit from NAFTA's provisions, apparel would have to be made in North America from North American cloth that was produced from North American fiber.[21] The American Textile Manufacturers Institute responded with a strong endorsement of NAFTA.[22]

The House vote was set for 17 November, and with each side looking to win, neither used parliamentary powers to delay it, even though the president did not actually submit the implementing bill until 4 November. Submission had been preceded by "nonmarkups" in the key committees, where members helped draft implementing bill's language, but this was subordinate to the larger public fight. In the final struggle for votes, attention focused particularly on members with sugar and citrus constituencies. On the former, USTR Kantor extracted from a very reluctant Mexican government a new commitment that would effectively limit sugar exports to the United States. On citrus, several concessions of lesser importance were made.

This policy bargaining provoked press and opposition cries that the administration was "buying votes." This characterization was accurate but oversimple, for the people being "bought" were, by and large, members who wanted to support NAFTA but needed a reason to justify doing so. By the time of the vote, it was widely recognized that a secret House vote would have endorsed NAFTA decisively; extracting concessions therefore cleared the way for on-the-fence members to vote their consciences! And while the sugar deal did change, significantly, how the agreement would affect that politically sensitive commodity, the total impact of the concessions on NAFTA's substance was modest.[23]

As the day of reckoning approached, with their "NAFTA creates jobs" case established, supporters began adding more traditional arguments:

---

21. Kenneth Oye has argued that regional free trade agreements that produce trade diversion are particularly capable of gaining domestic support because of the particularized benefits they convey. See his *Economic Discrimination and Political Exchange: World Political Economy in the 1930s and 1980s* (Princeton University Press 1992).

22. Congressmen from the most important single textile state, North Carolina, would shift from a 9–2 margin against fast-track extension in 1991 to 8–4 *support* of the agreement itself.

23. Some NAFTA promises concerned US positions in the Uruguay Round, raising concern that the global negotiation would be mortgaged to pay for the regional. In practice, the impact proved limited here also. A promise to the textile industry that the administration would seek an extension of the MFA phaseout period to 12 or 15 years (from 10) meant just that: the administration sought the extension, but other countries rejected it!

about how US-Mexican relations and US global leadership would be devastated by NAFTA's rejection and about the need to send the president off a winner to the upcoming summit of the Asia Pacific Economic Cooperation (APEC) forum in Seattle. And with the tide in Clinton's favor but the outcome not yet assured, the president took a giant gamble. He authorized his vice president, Albert Gore, to accept an invitation to debate Ross Perot on the national talk show "Larry King Live." A Perot "win" might conceivably have turned things around, but in fact the vice president dominated the encounter. He was relentless in challenging Perot, even presenting him with a joint portrait of Smoot and Hawley. The practical effect was to liberate some of the Republicans still on the fence.

Once a NAFTA victory appeared likely, a common assumption was that it would win just enough votes for passage—a frequent occurrence when marginal members favor a measure on its merits but see it as unpopular. Congressional action on Clinton's budget package followed this pattern. The final NAFTA vote of 234–200 was thus a surprise: 102 Democrats and 132 Republicans came down in favor. The margin was remarkably similar to the 233–194 vote in favor of fast-track extension two and a half years before. Comparing the two votes, 11 more Democrats supported NAFTA, and 10 fewer Republicans. The shift among the Democrats was virtually all within the southern delegations, which had opposed fast-track by 41–43 but backed NAFTA by 53–32. They were less affected by labor and more influenced by the textile provisions—and the deals of November.

For Clinton, the NAFTA vote was a big win—the biggest of his presidency. The budget vote was arguably more important, but it was eked out in a way that made the chief executive look weak. On NAFTA, by contrast, he was strong and persistent once he made his final commitment. In the spring and summer, he had dug himself one deep hole, but he and his team dug themselves out in the fall, turning the public debate around and winning the House of Representatives going away. The Senate followed as expected, clearing the way for the agreement to take effect in January 1994. Finally, and particularly important in the image-conscious 1990s, Bill Clinton had confounded press expectations that he would lose, and he had won by confronting major figures and interests within his party. His victory thus launched the most successful-seeming period of his incumbency.

Winning approval of NAFTA inaugurated what became a Clinton administration "triple play" on trade in November-December 1993. A day after the key House vote, the president flew to Seattle to host the first-ever summit meeting of Asia-Pacific states under the auspices of the Asia Pacific Economic Cooperation forum. And Mickey Kantor entered down-to-the-wire negotiations to win Uruguay Round agreement by the new deadline of 15 December.

Japan, China, and APEC

The APEC summit in December 1994 was the president's second major Asia venture of the year—the first was his trip to Tokyo in July,[24] in which the president sought to further his earlier commitment to "the rebalancing of our relationship" through "an elevated attention to our economic relations."[25] Administration officials declared repeatedly (and inaccurately) that previous negotiations to open Japan's markets had been uniformly unsuccessful. One important reason for failure, they insisted, was lack of agreed ways of measuring success: "specific results," in Clinton's words, for "specific sectors of the economy." Therefore, such measures should be included in future agreements. Two previous agreements had done so: the semiconductor arrangement of 1986 and the auto parts agreement of 1992. Both of these contained quantitative targets for import expansion—labeled "voluntary import expansion" targets (VIEs), or "temporary quantitative indicators" (TQIs)—and Clinton mentioned these two agreements explicitly in his April 1993 press conference as examples that "gave some hope that this approach could work."[26]

Japanese bureaucrats seized upon the evident US interest in VIEs and launched a successful national and international campaign against such "numerical targets," accusing the United States of seeking a new form of "managed trade." They thus united, against the US position, both those Japanese who had always resisted market opening and those who had frequently supported it. The two nations reached a compromise at the July summit, a "framework" agreement to negotiate on market opening and deregulation in specific market sectors that made no mention of targets, calling rather for development of agreed "qualitative and quantitative indicators" of import progress in each sector. But through the fall, Americans continued to advance proposals that could reasonably be construed as quantitative targets, and Japanese gave far more energy to resisting these than to devising alternative measures.

One problem was the range of administration actors visibly engaged on Japan policy. At USTR the lead actor was Deputy US Trade Representative Charlene Barshefsky, a purposive, knowledgeable trade negotiator. At the National Economic Council, Deputy Assistant to the President Bowman Cutter played a major Japan policy role, not just in development of strategy but in negotiations as well. Commerce was visibly engaged, as was State, and the Council of Economic Advisers was

---

24. The impetus for this trip was the seven-nation economic summit, but the administration also used the trip for important bilateral trade negotiations with Japan.

25. These words were spoken to Japanese Prime Minister Kiichi Miyazawa at their joint White House news conference of 16 April 1993.

26. Ibid.

active in internal debates. And Secretary of the Treasury Lloyd Bentsen was always a force to be reckoned with. The problem was not disagreement over the basic line—here there was exceptional agreement, at least by comparison with past administrations. But perhaps because of that agreement, tactical coordination was loose or nonexistent. Particularly neglected was the need to develop and present the policy in ways that would win allies in Japan and among other US trading partners.

US trade relations were also strained with Asia's other economic giant, the People's Republic of China. As a communist country (and a nonmember of GATT), China was subject to general provisions of US law denying most-favored nation (MFN) status to its exports. Under the provisions of the Trade Act of 1974, however, China had received, since 1980, MFN treatment through a presidential waiver, which had to be renewed annually. This was done without controversy until the brutal suppression of Chinese dissidents at Tienanmen Square in June 1989. In its wake, human rights advocates (among them congressional Democrats, including Senate Majority Leader George Mitchell) demanded that President Bush revoke MFN status or condition it explicitly on human rights improvements. Bush resisted but had to wage annual campaigns to prevent Congress from overriding his annual decisions extending China MFN.

Clinton had attacked Bush's softness on the matter during the presidential campaign, and thus entered office committed to linking China MFN and human rights. On 28 May 1993, he granted another one-year waiver but also issued an executive order setting forth human rights criteria for his forthcoming decision the following year. This order provided that the secretary of State "shall not recommend extension" in 1994 unless he determined that it would "promote freedom of immigration," that China was complying with a bilateral agreement concerning prison labor, and that the People's Republic had "made overall, significant progress" on such specifics as "releasing and . . . accounting for Chinese citizens imprisoned or detained" in the 1989 democracy campaign, "ensuring humane treatment of prisoners," "protecting Tibet's distinctive religious and cultural heritage," and "permitting international radio and television broadcasts into China."

With serious ongoing disputes with Japan and China, and facing a broader East Asian reaction to US trade aggressiveness, Clinton came to the APEC summit in Seattle bearing real burdens. But he was politically reinforced by his NAFTA success, which many pundits had labeled unlikely. Moreover, East Asians worried that NAFTA signaled a US shift from a strategy of global trade liberalization to one stressing regional blocs. By assuaging such fears, by committing the United States to open trade relations within the world's fastest growing region, by winning agreement on the goal of building a regional "community," and by simply hosting the first Asia-Pacific summit meeting ever, the president scored another triumph. And as the administration intended, movement in APEC raised alarms among Europeans, who feared the United States was turning away from its traditional Atlantic-first orientation.

Brussels and Geneva: Completing the Uruguay Round

Thus when Mickey Kantor flew to Brussels for the penultimate Uruguay Round talks, he did so with somewhat enhanced leverage. The European Union, pressed forward by its determined lead negotiator Sir Leon Brittan, was clearly committed to reaching agreement this time, and APEC was a force against backsliding. The basis remained the "Dunkel text," submitted by GATT Director General Arthur Dunkel in December 1991. And pressing the talks toward completion was Dunkel's aggressive Irish successor in Geneva, Peter Sutherland.

Agreement required further concessions to the French position on agriculture: in the end, the United States and the "Cairns Group" of farm product exporters settled for modest limits on European subsidies and slight opening of the Japanese and Korean rice markets in exchange for bringing agriculture as a whole under GATT discipline for the first time and for the requirement that agricultural quotas be converted to tariffs. Unable to budge the Europeans (again the French!) on treatment of cultural properties, but unwilling to risk the wrath of the US motion picture industry and its advocate, Jack Valenti, Kantor agreed to set the issue aside. Kantor won—from Japan, the Asian newly industrializing countries, and Canada—some modification of the Dunkel text on antidumping to ease its impact on petitioning US industries.[27]

Other major deals were firmed up: tariff cuts averaging nearly 40 percent; a 10-year phase-out of the Multi-Fiber Arrangement (MFA) on textile and apparel trade; a comprehensive agreement on trade safeguards, including an outlawing of voluntary export restraints (VERs); language restraining domestic subsidies, but with a "green light" for certain government support of research and development; a new General

---

27. According to GATT Director General Sutherland, "It was the United States versus the rest of the world" on the 11 antidumping changes it proposed. "But it had been made abundantly clear politically by Mickey Kantor from the very beginning that this was a crunch issue as far as the US was concerned." (Interview in *Inside US Trade*, Special Report: 24 December 1993, 4.) Nor should this have been a surprise, for Kantor was simply delivering on promises made to win approval of an unencumbered Senate extension of fast-track authority the previous summer. In a 29 June letter to Senator Ernest F. Hollings, he declared the administration's commitment to "a Uruguay Round agreement which preserves our antidumping and countervailing duty laws as effective remedies against unfair trade practices. We share Congressional concerns about certain provisions of the Draft Final Act [the Dunkel text], including those relating to antidumping methodology. . . ." The letter is reprinted in *Inside US Trade*, 2 July 1994, 15.

Agreement on Trade in Services (GATS), coupled with modest liberalization commitments in specific service sectors; a substantial new agreement on trade-related intellectual property rights (TRIPs); a major strengthening of dispute settlement procedures, which removed the ability of the party found "guilty" to block a decision; and the formal establishment of a new, umbrella institution—the World Trade Organization (WTO)—to succeed the GATT (which had evolved into an international organization despite its original establishment as a temporary device).

The United States had placed high priority on establishing "a more effective system of international trading disciplines and procedures,"[28] so the dispute settlement provisions constituted a major victory. The WTO, by contrast, was something to which the United States agreed only at the very end. Its most prominent advocate was an American, trade law authority John H. Jackson, but the proposal was in fact initiated by the Canadians and embraced by the Europeans as a means to constrain US unilateralism. US resistance was more tactical than strategic, however. After procedural improvements, the administration supported the WTO as consistent with its aim of a truly global, enforceable trade regime.[29] But because it emerged at the end of the negotiations, the WTO idea had received little attention in Congress, or in the broader public. This would cause problems during the implementation phase.

Perhaps most important was the sheer sweep of the Uruguay Round agreement. It was, for the most part, a "single undertaking" subscribed to by no less than 125 countries as of 15 September 1994. This meant that agreements on dispute settlement, intellectual property, and so on, were universal in their coverage and the discipline they imposed. By contrast, the Tokyo Round codes on issues such as subsidies applied only to nations specifically adhering to them. The substantive coverage was also comprehensive. Agriculture was brought into GATT rules effectively for the first time; the special MFA regime for textiles was to be phased out. And important new issues were incorporated in the regime: trade-related investment and intellectual property rights, and trade in services.[30]

The Uruguay Round agreement completed Clinton's "triple play" on trade in 1993. And the president's persistence paid political dividends.

---

28. This was one of three "overall US trade negotiating objectives" set forth in Section 1101 of the Omnibus Trade and Competitiveness Act of 1988, which authorized the round. A "more effective and expeditious dispute settlement" process was the first of the 16 more detailed goals spelled out in the same section.

29. See John H. Jackson, "The World Trade Organization, Dispute Settlement, and Codes of Conduct," together with comments by Julius L. Katz, in Susan M. Collins and Barry P. Bosworth, editors, *The New GATT: Implications for the United States*, (The Brookings Institution, 1994), 63–78.

30. For a comprehensive analysis of the round, see Jeffrey J. Schott, *The Uruguay Round: An Assessment* (Institute for International Economics 1994).

The NAFTA victory had shown him willing to take a stand and fight for what he believed; the follow-on achievements suggested a broader trade liberalization strategy. The press began treating the president with new respect. His public approval rating, below 40 percent through most of the summer, topped 50 in December.[31]

Unlike NAFTA, the Uruguay Round agreement generated little controversy in the United States when it was signed. House Majority Leader Gephardt, who had opposed NAFTA, endorsed it within a week. Organized labor did not take up arms and would remain largely on the sidelines throughout the next year. The administration entered 1994 determined to move expeditiously and avoid giving opponents the sort of open political field they had enjoyed during the NAFTA side agreement negotiations of 1993. USTR began working with congressional staff on implementing legislation in January, even as they were pinning down the details for the final Uruguay Round text to be signed in April.

But progress on the implementing legislation was slow. One reason was the complexity of certain issues, particularly the antidumping law revisions. Another was that the Clinton administration was giving top priority to the president's health care initiative. And this dominated the agenda of the key trade committees—Senate Finance and House Ways and Means—through the spring and into the summer. A third reason was the relative weakness of trade policy leadership in both House and Senate. A fourth was the lack of supportive pressure from business.

One reason business leaders were cool was Mickey Kantor's pursuit of a labor and environmental trade agenda not to their liking. More important was the priority that multinational firms were giving in early 1994 to another trade issue: MFN status for China.

US Business, Human Rights, and the China Market[32]

Business had been concerned about Clinton's potential China policy well before the 1992 election. Reacting to his criticism of Bush's refusal to link China's MFN status to its human rights performance, the National Association of Manufacturers (NAM) released a statement calling MFN "the minimum requirement of meaningful economic exchanges between two countries. It is the *sine qua non* of the US-China commercial relationship. As such, it cannot be the basis for the exercise of US leverage within

---

31. The figures are for positive responses to the *New York Times/CBS News* poll question: "Do you approve or disapprove of the way Bill Clinton is handling his job as President?"

32. This section draws upon the research assistance of Ning Shao, Ph.D. student at the University of Maryland.

that relationship."[33] After Clinton's victory, the NAM joined with other business organizations in the Business Coalition for US-China Trade. In May 1993, the coalition sent Clinton a letter signed by 298 companies and 37 trade associations opposing any conditioning or compromising of MFN status. Prominent were firms such as Boeing and General Electric, which feared loss of current and future export markets. Also active were wheat growers and footwear retailers; the latter "flooded the White House with letters from thousands of shoe store managers."[34]

There were many previous occasions when broad business coalitions had been formed to support the president on a critical trade-expanding vote. Typically, however, these were orchestrated by executive branch leaders. The 1992–94 China campaign was different, for here, a broad range of commercial interests united for a major, trade-expanding purpose. One reason was the fear of big losses in current business, something that often drives businesspeople to political action. But there was a strong, forward-looking element to the campaign as well. China loomed large—for exports, for investment—in almost all major multinationals' corporate plans. It was the most rapidly growing large economy in the world and potentially the dominant economy of the 21st century. Being shut out of that market could prove devastating for firms' broader competitiveness—in East Asia and throughout the world. This mix of hopes and fears produced what became known as "the new China lobby,"[35] perhaps the most formidable, pro-trade coalition ever sustained by US business on its own initiative.

As earlier recounted, Clinton responded in 1993 by extending MFN and establishing relatively moderate human rights criteria for his decision due in June 1994. This was widely perceived as a victory for commercial interests. But China's human rights performance on the specified criteria continued to be, at best, mixed, and Secretary of State Warren Christopher went to Beijing in early March 1994 to press the linkage policy. He was publicly rebuffed by Chinese officials. He was then rebuffed at home a day after his return, when the Council on Foreign Relations sponsored an unprecedented public forum in Washington in which three former secretaries of state and numerous other notables attacked the linkage policy.

With Chinese human rights cooperation at best partial and grudging, hard to square with the criteria in Clinton's executive order, business criticism of the policy intensified. During the president's trip to California to attend Richard M. Nixon's funeral, the Business Coalition present-

---

33. "NAM Statement on US-China Commercial Relations," 24 October 1992.

34. *New York Times*, 14 June 1993.

35. The original "China lobby," much feared in the 1950s and early 1960s, supported the "Republic of China" on Taiwan and opposed recognition of Beijing.

ed a petition signed by nearly 450 California-based companies saying MFN revocation would be "an additional devastating blow" to the state's economy.[36] The coalition also worked with supportive legislators to counter advocates of the human rights linkage led by Nancy Pelosi (D-CA); Jim McDermott (D-WA), who counted thousands of Boeing workers among his constituents, helped mobilize 106 representatives to sign a May letter to Clinton calling for MFN renewal.[37] Visibly aligned with business (and against the State Department's tough human rights position) were the economic agencies—Treasury, Commerce, USTR, and the NEC. Together they reinforced expectations that Clinton would not, could not, revoke MFN, effectively undercutting whatever leverage the threat might have had on Chinese human rights behavior.

Also influential in Washington was the argument that, over the longer term, trade and human rights were not competing but mutually reinforcing values. Market freedom and economic development and international engagement were more likely over time to promote democracy and basic freedoms in China, many believed, than heavy-handed US pressure. By this logic, it was important not only that the president continue MFN in 1994 but that the United States abandon the practice of linking its extension to annual human rights reviews.

As the early June deadline approached, therefore, Clinton faced a tough political choice. Even a selective denial of MFN—the choice of some human rights advocates—would have serious economic consequences, but an unconditional extension would violate the spirit, and perhaps the letter, of his own executive order. He opted for the latter, and played it straight. The secretary of State had concluded "that the Chinese did not achieve overall significant progress in all the areas outlined in the executive order. . . ." Clinton agreed with this assessment. Given this fact, he asked, "how can we best advance the cause of human rights and other profound interests the United States has in our relationship with China?" The answer he had reached was to "renew Most Favored Nation trading status," which "will permit us to engage the Chinese with not only economic contacts but with cultural, educational and other contacts, and with a continuing aggressive effort in human rights. . . . I am moving, therefore, to delink human rights from the annual extension of Most Favored Nation trading status for China . . . we have reached the end of the usefulness of that policy."[38]

There was some negative reaction from Democratic liberals, including

36. *Far Eastern Economic Review*, 12 May 1994, 16.

37. Congressman Matsui's office provided another sort of balance by sponsoring a May press conference for some Chinese students who had gathered more than 1,000 student signatures on a pro-MFN petition for the president and Congress.

38. Presidential remarks of 26 May 1994, *New York Times*, 26 May 1994.

Senate Majority Leader George Mitchell (D-ME), a champion of the linkage policy. But it proved short-lived, and ended with the decisive defeat of a House disapproval resolution. Clinton's decision commanded the political center, as Bush's similar decisions had not. And one major reason was the fierce business campaign that the possibility of MFN denial had brought forth. For liberal traders, this campaign suggested a new capacity for internationalist business to take the lead on a trade expansion issue when the administration was not leading the charge. In the context of early 1994, however, the campaign had a price. For it diverted business energy from support of the Uruguay Round and from specific struggles on implementing language.

Japan: Failure and Modest Success

As the China issue was moving toward resolution, fractious economic talks continued with Japan. The administration was united in its determination to press for major Japanese market-opening measures, as well as macroeconomic policy change (in the form of an income tax cut) to stimulate demand.[39] Offering hope—but also frustration—was the reform government of Prime Minister Morihiro Hosokawa, whose eight-party coalition had ended 38 years of Liberal-Democratic Party rule.

Hosokawa was committed, in principle, to economic deregulation and to the weakening of the special-interest influence that had made Japanese import liberalization so difficult to attain. But his government was also weak and inexperienced. This meant even greater power for Japan's traditionally strong bureaucracy. As discussed earlier, the way the administration had developed and described its proposal provoked a strong Japanese reaction, uniting that bureaucracy with Japanese business and liberal academics in opposing what they labeled a US campaign for "quantitative targets" for imports. US officials called this a misrepresentation of their goal; they just wanted agreements with meaningful "qualitative and quantitative indicators" of progress in specific sectors, as the Japanese government had agreed to seek in the "framework talks" launched in July 1993. It was Japan that "managed trade," Americans asserted.[40] But other nations joined Japan in denouncing the US position.

---

39. Japan's prolonged recession, in reaction to the "bubble economy" of the late 1980s, had produced new records in Japan's trade surpluses as demand for imports stagnated. The bilateral imbalance with the United States, which had shown significant improvement between 1987 and 1990, reached a new record of $59.4 billion in 1993.

40. Independent evidence in support of this argument can be found in C. Fred Bergsten and Marcus Noland, *Reconcilable Differences?* (Institute for International Economics, 1993), and Yoko Sazanami, Shujiro Urata, and Hiroki Kawai, *Measuring the Costs of Protection in Japan* (Institute for International Economics, 1995).

Matters came to a head at the Clinton-Hosokawa summit of February 1994. The sectoral negotiations were deadlocked, and the Japanese government was divided over economic policy—hence its macroeconomic package was weak. So in a joint news conference, Clinton and Hosokawa announced that the framework talks had failed, and they would not paper over the failure. Instead, the US administration indicated its readiness to consider unilateral action, including trade sanctions. Luckily, there was a particularly ripe issue: Japanese regulatory authorities had prevented Motorola, Inc., from competing effectively for market share in the lucrative Tokyo cellular telephone market, despite a previous official agreement. The Clinton administration threatened sanctions, and the Japanese regulators backed down.

Clinton also responded to the breakdown of the framework talks by issuing, in early March, what he labeled a "Super 301 executive order"—presumably meant to be a basis for pressing product issues with Japan. While the original "Super 301" had provided that the USTR name "priority foreign countries," Clinton's version referred instead to naming "priority foreign country *practices*" (emphasis added). This made it diplomatically more acceptable but less distinguishable from actions taken under the regular section 301. Essentially, the order simply established a timetable for USTR to follow in setting priorities and initiating Section 301 investigations, and it gave the president considerable latitude *not* to designate "priority foreign country practices."[41] "Not-so-Super 301" seemed a more appropriate label. It was nonetheless popular on Capitol Hill as another "shot across the bow" vis-à-vis Japan. In addition, it set a new target date, 30 September, by which USTR was to name these "priority practices."

In the weeks after the February summit, the Clinton administration refused to reopen the talks unless the Japanese made significant movement toward reaching an agreement. But as weeks became months, the benefits of this posture receded. Hosokawa resigned on 8 April over charges of shady financial practices in financing his governorship campaign 12 years before. A successor "reform government" under Tsutomu Hata took power. On 23 May the two nations reached a written understanding clarifying the framework and relaunching specific sectoral talks. The Japanese accepted new language on goals: "to deal with structural and sectoral issues in order substantially to increase access and sales of competitive foreign goods and services." The US side accepted an explicit statement that the "qualitative and quantitative criteria" to be developed "do not constitute numerical targets, but rather are to be used for the purpose of evaluating progress. . . ."[42]

---

41. Bayard and Elliott, *Reciprocity and Retaliation*, 48–49.

42. "US-Japan Agreement on Framework," published in *Inside US Trade*, 27 May 1994, 2.

Before summer was out, the United States would threaten sanctions on government procurement issues, following timetables in US law. But finally, after an all-night session, Kantor announced agreement the morning of 1 October 1994 on government procurement of medical technology and telecommunications equipment and on government deregulation of insurance. The agreement included a commitment to "evaluation of progress achieved" through specific quantitative and qualitative criteria: a US victory in compromise form. By this time, Japan had its fourth government in a year, under Socialist Prime Minister Tomiichi Murayama in coalition with the LDP. Disagreement remained on the long-festering issue of trade in automobiles and auto parts, and Kantor announced initiation of a case (under regular, not Super 301) to investigate closure in the aftermarket for auto parts. But together with steps the new government had taken on income tax reduction, the agreement resolved most of the issues in the original framework package. At the same time, USTR announced—almost unnoticed—that it was naming *no* priority foreign government practices under Clinton's Super 301 order. By then, the language of that order, effective through 1995, had been incorporated in the GATT implementing legislation, which Congress was considering. And all eyes were on the apparent crisis that legislation was facing.

Implementing the Uruguay Round: A Slow Start

Approval and implementation of the Uruguay Round was, of course, the major trade-political action of 1994. As noted earlier, the action began with staff-level discussions in January, as Mickey Kantor and his deputy, Rufus Yerxa, pursued the now-established "nonmarkup" process to get bipartisan consensus on the provisions of the nonamendable bill that the president would submit under the fast-track procedures. There was talk of rapid movement at both ends of Pennsylvania Avenue: agreement on the substance of a bill by April, and final congressional action before the August recess.

The reality proved very different. On the House side, the first formal Trade Subcommittee session on the agreement was a 26 May review of its agricultural provisions. Specific administration proposals on key issues were not available until mid-June. The full Ways and Means Committee did not hold its comprehensive, "walk-through" session with Mickey Kantor until 14 July. Senate Finance began its nonmarkups on 19 July.[43] It was not until 27 September that the president submitted his implementing bill for congressional action.

---

43. This contrasted to the Tokyo Round agreement, finalized in April of 1979—on that occasion, nonmarkups began in March, the "nonconference" was held in May, the bill was sent down in June, and the House and Senate votes came in July.

The most important cause of this delay was Washington's preoccupation with health care, which was the administration's absolute top priority until the failure of the Clinton-backed legislation in August, and which dominated the attention of the House and Senate leadership and the members of Ways and Means and Finance. Business gave enormous energy to it as well, largely opposing the administration. Hence USTR had to carry the trade issue pretty much alone for most of 1994.

Another problem was the weakness of congressional trade leadership, at least when compared with that of the year of the last major trade legislation, 1988. In May 1994, Congressman Dan Rostenkowski was indicted on long-pending charges of abusing his office for personal gain, forcing him (under Democratic caucus rules) to yield the Ways and Means chairmanship. The Illinois Democrat had achieved formidable effectiveness in this role: one senior colleague found his performance even more impressive than that of Wilbur Mills, if one factored in the reduced formal powers of chairs in the postreform era. Replacing him (on an "acting" basis) was longtime Trade Subcommittee Chair Sam Gibbons (D-FL), a committed and knowledgeable liberal trader who lacked Rostenkowski's bent for moving legislation. Succeeding Gibbons in the post of acting trade subcommittee chairman was Matsui, who was emerging as the most effective trade Democrat. Ranking Republican Bill Archer played an increasingly important role as the nonmarkup proceeded, but his capacity to speak for his party colleagues was not always clear. Most of all, the administration sorely missed having, at the top of the committee, a man who could cut policy deals and make them stick.

On the Senate side, the change had been of Clinton's making: his appointment of Lloyd Bentsen as secretary of the Treasury brought Daniel Patrick Moynihan into the key position of chairman of Senate Finance. The New Yorker was an erudite policy thinker of vast experience. He had voted against NAFTA, as had most Democrats with similar labor constituents, but his commitment to the liberal, multilateral trading system was deep and genuine. He knew trade history, including the failure of the International Trade Organization during the Truman administration, and he was generous enough to share this knowledge more than once with his colleagues. He lacked, however, Bentsen's power and focused approach, and his meandering reflections on substance and process entertained his audiences without instilling confidence. On the Republican side, ranking member Bob Packwood of Oregon was hobbled by charges of recurrent sexual harassment, though he would increasingly use the trade issue as a means to reestablish himself as a consequential substantive player in the Senate.

Another source of delay was the vexing matter of how to pay for the Uruguay Round. The financing problem arose because cutting tariffs reduced revenues, by roughly $12 billion over five years. Under congressional rules designed to hold down the fiscal deficit, any reduction in revenues had to be offset by other measures (e.g., spending cuts, tax increases). And the established counting rules allowed only for immediate budget impact, excluding dynamic effects such as the impact of increased trade on output and hence on revenues. Thus, though analysis indicated that GATT-stimulated economic activity would generate more than enough taxes to offset the tariff revenue losses, the administration had to find $12 billion in fiscal offsets or ask Congress to waive the budget rule.

The budget issue was tailor-made for posturing, with the administration squirming to find acceptable revenue increases and antitax Republicans quick to denounce them. Determined to maintain a strong posture on deficit reduction, President Clinton did not seriously consider seeking an overall waiver of the budget rules. But USTR excluded certain matters from the bill to limit the cost—the expiring system of trade preferences, for example, was extended for just one year, and a proposal to offset the negative impact of NAFTA on Caribbean nations had to be postponed. The administration did decide, however, to ask for exemption from a Senate rule requiring fiscal offsets for the *second* five years as well as the first. Such a waiver required 60 votes, and the Uruguay Round implementing legislation would thus need the approval of three-fifths of the Senate. (The House of Representatives had no such rule.) In any case, the specifics of the budgetary package were bound to generate controversy and some delay.

All these matters were outside the control of USTR Mickey Kantor. But he made his own contribution to GATT's slow legislative progress by his handling of two key matters: the revision of US antidumping law to comply with the Uruguay Round accord and the issue of providing fast-track authority for future trade negotiations.

Antidumping: Reversing the Round

As spelled out in chapter 6, the antidumping laws have become the best recourse for US industries seeking protection, with the rules so tilted that few petitioners fail to win dumping findings from the Department of Commerce. If they can also persuade the USITC that imports have caused them "material injury," imposition of an antidumping duty is automatic.[44] This trend continued into the 1990s: in 1990–93, only 4 out of 212 cases completed ended in "no dumping" findings (table

---

44. Douglas Nelson has argued, in a cogent essay, that the politics of antidumping resemble the pre-Smoot-Hawley politics of tariffs, with a built-in protectionist bias in the law arising from the asymmetrical activism of interests that were hurt by "dumped" imports. See his "Domestic Political Preconditions of US Trade Policy: Liberal Structure and Protectionist Dynamics," *Journal of Public Policy* 9, no. 1 (1989), 83–108.

6.2). The most dramatic use of the law was the 48 cases submitted by the steel industry on 30 June 1992, after the Bush administration had ended the negotiated quotas in the spring of 1992. Not one of these cases was rejected because no dumping was found, but 28 failed because the USITC did not find "material injury" to the petitioning producers.[45]

Antidumping law was among the major agenda items in the Uruguay Round. One might have hoped that US officials, at a disadvantage in fighting the protectionist tilt domestically, would have seized on international negotiations as an antiprotectionist counterweight, just as their counterparts in the 1930s did with the tariff. But they did not. Neither the Bush nor the Clinton administration was so inclined. Using international agreement to constrain use of this mechanism as a protectionist device does seem to have been in the mind of GATT Secretary General Arthur Dunkel, however, whose text—put forward in December 1991 to break a stalemate—contained provisions for antidumping law reform. In the climactic weeks of November-December 1993, US negotiators gave top priority to watering down these provisions, with some success, but substantial changes nonetheless remained in the final text—changes aimed at curbing practices that had tilted the process in favor of domestic protection seekers. Among the new requirements were the following:

- **Sunset**. An antidumping duty "shall be terminated on a date not later than five years from its imposition," unless a review establishes its continued justification. (US law has provided for antidumping duties to continue indefinitely unless a party requests and is granted a review.)

- **Start-up**. Costs were to be adjusted for nonrecurring items that occur in the start-up period. (US law has not deducted for start-up.)

- **Price averaging**. "The existence of margins of dumping shall normally be established" by comparing a weighted average of export prices with a weighted average of the exporter's home-country prices. (US practice has been to compare average home-country prices with individual export sales, increasing the chances that substantial dumping will be found.)

- **Standing**. Producers submitting a case must account for at least 25 percent of the domestic output of the product. (US law did not have such a minimum requirement.)

---

45. In 1990–92, the steel industry also filed 43 countervailing duty (CVD) cases, three-quarters of the total (58) for that period. Thirty-six of these cases were filed on 30 June 1992. None failed through a finding of no subsidy, but 25 of the 36 (and 27 of the 43) were rejected because the USITC did not find material injury.

- **De minimis.** An investigation must be terminated if the dumping margin is less than 2 percent or (in most cases) if dumped imports from the exporting country represent less that 3 percent to total imports. (US law included a 0.5 percent de minimis requirement for the dumping margin.)

None of these changes were as substantial as antidumping reformers had sought. But in the view of US experts on both sides of the issue, they would—if implemented in a straightforward manner—make it significantly more difficult for domestic petitioners to obtain protection under the antidumping statute.

Industries prone to employ the antidumping law fought back, steel in particular. They sought language that would limit the impact of the Uruguay Round changes. In this effort they had the sympathy and cooperation of the Clinton administration. Kantor made no bones about where he stood: he was convinced that the administration's (and his own) reputation for toughness, and hence its credibility in pushing trade expansion, depended on defense of the antidumping laws. Commerce, which administered the law, agreed. So ambiguities in the Geneva agreement were resolved in favor of the petitioning industry in drafting the implementing bill and the related "statement of administrative action." Users of the law also won certain changes in their favor on matters not covered by the Geneva agreement at all.

- **Sunset.** The legislation pushed the time for reviews as far back as possible within the five-year period. And capitalizing on ambiguities in the agreement, it specified that mandated reforms on price averaging would be applied only to new cases, not to reviews.

- **Start-up.** The administration's statement of administrative action explicitly limited the adjustment to fixed costs, excluding such things as advertising and other sales expenses. This seems a clear violation of the intention, and perhaps the letter, of the agreement.

- **Price averaging.** The bill mandated the agreed-upon "average-to-average" comparison rule for new cases (but not for reviews, which the agreement did not explicitly require). It also, however, established "a new fair comparison methodology that deducts an amount for the importer's profit from the US price,"[46] which has the effect of increasing the amount of dumping that is found.

---

46. *Uruguay Round Agreements Act*, Joint Report (#103-412) of the Committee on Finance, Committee on Agriculture, Nutrition, and Forestry, and Committee on Governmental Affairs of the United States Senate, to accompany S. 2467, 22 November 1994, 7.

■ **Standing** and **de minimus**. The bill included straightforward language implementing these provisions but limited the latter to new investigations.

The bill also included changes, beyond the Uruguay Round agreement, which benefited users of the law. These included toughened language on anticircumvention and a provision to exclude "captive production" (inputs manufactured by a firm for its own use) from the total US market for a product on which injury determinations are based. Critics of the AD laws, moreover, failed in their effort to win agreement on a provision to limit imposition of duties in "short supply" situations. Though a firm conclusion is difficult to reach, supporters of AD laws appear to have won back in Washington most, but probably not all, of the ground lost in Geneva. If so, this was not—as some have alleged—a protectionist takeover of US policy via the antidumping laws. It was a lost opportunity to make them significantly less restrictive.[47]

Why wasn't implementation of the Geneva agreement more straightforward? The major reason was that already cited—the choices made by the Clinton administration. The congressional committees were not especially protectionist, though Gibbons had shifted his position somewhat in this direction, and Representatives Sander Levin and Amo Houghton were active on the petitioners' side. Also unchanged from earlier periods was the relative weakness of internationalist firms and import users, each of whom had interests in changing the laws to bring treatment of import pricing closer to treatment of pricing of domestically produced goods. There had been dramatic cases showing the costs of high dumping duties to certain US firms—those on ball bearings and flat-panel displays were particularly telling. But in the main, CEOs of internationalist firms were preoccupied with other issues—especially China MFN. And some of them, companies such as Boeing, Kodak, or Motorola, had found the AD laws useful for their own purposes.

Whatever the full explanation, and whatever the exact balance, the rewriting of the dumping laws took time. Four months is normal for this, according to one experienced official. It could have been done more quickly, of course, if the drafters had limited themselves to straight-line implementation of the Geneva agreement, though detailed consultation with legislators and counsel for affected interests would still have been required. Finally, the administration's approach did apparently buttress

---

47. My effort to sort through the complexity of these issues was aided immensely by my research assistant, Steven Schoeny; by the summation in Jeffrey J. Schott (assisted by Johanna W. Buurman), *The Uruguay Round: An Assessment* (Institute for International Economics 1994); by the Senate Report, *Uruguay Round Agreements Act*; and by several conversations with experts on these issues. This does not mean that any of them will be satisfied with the balance struck here.

overall congressional support. Gephardt and Levin, two respected "tough on trade" Democrats, were solid supporters of the GATT bill.

The Loss of Future Fast-Track

The second issue where the administration approach cost precious time concerned future trade negotiations: whether fast-track authority for them would be included in the Uruguay Round bill. In this case, it cost USTR the substance as well. Mickey Kantor and his colleagues needed congressional authority to pursue their regional and global negotiating agenda. They did not get it in 1994.

Authority to employ fast-track procedures for the results of future trade negotiations had been included, almost unnoticed, in the 1979 legislation implementing the Tokyo Round. But the 1991 renewal debate had made fast-track a visible and controversial issue, particularly for members of Congress not on the principal trade committees. Kantor made the matter more controversial by delaying his specific proposal to mid-June, springing it on the trade community without full consultation, and including in it two provisions bound to provoke opposition. One was the duration of the proposal: it would cover essentially all trade negotiations completed by December 2001, seven years into the future. This seemed to many legislators an excessively long and broad request, particularly since the post–Uruguay Round trade agenda was only beginning to be developed. The second was a proposal to include trade-related labor and environmental issues among the specific negotiating priorities set forth in the fast-track extension. This got the business community up in arms.

In its post–Uruguay Round planning, USTR had placed very high priority on initiatives to reconcile trade liberalization and environmental protection and to bring internationally recognized labor standards into the trade dialogue. Politically, the latter was a peace offering to labor and its congressional allies, who had opposed NAFTA. Early in 1994, therefore, USTR launched an aggressive international campaign to include labor standards on the agenda of the new World Trade Organization. Specifically, Kantor pressed for agreement to be announced on this matter at the Marrakesh meeting on 15 April where final Uruguay Round agreements would be signed. He faced "overwhelming international opposition,"[48] particularly from developing countries, and in the end had to settle for agreement that the issue would be discussed by the Preparatory Committee, which was being established to help manage the transition from GATT to WTO. But Vice President Gore highlighted the issue in the address he delivered at Marrakesh.

---

48. *Inside US Trade*, 1 April 1994, 1.

Business interests had acquiesced only reluctantly in NAFTA labor and environmental side agreements, fearing they would increase regulation. They reacted very negatively to the administration's spring labor-standards campaign. Then USTR, with only limited consultation, unveiled its fast-track proposal in June, which made "labor standards" and "trade and the environment" the fifth and sixth of seven "principal trade negotiating objectives" for which the new authority was to be employed.[49] The business community reacted strongly. Before long, many Republicans were saying that they would only approve new fast-track if labor and environmental issues were explicitly *excluded*, a stance heartily endorsed by small and medium-sized businesses. Multinational firms in the Business Roundtable accepted the idea that some treatment of labor and environment issues might be appropriate in trade talks. But they felt frustrated. The administration, they believed, was undercutting its own cause by not working closely with the business allies upon whose support extension of fast-track would depend. With Moynihan and Packwood already skeptical about fast-track's inclusion in the implementing bill, the best hope was for the administration to win agreement in the House and then work hand-in-glove with business in persuading the Senate. But from the business standpoint, there was a lack of the close consultation and confidence that would make this possible.

The labor/environment issue, and the way Kantor was handling it, divided Congress along partisan lines—just the thing that he needed to avoid. The financing issue had a similar effect. Moreover, while Republicans remained generally supportive of free trade in general and the agreement in particular, their sights were increasingly set on the upcoming November elections, where they saw a chance for major gains. They feared that a Clinton "victory" on a major piece of legislation—or, worse yet, several major victories—would give him and the Democrats a political countermomentum like that which he had gained from the NAFTA vote. Their immediate target was health care, the predominant business of the second session of the 103rd Congress. But as Clinton's prospects on this issue receded, Republicans began thinking of denying him a trade victory also, or at least of making sure that the victory came on their terms. Thus, although the core Uruguay Round debate was never substantively partisan (like the budget in 1993 or health care in 1994), the issue became tactically partisan, and remained so through the November elections.

The WTO and US "Sovereignty"

The most prominent public issue was the creation of the new World Trade Organization. As noted earlier, US officials had initially been resis-

49. For the full text, see *Inside US Trade* Special Report, 21 June 1994, S-26.

tant to it, partly out of concern over its domestic reception. And once the WTO was agreed to, it became the target and mobilizing issue for an odd anti-GATT alliance, bringing together Ralph Nader, Pat Buchanan, and Ross Perot. The buzz word was "sovereignty," and whether the WTO would take it away from the United States. Newt Gingrich pressed the issue in the spring, partly because a Georgia primary opponent was raising it. He won a special hearing in House Ways and Means and won also a provision, in the implementing legislation, whereby the Congress could vote on withdrawal from the WTO every five years.

For the Buchanan-led hard right, the WTO was a new manifestation of the threat of a "world government." For the left, the WTO raised concerns that the new trade institutions and procedures would override US laws on such matters as environmental protection and product safety. For Senate Minority Leader Robert Dole, it was a rationale for withholding support until the politically opportune moment. Claiming he had had more phone calls to his Wichita office on WTO than on NAFTA, he asked why Congress couldn't wait until the issue was clarified and why there was the need to rush to a vote in 1994.[50] Supporters brought in conservative jurist Robert Bork to quash the sovereignty question, and Bork declared that the WTO took away no authority from US institutions, and could not force any changes in US law. The Heritage Foundation weighed in with a similar analysis. Together with the strengthened dispute-settlement procedures, however, the WTO could produce legitimate decisions that US laws violated US trade commitments. And while it could not force changes in these laws, it could sanction retaliation by other nations if the laws were not changed. A specific aspect of this issue receiving prominence was the impact on laws below the federal level. State attorneys general mobilized and won a provision to protect their participation in any changes of state laws required to conform to Uruguay Round agreements, or as a result of adverse WTO decisions.

Other issues also brought complications. The textile industry, whose quotas the agreement would phase out in 10 years, sought (and would win) short-term gains through promised changes in the "rules of origin" used to enforce those quotas. Senator John Danforth (R-MO) led an early Republican protest against rules governing subsidies, which gave a "green light" to those aimed at enhancing research and development. Curiously absent from the debate, however, was the issue of trade adjustment measures. One reason was that, with the AFL-CIO on the sidelines, the issue of "jobs" was as marginal to the Uruguay Round debate in 1994 as it had been central to the NAFTA debate in 1993.

---

50. See Keith Bradsher, "Dole Urges Postponement For Approval Of Trade Pact," *New York Times*, 31 August 1994. Kansas was a particular target of GATT opponents, who apparently orchestrated the phone calls. Dole presumably knew this at the time, and he admitted it later.

Delaying the Process: Dole, Hollings, and Gingrich

Thus, despite its determination to move fast on Uruguay Round implementation, USTR found itself bogged down on a variety of issues as spring became summer and summer approached fall. And the process seemed to maximize the leverage of those who stood in the way. If opponents' head start on NAFTA was the result of Clinton political strategy, on GATT a somewhat similar political pattern was rooted in the fast-track procedures themselves. The way in which policy bargaining was centered on the drafting of legislation gave business interests an incentive to delay or condition their support in order to extract the last bit of gain—in the wording of the antidumping laws, for example, or in rules of origin for textiles. Once the package was finally put together, time was short, the opposition was mobilized, and business could not simply turn on a dime to all-out support. Thus the internationalist interests that had come together so strongly on NAFTA and on China MFN were not a powerful counterweight when Republicans subordinated GATT approval to their determination to deny all victories to Clinton.

The original administration goal was to get approval—or at least a House vote—before the August congressional recess. But while health care dominated members' attention, negotiations on the implementing bill ran on endlessly—in particular on the budget, on future fast-track, and on antidumping. The first "nonconference" between Senate Finance and House Ways and Means was not held until 19 August, and the final one was on 20 September. Kantor struggled repeatedly to formulate a follow-on fast-track proposal acceptable to both Gephardt Democrats and Archer Republicans. He thought he had one in August, but by then Senate Finance was adamantly against including any such language. Under strong White House pressure, he continued to press the matter after its prospects had evaporated, delaying the process further. The administration finally gave up on future fast-track in September, without even gaining authority for the broadly supported free trade negotiations with Chile.

More important, the bill now faced a time bind that threatened its very enactment. The law allowed up to 90 legislative days for Congress to consider trade implementing legislation after its submission, and there were nowhere near 90 days between late September and the anticipated October adjournment. Of course, no previous fast-track bill had taken all of the 90 days, as steps had been skipped or statutory times truncated through leadership power (in the House) or unanimous consent agreements (in the Senate). The NAFTA bill was not even introduced until 4 November 1993, just 16 days before the final Senate vote, and the Senate skipped over the statutory requirement that the bill, after House passage, "shall be referred to the appropriate committee or committees" in that body. But that required acquiescence of key committee chairs, and support from the minority. For the Uruguay Round, neither was automatic. Dole was not helping at all, seeing political advantage in delay. Patrick Leahy (D-VT), chairman of the Senate Agriculture Committee, had threatened to use the 45 days the law allowed his committee if he did not win satisfaction on certain provisions. And after Leahy's agreement was won, there remained the chair of the Commerce Committee and one of the Senate's few out-and-out protectionists, Ernest Hollings of South Carolina.

Moreover, the predominant interpretation was that the administration could only submit a fast-track implementing bill once for each agreement. If the Uruguay Round legislation was stalled and never came to final vote in the 103rd Congress, approval would have to be sought by regular legislative procedures in the 104th—with the bill open for amendments and filibusters. And even if procedural cooperation could be attained, the key committees would all have new members, who were unlikely to acquiesce in all of the balances struck by the old.

Understanding Hollings's blocking power, USTR was solicitous and accommodating to him throughout—on antidumping laws, on textile rules of origin—although his committee's actual jurisdiction covered only a modest number of Uruguay Round provisions. Thus, in the frenetic late-September days prior to submitting the president's bill, USTR officials sought a commitment from the senator not to use his delaying power and explored at the same time the possibility of stripping from the bill the provisions under Commerce jurisdiction. They failed to win the first, and received overwhelming advice from friendly senators not to pursue the second, as it would alienate other senators now on the fence. They could, of course, have held off the bill until 1995, but that would have meant, in all probability, starting the nonmarkup process from scratch with a mix of old and new committee members. So they sent the bill down, and prayed! Hollings was considered a friend of the president. Would he play into Republicans' political hands by preventing a vote before the election?

The answer turned out to be yes. The implementing bill was sent to Congress on 27 September. After meeting with President Clinton, Hollings announced on 28 September that he would not waive his committee's prerogative; he would insist on his 45 days.

On trade policy, Hollings was best known as an advocate of textile protection: as described in chapter 4, he had been proposing textile quota legislation as far back as 1968. And he numbered among his constituents Roger Milliken, the most politically prominent of mill executives and a fierce opponent of liberal trade. But while Hollings's move was widely interpreted as doing textiles' bidding, the larger industry did not back him. The American Textile Manufacturers Institute was officially neutral on the agreement, and a number of firms were actually supportive—because of concessions they had won on textile tariffs and the details of the MFA phase-out, and because they, in some cases, had decided to go with the internationalist flow. Hollings, in turn, insisted he was fighting not just for textiles but for broader protectionist reasons: free trade had been ravaging American firms and workers for decades! He would use his 45 days for hearings to make this case to the American people.

The South Carolinian's action killed the chances of a Senate vote before October adjournment, but the administration had a procedural fallback: to call a "lame duck" session after the election. Clinton had made it clear that he would do so if necessary, perhaps hoping that the inconvenience caused to Hollings's colleagues might deter him from delaying the vote. It didn't. But Hollings did not press his procedural rights as far as he could have; the White House and Senate leader Mitchell were able to work with him on the details.

On 30 September, standing with Hollings on the Senate floor, Mitchell sought and received unanimous consent "that the time for committee consideration of S. 2467, the GATT implementing legislation, continue to be counted regardless of whether or not the Senate is in session." Hollings thus made a decisive procedural concession he did not have to make: that the 45-day clock would run while the Senate was in recess for the November elections! All he insisted on, at least in public, was "that I be recognized and have the floor and I can explain to my colleagues my position on this." With this key unanimous consent agreement, Mitchell was free to follow with a schedule consistent with giving Commerce its 45 days: the Senate would reconvene on 30 November for 12 hours of debate on GATT, and continue on 1 December with the remaining 8 hours that fast-track allowed—voting "at approximately 6 p.m." that day.[51] These arrangements minimized the inconvenience that the delay caused to senators, and they prevented further procedural maneuvers on Hollings's (and others') part.[52]

House committees had no comparable power to delay if the leadership wished to proceed. So the administration pressed the House to proceed with its scheduled vote on 5 October, with GATT supporters and editorialists joining in the call. But while the Uruguay Round never became as hot an issue as NAFTA, it had become more than controversial enough to make members reluctant to take a preelection vote that could be avoided, especially when their Senate counterparts were avoiding *their* vote.

---

51. Quotations are from *Congressional Record*, 30 September 1994, S13765.

52. For example, once the House delayed its vote to 29 November, the language of the fast-track authority indicates that Senate committees would have had a right to hold the House bill for an additional 15 legislative days. Had someone exercised this right, the earliest date for Senate action would have moved perilously close to Christmas. But the unanimous consent agreement, reached before the House deferred action, rendered this option moot.

The politics became further heated when it was revealed that *The Washington Post* Company had a private interest in enactment of the legislation, one that had not been acknowledged in its editorials calling for GATT's enactment. At issue was a Federal Communications Commission (FCC) license being granted to a *Post* subsidiary, American Personal Communications, Inc. (APC) to provide wireless telephone service. Originally, it had been promised free, as a reward for "pioneering" communications work, but in 1993 Congress established a policy that such licenses should be auctioned, and the FCC moved to charge APC and other "pioneers" the amount that it estimated an auction would bring. APC filed suit, claiming the government had no right to charge it anything. A compromise was negotiated, requiring APC and others to pay a total of $1.5 billion over five years.

The Clinton administration, needing revenue to offset GATT tariff losses and wishing to preempt possible court action denying the Treasury any payment, consulted with House Commerce Committee Chairman John Dingell and then included the agreed payment in the implementing bill sent to Congress. It was a substantial contribution to the $12 billion total required. A rival company, Pacific Telesis, was outraged—insisting that the license was worth more than the *Post* and the other pioneers were paying. So in early October, shortly after a *Post* editorial endorsed the implementing bill without mentioning the deal, PacTel published full-page ads in the *Post* and *The Washington Times* denouncing the arrangement. The day afterward, the Nader-backed, anti-GATT Citizens' Trade Campaign took out ads denouncing the "multi-million dollar giveaway to *The Washington Post*." Talk radio picked up the issue, reinforcing the idea—pressed by Nader, Perot, and their allies—that the GATT legislation was the very sort of secret, inside deal and back scratching among narrow interests in Washington that so incensed the public.[53]

The *Post* affair gave House politicians yet another reason to step aside until the issue could be resolved or had spent its course. And last but not least, Republicans were increasingly bullish on the fall election and increasingly caught up in their strategy of denying Clinton legislative victories, even partial ones. So House Minority Whip Newt Gingrich began talking of having Republicans oppose the *rule* that had to be passed to allow the House to vote on the legislation. If Republicans united with anti-GATT Democrats, they could block the vote. The administration and the House leadership kept calling for that vote up to its scheduled day, but they knew the political logic working against them, and ultimately they had to yield.

This additional setback unleashed a torrent of criticism. Carla Hills, USTR under Bush, who had been working with Clinton to win the House

---

53. This paragraph draws particularly on Mike Mills, "How an Editorial and an Ad Changed the GATT Debate," *The Washington Post*, 25 November 1994.

vote, accused the administration of a "major, major miscalculation in introducing the bill so late in the session," when it had been "ready to be acted on since the spring. I'm a lawyer and this borders on malpractice. If I were involved," she concluded, "I think I would have fired myself."[54] The 7 October *Journal of Commerce*, on the other hand, saved its main fire for Gingrich. In an editorial entitled "Gutless on GATT," it attacked the speaker-to-be as "too obsessed with pandering to Mr. Perot and bashing Bill Clinton to uphold his party's historical commitment to free trade. If this is the kind of leadership Mr. Gingrich intends to provide in the future, Republicans, Congress and the country are in trouble."

From Partisan Wrangle to Bipartisan Victory

Even as partisanship scuttled the vote, however, bipartisanship was paving the way for postelection action. In exchange for the postponement, Gingrich agreed to back a rule calling for a vote on 29 November, and this passed by a bipartisan margin of 293–123. He underscored his support in a letter to the president promising to work for approval of the legislation on that date.

Everyone agreed, however, that the harder test would be in the Senate: because a 60-vote super-majority would be necessary to waive the budget requirements for the second five years, and because minority leader Robert Dole remained on the fence.[55] Hoping to sway him was a curious left-right alliance signified by three prominent personalities—Ralph Nader, Ross Perot, and Pat Buchanan. Particularly energetic was Nader and his organization, Public Citizen. Even more curious was the thinness of visible opposition within Congress. Hollings was actively and vociferously opposed, but his position was familiar and therefore discounted. Jesse Helms would urge, after the election, that the legislation be held over until 1995, and Robert Byrd opposed it on grounds of budget process. But it was hard to find prominent names beyond these three.[56]

The business community was late getting organized and never really waged an all-out campaign, as they had on NAFTA. Business leaders did play an important role in October and November, however. Since

---

54. Quoted in *Journal of Commerce*, 7 October 1994.

55. "If the Uruguay Round legislation fails," remarked one key administration trade official around that time, "Bob Dole will bear a heavy share of the blame."

56. Although he voted in favor in committee and does not seem to have worked for the bill's defeat, Max Baucus, outgoing chair of the Finance Trade Subcommittee, ended up voting against passage, apparently in response to interests within his state. The vote discredited him as a trade policy leader.

Congress was not in session, they had to work through companies in the appropriate states and districts. They followed a two-stage strategy. Aware that the populist, antiestablishment tenor of the campaign did not tilt things in their favor on trade, the umbrella business organization, Alliance for GATT Now, asked members to withhold commitment during the campaign. This effort was generally successful; trade was not a front-rank issue in the campaign, despite Buchanan-Perot-Nader efforts to make it so. The second round, pushing for commitments, was also effective if judged by results. But "the business effort on GATT was not as vigorous, not as broadly based, and not as sustained as the effort on NAFTA a year earlier," according to one trade veteran deeply involved in both. And it was considerably less critical to the outcome than the administration's dialogue with key Republican leaders.

Bipartisan support is always necessary in trade policy. It was overridingly necessary for Bill Clinton after 8 November 1994. The result of that day's election—the remarkable Republican capture of both House and Senate—was a devastating repudiation of his leadership. Moreover, the vote was bound to raise questions as to the legitimacy of the rejected, Democrat-controlled 103rd Congress taking final action on the Uruguay Round in a lame-duck session. The only people who could give this process legitimacy were the Republican victors, and especially those with the new mandate: Newt Gingrich and Robert Dole.

Gingrich had, as earlier noted, signed on unambiguously in October, in exchange for the agreement to postpone the vote. He would deliver on this commitment, just as he had delivered on NAFTA the year before. Dole, by contrast, had promised nothing before the election—indeed, he had been nothing but trouble to the administration. So the spotlight was on him—what would he do? In postelection press conferences he expressed a hope that he could support GATT and suggested he might be able to do so if the president were to explain the importance of the agreement to the American people and counter the claims of those whose messages were flooding his Wichita office. Above all, he wanted some safeguard against adverse, arbitrary decisions against the United States in the WTO. In addition, he wanted some way to reopen the *Washington Post* deal embedded in the nonamendable implementing legislation. When the administration suggested willingness to address these issues, the senator upped the ante, proposing that if the Senate were to waive the budget rules for GATT, it should do likewise for reduction in the capital gains tax rate! For Republicans had long argued that this would trigger increased sales and hence larger tax revenues. In the spirit of bipartisan comity, wouldn't Clinton support that?

On this last item, the administration drew the line. It would not yield on an extraneous tax issue marked by strong partisan differences, just as Republicans earlier had rejected use of fast-track to pursue labor and environmental objectives. With the boundaries of bargaining thus set, the deal quickly followed. On the Wednesday before Thanksgiving, Dole announced, from a White House podium, that he had won concessions that "fixed this as much as we can." He admitted to getting nothing on capital gains, saying, "I never had it to give up." On the WTO, however, he won an administration commitment to support legislation to establish a "WTO Dispute Settlement Review Commission." This would be composed of "five Federal appellate judges, appointed by the president in consultation with [congressional] leadership." This commission would "review all final dispute settlement reports . . . adverse to the United States." If it found, within any five-year period, three such decisions in which a WTO panel "demonstrably exceeded its authority" or "acted arbitrarily or capriciously," then any member of Congress could introduce and force a vote on a joint resolution mandating US withdrawal from the organization.[57] On the *Washington Post* controversy, Dole won a promise of a review that could lead to a higher price being paid for the license.

The deal was vintage Washington politics: the "good" kind, because it brought adversaries together behind a larger objective, but, ironically, the sort of practice which November voters had resoundingly repudiated. The deal had enough substance to address real concerns about a runaway international entity wreaking havoc with US policy, and some liberal traders felt that the Review Commission might in fact play a constructive role: in providing legal discipline for the new procedures in Geneva and in discrediting groundless attacks on WTO decisions. In any case, by settling with the key fence-sitting Republican, Clinton and Kantor had secured the necessary votes and won legitimacy for the lame-duck proceeding. And Dole achieved what was presumably *his* broader purpose—to signal, on the first available issue, his central role as power broker in the new Washington.

After the Dole deal, victory in the Senate was assured. Both opponents and supporters concealed this: the former for obvious reasons, the latter because they wanted to keep the pressure on and win the largest possible margin. There were therefore the last-minute White House meetings with undecided congressmen and senators, and a few minor policy deals.[58] These reinforced the strong pro-GATT momentum of the final week, and when the House voted the Tuesday after Thanksgiving, both

---

57. Quotations are from Kantor's 23 November letter to Dole, reprinted in *Inside US Trade*, 25 November 1994, 23–24. A joint resolution is subject to presidential veto, however; thus a two-thirds majority of each house would be necessary to enforce withdrawal on an unwilling administration.

58. Because success was not riding on them, they were generally of minor consequence. For example, Senator Larry Pressler (R-SD) reportedly won an administration promise to push China to ease its import restrictions on soybeans (*The Journal of Commerce*, 2 December 1994).

parties supported the bill by margins of two-to-one, and the bill received at least 64 percent support from every region of the country.[59] GATT did even better in the Senate: the waiver passed with eight votes beyond the sixty required, and the count on final passage was 76–24, a happy surprise to the Clinton White House. In the Senate, the bipartisanship was mathematically perfect: as noted by Dole, each party voted 76 percent in favor: Democrats 41–13; Republicans 35–11.[60] There were some unexpected defections, most notably that of outgoing Trade Subcommittee Chair Max Baucus. Getting far more national notice, however, was the decision of labor Democrat Barbara Mikulski of Maryland to "vote for GATT."

> I am a blue-collar Senator. My heart and soul lies with blue-collar America. . . . And in the last decade, working people have faced the loss of jobs, lower wages and a reduced standard of living, and a shrinking manufacturing base, everything that the critics say. But voting against GATT will not save those jobs or bring those jobs back. . . . The Uruguay Round [will] cut tariffs and reduce trade barriers for many of Maryland's top export industries. . . . So I am voting for GATT to generate more exports, to create more jobs in my own State of Maryland and in the United States of America.[61]

In November before his GATT victory, Clinton had flown to Indonesia to sign an APEC summit declaration committing member states to achieving free trade by 2020 (by 2010 for the most advanced among them). In December the trade venue was Miami and the Summit for the Americas. The result there was a commitment to conclude a free trade arrangement for the hemisphere by the year 2005.[62]

As 1994 came to a close, President Clinton was still absorbing his crushing mid-term election setback. But he was also, in the words of one commentator, "compiling a more ambitious record of trade liberalization than any President since at least Harry S. Truman."[63] The road had been anything but smooth, and some of its obstacles had been of the administration's own making. One important battle was lost—that for fast-track extension. But in the end, with bipartisan support, the administration

---

59. The House split 288–146, with Democrats 167–89 and Republicans 121–56. Regional percentages in favor were: Northeast, 70%; South, 64%; Midwest, 66%; and West, 67%. (Calculations are from *The New York Times*, 30 November 1994.)

60. On the waiver, 69 percent of Democrats voted in favor, and 67 percent of Republicans.

61. *Congressional Record*, 30 November 1994, S15102.

62. This was the target date for agreement, not for the actual removal of barriers. This left ambiguous the question of which goal—APEC or Western Hemisphere—was more ambitious.

63. Ronald Brownstein, "Clinton Drawing Visionary Blueprint of Global Economy," *Los Angeles Times*, 5 December 1994.

came through. Mickey Kantor in particular had proved an adept "closer" of deals: with Mexicans on NAFTA issues, with the European Union on GATT, and with senators and representatives on both. Carla Hills and others had moved both enterprises very far along: completing the NAFTA pact and winning the key US-EC breakthrough at Blair House. Kantor had pushed them over the top. He was the first US trade representative called upon to deliver major results in his first two years. And he did.

Looking to the Future

Once again, the US trade policymaking system had worked. Congress played actively but allowed the administration to lead. On NAFTA, members came around because they were substantively persuaded, but also because they were unwilling to take the responsibility for its rejection. On GATT, direct rejection always seemed unlikely, but the limited enthusiasm of its backers made the agreement constantly vulnerable to other agendas. In the end, it received resounding bipartisan support. The trade policy process had once more overcome both partisan conflict and the separation of powers.

Kantor's USTR was less dependably antiprotection than the USTR of Carla Hills, reflecting the broader forces at play within Clinton's Democratic administration. It was responsive to a range of restriction-seeking industries: to steel on antidumping, to textiles on Uruguay Round and implementing bill details, to autos in seeking quantitative export targets vis-à-vis Japan. Its unrequited courtship of labor also fueled doubts over where Kantor and USTR stood. But these departures from free trade purity were well within the postwar trade-brokering tradition. The more important truth was that yet another administration had mastered the formula: firm commitment to negotiate and implement trade-liberalizing agreements and flexibility in accommodating key producer constituencies on the details. And trade continued to expand.

With NAFTA and GATT ratified, the biggest items had been removed from the US trade agenda. There remained unfinished Uruguay Round business and the need to launch the World Trade Organization. There loomed, on the horizon, hemispheric negotiations toward free trade and the APEC liberalization process as well. All this suggested a bright future for liberal trade.

Yet although the strong pro-GATT votes in Congress sent a powerful affirmative message around the world, the future remained murky. One reason was big tasks had been completed, the missions accomplished. If past periods following major GATT agreements are an indicator, the coming years will likely feature some backsliding, as protectionist forces are no longer held in check by the momentum of on-going talks. This need for momentum in trade policy—the so-called bicycle theory—made it all the more important for the Clinton administration and Congress to move forward in 1995 with a follow-on trade agenda. The failure to renew fast-track in 1994 has made this a necessity, but also an opportunity.

But the going would not be easy. For one thing, while trade votes may still be won by elites, the trade dialogue is no longer dominated by them. The threat of competition with Mexico triggered a gut-wrenching national debate over NAFTA in 1993, though the specifics of that agreement overwhelmingly favored the United States. The Uruguay Round never reached that degree of prominence, but the WTO engendered strong, vocal opposition in 1994, with opponents employing modern media methods—speaking to the grass roots, their voices amplified by talk radio. Supporters of liberal trade are not comfortable in such forums and have not done particularly well in them. They have coasted along, capitalizing on broad consensus among elites, comfortable that they would prevail in the inside politics of Washington—as they have generally prevailed throughout the postwar period. Unlike Cordell Hull, who initiated trade liberalization in the United States more than 60 years ago, free traders are not very good on the stump. They have not had to be. So they have gotten out of practice.

They will need to shape up, for their central procedural vehicle is threatened as well. The apparent reason Mickey Kantor failed to get future fast-track in the implementing bill was his effort to stretch the substance to cover trade-related labor and environmental issues. A deeper reason is that the process has been piling up opposition for years, especially since the vote of 1991 forced it into the light of day. Senate Finance Chairman Daniel Patrick Moynihan, whose jurisdiction stood to gain, opposed inclusion of follow-on authority in the implementing bill because he feared controversy over fast-track would jeopardize its passage. Senator Richard Lugar, a consistent supporter of liberal trade, declared during the final debate that "much of the opposition to the Uruguay Round has focused not [on] the specifics of the agreement, where the United States clearly stands to gain, but on the allegedly closed and corrupt nature of the congressional fast-track process." And some of this criticism was legitimate, he declared, for "the fast-track privilege has come to be seen as a vehicle for side deals, special-interest accommodations and provisions of questionable merit—none of which can be changed once included in implementing legislation, unless a Senator is prepared to defeat the entire agreement. . . ."[64]

There were other problems as well. With the strong US recovery, the trade deficit had ballooned again, to a record $166.3 billion in 1994 (table 3.1). Continued trans-Pacific conflict generated support for the notion that the United States should somehow pursue a two-track trade policy:

---

64. *Congressional Record*, 1 December 1994, S15321.

one for the bulk of nations and a second for Japan—as if a global trading system could somehow exclude the world's number-two economy and number-one creditor nation. There was continuing resistance abroad to "aggressive unilateralism" in US trade policy: in Europe, and across East and Southeast Asia. At home, the Republican sweep brought scores of militant newcomers to Capitol Hill—newcomers with unclear trade views, newcomers untutored in the Washington rituals that have deflected bad trade legislation.

In this new context, can the United States pursue forward-looking trade policies that accept the reality of an interdependent world and bring Americans the gains from competing effectively in that world? Chapter 10 explores how we might do so.

What to Do? A Framework
for Future US Trade Policy

Trade policy carries burdens that go beyond its capacities. The instruments at its disposal—measures impeding imports or encouraging exports—are weak and inappropriate when set against 12-digit trade deficits or crises in major American industries. Yet they are what US political leaders are typically asked to employ when such troubles come knocking at their doors. Nor do the tools get any sharper when alliances lose their enemies, and frustrations with Japanese and Europeans multiply.

This book has told the story of an American trade policymaking system confronting sharply altered circumstances at home and abroad, a system that has held up considerably better than most would have predicted. This chapter builds on that story but goes beyond it. It asks the prescriptive question: what should we do now? Granted the problems and changes recounted in previous pages, how should American officials and institutions respond? What set of policies, procedures, and institutions will best serve American interests in the new global environment?

The first section of this chapter answers these questions for the near term, in light of the challenges facing a Democratic president and a Republican Congress in 1995 and 1996. The remainder provides broader, longer-term prescription. It does so in two forms: a summary section offering concise analysis and recommendations, and a more extended section that treats matters more thoroughly. It includes remedies outside the trade policy sphere—steps to reduce the budget deficit and enhance productivity. And the entire chapter is built on the premise that, even in a world where many foreigners are "unfair" and some are gaining on us, a basically liberal trade approach remains the best policy option for today's United States.

Policy for the Near Term *terms for future*

To move trade policy forward in 1995 and 1996, the White House and Congress will need to come together on three central things:

■ **a substantive agenda** that simultaneously pursues multilateral, hemispheric, and APEC liberalization options and also nurtures the gradual development of the World Trade Organization and its dispute-settlement processes;

■ **A public argument** that highlights how internationalization is a fact of life, that trade brings gains that exceed its pains, and that broad protectionism is no longer a feasible policy option;

■ **A reformed trade policy process** that preserves the essence of fast-track but curbs abuses and promotes timely debate over major new initiatives.

A New Agenda?

The Clinton administration was understandably guarded about its post–Uruguay Round agenda in 1994, wishing not to lose votes on either side of the aisle. And the response to its trade-environment proposal hardly encouraged it to be more forthcoming. But in early 1995, it needed to be more forthcoming: ready to advance specific initiatives, yet aware that consensus had not yet formed on many matters.

On geographic priorities, there has been near-universal support for free trade with Chile—the Latin American country next in line—and broad backing for further moves toward Western Hemisphere free trade. There is more generalized support, tinged with wariness, for trade liberalization in APEC. Business is driven heavily in this direction, but Asian economies pose a far greater challenge to American workers than the Mexican economy ever can.

Moving to functional issues, the Clinton USTR has focused on three post–Uruguay Round matters—labor, the environment, and competition policy. It will need to adjust its priorities, for the election has further weakened support for the first two. They may not have to be abandoned entirely, but USTR will need to proceed cautiously, eschewing grand environmental and labor initiatives. US politics in the mid-1990s will not support them.

Fortunately for US officials who need to keep the initiative, there will remain other issues as well: left-over business from the round, such as trade in cultural properties and financial services, and questions of implementing the agreements and getting the WTO off to a solid start. The Dole deal is an expression of the limits of American tolerance for binding international dispute settlement. It will constrain both WTO panels and USTR trade officials seeking to influence them. There is also the distinct possibility that the implementing legislation has produced anti-dumping provisions that WTO panels will find inconsistent with the agreement signed in April 1994. One hopes such decisions will not be found arbitrary or capricious by Dole's WTO Dispute Settlement Review Commission. And if they are, Congress ought not seek to overturn the whole system in the interest of protecting a few steel producers. But in this, as in all trade policymaking, balance will be required: the United States should push for greater liberalization and internationalization, but not so fast as to put past achievements at risk.

More Effective Trade Advocacy

With 60 years of progress in trade liberalization, with negotiation after negotiation and vote after vote confirming this basic direction, US trade policy should be politically secure. The fact that it does not seem so is due, in important part, to the rising popular debate and the defensiveness of trade advocates within it. They have done very well within the analytic community—establishing standards for analysis and demolishing the sweeping claims of Ross Perot and Pat Choate. They have done less well debating Ralph Nader on the national media. And they have failed to convey a realistic sense of today's world: that internationalization is a fact, no longer a choice; that imports as well as exports benefit a nation; that with the increased trade in components as well as final products, producers are importers too; that to gain maximum advantage from trade liberalization, we must be prepared to attack—as protectionist—all laws and practices, however they are labeled, that treat foreign and domestic producers differently.

As Bill Clinton and Mickey Kantor have noted, much of the American public is predisposed against trade because it is afraid of change—with reason. Trade has hurt many workers and will likely continue to disadvantage those with the least skills by putting them in competition with lower-wage foreign counterparts. But the answer is not to protect but to upgrade, for there is no durable way for worker welfare to advance unless productivity advances first. And a better educated, better trained work force is a key to improving productivity.

These and other arguments need to be made, with empathy for those who fear becoming losers in the global economy, but with determination to maintain and broaden policies of trade openness. And trade experts as well as trade-supporting politicians need to be bolder about making them.

A Trimmed-Down Fast-Track Process

Finally, there is a need for significant reform of the fast-track process. Here, too, the insider community has coasted for 20 years with the basic law of 1974, as agreements became more complex, as the drafting process became more cumbersome, as trade politics became more public. Extension of the law in 1988, intended for the Uruguay Round, was applied also to NAFTA, denying Congress as a whole any single occasion to stop it before the NAFTA train had left the station.[1] The joining of fast-track rules with budgetary requirements has led to embarrassments such as the APC-*Washington Post* provision, inserted at the eleventh hour because it brought needed revenue, yet immovable when it provoked understandable attack after the bill was formally submitted. And efforts have been made to broaden the substance of policy covered by fast-track beyond what today's trade policy consensus permits.

Because the administration failed to win extension of the process in 1994, Congress will be considering fast-track on a non-fast-track basis—in a bill open to amendment. With both houses now under Republican control, the administration will need to proceed very carefully. As they both play their roles, the executive and Congress should consider statutory changes that would narrow fast-track's potential for use and abuse, in order to make it a still more effective vehicle for trade agreements that Congress has explicitly authorized.

Like its predecessors, any bill extending the procedures will delimit the substantive purposes served by negotiations whose outcomes receive fast-track treatment. The administration should not repeat its effort to extend the procedure to cover, explicitly, negotiations on labor and environmental matters. These issues, however important, are currently subjects of sharp partisan division, not bipartisan consensus. And fast-track can work only on issues for which this consensus exists.

Departing from its predecessors, forthcoming fast-track legislation should incorporate **three major changes** in the process:

- First, the bill should **narrow the range of matters a fast-track bill can cover**, perhaps limiting it to measures "necessary" for implementation, rather than the more permissive "necessary or appropriate" in previous laws. The latter has given administration officials the leeway to broaden support by adding ancillary measures, but at the cost of lengthening the drafting process, inviting new special-interest demands, and encouraging international business to hold off lobbying for an agreement until all details on which it has an interest have been resolved. As part of this limitation, it could allow amendment of budgetary provisions included not to implement the agreement but to square with congressional rules.[2]

---

1. The legislation did give the Senate Finance and House Ways and Means Committees a veto over the launching of bilateral free trade negotiations, one which Senate Finance came within one vote of exercising on the US-Canada negotiation in 1986.

2. Senator Lugar suggested this in his Uruguay Round statement, on which this concluding proposal draws in other respects also.

- Second, the bill should **give committees their right to review** **the text of the bill is set in concrete** and establish a more expedit[e] timetable thereafter. The 45-day review period, which was Senator Hollings's statutory right in 1994, came after the final bill was drafted and submitted and unamendable. More appropriate would be to put into law some features of the nonmarkup process as now practiced: allowing committees of jurisdiction, for example, a specified length of time to hold hearings and make detailed statutory recommendations between the signing of an agreement and the presidential submission of implementing legislation.

- Third, **the bill should provide for explicit congressional authoriza-** **tion of the specific negotiations where the procedure applies.** It should not be written so broadly that an administration can launch a major negotiation such as NAFTA without explicit congressional action. Rather, fast-track should be amended so as to facilitate debate over such a negotiation, and provide for an explicit up-or-down vote, before it gets started.

One way to legislate this last limitation would be for the Congress to enact, without a termination date, a slimmed-down fast-track process of the sort proposed here—or in Senator Lugar's floor statement. Specific negotiations would qualify for the process, however, only if explicitly authorized by the Congress.[3] Matters that are ripe—Chilean adherence to NAFTA, for example—could be included in the bill that establishes the broader process. But any matter not explicitly authorized therein would need to be voted later. The bill might also specify procedures under which the administration could request and win a timely vote. More important is the need to require one.

Finally, to ensure that the fast-track process will be employed for major negotiations—where it is vital—USTR and Congress should eschew the temptation to negotiate and implement less complicated, specific country negotiations under the normal legislative process. This would be a terrible precedent, for it would create the erroneous impression that fast-track is not generally necessary and undercut the case for its renewal. In early 1995, for example, there has been talk of handling Chilean accession to NAFTA in this manner. This temptation should be resisted. The Chileans have been waiting several years to negotiate with the United States, and it is not unreasonable to *begin* talks with them in anticipation of fast-track legislation. Both the Tokyo and Uruguay Round negotiations were launched before Congress had enacted laws authorizing them. But a Chile negotiation should not be *completed* unless and until Con-

---

3. This should normally include dates for their completion, so as to create the action-forcing target that has often proved essential.

track and implementation can proceed under that au-

e fast-track law, and applying it to all significant trade
would retain what has proved so important: the need to
essional renegotiation of an accord, and hence to assure
ns that our negotiators possess sufficient authority to deal
vely with issues at hand. But it would also enhance democratic .bate. Both are important. The latter is becoming more so as
trade becomes central to American economic life.

These specific measures should be considered as part of a broader
approach to US trade policy, one built on good economics *and* good
politics. The remainder of this book sets forth such an approach.

Managing Trade Policy: A Basic Prescription

The fundamental prerequisite for sensible trade policy is *macroeconomic
balance*. If a nation is consuming more than it is producing, if investment
within its borders exceeds saving, it runs—by definition—a trade deficit.
If that deficit is large, it will affect the balance of trade politics by increasing the number of producers hurt by imports relative to the number of those helped by exports. It will multiply the number of demands
for trade restrictions, making it far harder for officials and legislators to
resist.

Although a trade deficit thus exerts a major impact on trade policy,
the converse is not the case. Action specifically directed toward imports
and exports has little effect on the balance between them. **Trade measures can affect the volume of trade. They can influence the composition of trade. But unless coupled with other measures, they will have
little impact on the overall surplus or deficit of a nation.**

Rather, the appropriate remedies for a trade deficit are *macroeconomic*
actions that increase saving relative to investment and production relative to consumption. For the United States, the most promising course
by far is action to reduce the federal budget deficit, because that represents massive dissaving for the American economy. Under conditions of
slack domestic demand, there can also be a role for *exchange rate policy*,
meaning direct efforts to influence the value of the dollar.[4]

---

4. In these circumstances, decline in the value of the dollar will increase demand for
exports and replace imports with domestic products, thus increasing production relative
to consumption (and bringing the economy closer to full capacity). At full capacity,
however, the main product of dollar devaluation will be inflation. For elaboration, see
I. M. Destler and C. Randall Henning, *Dollar Politics: Exchange Rate Policymaking in the
United States* (Washington: Institute for International Economics, 1989), esp. 10–11 and
148–49.

Within a condition of overall balance, the United States should expect to run surpluses with some trading partners—such as the European Union—and deficits with others—such as Japan.[5] **These bilateral imbalances are normal, even beneficial: they are one way that nations maximize the gains from trade. Measures that seek to regulate or eliminate them make no economic sense whatsoever.**

Macroeconomic policy can help the United States balance its global trade account and thereby bring pressures down to a more manageable level. It cannot, however, determine the exchange rate at which balance will take place. And unless productivity within the United States grows at a rate comparable to that in the rest of the world, it can only achieve external balance at a progressively lower (real) exchange rate. This means a declining living standard for Americans relative to the citizens of other nations, because it will take more US currency to buy foreign products and less of foreigners' currency for them to buy US products.

Hence there is a need for *productivity and competitiveness policies* that improve the quality and profitability of economic activity in the United States. These include measures to improve the quality of the work force (education and training), actions to strengthen the US economic infrastructure, steps to increase private saving and investment, and *technology policy* aimed at encouraging innovation and the efficient application of new ideas to the production process. The aim of such *microeconomic* measures is to make the economy both more productive and more flexible. The result, if successful, is greater gains from trade and a higher living standard for Americans.

Trade policy is not an effective instrument for addressing these broad, economywide problems of international balance and domestic productivity growth. It can have two very important goals, however. Its positive goal is to increase the volume of trade—and hence the gains from trade—through opening markets abroad and at home. Its negative goal is damage limitation: minimizing the harm to the overall US economy, and to the international trading system, from successful attempts by special interests to win import protection. In practice, the two are related. Damage limitation requires mobilization of counterpressure to offset the normal political imbalance favoring the concentrated interests hurt by trade. And one of the best means of creating such counterpressure is through negotiations aimed at increasing export opportunities, because these bring the export interests that gain from trade expansion more actively into the political fray.

This underscores the importance of the success in the complex, multi-

---

5. C. Fred Bergsten and William R. Cline, *The United States–Japan Trade Problem*, POLICY ANALYSES IN INTERNATIONAL ECONOMICS 13 (Washington: Institute for International Economics, 1985), 32–41.

nation, multi-issue Uruguay Round. The agreement will bring new export opportunities for American farmers and producers of other goods and services, as well as multilateral constraint on protectionist measures. And the new World Trade Organization offers opportunities to press for further market opening that US officials should exploit. Regional free trade is not a good substitute. For a nation two-thirds of whose exports go across the two great oceans, a hemispheric trade bloc offers a much narrower range of economic opportunities, and hence less counterpressure against trade restrictions.[6] And it brings risks of precipitating conflict among regional blocs unless accompanied by progress in the global GATT system.

There are specific economic and political gains to the United States from special arrangements with Canada and Mexico. But US priority should continue to go to *global* trade liberalization. In pursuit of regional liberalization opportunities, moreover, the United States should balance initiatives within the Americas with those elsewhere, particularly East Asia. As a general principle, **Western Hemisphere nations beyond the current NAFTA partners should not be offered free trade arrangements unless the United States is simultaneously moving toward free trade with nations outside the hemisphere.**

To conclude major trade-liberalizing agreements, fast-track procedures remain essential—as they were for the Tokyo Round of the 1970s and the Uruguay Round. The Bush administration and its congressional allies won a major victory in May 1991 when both houses acquiesced in their extension through June 1993. But in the course of that debate, fast-track became a broad congressional and public issue for the first time since its creation in 1974, with critics protesting loudly that it tied legislators' hands. Due in part to this concern, the Clinton administration failed to win such authority for new negotiations in the Uruguay Round legislation of 1994. As discussed earlier in this chapter, **it will be difficult to get fast-track procedures extended without some limitation on their scope and/or some buttressing of the congressional role within them.**

Ever since the Reciprocal Trade Agreements Act of 1934, international barrier-reducing negotiations have been a major counterweight to protectionism here at home. Multilateral talks may not play this role as effectively in the future. The pain attendant to the completion of the Uruguay Round of negotiations does not encourage leaders in the United States, Europe, or Japan to plunge quickly into another. And if a forthcoming round addresses trade and the environment, as widely predicted, its primary goal will not be further trade-barrier reduction but rather the reconciling of two strong, and sometimes compet-

---

6. See Jeffrey J. Schott, *More Free Trade Areas?* POLICY ANALYSES IN INTERNATIONAL ECONOMICS 27 (Washington: Institute for International Economics, 1989).

ing, policy frameworks. Thus it may not play the same protection-constraining role in the US political process. **Advocates of liberal trade policy must be prepared to rely less on major international negotiations and more on specific antiprotectionist interests based within the United States.**

Such trade-dependent interests—including retailers and industrial users of imported inputs—have grown stronger and more active in US trade politics.[7] Enmeshed as they are in an interdependent global economy, they can and should bear more of the political burden for supporting liberal trade policies. **US trade-remedy laws should be amended to reflect their growing trade interest and economic importance.**

This should be part of a broader reshaping of the statutes governing administrative trade relief. Before the 1970s, it was too hard for firms to get action under these statutes; now, it is too easy (at least under current US antidumping law as implemented). The result is too much protection and too many cases diverted from consideration under the escape clause to the laws that highlight alleged foreign "unfairness." And as spelled out in chapter 9, the Clinton administration acted to weaken Uruguay Round reforms in these procedures.

The best solution would be an international agreement on competition policy, with rules on predatory pricing that apply to both foreign and domestically produced goods. But absent such an agreement, the United States should adopt the following reforms as a package:

- The threshold for proving injury under the escape clause (Section 201) should be eased, but relief should be tied to an explicit adjustment commitment by the petitioner.

- The threshold for proving dumping should be toughened, returning to the original standard of comparing selling prices here to selling prices in the producer's home market.

- In dumping or countervailing duty cases in which dumping or subsidy and injury are found, a follow-on procedure should be created whereby users and other affected interests could seek a reduction in the level of penalty duty assessed by demonstrating that its full imposition would cause them serious injury.

Congress will continue to insist on export assertiveness, and the US Trade Representative (USTR) will continue to find tough, market-opening negotiations important in establishing its credibility and deflecting

---

7. I. M. Destler and John S. Odell, *Anti-Protection: Changing Forces in United States Trade Politics*, POLICY ANALYSES IN INTERNATIONAL ECONOMICS 21 (Washington: Institute for International Economics, 1987).

US protectionism. Thus there is an ongoing need for unilateral initiative, such as Section 301 provides for under current law.

Such procedures ought to be legitimated and regulated internationally, and the Uruguay Round agreements advanced this objective by broadening the range of trade issues subject to multilateral discipline and by strengthening dispute-settlement procedures under the new World Trade Organization. (US law provides that Section 301 cases must be pursued under GATT/WTO rules if they apply to the case at hand.) Moreover, the original Super 301 was counterproductive in its targeting of entire countries rather than specific trade practices. **But continuation of a case-initiating authority like that provided by Section 301 offers an important instrument for the USTR to retain trade policy initiative—with foreign countries, within the executive branch, and vis-à-vis the Congress.** And since the net effect of Section 301 to date has been trade liberalization, not trade restriction, its continuation is not an excessive burden for the international trading system to bear.[8]

Section 301 should be employed not to balance trade with particular countries or within particular sectors, but for products for which US producers are world-class competitors but find their comparative advantage thwarted by foreign restrictions. Section 301 should not be deployed to support an American "strategic trade policy," but it is an appropriate weapon for thwarting other nations' efforts to pursue such policies. To this end, it will occasionally be useful to employ two devices in negotiations with Japan: "sectoral reciprocity," that is, conditioning access to the US market on comparable access to the Japanese market in the same product area; and quantitative targets for import expansion. But their use should be the exception, not the rule. **Most important, the United States should resist the notion of developing a split-level trade policy: managed trade with Japan and liberalism with all other countries.** The need is to bring the world's number-two capitalist economy more fully *into* the global trade order, not to draw lines against it.

All these recommendations assume continuation of a trade policymaking system where Congress makes great noise and exerts considerable influence but delegates final decision power elsewhere. Congress reinforced this system in 1988 by eschewing product-specific measures and by transferring important authorities to the USTR, particularly the authority to impose sanctions in Section 301 cases. The grand successes of 1992–94, in completing and ratifying NAFTA and the Uruguay Round, suggest that the basic institutional mechanism remains sound.

Nonetheless, the following reforms would be useful at both ends of Pennsylvania Avenue to consolidate authority and deal with changes in personalities that come with changes in administrations:

---

8. Thomas O. Bayard and Kimberly Ann Elliott, *Reciprocity and Retaliation in U.S. Trade Policy* (Washington: Institute for International Economics, 1994).

- In the executive branch there have twice been occasions of sharp conflict between the USTR and the secretary of Commerce. Such conflict is built into the current structure, because trade is the most important of the Commerce secretary's policy responsibilities. The appropriate response is to **transfer, from Commerce to an operating agency reporting to the USTR, the functions of the current International Trade Administration.**

- On Capitol Hill, decentralization of power and internationalization of the US economy have weakened the impact of the key trade committee, House Ways and Means. Former chairman Dan Rostenkowski (D-IL) limited that erosion through a combination of committee role and personal power. But his successor, Bill Archer (R-TX), may find the going harder. It would be useful, therefore, to **create a House Trade Steering Group, headed by the Ways and Means chair and including representatives of other committees with trade jurisdiction, including Energy and Commerce, Banking, Foreign Affairs, and Agriculture.** The role of the Steering Group would be to coordinate omnibus trade legislation, including bills to implement major trade agreements.

Other reforms would also buttress the United States' capacity to pursue rational trade policies, including a restored trade adjustment assistance program and new means to analyze and publicize the gains from trade and the costs of trade protection. All will only work over the long term, however, if the United States can compete effectively in the world economy. And all will work *well* only if Americans understand the limits of trade policy: what it can and cannot do. That is a major purpose of this summary, and of the broader analysis that follows.

How Not to Cure Trade Imbalances

On 4 November 1991, the House majority leader introduced a new "Gephardt amendment." If it had been enacted, the measure would have "put on a Super 301 list for priority trade negotiations" any country that had bilateral trade accounting for "not less than 15 percent" of the US merchandise trade deficit, that ran a global current account surplus at least as large as its bilateral deficit with the United States, and that engaged in "protectionist practices which limit market opportunities."[9]

---

9. Quotations in this and the following paragraph are from the proposed "Market Opportunity and Reciprocal Enforcement Act of 1991" and the Statement of Majority Leader Richard A. Gephardt (D-MO) on its introduction, News Release of 4 November 1991.

No specific nation appeared by name in Gephardt's statutory language, but Japan was the obvious and admitted target. "For years," Gephardt declared in his statement introducing the measure, "we have been trying to get Japan and other countries to be more like us, to play by our rules. This legislation will continue this fight. But, at the same time, if a country wants to exclude our products, they will face similar restrictions on access to the U.S. market."[10]

Like the original Gephardt amendment of 1986–88, this proposal exploited two widely shared beliefs: that nations *ought* normally to balance their trade bilaterally, and that deficits were caused, in important part, by the surplus country's barriers to imports. The majority leader was too sophisticated to make such arguments directly; indeed, he had stated on other occasions that foreign trade barriers were *not* the prime source of the US deficit. But in late 1991 he was clearly implying that they were— at least where Japan was concerned. Responding to questions after an earlier address announcing his intent to submit the bill, Gephardt declared that "with Japan we continue to have a $40 billion trade deficit out of a [global] total of a $60 billion trade deficit"; had his amendment been adopted in 1988, we "would have probably brought down the Japanese trade deficit more quickly and we'd be in a different position with regard to Japan than we are today."[11] And in December, Gephardt joined with Michigan colleagues in putting forward a bill calling on Japan to eliminate the bilateral deficit entirely over a five-year period, against the threat of a curtailment of the total number of Japanese-label cars and light trucks sold in the American market.[12]

Trade With Japan: Right Problem, Wrong Solution

Bilateral trade deficits are bad; they are caused by foreign barriers against US products; target these barriers and the deficits will come down— Gephardt was far from alone in advancing or exploiting such logic in the 1990s. As 1991 drew to a close, business executives preparing to visit East Asia with President Bush were stressing that "Japan and the other

---

10. Moreover, the bill had a specific sectoral target: trade in automotive vehicles and parts. For any country put on the new Super 301 priority list, the USTR would be required to address, under Section 301, any and all restrictive practices affecting any sector that accounted for at least 10 percent of the bilateral deficit. This criterion was intended to respond to the recession-worsened crisis in the US auto industry—and to the fierce competition US auto parts manufacturers were facing from imports and from production by Japanese transplants.

11. Address to the Institute for International Economics on US Trade Policy, 10 September 1991, Reuters transcript, 10.

12. *Washington Post*, 21 December 1991, C1.

nations of the region—which account for 80 percent of the US trade deficit—must open their markets wider to American companies."[13] And in pursuing its "framework negotiations" with Tokyo, the Clinton administration was driven, in part, by the rise of the bilateral imbalance to a new record level. It seems like elementary common sense to blame a trade imbalance on foreign import restrictions or on weak-kneed American trade bargaining. If the United States is selling less than it is buying, it must be because the US market is open, drawing others' goods in while they are blocking US goods. If the situation is to be corrected, it seems to follow that the United States will have to "get tough"—really tough—with its trading partners.

Of course, prominent Americans had spoken in this manner before the 1990s. In the spring of 1985, the US Senate literally unloaded on Japan. In the previous year, the US trade deficit had topped $100 billion for the first time, and the value of imports had ballooned to 50 percent above that of exports. Little wonder that producers of internationally traded goods flocked to Washington—not just those feeling pressure from imports, but those like Caterpillar, who were losing market share in formerly lucrative export markets. Such companies saw the trade imbalance growing even worse. They saw the dollar continuing to rise. Perhaps worst of all, they saw a Reagan administration with no credible program for dealing with the trade crisis, and a president who, to judge by his words, looked upon the American economic landscape and saw nothing but good. Finding the White House deaf to their appeals, they redoubled their efforts at the other end of Pennsylvania Avenue.

Senators responded by going after Japan. By a 92-to-0 vote on 28 March 1985, they passed a resolution attacking the "bilateral trade imbalance" that was "costing the United States hundreds of thousands of jobs every year."[14] Japan had "extensive access to the United States market," the resolution declared. US exporters "lack access to the Japanese market for manufactured goods, forest products, key agricultural commodities, and certain services in which the United States has a comparative advantage." Years of market-access negotiations with Japan had been "largely unsuccessful." Therefore, the resolution called upon the president to retaliate against unfair Japanese trading practices.

In the one-sided debate on the measure, Finance Committee Chairman Bob Packwood (R-OR) announced he had reached "the limits of my patience with the Japanese." Trade Subcommittee Chairman John C. Danforth (R-MO) declared that, regarding Japan, "the time has come to

---

13. *Washington Post*, 20 December 1991, B10.

14. The text of Senate Concurrent Resolution 15 appears in *Congressional Record*, Daily Edition, 28 March 1985, S3573. The quotes in the following paragraph come from the debate that preceded its adoption, S3556-73. See the first edition of *American Trade Politics* for a fuller account of this episode.

act—not talk, not complain, not insult, but act." His Democratic counterpart, Senator Lloyd Bentsen (D-TX) declared himself "a reluctant supporter of this resolution . . . because I do not think it goes far enough." "We are in a trade war, and we are losing it," he declared.

Congressional frustration with Japan had ample factual basis—in 1995 as well as 1985. Tokyo ran persistent global trade and current account surpluses, and while Gephardt did not acknowledge, in his 1991 proposal, the major improvement that took place between 1987 and 1990, Japan's surplus would reach new record levels in the years thereafter.[15] And its market did not thwart only Americans. To quote one oft-cited statistic, in 1984 Japan took just 8 percent of the manufactured exports of the developing countries, compared to 58 percent taken by the United States—although this percentage rose with the yen appreciation of the late 1980s. While Japan had dismantled most of its formal trade barriers rapidly in the 1970s, strong import resistance clearly remained, and it was entirely proper for the United States to press a country that had so benefited from liberal trade to practice at home what it took such adept advantage of abroad.[16]

But there was one small difficulty. Japanese trade policies had very little relation to the American trade imbalance that generated such enormous pressure on Capitol Hill in 1985, and that remained Gephardt's target in the 1990s. Japan had not created it, and improvements in Japan's trade behavior would not solve it, however desirable such improvements might be on other grounds. Even the bilateral imbalance was not, to any significant degree, the product of Japanese import barriers. To demonstrate why, let us analyze the situation that existed in the spring of 1985.

- The trade deficit with Japan was America's largest, but it had not worsened any faster between 1981 and 1984 than US trade balances with Europe or the developing countries.[17]

---

15. Between 1986 and 1990, US exports to Japan nearly doubled, rising from $26.9 billion to $48.6 billion. Over this same period, US imports from Japan rose just 9.5 percent, from $81.9 billion to $89.7 billion. Japan's current account surplus peaked at $87.0 billion in 1987 and fell to $35.8 billion in 1990.

In 1991, however, this improvement ceased. By 1993, Japan's current account surplus had reached a new record of $131.4 billion, and in 1994 the bilateral trade imbalance hit $65.7 billion, with US exports at $53.5 billion and imports at $119.1 billion.

16. For a comprehensive analysis, see Edward J. Lincoln, *Japan's Unequal Trade* (Washington: Brookings Institution, 1990).

17. Comparing US bilateral trade balances with 24 major trading nations, Bergsten and Cline found that for 17 of them, the proportionate change from 1980–81 to 1984 was greater than that with Japan. Bergsten and Cline, *United States–Japan Economic Problem*, 23. For the decade as a whole, changes in the US-Japan trade deficit were proportionate to those in the global US trade deficit.

- This suggested that the trade imbalance was, in essence, "made in America." And it was. But it was not a product of US trade policies: these had in fact grown more restrictive since 1981, when the overall US current account was in balance.

- Instead, experts generally agreed, the $80 billion increase in the US trade deficit between 1981 and 1984 was the product of three macro-economic developments: the developing-country debt crisis, which caused Latin American capital and merchandise imports to plummet; the "growth gap" of 1983 and 1984, with the United States leading the advanced industrial world in emerging from recession (and therefore in growth of its import demand); and most important, the remarkable rise in the value of the dollar.[18]

- Why had the dollar risen, despite growing US trade deficits? The operative force had been international capital flows—the readiness of both domestic and foreign investors to shift their funds out of foreign assets and into US assets. The United States needed them to do so in order to finance its suddenly enormous budget deficits without "crowding out" private business investment. High real US interest rates were a powerful inducement. These were being encouraged by the tight monetary policy of a Federal Reserve Board determined to quench inflation.

- Finally, during the same period when the United States had been developing a capital shortage, Japan and the European Community had been developing capital surpluses. They had been cutting their government budget deficits. In Japan, this had created a substantial excess of savings. Its outflow, much of it directly to this country, helped finance the US deficit and the Reagan-era boom, but it weakened the yen and thereby fueled the very Japanese trade surplus that was bringing denunciation down upon Tokyo.

Given this situation, suppose that in 1985 Japan had made the sort of broad, immediate trade concessions that Americans sought. Suppose that, as the Commerce Department estimated at the time, such opening of Japanese markets resulted in $10 billion in additional US sales. Suppose also that these openings benefited other exporting nations also, to the tune of an additional $10 billion. But suppose that the Japanese savings-

---

18. For the most comprehensive analysis, see Stephen Marris, *Deficits and the Dollar: The World Economy at Risk*, POLICY ANALYSES IN INTERNATIONAL ECONOMICS 14 (Washington: Institute for International Economics, revised edition, 1987), chap. 1. Bergsten and Cline (*United States–Japan Economic Problem*, 50) found that "the main driving force behind the growing imbalance in the bilateral US-Japanese trade relationship has been the overvaluation of the dollar," followed by the slowdown in Japan's growth relative to the United States. See chapter 3 for more on exchange rate misalignment and its impact on trade flows.

capital surplus remained substantially unchanged. The increased import demand, combined with the continuing capital outflow, could be expected to weaken the yen further, reducing other imports and increasing exports until most or all of the trade balance improvement was offset.[19] The volume of Japanese trade would almost certainly be larger, the world economy would be more efficient, and US exporters would benefit. But the *balance* of trade would be little changed.[20]

One could, by this logic, still criticize the Japanese government for policies that resulted in large trade and current account surpluses, just as one could criticize the Reagan administration for the opposite. But the policies needing alteration would be macroeconomic. As Secretary of State George P. Shultz put it in the trade-contentious spring of 1985, "Japan must deal with its saving-investment imbalance if its chronic imbalance in trade is to be corrected."[21]

Similarly, if the United States had then imposed trade barriers without reducing the saving-investment imbalance that was causing it to import capital, it might succeed in reallocating the trade pain among import-impacted industries, and between them and the export sector. But it would not, in a floating exchange rate regime, reduce the US trade deficit to any significant degree.

In the years thereafter, of course, the US trade imbalance did come down significantly—from the 1987 peak of $159.6 billion to $74.1 billion in 1991 (table 3.1). Improvement was even greater in the deficit as a proportion of total US trade: from 24.5 percent in 1986 to 8.2 percent in 1991, a level last seen in 1982. The bilateral deficit with Japan declined also: from $56.3 billion in 1987 to $41.1 billion in 1990, and from 50 percent to 30 percent of total bilateral trade. By 1994, however, the global US deficit had risen again, to a new record total of $166.3 billion, though total US trade had so expanded since the mid-1980s that the deficit's proportion of total trade was now just 14.2 percent, far from the peak. For Japan, the deficit also reached a peak total—$65.7 billion—and also not a peak share of bilateral trade—38.1 percent.

The causes of the improvement between 1987 and 1991 were macroeconomic: a sharp decline in the dollar; a reversal of the growth

---

19. By definition, a nation's net capital outflow has to be equaled by its current account surplus. Or, in the case of the United States, the present current account deficit has to be equal to, and financed by, an inflow of capital.

20. As the president's Council of Economic Advisers put the matter in 1990, "removal of import barriers is likely to increase both Japanese imports and Japanese exports. The net effect on overall trade imbalances is unclear." *Economic Report of the President,* February 1990, 249.

21. George P. Shultz, "National Policies and Global Prosperity," address at the Woodrow Wilson School of Public and International Affairs, Princeton University (11 April 1985).

gap, with Japan in particular growing faster in the late 1980s; modest improvement on the US fiscal front;[22] and the US recession, which depressed import demand in 1990–91. Paul R. Krugman, frequently a challenger of the conventional wisdom on trade economics, concluded that, in this instance, mainstream theory had been vindicated:

> During the 1980s, and in particular as the US trade deficit continued to widen after 1985, it was widely argued that . . . strategic behavior by foreign firms in general and Japanese firms in particular meant that exchange rates no longer worked to reduce imbalances. Yet two years after the dollar began its decline, the United States experienced an export boom; this happened just about when and in the magnitude that the traditional models would have predicted. . . . the evidence seems overwhelming that exchange rate changes do indeed work.[23]

Robert Z. Lawrence reached similar conclusions, adding that "both export and import performance indicate that Japan has adjusted more than Europe and other trading partners of the United States."[24]

But after 1992 the same macroeconomic forces were working in the opposite direction—in particular a new growth gap between a recovering America and its sluggish industrial partners. The trade results gave new legitimacy to proposals that targeted that imbalance, even Gephardt's proposal to reduce it to zero.

The means for achieving this remain unclear. Moreover, unlike the goal of eliminating the overall US trade deficit, making exports equal imports in bilateral US-Japan trade makes absolutely no economic sense. The advantage of a multilateral system is that nations do not have to balance two-by-two: they can run surpluses with certain countries and deficits with others, taking full advantage of the gains from trade. Any effort to limit or eliminate the overall US-Japan deficit would be incredibly disruptive to consumers and marketers and industrial users of Japanese-made products in the United States. And assuming no change in the two nations' saving-investment balances, the bilateral deficit reduction would be offset by changes in the two nations' trade accounts with other nations, leaving the global US deficit (and the global Japanese surplus) unchanged.

---

22. Among the inadequate, partial steps which produced *some* fiscal constraint were the Gramm-Rudman-Hollings legislation of 1985, the tax reform law of 1986, which brought a one-time revenue rise in 1987, the executive-legislative agreement in the wake of the October 1987 stock market crash, and most important, the comprehensive budget agreement of October 1990.

23. *Has the Adjustment Process Worked?* POLICY ANALYSES IN INTERNATIONAL ECONOMICS 34 (Washington: Institute for International Economics, 1991), 46.

24. "U.S. Current Account Adjustment: An Appraisal," *Brookings Papers on Economic Activity*, 1990: 2, 372.

Getting Serious About Trade Imbalances

What then should be done about trade imbalances? The first need is for education, to spread understanding of their causes and why trade actions cannot cure them. The second, at the boundaries of this book's reach, concerns macroeconomic policy, or specifically what might be done to set such imbalances aright.

Education

Experience may be a hard school, but the 1980s brought many learners. By early 1983, for the first time in memory, a major US industry group, the Business Roundtable, was pointing to the dollar-yen rate as a primary source of trade ills. By 1985, precious few trading interests were still insensitive to the impact of exchange rates on their international competitiveness. And since this new awareness extended to most congressional trade activists, it bought time for US trade policymakers when, in the fall of 1985, the yen began a sharp rise. In fact, the trade legislation of 1988 contained a subtitle on "Exchange Rates and International Economic Policy Coordination."

But this connection, however crucial, is not all that needs learning and remembering. The larger lesson is that, in a world of floating exchange rates and large-scale capital flows, **trade imbalances are largely immune to treatment by trade policy measures.** They can be reached only by other means, mainly macroeconomic measures that influence total demand and affect the saving-investment balance within trading nations. Also, when circumstances are favorable, trade imbalances can be influenced by official intervention in foreign exchange markets.

Trade measures can affect the volume of trade. They can influence the composition of that trade, and the fortunes of individual companies and workers. But unless coupled with other measures, they will have little impact on the overall surplus or deficit run by a nation.

This negative lesson has its limits. It is, as earlier noted, counterintuitive. If Japan restricts market access *and* runs trade surpluses, it is an uphill argument to assert that the two are essentially unrelated. If the United States is running record trade deficits and its firms are facing trade barriers abroad and subsidized foreign competition at home, it is hard to resist arguments that the former are *caused* by the latter. And even those who are persuaded that trade deficits are macroeconomically driven may become unpersuaded if a significant trade imbalance remains after a major macroeconomic change like the 1985–87 decline of the dollar.

More important, it is not enough, in responding to industries under stress and to politicians feeling their heat, to argue that a particular remedy will *not* minister to their ills. For in policy, as in sports, it is hard to beat something with nothing. Politicians facing daily pressure need at some point to respond, to "do something." If constructive action is not available, they may be driven to destructive actions. This was true during the record trade imbalances of the mid-1980s; it was also true of the (proportionately) lesser imbalances during the recession environment of the 1992–94.

So one must ask further: if trade measures will not cure trade imbalances, what will? The short answer is the obvious one: changes in macroeconomic policy.

Macroeconomic Policy

Federal Reserve Chairman Alan Greenspan brought the bad news to the House Ways and Means Committee in December 1991. To members under pressure to do something about a recession that would not end, he argued against a "quick fix" tax cut that would further increase the federal budget deficit. The need was the opposite: to increase national saving. And the surest way to achieve that would be to reduce the size of the federal budget deficit. Only in this fashion could the United States begin to put the US economy on a sound, long-term basis.[25]

As with the budget deficit, so also with the trade deficit. A nation importing more than it exports is consuming more than it produces. This can only be financed by borrowing, or by drawing down assets. Either way, we purchase enjoyment in the present at cost to the future.[26]

Attacking the trade deficit ultimately requires attacking the saving-investment imbalance that lies at its roots. There are times when other measures will help temporarily—Treasury Secretary James A. Baker, for example, exploited a period of economic leeway to "manage" a substantial decline in the dollar after the Plaza Agreement of September 1985, without major fiscal adjustment and without the inflation many feared would result.[27] But ultimately it is necessary to eliminate overconsumption. Americans can do this either by increasing private saving or by

---

25. Greenspan testimony as reported in *Washington Post*, 19 December 1991, A1. The Fed chairman made this pill a bit easier to swallow by orchestrating, two days later, a major easing of monetary policy: a full-point drop in the discount rate.

26. A *Washington Post* editorial of 2 January 1992 reiterated the "basic but inconvenient reality" that "the American trade deficit is made in the U.S.A. It reflects policy decisions here to keep consumption and the standard of living higher than the country's productivity can support. That requires a flow of imports larger than the country's exports." Of course, trade deficits may serve long-term objectives if the borrowing finances investment leading to greater future productivity. But in the 1980s, the United States borrowed mainly to finance consumption.

27. See I. M. Destler and C. Randall Henning, *Dollar Politics*, esp. chaps. 3 and 4.

reducing government dissaving. We know little about how to do the first, at least at the household level. Thus, as Greenspan told the Ways and Means Committee, the United States needs to do the second, by cutting the federal budget deficit. The Fed could offset the depressive fiscal effects by easing up on interest rates. Together these moves could bring down the value of the dollar, promoting exports and replacing imports, so that improvement in the international balance compensates for total reduction in domestic demand.

The good time to do this, of course, is when the domestic economy is strong and unemployment is low. That way the pain of adjustment is reduced. President George Bush entered office at just such a time. He inherited six straight years of economic growth, and the unemployment rate in 1989 was the lowest since 1973. Bush was also greeted with advice to act at once, "to move preemptively early in his new term . . . rather than being forced to react to a crisis later,"[28] to "take bold action" in an expanding economy "to reduce the deficit."[29] And Congress had even provided political protection in the form of a bipartisan National Economic Commission to share the political pain.

Unfortunately, the president had already mortgaged *his* future with his endlessly repeated presidential campaign pledge: "Read my lips. No new taxes!" So he temporized for 15 months and did not declare himself ready to compromise on revenues until June 1990. Fractious budget negotiations took four additional months to reach a conclusion, and the significant (albeit insufficient) new taxes and spending constraints agreed to in October hit an economy sliding into recession.[30] When recovery proved elusive, Bush faced the worst of all political-economic worlds as he approached election day 1992: a weak economy and a budget deficit that had soared to a record $340 billion, and a challenge from the right drawing blood for his broken tax promise![31] There was enormous pressure from politicians in both parties to take short-term, stimulative actions that would shift money from saving to consumption and hence make the long-term problem worse—the very sort of actions Greenspan had warned against.

At last, the nation was paying the price for the consumption binge of the 1980s. Bush paid it personally, in his resounding electoral defeat. And Clinton paid a price also, when his moderate program to reduce

28. C. Fred Bergsten, *America in the World Economy: A Strategy for the 1990s* (Washington: Institute for International Economics, 1988), 6.

29. C. Michael Aho and Marc Levinson, *After Reagan: Confronting the Changed World Economy* (New York: Council on Foreign Relations Press, 1988), 25.

30. The October 1990 budget agreement increased taxes and constrained spending to some degree, lowering the projected annual deficit by roughly $100 billion a year.

31. This fiscal 1992 figure was ballooned by both the recession and the enormous budgetary cost of the collapse of many federally insured savings and loan institutions.

the deficit was denounced by Republicans as the greatest tax increase in history and played some part in the GOP's mid-term election triumph of 1994. The president then backed away from further serious budget action in 1995, while Republicans proposed both tax and spending cuts, with uncertain net result. Still the sad fact remained: durable resolution of the trade imbalance would require serious, painful budget action during the Clinton administration and beyond.

If the United States were to finally get out of the budget imbalance/trade imbalance mess, would there be any way to reduce the chances of recidivism in the future? Is there any way, within the governmental process, to institutionalize consideration of policy linkages, to increase the chances that US leaders will address the connection between trade and macroeconomic policies in a timely manner?

There is certainly a clear need for the president's senior advisers to focus on the global impact of such far-reaching measures as the Reagan tax-and-budget package of 1981. And a president needs mechanisms of political burden sharing when he contemplates remedial action. The problem is that one cannot legislate presidential advisory processes. In 1981 the Reagan administration did establish a senior committee that ought to have addressed these policy connections: the Cabinet Council on Economic Affairs. The fact that it did not do so reflected not lack of jurisdiction but lack of understanding and will; administration minds and priorities were elsewhere. Similarly, President Bush did not take advantage of the bipartisan National Economic Commission because of his ill-advised campaign commitment on taxes. One is left with a modest but useful recommendation: that any administration ought to place within its policy coordination staff a senior aide with presidential access and a broad international economic policy mandate.[32] The Clinton administration in fact did so through the creation of the National Economic Council, staffed by an assistant to the president for economic affairs.

Finally, could changes in congressional procedures encourage legislators to target the real causes of unbalanced trade? One reason legislators have stressed trade policy responses is that they have clear power to impose them, whereas the exchange rate, for example, is beyond legislative reach. The 1988 act provides a potentially useful vehicle for refocusing congressional attention: a requirement that the secretary of the Treasury deliver every six months, to the Senate and House banking committees, "a written report on international economic policy, including exchange rate policy," one which is to include "recommendations for

---

32. For considerations governing where this aide can best be placed, see I. M. Destler, *Making Foreign Economic Policy* (Washington: Brookings Institution, 1980), 217–28. For a comprehensive analysis based on the Ford administration experience, see Roger Porter, *Presidential Decisionmaking: The Economic Policy Board* (Cambridge: Cambridge University Press, 1980).

any changes necessary in United States economic policy to attain a more appropriate and sustainable balance in the current account."[33] But the report is also required to address "bilateral negotiations," particularly regarding countries that may "manipulate the rate of exchange." With congressional acquiescence, the Treasury has used this mandate to deal lightly with the problem of the US imbalance, spotlighting instead the exchange rate policies of Korea, Taiwan, and the People's Republic of China. This underscores how any such mechanism is dependent on the enforcement attention given it by members of Congress. A stronger vehicle might be what this author has suggested elsewhere: creation, in each house of Congress, of a Select Oversight Committee on the Dollar and the National Economy.[34] The aim is to put constructive pressure on an administration and to channel congressional energy away from the wrong answers and toward the right ones.

Using corrective macroeconomic policy measures, as well as reforms in structure and process like those suggested here, government can attack those large imbalances that so burden trade policymakers. For these economywide "trade" problems have, by their nature, no trade policy solutions. If macroeconomic policy changes help bring an end to the saving-investment imbalance, and if national policies and international cooperation can reduce future exchange rate fluctuations, American firms and workers can function in a far more stable, predictable economic environment. If adjustment within the US economy were then smooth, so that workers and capital could flow efficiently into enterprises with international comparative advantage, and if US productivity growth were robust—bringing rising average income to American workers—then trade policymakers could rest truly easy.

Unfortunately, major adjustment is seldom smooth. And productivity growth has not been strong: the average real wages of the American worker have not risen over the past two decades. Hence macroeconomic policy correction needs to be accompanied by *microeconomic* measures that buttress the long-term competitiveness of firms and workers operating within US borders.

Microeconomic Policy: Promoting Adjustment and Productivity Growth

Over the past quarter-century, US producers have lost global supremacy in a succession of sectors: steel, consumer electronics, automobiles, and

---

33. Omnibus Trade and Competitiveness Act of 1988, Public Law 100-418, Title III, Sec. 3005.

34. Destler and Henning, *Dollar Politics*, 155–58.

high-technology products such as semiconductors. These successive declines evoked a broader pessimism: could the US economy have much of a future if industry after industry was being bested in its home market by foreign competitors, particularly Japanese? Some argued that the United States was deindustrializing, that international trade was relentlessly transforming the nation into a postindustrial, service economy. This was demonstrably not true in the late 1970s, when the issue was first raised—manufacturing employment reached an all-time high of 21.1 million in the summer of 1979. But in the decade that followed, the trade deficit and broader structural transformation took a significant toll. At the end of 1994, after three years of steady economic recovery, US factory jobs were 2.9 million fewer.

As discussed in chapter 7, these developments raised the question of industrial policy: whether the United States should invest public resources to influence the sectoral composition of the US economy, to buttress certain industries viewed as important for the national future. Other nations had clearly done so, albeit with mixed effectiveness. So, willy-nilly, had the United States. Agriculture had long benefited from research and educational support and from programs to aid producers of specific commodities. Aircraft, computer, and semiconductor firms had gained enormously from Pentagon research and development funding. The US textile and apparel industries were larger because of quota protection. But all this was ad hoc. Unlike countries such as Japan and France, the United States had never targeted particular industries or sectors for purposes of economic development. But there were many who saw such action by foreign governments as a threat to the United States. They felt that the United States should counter other nations' industrial policies or respond in kind to their governmental efforts to create future comparative advantage, or both.

Much of the campaign focused on trade action: making industrial targeting an unfair trade practice under US countervailing duty law, as proposed by Representative Sam M. Gibbons (D-FL), or threatening import restrictions for products such as telecommunications from nations whose markets denied US firms reciprocal access. Or, for basic industries, the policy advocated was frequently one of protection, because imports were subsidized and this was unfair, or because the industry needed time to restructure itself so that it could face foreign competition more effectively in the future, or both.

From the vantage point of a particular industry, such an approach has substantial attractions. An industry loses when foreign competitors are subsidized, as in certain cases they have been; it gains, at least in the short run, from any form of benefit bestowed by its government, whether it be a direct subsidy, import protection, or favorable treatment in the tax code. There will also be, from time to time, strong welfare arguments for providing import relief and related assistance to individuals and communities absorbing acute trade pain. If, for certain large industries, the burden of trade impact is regionally concentrated in the Northeast-Midwest rust belt; if plant closings have a multiplier effect by drying up businesses that depend on their spending and that of their employees; and if the geographic mobility of many residents of these communities is limited, this may argue for redevelopment programs with a geographic focus.

But such programs need to be limited to cases of very severe need. For their net impact will almost always be to weaken, not strengthen, the American economy taken as a whole.

From an economywide perspective, any help to a particular industry represents resources diverted from other uses, however the subsidy may be provided. If the aim is to arrest or slow an industry's decline, it is, by definition, a grant to the competitively inefficient, to a current economic loser. Even at the high-tech, high-growth end of the industrial spectrum, public support makes economic policy sense only if it promises to spur future productivity or market gains commensurate with public investment. And if it does, one must then ask why government is better able than private capitalists to anticipate these gains and finance them.

There will be instances, of course, in which a particular industry produces spillover benefits, "external economies" in economists' lingo, meaning that its success produces gains for the broader economy and society beyond those captured by the firms' owners. Such public gains can justify public investments. But these gains must be weighed against negative spillovers. If government policies result in US steel (or semiconductor) prices being substantially above international norms, for example, these will create international competitive disadvantages for firms that use these products as inputs, such as makers of autos (or computers). Moreover, while public help can increase the capacity of an industry to compete internationally, it can reduce the incentive to make the hard, cost-cutting decisions that will ultimately prove necessary.

To the limits of industry-specific interventions in terms of overall economic efficiency must be added problems of political efficacy. Will the US system of government allow officials to allocate resources to those select cases in which the spillover gains for the overall economy are strongest? It may when these gains are coincident with other policy purposes, as in the case of certain defense research, for example. But the normal political process tends to produce the opposite result. It is the losers (Chrysler Corporation, the steel industry) that come to Washington for help, and government frequently responds to them—because of their evident hardship, as well as their political power. In Japan, too, it is agriculture that wins the most blatant government favor, to the detriment of the economy as a whole. In the United States, which lacks a policy tradition of trying to generate visions of future industrial structure and bring these visions into being, the losers are likely to do even better.

For all these reasons, even strong proponents of an industrial-policy focus tend to see sector-specific policy actions as the last resort. As Laura Tyson and John Zysman put it, "When we confront either a sector problem or a shift in international trade that is of broad national concern, there should be a clear order of policy preferences: aggregate policies first; policies to improve the workings of markets second; and finally—and only as a last resort—industry-specific policies."[35] And in undertaking such interventions, to repeat the words of Robert B. Reich, the motivation should be pro-adjustment, supportive of the "transformation of all nations' industrial bases toward higher-value production."[36]

But there remains a broader concern about American industrial competitiveness. In the world of international trade, a nation cannot, by definition, be competitive in all industries. The whole purpose of trade is to benefit from the international division of labor, to buy from abroad what is less expensive there, and to produce what we produce most efficiently here. But the position of the US economy overall, and the living standards of American citizens, are ultimately functions of the productivity of US economic enterprises. Unless their output per worker continues to increase, there is no way, in the long run, for the real incomes of Americans to grow. And there is no way to avoid falling behind, in relative terms, if productivity in other nations, broadly defined, is increasing faster.

Here there is reason for long-term worry. Paralleling the relative decline of specific US industries has been a sharp longer-term drop in the rate of growth of output per hour per worker: from 1958 through 1973 it rose by 51 percent; in the ensuing 15-year period, 1973 through 1988, it grew by only 16 percent. Since 1988, US productivity performance has been slightly better.[37] Still, average weekly earnings in private industry actually declined in the 1970s and 1980s, remaining flat since then.[38] The postwar American escalator that brought steady rises in average living standards has ceased to function.[39] Other nations have experienced similar declines—the "productivity slowdown" has been present in all ad-

---

35. "Conclusions: What to Do Now?" in John Zysman and Laura Tyson, eds., *American Industry in International Competition: Government Policies and Corporate Strategies* (Ithaca, NY: Cornell University Press, 1983), 423.

36. Robert B. Reich, "Beyond Free Trade," *Foreign Affairs* 61, no. 4 (Spring 1983): 790.

37. Changes in "output per hour for all persons," in 1982 dollars, computed from *Economic Report of the President*, February 1995, table B-47.

38. *Economic Report of the President*, February 1995, table B-45.

39. Frank Levy, *Dollars and Dreams: The Changing American Income Distribution* (New York: Russell Sage Foundation and W. W. Norton, 1988).

vanced industrial nations. Nonetheless, "by the 1980s foreign productivity levels had converged close to those in the United States."[40] In Japan, productivity growth continues to be significantly greater. And according to a committee of the National Academy of Sciences, experts in both countries "share the conclusion that Japan's high technology capabilities are now on par with or ahead of the United States in many areas."[41] In future years, unless US relative productivity performance improves, the United States could return to, and maintain, a reasonable export-import balance, but only at the cost of a gradual, continuing devaluation of the dollar, which would mean lower (relative) living standards for the American people.

The United States therefore needs policies to speed adjustment by industry and labor and to encourage movement of resources from less-productive to more-productive enterprises and regions. This should be joined with efforts to enhance the productive base for the economy as a whole: education and training for the 21st century work force and public investment in the United States' eroding economic infrastructure. There is also a strong need for policies, in Charles Schultze's words, "designed to make the economy in general more flexible, more dynamic, more productive, and more capable of adjustment to technological change."[42] These policies can include tax code changes that favor productivity-enhancing forms of investment and that favor the domestic saving that must ultimately finance such investment. And since private firms typically underinvest in research and development, because it is difficult for them to capture the full social return on such investment, the United States needs government policies that support the development and application of new technology.[43]

Among liberal trade advocates, it is common to view industrial policy as a stalking horse for protection. And among proponents of laissez-faire in general, it is seen as counterproductive meddling in domestic markets. It can be either, or both. A label like "industrial policy" can lend respectability to trade-restrictive proposals for politicians who view "protectionism" as something bad. Even if no trade protection is initially involved or intended, it can create a governmental stake in a particular

40. Robert Z. Lawrence, "Innovation and Trade: Meeting the Foreign Challenge," in Henry J. Aaron, ed., *Setting National Priorities: Policy for the Nineties* (Washington: Brookings Institution, 1990), 147.

41. Committee on Japan, National Research Council, *Science, Technology, and the Future of the U.S.-Japan Relationship* (Washington: National Academy Press, March 1990), 7.

42. Charles L. Schultze, "Industrial Policy: A Solution in Search of a Problem," *California Management Review* 24, no. 4 (Summer 1983): 6.

43. See Martin Neil Baily and Alok K. Chakrabarti, *Innovation and the Productivity Crisis* (Washington: Brookings Institution, 1988), chap. 6; and Lawrence, "Innovation and Trade."

industry's prosperity that may lead to such protection in the future. And industrial policy involves, by definition, government microeconomic intervention that may well prove unwise from an economywide perspective.

But these problems notwithstanding, a focus on competitiveness and industrial productivity can be enormously constructive. It can offer an alternative to protection, or Japan bashing. It can turn American attention away from nefarious-seeming foreigners, toward self-help at home. It can focus US energies on creating an appropriate, stimulative policy environment for productive enterprises. It can encourage a creeping recognition that many of the problems of American producers are, in important part, "made in USA."[44]

The Role of Trade Policy

Changes in macroeconomic policy can help redress trade imbalances and ease the pressure they generate for import restrictions. Steps to improve overall industrial competitiveness can help make adjustment to economic dislocations more humane and efficient and hopefully renew the growth in American wage levels, reducing the temptation to blame foreign devils for domestic ills.

By contrast, *trade* policy—actions directly affecting imports and exports—is not an efficient instrument for addressing these broad, economywide problems. Import barriers can, of course, affect the composition of trade, and thus, over time, the sectoral composition of the domestic economy. But the gains such barriers provide to some industries will be at the expense of other industries, and the economy as a whole will suffer from favoring enterprises that are less competitive internationally.

We are left, then, with two primary trade policy goals: one positive and one negative. The positive aim is to increase the *volume* of trade,[45] through opening markets abroad and at home, and thus to increase the gains from trade to the American economy as a whole.[46] The negative aim is damage limitation—minimizing the harm to the overall US econ-

---

44. For a comprehensive analysis, see *Building A Competitive America, First Annual Report of the Competitiveness Policy Council* (Washington: Government Printing Office, March 4, 1992).

45. Of course, an expansion of exports through subsidization is just as trade-distorting as a restriction of imports. Thus, countervailing duties to offset foreign subsidies have an economic, as well as a political, rationale.

46. US gains will be particularly strong if the newly liberalized foreign markets are for products where American producers have a strong comparative advantage. Hence there is strong economic *and* political interest in responding to market-opening pressures from export interests.

omy, and the international trading system, from successful attempts by special interests to win import protection.

The latter remains the core problem of American trade politics. Even after current trade storms pass, even after the value of American exports comes to equal the value of its imports, substantial demands for trade restrictions will remain. Between 1970 and 1990, trade doubled as a share of US gross national product. Hence more industries are exposed internationally, and more are hurt by import competition. Of course, there are also more that gain from trade—and their interests offer a check against across-the-board protectionism. Still, relief from imports retains a political legitimacy that government protection from domestic rivals does not have. For products like steel, the case for protection is strengthened by the actions of some foreign governments to subsidize and protect their own domestic producers.

In form, this is basically the Schattschneider problem that opened this book: the problem of political imbalance. The US Congress, recognizing its vulnerability to one-sided pressure for import restrictions, cooperated with successive administrations in developing means of coping: a range of devices that facilitate voluntary legislative restraint on product-specific trade policy. America's political leaders developed a system to divert and channel pressures and to deal separately with the most trade-afflicted among the major US industries. Throughout the postwar period, this system has generally avoided major public confrontations on trade that pit industry against industry or political party against political party. It has tilted policy outcomes toward open trade by tilting process toward closed politics.

Can the System Be Salvaged?

Can such an approach still work for the United States in the 1990s? At least four trends, spelled out in the body of this book, make the going harder:

- trade has become more important economically;

- Congress is now more open procedurally;

- the trade-remedy procedures have proved more exploitable politically;

- politicians have brought the issue back into partisan national electoral politics.

Taken together, these four trends have made trade policy a much more public matter. Rhetoric has escalated. Legislative activity has increased, whether it is measured in the number of bills introduced or in the number given committee or floor consideration. There are more efforts to draw trade policy lines for partisan advantage.

Such developments might lead to a judgment that the old system has run its course, that it is futile to keep trying to patch it up, that the United States should instead look to create an entirely different set of trade policy institutions. One sophisticated recent analysis asked whether the American trade policymaking system had not become "an obsolete bargain."[47] Representative Richard A. Gephardt, in introducing the bill discussed earlier, declared an interest in "reclaiming some of the power which has been delegated to the president and his administration."[48]

Yet even the Congresses of the 1980s, faced with a trade imbalance beyond previous imagination, proved reluctant to seize product-specific trade responsibility. In fact, most congressional trade leaders have sought not weaker but stronger executive branch leadership. Senator John C. Danforth (R-MO) suggested openly in his spring 1985 Japan offensive that his prime target was the White House: he wanted the administration to take the trade problem seriously. When Senate Finance Committee Chairman Lloyd Bentsen took the Senate floor seven years later to declare that a draft Uruguay Round text "just won't pass muster" in the Congress, his aim was not to bury the agreement but to salvage it.[49] Between those two occasions Congress passed three textile quota bills, but each with the comfort of knowing that the president was committed to vetoing them, and with House override votes that somehow fell eight—and eleven, and ten—votes short of the two-thirds required.

This suggests a strong continuing market on Capitol Hill for political insulation, a will to continue a trade policymaking relationship in which legislators can make noise, pressure the administration, claim credit for specific actions it takes, but avoid final responsibility themselves. It suggests that "protection for Congress" lives on.

If a system that insulates members continues to reflect political reality on Capitol Hill, it also represents political necessity for those who favor open trade policies. As illustrated by House votes for domestic-content legislation in 1982 and 1983 and the substantial margins in both chambers for the textile bills of 1985 through 1990, legislators remain vulnerable to unbalanced pressure for import restrictions. In neither autos nor textiles was the number of representatives who wanted the legislation to become law anywhere near equal to the number who voted "aye" at roll call time.

---

47. David B. Yoffee, "American Trade Policy: An Obsolete Bargain?" in John E. Chubb and Paul E. Peterson, eds., *Can the Government Govern?* (Washington: Brookings Institution, 1989), esp. 118ff.

48. Statement of 4 November 1991.

49. Statement of 2 February 1992.

Many of them, in fact, would rather not have voted at all. But the erosion of internal congressional constraints makes it harder today for leaders to protect members by stopping such proposals before they reach the floor.

All of this places even more burdens on the "executive broker," in both meanings of that phrase: the central function that needs buttressing and the downtown institution that must perform it. Both damage limitation at home and trade expansion abroad require the balancing of economic interests and policy concerns. When an industry seeks protection from imports, government needs to seek out other interests that would be affected by such protection—industrial users of products affected, retailers, exporters—and encourage them to enter the political arena. And ever since the "bargaining tariff" of the 1930s, one of the best ways to resist closing markets at home has been to press for opening markets overseas.

Not by coincidence, successive congressional trade leaders have created, strengthened, and protected the executive branch brokering institution—the Office of the US Trade Representative. They placed it where they hoped its chief would have the ear of the president and the leeway to balance domestic and foreign concerns, micro and macro issues, legislative and executive branches. And if presidents have seldom given trade policy the priority that legislators sought, they have regularly chosen strong USTRs: adroit senior politicians with strong ties on Capitol Hill like Robert S. Strauss and William E. Brock and seasoned professionals like Carla A. Hills and Mickey Kantor. And their successes have come from immersion in the politics of trade.

All learned quickly the bedrock need to establish credibility as defender of US interests; only then will broad business and congressional support for a liberal trade regime and market-expanding policies be maintained. This requires the aggressive and visible practice of "export politics," pressing particular foreign-market issues in which there are good prospects for success and issues in which the United States can maintain a tough stance—a stance that threatens trade sanctions if meaningful foreign concessions are not forthcoming.

Finally, trade policy needs to be managed, insofar as is possible, in a bipartisan manner—as STRs and USTRs generally have done. A bipartisan approach is necessary because the immediate electoral payoffs will often seem to be on the trade-restrictive side, and the alternative is a bidding war in which Democrats and Republicans compete for special-interest support at the expense of overall national welfare. A bipartisan approach remains possible because protectionism is still a risky party platform, costly in respect and in reputation—as John Connally learned in the late 1970s in his quest for the Republican presidential nomination, and as Democrats have discovered more than once during the 1980s. And a bipartisan approach can bring great trade victories, as shown in congressional action on the NAFTA and GATT accords.

Policy Tools: International Negotiations

The old trade policymaking system leaned heavily on international negotiations to achieve global reductions in trade barriers. Such negotiations remain the most obvious political means of expanding the volume of trade. They also perform three valuable functions in US trade politics. They offer a basis for bringing export interests actively into the political process, offsetting the ever-present pressure from producers who would restrict imports. They provide a rationale for resisting that protectionist pressure. And they reinforce the position of the central trade broker who has the lead in conducting them.

Thus, USTR William Brock was advancing both national and institutional interests when, during President Reagan's first term, he sought to initiate a new global trade negotiation. His successor, Clayton Yeutter, brought this goal to fruition in September 1986 by winning agreement at Punta del Este to launch the "Uruguay Round" of multilateral trade talks. *His* successor, Carla Hills, brought these complex, multination, multi-issue talks near completion. *Her* successor, Mickey Kantor, closed the deal. The agreement is expected to produce new export opportunities for American agriculture, and for manufacturing and service industries. It signals that the end of the Cold War does not mean the end of trade cooperation.

Over this same period, the United States also negotiated trade liberalization regionally: a free trade agreement with Canada and Mexico, and target dates for barrier elimination for both the hemisphere and the Asia-Pacific community. These talks also energized US producers seeking trade expansion and helped deflect protectionist pressures. And the Clinton administration avoided the dangers of a world of regional trade blocs through parallel agreements in APEC and the Americas. Trade diplomacy in both arenas brings economic and political gains, helping build collaborative structures for the post–Cold War world. But the fundamental US interest is in the global system. The United States is a global trader, two-thirds of whose exports go *outside* the Western Hemisphere. US trade with Korea, for example, is more than double that with any American nation outside NAFTA. The European Union and Japan, moreover, are the economic power centers with which the United States will define the future world economic order.

US trade policy priority should therefore continue to go to *global* trade liberalization. To this end, high priority should be given to *using* the WTO and its dispute-settlement procedures to open foreign markets. The United States should pursue unresolved trade issues on a multilateral, MFN basis to the extent feasible. And where the United States chooses to pursue regional negotiations, it should balance initiatives within the Americas with those elsewhere, particularly East Asia. As a general principle, the United States should not offer free trade arrangements to other Western Hemisphere nations beyond the present NAFTA unless the United States is simultaneously moving toward free trade with nations outside the hemisphere.

Flexibility on Fast-Track

Success on NAFTA and the Uruguay Round depended on the fast-track procedures, by which Congress committed itself to an expeditious up-or-down vote on the implementing legislation as submitted by the president. But both exposed fast-track to broad congressional and public scrutiny for the first time since its invention in 1974. On previous occasions, the key action on the procedures was taken in committee. The trade debates of the 1990s brought chamberwide attention to fast-track, with critics highlighting the limitations it places on congressional power. This was one important reason Clinton failed to win extension of fast-track during the debate over the implementing legislation for the Uruguay Round in 1994 (see chapter 9).

The resulting lack of such authority poses a serious threat to trade negotiations, since it remains unrealistic to expect others to reach complex trade agreements with the United States if the Congress has the power to amend them, or to pick and choose among their provisions. So supporters of multilateral trade negotiations need to explore compromises that respond to critics' concerns while preserving the core principle. Some of these compromises need to be procedural: trimming back the permissible substance of a fast-track bill and giving explicit statutory recognition to the congressional role in its drafting. Others involve the substance of future negotiations, with liberals seeking explicit authorization of trade-related labor and environmental agreements and conservatives seeking to exclude these subject matters entirely. Specific suggestions are included earlier in this chapter.

The point of these suggestions is to preserve the essence of the fast-track process. What is crucial is that the Democratic administration and the Republican Congress reach agreement on a practical extension formula, just as a Republican administration and a Democratic Congress initiated the process 21 years ago. And the administration should avoid the temptation to do without it—to complete a free trade negotiation with Chile, for example, and bring it up for approval under normal legislative procedures. It is doubtful this would work. And even if it did, it would set a terrible precedent for future multilateral agreements.

Revising the Trade-Remedy Laws

NAFTA and the Uruguay Round were dramatic breakthroughs, but they left many issues unresolved. It will take time, however, to get major new talks under way. The 1994 impasse over fast-track is only one of the reasons.

In years to come, therefore, major international negotiations may play a diminished role in countering US protectionism. Advocates of open markets will need to rely less on such international negotiations and more on specific, antiprotectionist interests that gain from exports and imports. Such trade-dependent interests—including retailers and industrial users of imported inputs—have been growing more active in US trade politics. Enmeshed as they are in an interdependent global economy, they can and should bear more of the political burden for supporting liberal trade policies than they did during the relatively "closed" US economic past.

US trade law is sometimes written as if the only particularized interests of concern are US-owned, US-based producers of the specific products whose trade is at issue. But the real world has long since departed from this model. A firm's capacity to export may rest upon its capacity to import—as Caterpillar has argued in resisting steel import restraint. And in certain product areas like TV production, foreign-owned companies may be more likely than their domestic counterparts to have their products "made in USA."[50]

One area of policy particularly embedded in obsolete assumptions is US trade-remedy laws. As illustrated by the case of flat-panel display panels for computers, discussed in chapter 6, US dumping laws ask only whether products priced below an arbitrarily set "fair value" hurt competing US producers (who do not have to follow the same pricing rules). They do not ask whether imposition of a duty will damage US firms that use the imported products as inputs—perhaps forcing them, as in this case, to move entire operations overseas.

For most of the postwar period, it was very difficult for firms to get relief under US trade-remedy laws. Now, in dumping cases, it is too easy. Of the 539 antidumping cases carried to completion since 1980, only 27—or 5 percent—failed because dumping was found not to have occurred.[51] One apparent cause is "practices and procedures which tend systematically to favor higher rather than lower dumping . . . 'margins,' "[52]

---

50. In 1988, foreign-owned firms employed over 15,000 Americans engaged in TV manufacturing in the United States, compared with 2,500 for Zenith, the sole US producer. See Robert B. Reich, "Who Is Us?" *Harvard Business Review* (January-February 1990): 61. Reich's broader analysis on this issue is *The Work of Nations: Preparing Ourselves for 21st Century Capitalism* (New York: Alfred A. Knopf, 1991).

51. Forty-three percent were concluded with a finding of no injury, and an additional 134 cases were withdrawn before final action was taken—in most cases because of voluntary export restraint arrangements.

52. Richard Boltuck and Robert E. Litan, eds., *Down in the Dumps: Administration of the Unfair Trade Laws* (Washington: Brookings Institution, 1991), 13.

procedures that are encouraged—though not always required—by US antidumping law. The result is unjustified or inflated penalty duties, which turn the spotlight on alleged foreign unfairness, poisoning the international dialogue by turning international commercial contests into battles of good versus evil. The United States also provokes foreign emulation, as the European Union and other trading partners impose mirror-image penalties on it. Finally, easy access to antidumping relief undercuts what is supposed to be the primary channel for import relief and adjustment, the "escape clause" (Section 201). For if dumping findings are quasi-automatic, why should a company seek action under a statute with a more demanding injury standard, a time limit for any protection, and a presidential right to deny relief even if statutory criteria are met?

It is difficult to muster domestic support to restore balance to the trade-remedy laws, since politicians are understandably wary of being labeled as advocates of "unfair trade."[53] The best approach is through international negotiations over competition policy, which would ideally bring the law on pricing practices by foreign producers closer to that governing practice by domestic producers—barring predatory pricing, but allowing greater flexibility in pricing to specific markets. Moreover, trade officials could use international negotiations as a counterweight to the narrow, intense interests that have skewed antidumping laws in the protectionist direction. Unfortunately, Mickey Kantor did the opposite in the Uruguay Round. He leaned against the forces of reform in order to build industry confidence in administration "toughness" and to broaden support for the implementing legislation (see chapter 9). So while the round did bring some useful changes, the net impact on US practice is likely to prove small.

There remains, therefore, a need for comprehensive reform of the trade remedy laws. The governing statutes should be amended: to lower the injury threshold for the escape clause, while tying relief to a specific, enforceable adjustment commitment from the petitioner; to raise the threshold for proving dumping, returning at minimum to the original standard of comparing prices here to those in the exporter's home market; and to create, in dumping or countervailing duty cases where dumping or subsidy and injury are found, a follow-on procedure whereby users and other affected interests could seek a reduction in the level of penalty duty assessed by demonstrating that its full imposition would cause *them* serious injury. In the increasingly trade-dependent US economy, it is high time to recognize that there are American economic interests on both sides of these cases. Resolving them requires balancing such interests, not specifying—in ever-tighter form—the "rights" of one side.

---

53. In our study of antiprotection lobbying, John S. Odell and I found that activity in opposition to trade restrictions was "significantly lighter or absent" in cases "where charges of unfairness were . . . prominent." See Destler and Odell, *Anti-Protection*, 73.

Keeping Section 301

On "unfair trade," US law and administrative processes have become skewed in favor of petitioners, moved by the ideological triumph of those who champion these remedies. For use of Section 301 to attack foreign market barriers, however, there is greater justification for the course that Congress and successive administrations have taken. Substantively, there remain many arbitrary foreign practices that close potentially lucrative export markets; institutionally, the GATT process has not proved a strong means of addressing them, though the strengthened WTO dispute-settlement procedures offer hope for the future. Moreover, for the typical member of Congress the political alternative to toughness on exports is not likely to be unabashed laissez-faire liberalism, but greater protectionism on imports.

There is thus a continuing need for export assertiveness, even (to use the critics' label) "aggressive unilateralism."[54] Producers sometimes need such assertiveness to crack foreign markets; Congress needs it to press for executive activism; the USTR needs it to retain the initiative.

The statutory vehicle for unilateral initiative is Section 301 of the Trade Act of 1974, as amended. Critics have protested that this provision has no specific GATT sanction and that retaliation under its authority therefore violates US GATT obligations (unless it is pursuant to a specific GATT finding that foreign trade restrictions constitute "nullification and impairment" of the offending nation's previous trade concessions). The authority granted to the president under Section 301 is quite sweeping: an administration predisposed toward trade restrictions or trade sanctions could do much damage with it. So the best route to reform here, as with excesses in antidumping law, would be international agreement on criteria for Section 301–type cases, and resolution of such cases—as far as possible—within a strengthened WTO dispute-settlement mechanism. This would have the added advantage of subjecting "unreasonable and unjustifiable" US practices to reciprocal attack from abroad.

Constraining American unilateralism was an important Uruguay Round goal for US trading partners, and the agreement did achieve this to some degree: by strengthening the WTO's capacity for dispute settlement and broadening the range of agreements to which it can apply. Since US law already provided that 301 cases should be pursued through such channels where applicable, this has the effect of bringing more

---

54. Jagdish Bhagwati and Hugh Patrick, eds., *Aggressive Unilateralism: America's 301 Trade Policy and the World Trading System* (Ann Arbor: University of Michigan Press, 1990). See especially the extended reflection by Robert Hudec, subtitled "Beyond Good and Evil," concerning whether Section 301 represents justifiable "civil disobedience" for achieving change in a sluggish, often unresponsive international system.

such cases within the multilateral system. It also provides international legal sanction for US retaliation, in cases where the system finds that 301 claims are justified. The result has been to improve a mechanism that has been, on balance, a force for trade liberalization.[55] So Section 301 should be retained: despite the heat that it generates, it is not an excessive burden for the international trading system to bear. "Special 301" on intellectual property protection should be retained as well.

Super 301 is another matter. There seems little doubt that the direct impact of the original, 1989–90 version was constructive: Korea and Taiwan made substantial concessions to avoid the "priority foreign country" designation, and agreements were reached with Japan in 1990 covering the supercomputer, satellite, and wood-product markets targeted under Super 301 in 1989. And Super 301 was indirectly responsible for the useful Structural Impediments Initiative, or SII talks, between the United States and Japan. Still, as in child rearing and social relations, it is better in trade policy and interstate relations to attack the practice rather than denounce the culprit ("you did a bad thing," not "you are a bad boy"). In this sense, President Clinton's "Super 301" executive order of March 1994 targeting foreign country *practices* was an improvement. But this welcome change made it indistinguishable from regular 301, except that the administration was giving itself a new set of deadlines! The Clinton administration's not-so-Super 301 was included in the Uruguay Round implementing legislation, continuing through 1995. No substantive purpose is served by extending it further, but if further extension proves politically useful, it will do little harm.

Using Section 301: Strategic Trade Policy or Sectoral Reciprocity?

The authority to initiate cases raises the question of how they should be selected. The United States should certainly *not* follow Representative Gephardt's proposal to base the decision on a mechanical formula highlighting bilateral trade deficits or imbalances within specific sectors. It makes no economic sense to balance trade bilaterally; moreover, such a formula would typically focus US energies on product areas in which it had comparative *disadvantage*! The USTR should instead give priority to product areas where US producers are clearly world-class competitors and where foreign impediments are preventing this advantage from being realized. The rapidly emerging biotechnology industry is one very strong candidate. In such cases, successful negotiations are most likely to result in significantly increased markets for efficient American firms, and

---

55. Bayard and Elliott, *Reciprocity and Retaliation*.

hence gains for the US (and global) economies. It is also likely to build support for liberal trade policies.[56]

Should US policy go further? Should the United States embark on a "strategic trade policy" that systematically selects key industries and seeks to buttress their position in international markets? In general, policies that subsidize or protect particular firms or sectors impose a net cost to the nation—the industrial problem treated earlier. But as discussed in chapter 7, recent economic research has suggested there may be exceptional cases—involving oligopolistic markets, short product cycles, and increasing economies of scale—where "strategic" government intervention can bring durable trade advantages that exceed and outlast the governmental help provided. Further research has suggested, however, just how difficult it would be for officials to identify such industries in a timely manner and choose the appropriate means of government action. There is, however, a stronger case for defensive policies aimed at thwarting other nations' efforts to confer international market advantage on their favored industries, at heading off foreign industrial targeting before it has an impact on US industries.[57]

Once the United States has decided which export cases to press, two further questions repeatedly arise. The first concerns what is labeled "specific" or "sectoral" reciprocity: whether the openness of the US market for a product should be conditioned on foreign market access for the same product. The second is whether negotiators should go beyond seeking removal of import barriers and insist on fulfillment of quantitative targets for import expansion—as in the US-Japan semiconductor agreement.

Carried to its logical extreme, "sectoral reciprocity" makes little trade sense. If negotiators must limit themselves to a series of narrow bargains within sectors—balancing US import restrictions on wine against those of the European Union, for example—the chance for broad, mutually beneficial, cross-industry trade-offs disappears, and with it the prospect for major trade liberalization.

There is, however, a strong circumstantial case for selective application of the "sectoral reciprocity" principle in negotiations with Japan. If one believes, for example, that industries such as semiconductors and telecommunications are important to future US industrial strength, and that the ability to sell in one of the two biggest markets in the world is an important contributor to the strength of these industries, then it follows

---

56. Seeking to balance auto sector trade with Japan, as the Gephardt proposal would have us do, would predictably—and perhaps intentionally—undermine support for liberal trade. Balance will not be achieved, and this "failure" will legitimize protection of the domestic market.

57. Laura D'Andrea Tyson elaborates on these issues from the perspective of a "cautious activist" in *Who's Bashing Whom? Trade Conflict in High-Technology Industries* (Washington: Institute for International Economics, 1992).

that these products should have priority in bilateral trade talks. In the quest for leverage over the Japanese government on these issues, the question arises of how to affect the interests of Fujitsu or Nippon Electric or Hitachi, integrated electronics firms that will have an important influence on Japanese policy. Generally speaking, they will have no interest in opening home markets to competitive imports unless failure to do so is likely to cost them sales in the lucrative American market. Thus, a capacity to threaten market closure here can be important in achieving market openness across the Pacific. In 1980 the United States won its initial concessions from Japan on telecommunications by threatening to deny Japanese firms the right to bid on US government contracts under the just-completed Tokyo Round government procurement code.[58]

This principle of sectoral reciprocity was at the core of the US-Japan semiconductor agreement reached in 1986 and renewed in 1991. Senator Danforth also succeeded in attaching to the 1988 act a set of provisions applying the principle to telecommunications trade. Such "reciprocity" has won the support of both practitioners and scholars who see it as a practical, politically manageable means of handling thorny trade issues with Japan.[59]

The risk of sectoral reciprocity, as William R. Cline has pointed out, is that if the United States actually comes to deliver on such threats, the likely outcome is greater protection and lower welfare in both countries.[60] Or it may lead to a market-sharing, cartel-type arrangement, as the US-Japan semiconductor arrangement has become in some respects, strengthening the very government-business collusion the United States normally seeks to eliminate. This risk is increased if an agreement includes explicit import-expansion commitments or targets, as recommended by advocates of "results-oriented trade policy," since these force collaboration among firms—and with government—to allocate the import "burden."[61] They can thus be attacked as a new form of "managed trade,"

---

58. Timothy J. Curran, "Politics and High Technology: The NTT Case," in I. M. Destler and Hideo Sato, eds., *Coping with U.S.-Japanese Economic Conflicts* (Lexington, MA: Lexington Books, 1982), 231–39.

59. Clyde V. Prestowitz Jr., *Trading Places: How We Allowed Japan to Take the Lead* (New York; Basic Books, 1988), esp. chap. 11; Stephen D. Krasner, *Asymmetries in US-Japanese Trade Relations: The Case for Specific Reciprocity*, Policy Papers in International Studies 32 (Berkeley: University of California, Institute of International Studies, 1987).

60. William R. Cline, *Reciprocity: A New Approach to World Trade Policy*, POLICY ANALYSES IN INTERNATIONAL ECONOMICS 2 (Washington: Institute for International Economics, 1982).

61. Advisory Committee on Trade Policy and Negotiations, *Analysis of the U.S.-Japan Trade Problem*, transmitted to USTR Carla A. Hills, February 1989. Jagdish Bhagwati has labeled such agreements "voluntary import expansions," or VIEs. See Bhagwati, *Protectionism* (Cambridge, MA: MIT Press, 1988), 82–84. Bergsten and Noland, in *Reconcilable Differences?*, advocate use of VIEs in exceptional cases.

and the Japanese did precisely this in response to Clinton administration proposals in 1993. Thus the presumption should normally be against the use of such targets. There are times, however, when they become the only practical way of addressing a situation where private-sector import resistance is the core problem in the target country, and they are generally preferable to the alternative of limiting sales to the US market. The semiconductor agreement of 1986 is a case where such targets seem to have brought about increased foreign sales in the Japanese market.

A Separate Trade Policy Toward Japan?

As such examples show, many of these thorny policy problems arise most frequently in US trade dealings with Japan. In industry after industry, Japanese firms are American firms' toughest rivals. The enormous impact of Japan on the world trading order, the combination of formidable competitiveness on exports and embedded resistance to imports, has drained the patience of team after team of US trade negotiators. It has also led some veteran trade practitioners to conclude— usually not for attribution—that the United States should respond to this challenge by pursuing a split-level or two-track trade policy: managed trade or tit-for-tat reciprocity with the Japanese, and multilateral liberalism with everyone else. This sentiment—that Japan is different and should be treated differently—finds support in the writings of so-called Japan revisionists (and in Japanese self-perceptions of uniqueness). Clyde Prestowitz argues, for example, that the concept of trade openness is alien to Japanese culture and practice, so efforts to apply this principle to trans-Pacific dealings must inevitably fail.[62]

Conflicts with Japan regularly threaten the political base for liberal policies. Why not therefore jettison the most vulnerable part of the US "free trade" policy in order to preserve the rest? If the United States did so, Europeans would certainly follow: the Japanophobia of leading continental politicians far exceeds that of the United States. But it is hard to see how one can exclude the world's number-two market economy from the global system without crippling that system. It would be reckless to abandon the substantial trade gains stemming from Japan's GATT commitments in the hope that the United States could somehow work a better deal outside them. It would be foolish to discard the potential leverage that US-Japan cooperation gives against EU protectionism.

Moreover, while "the Japan problem" is real, it is typically misspecified and exaggerated. Many point to the bilateral trade deficit, but this is not per se a detriment to the American economy, and it is, as earlier stated,

---

62. See Prestowitz, *Trading Places*.

an inappropriate target for US trade policy. Many decry the loss of "good jobs" to Japanese competition—and many US workers have indeed suffered from the internationalization of the US economy—but as Japan's former Minister of Labor Tetsuo Kondo recently noted, the average productivity of American workers still exceeds, substantially, that of their counterparts across the Pacific.[63] Many bemoan the *keiretsu* ties among Japanese firms—which make getting a foothold in that market particularly difficult. Yet Japanese management and production methods are being widely emulated by American firms, and one key driving force for this emulation is the success of companies like Honda and Sony in manufacturing within the United States. Moreover, the notion that Japanese gains equal American losses is wrong and obsolete. In the global, interdependent world market that has emerged from the ashes of World War II, gains by one nation bring gains to others, provided they remain open and exploit competitive pressure to improve efficiency within their own borders.

The rise of Japanese economic power has not been easy for Japan's partners and rivals to accommodate. And the problem will certainly continue, the recession of 1992–94 notwithstanding, since Japan's growth performance may well continue to exceed that of America and Europe into the 21st century. But the problem will hardly be ameliorated if the United States tries to manage global economic relations with the Japanese off to one side. Instead, the need is to bring Japan more fully into the world system. The United States needs to use aggressive policy tools where necessary in particular product cases, but only in order to facilitate trade, not to impede it. Most important, the need is to build a positive-sum relationship and avert the sort of geostrategic conflict in which we—and the Japanese—would be losers.[64]

A USTR-Based Trade Reorganization

The analysis and recommendations in this chapter assume that the postwar interbranch division of labor will be maintained: senators and repre-

---

63 "On the key measure of purchasing power per hour of manufacturing work, the [Japan Productivity Center/OECD] figures showed that Americans outproduced the Japanese by 62 percent and led the European countries by smaller margins." *Washington Post*, 8 February 1992, C1.

64. For a more comprehensive look at US-Japan relations in the altered global environment, see I. M. Destler and Michael Nacht, "Beyond Mutual Recrimination: Building A Solid U.S.-Japan Relationship in the 1990s," *International Security*, 15, no. 3 (Winter 1990/91): 92–119. See also *Beyond the Framework Talks: Building a Mature U.S.-Japan Relationship*, Final Report of the Maryland/Tsukuba Project (I.M. Destler and Hideo Sato, co-directors), Center for International and Security Studies at Maryland, School of Public Affairs, University of Maryland at College Park, November 1994.

sentatives will be visible and influential participants in the process, but the primary decision locus for specific product and negotiating cases will remain the executive branch. The Omnibus Trade and Competitiveness Act of 1988 moved to strengthen this system, not to transform it, by avoiding product-specific measures and buttressing the authority of the USTR, even transferring to the USTR from the president the power to decide upon sanctions in Section 301 cases.[65] Congressional approval of landmark agreements in 1993 and 1994 gives testimony to the fact that the system continues to work. Still, it could be further strengthened by moderate reforms at both ends of Pennsylvania Avenue.

The reason for moderate trade reorganization is *not* the fact that many federal agencies have *some* role in trade policymaking. This simply reflects the range of governmental concerns that trade policy affects. In any conceivable organizational arrangement, the United States would continue to have the State Department and the National Security Council stressing trade's importance to alliance relations, the Defense Department worrying about the defense industrial base, the Treasury Department and the Council of Economic Advisers responsible for linking trade policy to the overall domestic economy and developing-world debt, and the Department of Agriculture stressing the connection of grain exports to commodity programs and overall farm welfare.

All government activities that have a "trade" label do not require a common home. As a day-to-day matter, for example, export promotion through technical aid to firms need not be housed in the same agency that handles import regulation or trade negotiations. Nor, contrary to myth, are other governments united on trade policy. Americans negotiating trade issues with Japan during the past 15 years have dealt not only, and not always mainly, with the Ministry of International Trade and Industry. They have found themselves confronting the Agriculture Ministry on beef and citrus, the Ministry of Posts and Telecommunications on the deregulation of Nippon Telephone and Telegraph, and the Finance Ministry on a range of matters, not to mention the Office of the Prime Minister, the Foreign Ministry, and, intermittently, a special Minister for International Economic Relations.

Reorganization proposals also suffer from exaggeration of what trade policy can accomplish. Proponents of a US "department of trade" have had ambitious goals: to redress the trade imbalance, to bolster industrial competitiveness generally.[66] Their reach exceeds trade policy's grasp.

---

65. The first edition of this book argued against such transfers of authority, warning that they might *weaken* the USTR by distancing her/him from the president (page 205). To date, this does not seem to have occurred.

66. See, for example, the opening statements of Senator William V. Roth Jr. (R-DE), and his colleagues in US Congress, Senate Committee on Governmental Affairs, Trade Reorganization Act of 1983, 98th Cong., 2nd sess., 17 March 1983, S. Hearing 98-474, 1-10.

But if substantial dispersion of US governmental trade responsibility is inevitable, the current bifurcation of central trade responsibility is not. In fact, the current organization has at least four serious flaws:

■ The current USTR-Commerce division of labor asks for trouble. Assigning "policy," "coordination," and "negotiations" to one official and "nonagricultural operational trade responsibilities" to a cabinet colleague invites competition and conflict.

■ This is exacerbated by the fact that international trade is the only subject in the Commerce secretary's portfolio that offers an opportunity for important policy leadership. Thus, any ambitious incumbent with decent White House connections becomes a rival of the USTR.

■ The numerical expansion of the Office of the USTR in 1980 created an organizational hybrid, too large for a flexible coordinating-negotiating staff but too small to be the central executive branch repository of line expertise and responsibility. And the USTR's size makes it a target of White House reorganizers seeking to trim overall staff.

■ Presidential support for the USTR, particularly important at times of trade policy crisis, has often in the past been tenuous.

This situation has led some legislators, notably Senator William V. Roth Jr. (R-DE), to propose replacing this "two-headed monster"[67] with a Department of Trade. They argue that this would create strength. Indeed, the Reagan administration endorsed this view in 1983–84, though largely because of a prior commitment by senior aide Edwin Meese III to Secretary of Commerce Malcolm Baldrige. In fact, however, a secretary of trade would more likely become what most heads of executive departments currently are: an official with a prestigious title but modest power, all too close to the interests his department affects, and distant from the president. On trade, this would mean a department overly responsive to the protection-seeking complainers and unable or disinclined to balance their concerns against those of others.

The better answer is to build on what has been, across a number of administrations, an organizational success story—the Office of the US Trade Representative—and to do so in a way that might improve the incumbent's presidential connection. Three simple steps are needed:

■ Convert the USTR into a small, elite Executive Office of the President (EOP) unit, with a professional staff totaling about 25, with responsi-

---

67. The phrase is Senator Roth's. See, for example, US Congress, *Trade Reorganization Act of 1983*, 2.

bility for leading international negotiations, brokering on Capitol Hill, and coordinating interagency trade.

- Create outside the EOP, as a noncabinet executive branch agency, a United States Trade Administration (USTA) headed by a deputy USTR for operations, and merge within this new unit the remaining staff of the current USTR and that of Commerce's International Trade Administration.

- Abolish the Department of Commerce.[68]

Creating a two-tiered USTR-USTA structure would have several obvious advantages. It would build on an organization with a generally successful track record, one that retains substantial support on Capitol Hill and in the broader trade community. It would establish the US trade representative as the only cabinet-level official for whom international trade was the primary policy responsibility. It would reduce conflict below cabinet level by consolidating, under one of the USTR's deputies, the staffs responsible for providing detailed backup to negotiations and enforcing the trade laws. Within the executive branch, trade policy would continue to be an interagency process at both the USTR and the USTA level, but management of this process would be easier with a clear locus of leadership.[69]

Trade policymaking could also benefit from modest reform at the other end of Pennsylvania Avenue. The USTR has been, in important respects, a creature and ally of the Senate Finance and House Ways and Means committees. A strong role for these committees remains critical, particularly for Ways and Means, which has faced increasing jurisdictional challenge. But it cannot regain the dominance of Chairman Wilbur D. Mills's day. With increased congressional interest in trade, and with major trade-affecting action now involving spheres like exchange rate, regulatory, or industrial policy, other committees will inevitably play important roles. For instance, other committees partici-

---

68. This final step would not be required for trade reorganization, since removal of the Commerce Department's trade functions would presumably end the secretary's threat to USTR primacy. But it would be a logical step, for what remained would be a set of autonomous technical agencies—National Oceanic and Atmospheric Administration, Bureau of the Census, National Institute of Standards and Technology, and Patent and Trademark Office are the largest. These could exist as free-standing federal agencies, but cabinet status would be inappropriate. Of course, if the United States were to embark on an active, industry-specific microeconomic policy, a revamped Commerce Department might be an appropriate base. On this point, see the Competitiveness Policy Council report, *Building a Competitive America*.

69. For a more extended argument supporting this recommendation, see pages 201–206 of the first edition of this book.

pated in review of the Tokyo and Uruguay Round agreements of 1979 and 1994, and the Omnibus Trade and Competitiveness Act of 1988 engaged 11 different House committees, while the conference committee contained no less than 155 representatives and 44 senators; action was coordinated by the office of House Speaker Jim Wright (D-TX). Former Ways and Means Chairman Dan Rostenkowski (D-IL) was able to play a very strong leadership role—because of his personal power, and because many of the most contentious issues were under his committee's jurisdiction. But his successors may not be so fortunate.

There is a need to protect that central role while accommodating pressures for broader participation. For future general trade legislation, it would be desirable for the speaker of the House to formalize the first-among-equals role of the Ways and Means chair by designating him as head of a House Trade Steering Group that included representatives from other appropriate committees, including Banking, Finance and Urban Affairs (to cover international monetary issues), Energy and Commerce, and Foreign Affairs. Such a group could manage future omnibus legislation and implementation of major trade agreements, farming out sections of a bill to the appropriate panels, with the Ways and Means chair retaining overall policy responsibility for coordinating their work and managing the bill that emerged.

Another possible congressional reform would be a trade reconciliation procedure parallel to that employed on budget matters since 1974. Bills and amendments diverging from existing trade policy (as interpreted by Senate Finance, House Ways and Means, the proposed Steering Group, or any other committee with established authority over its subject matter) would be subject to a point of order on the Senate or House floor. Through such a procedure, congressional leaders could block floor votes on product-specific, trade-restrictive proposals that had not been recommended by the committee with jurisdiction.

Policy Tools: New Approaches to Trade Adjustment

Just as trade policymakers need opportunities to expand US markets abroad, they need alternatives at home for firms and workers fighting losing battles against import competition.

In principle, of course, the plight of a worker displaced by foreign competition is no different from that of one whose job disappears because his firm moves to Texas or South Carolina. In practice, however, "foreign" competition creates pressure for government intervention, while domestic competition does not. When there are no alternatives, that intervention is likely to be focused on restricting imports. Thus, the argument for treating trade-generated displacement differently is that the US political system treats trade differently.

In the 1960s and 1970s, the United States recognized this difference by establishing and expanding the program known as Trade Adjustment Assistance (TAA). This broadened support for major trade legislation and provided Presidents Gerald R. Ford and Jimmy Carter something to give industries like shoes and automobiles while denying or deferring import relief. TAA did not, however, prove very effective in retraining workers and helping them move out of the trade-injured industry. Many auto workers, for example, seem to have used the program to maintain an income near that to which they had become accustomed, while waiting for their old companies to hire them back! No wonder many of TAA's former congressional champions turned skeptical, or that it proved an easy target for the budget-cutting initiative of the incoming Reagan administration. Since 1981, the authorizing legislation has twice been extended, but funding and eligibility have been curtailed.

TAA's demise was unfortunate for two important reasons. First of all, government should be seeking ways to facilitate workers' adjustment to economic change. These workers are losers in a broader international competitive process that brings large overall benefits to their nation. In return, that nation ought to give some attention to helping these workers train for and find other jobs. Public officials have not found this easy to do, but the federal government should continue to experiment in this area, together with private firms and state agencies. A moderately financed TAA program can carry out such experimentation, and approaches that prove successful can then be extended also to workers displaced by home-grown economic change.

The second reason to regret TAA's decline is political: TAA dilutes pressure for trade restrictions, and thus it strengthens the national capacity to pursue open trade policies, which produce gains for the nation far greater than TAA's costs.

But how could one hope to fund trade adjustment at more than a token level, at a time of record budget deficits and tight spending limits? One promising approach, developed in detail by Gary Clyde Hufbauer and Howard F. Rosen,[70] applies particularly to those industries to which trade protection is also being provided. They would channel revenues from tariffs to the financing of adjustment programs. If the protection were in the form of quotas, these would be auctioned off and the proceeds devoted to the same purpose.[71] The aim would be not to invest

---

70. Hufbauer and Rosen, *Trade Policy for Troubled Industries*, POLICY ANALYSES IN INTERNATIONAL ECONOMICS 15 (Washington: Institute for International Economics, 1986), chap. 5. See also Robert Z. Lawrence and Robert E. Litan, *Saving Free Trade: A Pragmatic Approach* (Washington: Brookings Institution, 1986).

71. C. Fred Bergsten et al., *Auction Quotas and United States Trade Policy*, POLICY ANALYSES IN INTERNATIONAL ECONOMICS 19 (Washington: Institute for International Economics, 1987).

public funds in new production facilities but to facilitate downsizing, a movement of resources out of the industry. This approach is easiest to apply in cases of new protection. By opting to participate in such a program, firms and workers would get temporary import relief, but it would be degressive, diminishing over time. And they would have to choose between this sort of comprehensive but temporary protection and other remedies such as the unfair trade statutes.[72]

The political risk of such a program, addressed to (and shaped by) a particular industry or sector, is that it may be captured by antiadjustment industry and labor interests, who may convert it into an instrument of indefinite protection and support. It would then no longer facilitate an orderly outflow of resources from the industry; it would instead become a means for an industry to remain uncompetitively large with perpetual government help. European adjustment programs have frequently experienced such capture. One means of resisting this tendency would be to ensure that antiprotection interests, including users of an industry's products, were represented in the development and oversight of any adjustment program. Also important is active monitoring by executive branch trade leaders determined to limit trade restrictions. This is another argument for housing executive branch leadership in the White House-based USTR, rather than in a department that would be vulnerable to special-interest pressure and disadvantaged in mobilizing counterweights.

In balancing pressures for import relief in specific industry cases, one final device would be most helpful: an analytic agency, free of short-run dependence on either the White House or the Congress, whose job would be to measure, as objectively as possible, the real impact of present and prospective cases of trade protection on all major affected US interests and on the economy as a whole.

As an operating agency, the USTR could not give priority to such analysis, nor would the proposed USTA under it. The US International Trade Commission must, under present law, limit its injury investigations to the petitioning industry, although it can and does consider broader effects when it decides what form of trade relief to recommend. One approach would be to widen the USITC's mandate so that it would be required to publish a more comprehensive assessment of the impact of import restrictions, as well as the industry-specific findings on which its injury determination is based. This would include, but go beyond, the

---

72. The Reagan and Bush administrations were resistant to such trade adjustment; TAA was kept alive in the 1980s, and operated with modest funding, only through the persistent efforts of senators like the late John Heinz (R-PA). President Bush promised, in the 1991 campaign for continuation of fast-track authority, an "adequately funded" worker adjustment program as a complement to a North American Free Trade Agreement. Such a program was part of the final NAFTA package. But the Clinton administration has favored general-purpose worker adjustment programs over those specifically targeted at the effects of trade.

proposal of Senator John H. Chafee (R-RI) that the USITC evaluate the impact of trade relief on consumers.

If it were judged difficult for the USITC to pursue such contrasting analytic tacks simultaneously, an alternative would be to create a new Trade Barrier Assessment Agency. Its task would be to issue annual, public reports on the extent and impact of existing US import barriers and other trade-distorting practices, and ad hoc reports when specific new cases arose.[73] A model would be the Australian Industry Commission (formerly the Industries Assistance Commission), which has performed this function with high credibility.[74]

In Defense of Trade Brokering

In the end, much will depend on the quality and assertiveness of the trade leadership of the executive branch. Greater decentralization and activism on Capitol Hill have increased the USTR's burden and her/his need to keep the initiative. To cope with trade policy pressures effectively requires building confidence in the system, so that it is responsive to trade-created problems even when resisting the relief sought. It requires knowing the petitioners and their political patrons.

Brokering in the trade sphere is not an end in itself, but a means to maintain relatively open US policies. It is an appropriate means for trade because achieving this goal is importantly a matter of avoiding or limiting government interventions in the US economy. Such a trade-expanding purpose is what gives officials a basis for taking the initiative and a capacity for dealing with specific interests without being engulfed by them. If they act as if government policy is simply a function of the balance of outside pressures, they will invite still more pressure, together with contempt for their weakness. But if they demonstrate commitment to this purpose, and skill in its pursuit, they will command respect—as have, in fact, many US trade officials in the half-century since Secretary of State Cordell Hull.

Trade officials' posture should be that they know where the trade policy train should go, and that they have the political capacity to steer it in that direction, together with the readiness to plan and execute the journey in ways that maximize the gain and minimize the pain for spe-

---

73. Jeffrey J. Schott would have such a "domestic surveillance body" work in tandem with a strengthened GATT "trade policy review mechanism." *The Global Trade Negotiations: What Can Be Achieved?* POLICY ANALYSES IN INTERNATIONAL ECONOMICS 29 (Washington: Institute for International Economics, 1990), 38.

74. Lawrence B. Krause, "Australia's Comparative Advantage in International Trade," in Richard E. Caves and Lawrence B. Krause, eds., *The Australian Economy: A View from the North* (Washington: Brookings Institution, 1984), 290.

cial interests. Only then will private actors find it to their advantage to climb on board. Only with a balance of strength and responsiveness can trade leaders cope effectively with the inevitable pressures of an internationalized American economy.

In cases of major industry campaigns for import relief, like steel in 1984 or textiles in 1985–90, the USTR needs to tilt against them, to encourage all major interests affected by proposed trade restrictions to make their voices heard. When the political game is broadened to include players on the other side—industrial users of imports, retailers, exporters, foreign governments—an administration gains leeway to resist extreme demands and to opt for moderate trade restrictions when some action is required.

By contrast, in cases in which industries seek legal trade remedies, the USTR needs to show sympathy and empathy, with overt presidential backing—to press Section 301 cases where egregious foreign practices are involved, and to lean toward granting temporary relief under the escape clause (Section 201) where it would seem to make a nontemporary difference for a trade-injured industry.

In the end, there is no attractive alternative to the classic, liberal-leaning trade policy that was pursued by those who shaped the old American trade policymaking system. Now, as in earlier decades, the United States needs institutions designed to limit and balance restrictive pressures while leading the United States and the world toward a more open and mutually rewarding international economy. Yet these institutions must be adapted to changes in US economics and politics. If the United States is to maintain the benefits of trade and the stimulus of a relatively open international system, it must continue to find ways of coping with trade pressures, ways of converting import-reducing issues to export-expanding issues when it can, and putting together limited protection packages when it must.

Finally, if Americans are to support continuation of such policies, they must believe that they can compete and prosper in today's difficult trade world.

Most critical to restoring such a belief are the macroeconomic and microeconomic measures stressed at the outset of this chapter, for only when US imports stop regularly exceeding its exports, and only with greater improvement in productivity, will it be possible to sell the notion that the United States is "holding its own." Also important, however, is a sustained effort by government and business leaders to put forward a broad, pro-trade rationale that can play in the domestic arena.

That rationale would go something like this: The world is a tough place, with a great deal of unfairness (here as well as overseas), but:

■ America is competing and can compete with any nation in the world, as long as its macroeconomic policies keep saving and investment—

and currency relationships—in reasonable balance and US workers and firms grow in productivity.

- The way to keep competing is by maintaining a dynamic, flexible economy that rewards US industrial winners, not its losers.

- To do this, the United States needs to keep its economic borders as open as possible and press other nations to do likewise.

To those hurt by the economic change that trade will bring, the United States should offer aid to facilitate adjustment, but not lock itself into outmoded production facilities or overpriced products.

With persistence and luck, Americans can hold their own in a relatively open trade world. Americans ought to be able to handle internal politics so as to make that happy outcome possible. And day by day, as they grapple with the specifics of trade politics, executive branch and congressional trade leaders could do worse than bear in mind the admonition with which E. E. Schattschneider closed his book about Smoot-Hawley 60 years ago: "To manage pressures is to govern; to let pressures run wild is to abdicate."[75]

75. Schattschneider, *Politics, Pressure and The Tariff* (New York: Prentice-Hall, 1935), 293.

Glossary

American selling price (ASP)

A method of calculating US import duties, under which those for certain categories of products—benzenoid chemicals, rubber footwear, canned clams, and wool-knit gloves—were computed by multiplying the tariff rate not by the price of the imported product, as is standard practice, but instead by the (usually much higher) price of the US product with which the import competed. This typically resulted in a much higher effective tariff. The United States agreed in the MTN, or Tokyo Round, to phase out ASP, effective in 1981.

Antidumping (AD) investigation

An investigation instituted by an importing country in response to a claim that a foreign supplier is selling merchandise at "less than fair value." (See "dumping.") In the United States, if the Department of Commerce finds dumping has occurred, and the US International Trade Commission finds that US firms have been materially injured, the law provides that customs officials levy an additional import duty equal to the calculated price discrepancy. GATT Article VI authorizes such measures. The Uruguay Round antidumping code, signed in 1994, aims to standardize and discipline national government practices.

Asia Pacific Economic Cooperation (APEC) forum

An informal grouping of 18 Asian and Pacific Rim nations that provides a forum for discussing economic and trade issues. The members include Australia, Brunei, Canada, Chile, China, Hong Kong, Indonesia, Japan, Malaysia, Mexico, New Zealand, Papua New Guinea, Philippines, Singapore, South Korea, Taiwan, Thailand, and the United States. Originally, meetings were at the ministerial level; however, the November 1993 meeting, hosted by President Clinton in Seattle, brought together the heads of state of almost all members. At the 1994 summit, the leaders agreed to eliminate barriers to trade and investment among industrialized members by 2010 and among all members by 2020.

Burke-Hartke quota bill

Legislation introduced in Congress in 1971, widely interpreted as reflecting a major swing toward protectionism. Its provisions included broad-ranging import quotas and measures to discourage overseas investment by multinational firms based in the United States.

Comparative advantage

Relative efficiency in production of a particular product or class of goods. Trade theory holds that a country should export those goods in which it has the greatest comparative advantage and import those goods in which it has the greatest comparative disadvantage, regardless of its general level of productivity or its overall labor costs relative to other countries.

Cost-insurance-freight (c.i.f.)

A system of valuing imports that includes the cost of moving them from their port of embarkation to their destination. The Trade Agreements Act of 1979 required the US Department of Commerce to report c.i.f. import statistics "no later than 48 hours before the release of any other [import] statistics" (Sec. 1108). This provision was repealed in 1988.

Countervailing duty (CVD) investigation

An investigation instituted by an importing country when given evidence that foreign goods sold within its borders are subsidized by the government in the country of production. If a subsidy is found by the US Department of Commerce, and the US International Trade Commission finds that US firms have been materially injured, US law generally requires imposition of a duty to offset the subsidy. The Uruguay Round code on subsidies and countervailing measures, signed in 1994, aims to standardize and discipline national practices on subsidies and offsetting duties.

Current account balance

A measure of a country's international transactions which includes trade in goods and services and unilateral transfers. A "negative" balance on current account, or current account deficit, means that outflows of currency resulting from these transactions exceed inflows. (A current account deficit is offset and financed by a capital account surplus, representing a net inflow of investment funds.)

Customs value

A method of valuing imported goods which, in traditional United States practice, excludes shipping costs from their price.

Domestic-content requirement

A requirement that firms selling a particular product within a particular country must use, as a certain percentage of their inputs, goods produced within that country. The United Auto Workers sought unsuccessfully to limit imports of foreign cars and parts through enactment of domestic-content legislation for automobiles sold in the United States.

Dumping

The sale of a commodity in a foreign market at "less than fair value." Fair value is usually considered to be the price at which the same product is sold in the exporting country or to third countries, but under US law dumping can also be established by comparing the export price to the estimated costs of production of the merchandise in question. When dumping occurs, the legal remedy is imposition of a special duty equal to the "margin" of dumping, the difference between fair value and the actual sales price.

Escape clause (Section 201, Article XIX)

A provision of the GATT articles, and of US law, authorizing import relief as a temporary "safeguard" for domestic producers injured by import competition. Originally limited to those whose losses resulted from prior US trade concessions, escape clause eligibility was extended in Section 201 of the Trade Act of 1974 to all who could establish that imports were "a substantial cause of serious injury, or the threat thereof." The Omnibus Trade and Competitiveness Act of 1988 stipulated that the goal of any relief must be "positive adjustment." If the US International Trade Commission finds injury and recommends relief, the president must grant it or report to Congress why, after reviewing the "national economic interest of the United States," he has decided there is "no appropriate and feasible action to take." Congress may then override his decision through enactment of a joint resolution, imposing thereby the remedy recommended by the USITC.

Exon-Florio amendment

A measure attached to the 1988 Trade Act to provide a means of monitoring foreign direct investment in the United States. The amendment authorizes the president to block mergers and joint ventures with, or acquisitions or takeovers of US companies by foreign interests, on national security grounds.

Fast-track procedures

Legislative procedures set forth in Section 151 of the Trade Act of 1974, stipulating that once the president formally submits to Congress a bill implementing an agreement (negotiated under the act's authority) concerning nontariff barriers to trade, both houses must vote on the bill within 90 days. No amendments are permitted. The purpose of these procedures is to assure foreign governments that Congress will act expeditiously on an agreement they negotiate with the US government. The deadline for negotiations under the fast-track procedures was extended until 1991 by the 1988 Trade Act, and then (with congressional acquiescence) until 30 June 1993. The deadline for Uruguay Round negotiations was subsequently extended to 16 April 1994. There was no extension of fast-track authority in the Uruguay Round implementing legislation.

Free-alongside-ship (f.a.s.)

A contractual basis for trade by which the seller delivers goods to the buyer at the port of embarkation and the buyer assumes responsibility thereafter; hence, a method of valuing internationally traded goods that does not include the cost of their shipment from the exporting to the importing country.

Free trade agreement

An arrangement between two or more nations to remove barriers to the trade they conduct with one another. An FTA also usually addresses trade-distorting practices such as government subsidies.

Under such an agreement, concessions are not on an MFN (most-favored nation) basis, but only to the parties to the FTA. Since such agreements were authorized by the Trade and Tariff Act of 1984, the United States has negotiated FTAs with Israel and Canada, and a North American Free Trade Agreement (NAFTA) with Canada and Mexico.

General Agreement on Tariffs and Trade (GATT)

Early postwar multilateral agreement on trade rules, completed in 1947 as an interim arrangement pending establishment of the projected International Trade Organization (ITO). After Congress failed to ratify the ITO agreement, the articles of the GATT agreement became the basic rules of international trade, and the GATT organization at Geneva the central international institution supporting international negotiations and the reduction of trade barriers. As part of the Uruguay Round agreement, the GATT was superseded by the World Trade Organization (WTO) on 1 January 1995, with all bodies and rules of the GATT as modified by the Uruguay Round agreements becoming part of the WTO.

Generalized System of Preferences (GSP)

A system under which industrial nations give preferential rates of duty on imports from less developed countries without receiving trade concessions in return. The United States began extending preferences in 1975, and renewed them in the Trade and Tariff Act of 1984.

Gephardt amendment

Authored by Representative Richard A. Gephardt (D-MO), this legislation threatened retaliation against countries running large trade deficits with the United States. Initially passed by the House in 1986 and 1987, it was supplanted, in the 1988 act, by Super 301. The congressman, as House majority leader, introduced a "new Gephardt amendment" in 1991 targeted mainly at Japan.

Industrial policy

Governmental actions affecting, or seeking to affect, the sectoral composition of the economy by influencing the development of particular industries.

Industrial targeting

The selection, by a national government, of industries important to the next stage of that nation's economy, and encouragement of their development through explicit policy measures. A frequent goal of such targeting is competitiveness in export markets.

Injury — The requirement, under GATT, that an industry seeking trade relief establish that it has been hurt by foreign competition. In the United States, a finding of injury has always been required for escape clause relief, and since 1979 for the bulk of CVD and antidumping cases as well.

Intellectual property — See TRIPs.

International Trade Commission — See US International Trade Commission.

Kennedy Round — The popular name for the sixth round of trade negotiations under the aegis of the GATT, conducted during 1963–67, which produced major cuts in tariffs.

Liberal trade — The policy or practice of reducing import barriers and expanding the volume of international trade.

Macroeconomic policy — Policy geared toward influencing the overall aggregates of the economy, such as employment, production, and the rate of inflation, through measures affecting the fiscal balance and the supply of money and credit.

Mercantilism — Historically, an economic philosophy that equates national wealth with the accumulation of gold or other international monetary assets, and hence with running a trade surplus. In today's world, mercantilism refers to a belief that running a consistently positive trade balance contributes to a nation's economic strength and moral virtue, and also to policies aimed at this goal.

Ministry of International Trade and Industry (MITI) — The Japanese cabinet agency that is concerned with that nation's industrial development, and that shares with other ministries responsibility for international trade.

Most-favored nation (MFN) — The principle of nondiscrimination in international trade. For a nation, receiving "most favored" treatment from another means that the products it exports are subject to tariffs no greater than those imposed on imports from any other country. Under GATT Article I all contracting parties pledge most-favored nation treatment to one another. MFN is frequently circumvented by voluntary export restraints (VERs), however, and preferences (GSP) constitute an exception to MFN. So do free trade agreements (FTAs) between two or more nations.

Multi-Fiber Arrangement (MFA)

An international trade compact, dating from 1973, that establishes a framework for negotiating bilateral orderly marketing agreements (OMAs) under which exporting nations undertake to limit their shipments of textile and apparel products. Under the MFA, importing nations can impose quantitative import restrictions when unable to negotiate such agreements or to counter market-disruptive import surges. The MFA succeeded the LTA (Long-Term Arrangement), which took effect in 1962 and applied only to cotton textiles. The MFA broadened controls to include products made from wool or synthetic fibers. As part of the Uruguay Round agreement, the MFA will be phased out in three stages over 10 years. After 3 years, the quotas on 17 percent (by volume) of textile imports must be removed. The quotas on an additional 18 percent of textile imports must have the quota removed within 7 years, and the remaining 65 percent must be free from quotas within 10 years.

Multilateral trade negotiations (MTN)

Technically any of the postwar series of barrier-reducing negotiations under GATT auspices, the MTN commonly refers to the Tokyo Round of 1973–79.

Newly industralizing countries (NICs)

Developing countries (for example, Hong Kong, Korea, Singapore, and Taiwan) experiencing rapid industrial development and, hence, expanding exports of their industrial products.

Nontariff barriers (NTBs)

Government measures other than tariffs—i.e., import quotas, buy-national procurement regulations, product standards, subsidies—that impede or distort the flow of international commerce. The Tokyo Round was devoted primarily to limiting and disciplining national use of NTBs.

North American Free Trade Agreement (NAFTA)

Agreement establishing free trade among the United States, Mexico, and Canada. Negotiated by President Bush and signed on 17 December 1992,

NAFTA removes barriers to trade and investment and improves the protection of intellectual property rights. Prior to seeking congressional implementation of NAFTA, President Clinton negotiated side agreements on labor and environmental issues. Congress approved implementation of NAFTA in November 1993.

Omnibus Trade and Competitiveness Act of 1988

The 1988 Trade Act was the first comprehensive trade legislation initiated by the Congress since before the Smoot-Hawley Act of 1930. Its important features included the strengthening of unilateral trade retaliation instruments, particularly Section 301, provision of fast-track negotiating authority for the Uruguay Round of GATT negotiations, and enhancement of the authority of the US Trade Representative.

Orderly marketing agreement (OMA)

A formal agreement in which an exporting nation undertakes to limit its sales of specified "sensitive" products to specific levels, so as not to disrupt, threaten, or impair competitive industries or workers in an importing country or countries.

Plaza Agreement

An agreement in September 1985 among the "Group of Five" advanced industrial nations (France, Germany, Japan, the United Kingdom, and the United States) to encourage depreciation of the US dollar.

Protectionism

The imposition of substantial tariffs or other limitations on imports in order to insulate or "protect" domestic producers from foreign competition; hence, support of the imposition of such import barriers.

Quasi-judicial procedures

Procedures through which law is made by regulatory agencies applying general statutes to specific cases. On trade, procedures administered by the US International Trade Commission and the Department of Commerce determine the eligibility of petitioners for import relief under the escape clause, countervailing duty, antidumping, or other trade statutes.

Quota

A limit on the quantity of a product that may be imported by (or sold to) a country. Import quotas are enforced by the receiving nation, export quotas by the country of origin.

Reciprocal Trade Agreements Act of 1934	The law that provided authority for the US government to enter into bilateral agreements for reciprocal tariff reductions. Through successive extensions and amendments, it also authorized US participation in the first five GATT rounds of multilateral trade negotiations. It was superseded by the Trade Expansion Act of 1962.
Reciprocity	The general principle or practice of nations' negotiating mutual reductions in import barriers. See also sectoral reciprocity.
Retaliation	Import-restrictive action taken by a country in response to similar measures by a trading partner. GATT rules permit a country whose exports are hurt by new restrictions to retaliate by imposing trade barriers on products sold by the nation taking the initial protectionist action. In principle, the volume of trade affected by retaliation should be comparable to that affected by the measures against which it is targeted.
Safeguards	See Antidumping investigation; CVD investigation; Escape clause.
Section 201	See Escape clause.
Section 301	Under this provision of the Trade Act of 1974, as amended by the Omnibus Trade and Competitiveness Act of 1988, the USTR is required to take all appropriate action, including retaliation, to obtain the removal of any act, policy, or practice of a foreign government that violates an international agreement or is unjustifiable, unreasonable, or discriminatory, and burdens or restricts US commerce. In practice, it has been employed increasingly on behalf of American exporters fighting foreign import barriers or subsidized competition in third-country markets.
Sectoral reciprocity	The principle or practice of comparing the openness of national markets to imports sector by sector, and negotiating restraints sector by sector, rather than across entire economies. US advocates of a sectoral reciprocity approach to trade in telecommunications or wine, for example, propose to compare the levels of US and foreign barriers to imports of these products, and to equalize them, either by negotiating reductions in foreign restraints

or by raising our own. A modified version of sectoral reciprocity was enacted into law as Title III of the Trade and Tariff Act of 1984.

Semiconductor Trade Arrangement (STA)	Bilateral agreement between the United States and Japan on foreign access to the Japanese semiconductor market and dumping by Japanese companies in the United States and third-country semiconductor markets. The STA, which went into effect in 1986 and was extended in 1991, is important in its use of numerical targets. The 1991 agreement set an explicit market share of 20 percent for foreign suppliers in the Japanese market by the end of 1992.
Smoot-Hawley Act	The Tariff Act of 1930, which raised US tariffs on over 20,000 dutiable items to record levels and contributed to the deepening of the Great Depression.
Special Representative for Trade Negotiations (STR)	See United States Trade Representative.
Special 301	This clause in the 1988 Omnibus Trade Act requires the USTR to investigate countries determined to have a history of violating existing laws and agreements dealing with intellectual property rights. Such countries must have their current practices reviewed each year, and, if they are not found to be improving, are subject to mandated retaliation under Section 301.
Structural Impediments Initiative	A series of negotiations begun in 1989 by the United States and Japan to identify and attempt to reduce structural impediments to trade between the two countries. The SII has focused on issues such as marketing and distribution systems, saving and investment patterns, and government-business relations. The United States has used the negotiations to seek Japanese government actions that would increase Japanese imports of American goods.
Subsidy	A bounty or grant conferred upon the production or exportation of an article or merchandise by the government in the country of origin. Foreign subsidies affecting trade are subject, under US law, to countervailing duties (CVDs).
Super 301	Under this amendment to Section 301 of the 1988

Trade Act, the USTR was required in 1989 and 1990 to designate "priority foreign countries," chosen for the "number and pervasiveness" of their "acts, policies or practices" impeding US exports, and for the US export gains that might come from the removal of these practices. The law called for retaliation if foreign action was insufficient or not forthcoming. In March 1994, President Clinton issued a so-called "Super 301" executive order targeting "priority foreign country *practices*." Its provisions, carrying through 1995, were codified in the Uruguay Round implementing legislation.

Targeting

See Industrial targeting.

Tariff Act of 1930

See Smoot-Hawley Act.

Tokyo Round

The GATT negotiations formally initiated by the Tokyo Declaration in 1973 and completed in 1979. The Tokyo Round, also called the multilateral trade negotiations (MTN), differed from previous GATT rounds in its primary focus, which was reducing and regulating nontariff barriers (NTBs). It yielded a number of multilateral codes covering, among other subjects, subsidies and countervailing measures, antidumping, customs valuation, government procurement, and technical barriers to trade. Participating nations also agreed to a substantial further reduction in tariff rates.

Trade Act of 1974

Legislation signed into law on 3 January 1975 which granted the president authority to enter the Tokyo Round and negotiate international agreements to reduce tariffs and NTBs. (See also fast-track procedures.) The act also amended US law governing the escape clause, antidumping, and countervailing duties; expanded trade adjustment assistance; established guidelines for granting MFN status to East bloc states; and granted limited trade preferences (GSP) to less developed countries.

Trade Adjustment Assistance (TAA)

Originated under the Trade Expansion Act of 1962 and expanded under the Trade Act of 1974, this is a program designed to provide retraining and financial benefits to workers and firms that are injured as a result of increased imports. TAA eligibility and funding have been cut back sharply since 1981.

Trade Agreements Act of 1979	Legislation, adopted under the fast-track procedures, that approved and implemented the trade agreements negotiated during the Tokyo Round. It made US law consistent with the MTN agreements, while at the same time rewriting the countervailing duty and antidumping laws, extending the president's authority to negotiate NTB agreements, and requiring the president to reorganize executive branch trade functions.
Trade and Tariff Act of 1984	An omnibus trade bill whose provisions included extension of the president's authority to grant trade preferences, authorization for negotiating bilateral free trade agreements, and authority to enforce export restraint agreements on steel.
Trade balance	The total value of a nation's merchandise exports minus the value of its merchandise imports, globally or vis-à-vis specific countries or regions. A "negative" trade balance is one in which imports exceed exports.
Trade Expansion Act of 1962 (TEA)	Legislation authorizing the Kennedy Round of trade negotiations, which also amended US escape clause procedures and established the Trade Adjustment Assistance (TAA) program.
Trade-related intellectual property rights (TRIPs)	Issues involving the treatment of intellectual property owned by foreigners. The United States has focused on preventing the piracy of intellectual property in foreign nations. Improved protection of intellectual property has been an objective of the United States in Section 301 cases and in the Uruguay Round. Specific areas covered by the Uruguay Round agreement on TRIPs include copyrights, patents, trademarks, industrial designs, design of integrated circuits, and anticompetitive practices in licensing.
Trade-related investment measures (TRIMs)	Issues involving restrictions on the operations of foreign firms—requiring, for example, foreign firms to produce a certain percentage of the final product locally or export a certain percentage of their output. Although the TRIMs agreement was less ambitious than the TRIPs agreement, the Uruguay Round did produce the first GATT agreement on investment measures. The Uruguay Round agreement on TRIMs focused on providing national treatment and eliminating quantitative restrictions.

Trade-remedy procedures	See Quasi-judicial procedures; Section 301.
Trigger price mechanism (TPM)	A system, developed and enforced during the Carter administration, of restraining steel imports by monitoring them for possible dumping. Under the TPM, an antidumping investigation was to be "triggered" if the price of an imported steel product was below the production costs of the world's most efficient producer of that product.
Tuna-dolphin cases	GATT disputes over whether the United States can use a tuna import prohibition to enforce limits on the killing of dolphins during tuna harvesting. In 1991, a GATT dispute between the United States and Mexico over Mexican tuna fishing practices led to a GATT panel finding that the US Marine Mammal Protection Act (MMPA) violated US obligations under the GATT. Among other things, the panel concluded that the United States could not impose import restrictions to protect animal life or natural resources outside the United States. However, Mexico declined to have the decision adopted by the GATT Council. Thus, the decision is not considered a formal part of GATT law or precedent. In 1994, the European Union challenged the MMPA's embargo on tuna imported from countries that trade in tuna with Mexico. A second panel found that the United States had violated its GATT obligations by acting unilaterally.
UN Conference on Trade and Development (UNCTAD)	A quasi-autonomous body within the United Nations system, intended to focus special attention on measures that might be taken to accelerate the pace of economic development in the developing countries. The conference was first convened in Geneva in 1964, and has met quadrennially since that date.
US International Trade Commission (USITC)	An independent US fact-finding and regulatory agency whose six members make determinations of injury and recommendations for relief for industries or workers seeking relief from increasing import competition. In addition, upon the request of Congress or the president, or on its own initiative, the USITC conducts comprehensive studies of specific industries and trade problems, and the probable impact on specific US industries of proposed reductions in US tariffs and nontariff trade barriers. The USITC was created by the Trade Act

of 1974 as the successor agency to the US Tariff Commission, which was created in 1916.

United States Tariff Commission

See US International Trade Commission.

US Trade Representative (USTR)

An official in the Executive Office of the President, with cabinet-level and ambassadorial rank, charged with advising the president, working with Congress, and leading and coordinating the US government on international trade negotiations. (USTR also designates the White House office that the representative heads.) Established by the Carter administration in 1980, the USTR was given increased authority in the Omnibus Act of 1988. It succeeded the Special Trade Representative (STR), created (at congressional insistence) in the Trade Expansion Act of 1962, and whose status and authority were strengthened in the Trade Act of 1974.

Uruguay Round

The comprehensive GATT negotiations initiated by the Punta del Este agreement of September 1986. The negotiations were originally to be completed by the end of 1990; however, a final agreement was not reached until December 1993, with the formal signing in April 1994. Substantial new agreements were reached on general tariff reduction, agricultural subsidies and quotas, textiles, safeguards, antidumping and countervailing duties, trade-related investment measures (TRIMs), rules of origin, standards, services, trade-related intellectual property rights (TRIPs), and government procurement. An unprecedented number of nations adhered to the major Uruguay Round accords—123 as of mid-1994. The Uruguay Round also created the World Trade Organization (WTO) to supersede the GATT structure and modified dispute-settlement procedures so a single country can no longer block the adoption of a panel report, although panel findings can be appealed.

Voluntary export restraint (VER)

An arrangement under which exporters voluntarily limit exports of certain products to a particular country. Such restraints (also known as voluntary restraint agreements, or VRAs) are typically undertaken under threat of that country's imposition of import restrictions. VERs circumvent the GATT MFN principle, and the obligation on the part of the importing country to provide compensation to the exporting country when it imposes new import restrictions. The Uruguay Round agreement on safeguards bans the use of VERs.

World Trade Organization (WTO)   A new organization created by the Uruguay Round agreements to oversee the global trading system and monitor implementation of trade accords. The WTO is the successor organization to the GATT; unlike the GATT, however, it was explicitly established to play this role. The WTO encompasses and extends the GATT structure. It came into being in 1995.

Index

Free trade agreements, 77. *See also specific*
    agreements
  beyond NAFTA, 266
  definition of, 312–13
Free trade doctrine, challenges to, 185–91
Frenzel, William, 225
Friends of the Earth, 224n
Fukuda, Takeo, 110

Gallup polls, 182–83
GATS. *See* General Agreement on Trade in
    Services
GATT. *See* General Agreement on Tariffs and
    Trade
General Agreement on Tariffs and Trade
    (GATT), 6–7, 12, 22, 26, 27, 33–34, 41,
    313. *See also specific trade rounds*
  antidumping code, 72, 231n
  Article VI. *See* Countervailing duties
  Article XIX. *See* Escape clause
  bipartisan support, 251–55
  Brussels ministerial meetings, 135
  Dunkel text, 231
  erosion of, 44, 53–54, 63
  ministerial conferences, 83, 99
  Punta del Este ministerial talks, 126
  waivers, 33
General Agreement on Trade in Services
    (GATS), 231–32
General Electric Co., 234
Generalized System of Preferences (GSP), 54,
    85, 313
  renewal of, 86, 240
General Motors, 77
Geneva agreement, 231–33
  implementation of, 243
Gephardt, Richard A., 80, 180, 208, 208n
  as House majority leader, 98
  on House Ways and Means, 89–90
  and NAFTA, 101–02, 224, 226
  protectionism, 181
  support for GATT, 244
  support for Uruguay Round agreement, 233
Gephardt amendment, 86, 91, 93, 103, 269,
    287, 295n, 313
Germany, 91
  income per capita, 47
  unemployment rates, 56
Gibbons, Sam M., 78, 80, 87, 90, 162, 239, 243,
    281
Gibbons bill, 162–64
Gilpin, Robert, 62
Gingrich, Newt, 252
  NAFTA debate, 224, 226
  Uruguay Round implementation, 246–51
Goldstein, Judith L., 181
Gore, Albert, 222, 228, 244–45
Gramm-Rudman-Hollings legislation of 1985,
    275n

Greenspan, Alan, 277–78
GSP. *See* Generalized System of Preferences
Gulf War, 61–62

Harris surveys, 182–83
Hartke, Vance, 81, 178
Hata, Tsutomu, 237
Hathaway, William D., 111
Havana Charter, 34
Heinz, John, 76, 82, 149, 158n
Helms, Jesse, 158, 251
Heritage Foundation, 246
Herter, Christian A., 20, 108
Hewlett-Packard Co., 192
Hills, Carla A., 98, 101, 104, 106, 207, 250–51,
    255
  Super 301, 132–34
  and textile industry, 198
  trade priority, 218
  Uruguay Round negotiations, 134–37, 289
Hollings, Ernest F., 29, 69, 90
  Uruguay Round implementation, 247–51
Holmer, Alan, 94, 131
Hong Kong, 53, 85
Hoover, Herbert C., 177
Horlick, Gary, 154
Hosokawa, Morihiro, 236–38
Houdaille case, 163, 163n
Houghton, Amo, 243
Hufbauer, Gary Clyde, 144, 171, 210, 303
Hull, Cordell, 5–6, 14–15, 18, 119
  bilateral trade agreements, 12, 17
Human rights, and MFN status for China,
    230, 233–36
Humphrey, Hubert H., support for textile
    industry, 197

IBM Corp., 172
Imports. *See also* Voluntary export restraints
  quotas, 195–96, 206, 210
  steel stabilization bill, 86–87
  sugar quotas, 210
  textile, 24–26, 69–70, 69n, 212n
  tobacco restrictions, 127
  US, 45t, 45–46, 61, 205n, 208, 208n
Imports-production ratio, 205, 206n
Import statistics, reporting, 49n
India, Super 301 target, 133, 134n
Industrial policy, 185–89, 280–85
  activist, 188
  definition of, 313
  spillover benefits as argument for, 282
Industrial targeting, 163
  definition of, 313–14
Industries Assistance Commission. *See*
    Australian Industry Commission
Informatics policy, Brazilian, 127
Injury test, for CVDs, 113, 149, 314

Local content legislation, 79
Lodge, George C., 187
Long, Russell B., 20, 30, 42, 49n, 67, 109, 115–16, 164
Long-Term Arrangement Regarding International Trade in Cotton Textiles, 26
LTA. *See* Long-Term Arrangement Regarding International Trade in Cotton Textiles
Lugar, Richard, 256, 262n
Lyng, Richard E., 126

Machine-tool makers, import relief, 210
Macroeconomic balance, 264
Macroeconomic policy, 265
  definition of, 314
  proposal for, 277–80
Madrid Hurtado, Miguel, de la, 135
Malmgren, Harald B., 20, 108
Managed trade, 296–97
  expansion of, 210
  in semiconductors, 212
Marine Mammal Protection Act of 1972, 223
Market-Oriented, Sector-Specific (MOSS) talks, 128–30
Marrakesh signing of Uruguay Round agreements, 244
Material injury test, for CVDs, 113, 149, 314
Matsui, Robert, 222n, 224, 226, 235n, 239
McDermott, Jim, 235
McDonald, Alonzo L., 109
McDonald, David J., 23
McKinley Tariff Act of 1890, 12, 16n
McLarty, Mac, 226
Meany, George, 178
Meese, Edwin III, 118, 125, 300
Mercantilism
  definition of, 314
  history of, 8
  selective, 189
Merchandise trade balance, US, 115
Mexico, 98–103
  fast-track time period, 77
  NAFTA talks, 135
  US free trade agreement, 207
  US negotiations, 54, 212
MFA. *See* Multi-Fiber Arrangement
MFN status. *See* Most–favored–nation status
Microeconomic policy
  measures, 265
  proposal for, 280–85
Middle-class income, decline in, 47n
Middle East, October War, 55
Mikulski, Barbara, 254
Milliken, Roger, 248
Mills, Wilbur D., 19, 28–29, 33, 88
  fall from power, 66–67
  textile quota bill, 29–30, 68, 69, 108
  trade protectionism, 29–30

Mills bill, 29–30, 68, 108
Minilateralism, 212n
Ministry of International Trade and Industry (MITI), 21, 78, 130, 212, 314
Minivans, 221, 221n
Misery index, 55
Mitchell, George, 98, 230, 236, 249
Miterrand, François, 135
MITI. *See* Ministry of International Trade and Industry
Moffett, A. Toby, 75
Mondale, Walter F., 87, 178–79, 179n–180n, 181
Mosbacher, Robert, 132
MOSS talks. *See* Market–Oriented, Sector–Specific talks
Most-favored nation (MFN) status, 17, 314–15
  for China, 217, 230, 233–36
Motorcycles, escape clause proceedings, 210
Motorola, 192, 237, 243
Moynihan, Daniel Patrick, 239, 245, 256
MTNs. *See* Multilateral Trade Negotiations
Multi-Fiber Arrangement (MFA), 26, 76, 197, 315
  phase-out, 231–32
  renewal negotiations, 90
  talks, 70n
Multilateral trade agreements, 134
Multilateral Trade Negotiations, 13, 54, 73–74, 266. *See also* Tokyo Round
  definition of, 315
  final stage, 113
Multilateral trade system, advantages of, 275
Murayama, Tomiichi, 238

Nader, Ralph, 194, 218, 246, 250–51, 261
NAFTA. *See* North American Free Trade Agreement
Nakasone, Yasuhiro, 89, 123
NAM. *See* National Association of Manufacturers
National Association of Manufacturers (NAM), 195, 233
National Bureau of Economic Research (NBER), 187
National Economic Commission, 278
National Economic Council (NEC), 221, 279
National Electrical Manufacturers Association, 196
National Resources Defense Council, 224n
National Wildlife Federation, 224n
Natural resource subsidies, 163
NBER. *See* National Bureau of Economic Research
NEC. *See* National Economic Council
Neustadt, Richard E., 121
New China lobby, 234
New Deal, 6, 31

Newly industrializing countries
definition of, 315
rise of, 63
New York Times/CBS News polls, 183
NICs. *See* Newly industrializing countries
Nippon Telephone and Telegraph (NTT),
111–12
Niskanen, William A., 160*n*
Nissan Corp., 79
Nixon, Richard M., 29
ambivalence toward USTR, 120–21
devaluation of dollar in 1971, 41–44, 57
support for textile industry, 34, 177, 197
trade policy, 32, 34
Nixon administration, 26
nontariff barriers, 72
subsidies, 144
support for STR, 108
textile wrangle with Japan, 108
trade reorganization, 105
Nixon-Ford trade bill, 193
"Nixon" Round, 105
Nonconferences, 73, 75, 97, 247
Nondiscrimination principle, erosion of, 54
Nonmarkups, 73, 75, 97, 238–39
Nontariff barriers, 36, 71, 75, 315
North American Development Bank promise,
226
North American Free Trade Agreement
(NAFTA), 99, 101, 217, 315–16
Clinton and, 219, 222, 224–29
congressional vote, 228
content requirements, 219, 227
debate, 222–29
fast-track extension vote as precursor, 219,
223, 226, 227*n*, 228
implementation bill, 227, 247–48
negotiations, 135, 180, 216, 218–19, 222, 224
signing, 219
North Carolina, support for NAFTA, 227*n*
NTBs. *See* Nontariff barriers

October War, 55
Ohmae, Kenichi, 196
Oil
Alaskan provisions, 95
import quotas, 25
prices, 55
Oilseed subsidies, US-EC dispute, 219–20
Oliver, Geoffrey, 154
Olmer, Lionel H., 119, 125
Olson, Mancur, 4*n*, 186*n*
OMAs. *See* Orderly marketing agreements
Omnibus Budget Reconciliation Act of 1981,
153
Omnibus Trade and Competitiveness Act of
1988, 66, 84, 90–91, 164–66, 299, 316
committee review, 302
draft legislation, 92–98

Exon-Florio amendment, 95, 189, 312
passage, 96
Section 1101, 232*n*
Special 301, 294, 318
Super 301, 93, 95, 98, 132–34, 294, 318–19
O'Neill, Thomas P. "Tip", 90, 180
OPEC. *See* Organization of Petroleum
Exporting Countries
Openness, versus intervention, 35–36
Opinion leaders surveys, 184
Opinion Research Corporation (ORC), 184
Orderly marketing agreements (OMAs), 54,
146, 316
Organization of Petroleum Exporting
Countries (OPEC), 55
Organized labor, 43, 218
opposition to NAFTA, 223
protectionism, 193–94
Ottinger, Richard L., 79

Pacific Telesis (PacTel), 250
Packard, David, 192
Packwood, Bob, 94, 239, 245, 271
Panama Canal treaties, 222*n*
Panetta, Leon, 223
Paster, Howard, 225
Pearce, William R., 20
Pease, Donald J., 100*n*
Pelosi, Nancy, 235
People's Republic of China. *See* China
Perot, Ross, 218, 222–23, 225, 228, 246, 250–51,
261
Petersen, Howard C., 19
Peterson, Peter G., 108
Plant-closings provisions, 95
Plaza Agreement, 59, 316
Politics, Pressures and the Tariff
(Schattschneider), 3–4
Preferences. *See* Generalized System of
Preferences
Presidential elections, 177
Presidents, ambivalence toward USTR, 106,
120–22
Pressler, Larry, 253*n*
Prestowitz, Clyde V., Jr., 188, 297
Trading Places, 52
Price averaging, antidumping, 241
Process protectionism, 91
Product safety, 246
Productivity and competitiveness policies,
265
Productivity performance, US, 283
Property rights, intellectual, 232, 320
Protectionism, 7, 175, 177, 179. *See also specific
devices and industries*
America First campaign, 181, 204, 216
definition of, 316
Democrats and, 216
early 1980s, 210–11

Other Publications from the
Institute for International Economics

POLICY ANALYSES IN INTERNATIONAL ECONOMICS Series

1 **The Lending Policies of the International Monetary Fund**
John Williamson/*August 1982*
ISBN paper 0-88132-000-5   72 pp.

2 **"Reciprocity": A New Approach to World Trade Policy?**
William R. Cline/*September 1982*
ISBN paper 0-88132-001-3   41 pp.

3 **Trade Policy in the 1980s**
C. Fred Bergsten and William R. Cline/*November 1982*
(out of print)   ISBN paper 0-88132-002-1   84 pp.
Partially reproduced in the book *Trade Policy in the 1980s.*

4 **International Debt and the Stability of the World Economy**
William R. Cline/*September 1983*
ISBN paper 0-88132-010-2   134 pp.

5 **The Exchange Rate System, Second Edition**
John Williamson/*September 1983, rev. June 1985*
(out of print)   ISBN paper 0-88132-034-X   61 pp.

6 **Economic Sanctions in Support of Foreign Policy Goals**
Gary Clyde Hufbauer and Jeffrey J. Schott/*October 1983*
ISBN paper 0-88132-014-5   109 pp.

7 **A New SDR Allocation?**
John Williamson/*March 1984*
ISBN paper 0-88132-028-5   61 pp.

8 **An International Standard for Monetary Stabilization**
Ronald I. McKinnon/*March 1984*
(out of print)   ISBN paper 0-88132-018-8   108 pp.

9 **The Yen/Dollar Agreement: Liberalizing Japanese Capital Markets**
Jeffrey A. Frankel/*December 1984*
ISBN paper 0-88132-035-8   86 pp.

10 **Bank Lending to Developing Countries: The Policy Alternatives**
C. Fred Bergsten, William R. Cline, and John Williamson/*April 1985*
ISBN paper 0-88132-032-3   221 pp.

11 **Trading for Growth: The Next Round of Trade Negotiations**
Gary Clyde Hufbauer and Jeffrey J. Schott/*September 1985*
(out of print)   ISBN paper 0-88132-033-1   109 pp.

12 **Financial Intermediation Beyond the Debt Crisis**
Donald R. Lessard and John Williamson/*September 1985*
(out of print)   ISBN paper 0-88132-021-8   130 pp.

13 **The United States-Japan Economic Problem**
C. Fred Bergsten and William R. Cline/*October 1985, 2d ed. January 1987*
(out of print)   ISBN paper 0-88132-060-9   180 pp.

BOOKS

SPECIAL REPORTS

WORKS IN PROGRESS

The list below describes research in progress at the Institute. It is intended to inform our customers about our current research agenda. We do not accept back orders for books in this section because of the uncertainty about publication dates.

Reciprocity and Regulation
Thomas O. Bayard

Global Firms and National Governments
C. Fred Bergsten and Edward M. Graham

The World Economy in Disarray
C. Fred Bergsten and C. Randall Henning

Trade, Jobs, and Income Distribution
William R. Cline

Environment in the New World Order
Daniel C. Esty

Trade and Labor Standards
Kimberly Ann Elliott and Richard Freeman

Regionalism and Globalism in the World Economic System
Jeffrey A. Frankel

The Exchange Rate System and the IMF
Morris Goldstein

Overseeing Global Capital Markets
Morris Goldstein and Peter Garber

Global Competition Policy
Edward M. Graham and J. David Richardson

Toward an Asia Pacific Economic Community?
Gary Clyde Hufbauer and Jeffrey J. Schott

The Economics of Korean Unification
Marcus Noland

The Case for Trade: A Modern Reconsideration
J. David Richardson

Managing Official Export Credits
John E. Ray

The Future of the World Trading System
John Whalley, in collaboration with Colleen Hamilton

Standards and Conformity Assessment in APEC
John Wilson

For orders outside the US and Canada please contact:
> Longman Group UK Ltd. Telephone Orders: 0279 623923
> PO Box 88 Fax: 0279 453450
> Fourth Avenue Telex: 81259
> Harlow, Essex CM 19 5SR UK

Canadian customers can order from the Institute or from either:
> RENOUF BOOKSTORE LA LIBERTÉ
> 1294 Algoma Road 3020 chemin Sainte-Foy
> Ottawa, Ontario K1B 3W8 Quebec G1X 3V6
> Telephone: (613) 741-4333 Telephone: (418) 658-3763
> Fax: (613) 741-5439 Fax: (800) 567-5449

- Book work in 1995-
- Before All the struggles
  of 9/11. Good Background
  + all of Detail